W9-CKH-675

COMPLETE OUTDOOR LIVING COOKBOOK

WILLIAMS-SONOMA

COMPLETE OUTDOOR LIVING COOKBOOK

GENERAL EDITOR

Chuck Williams

RECIPES

Charles Pierce, Tori Ritchie
and Diane Rossen Worthington

PHOTOGRAPHY

Chris Shorten

First published in the USA, 1998–1999,
by Time-Life Custom Publishing

Originally published as Williams-Sonoma Outdoors series:
Beach House Cooking (© 1999 Weldon Owen Inc.)
Cabin Cooking (© 1998 Weldon Owen Inc.)
Picnics and Tailgates (© 1998 Weldon Owen Inc.)
Snow Country Cooking (© 1999 Weldon Owen Inc.)

Oxmoor House.

Oxmoor House Inc.
Oxmoor House books are distributed by Sunset Books
80 Willow Road, Menlo Park, CA 94025
Phone: 650.321.3600 Fax: 650.324.1532
Vice-President/General Manager: Rich Smeby
Director of Special Sales: Gary Wright
Oxmoor House and Sunset Books are divisions of
Southern Progress Corporation

In collaboration with Williams-Sonoma Inc.
3250 Van Ness Avenue, San Francisco, CA 94109

Williams-Sonoma
Founder & Vice-Chairman: Chuck Williams
Book Buyer: Cecilia Michaelis

Produced by Weldon Owen Inc.
Chief Executive Officer: John Owen
President: Terry Newell
Chief Operating Officer: Larry Partington
Creative Director: Gaye Allen
Vice President International Sales: Stuart Laurence
Sales Manager: Emily Jahn
Publisher: Hannah Rahill
Editor: Sarah Lemas
Consulting Editors: Lisa Atwood, Norman Kolpas
Copy Editors: Judith Dunham, Sharon Silva
Editorial Assistant: Donita Boles
Art Director: Catherine Jacobes
Design Director: Diane Dempsey
Designer: Kyrie Forbes
Production Manager: Chris Hemesath
Production Coordinator: Libby Temple
Production: Joan Olson
Photography: Chris Shorten
Food and Prop Stylist: Heidi Gintner
Front Cover Photographer: Daniel Clark
Front Cover Food Stylist: George Dolese
Front Cover Prop Stylist: Amy Denebeim

The Williams-Sonoma Complete Cookbook series
conceived and produced by Weldon Owen Inc.

A Weldon Owen Production

First printed in 2002
10 9 8 7 6 5 4 3 2 1

Library of Congress Cataloging-in-Publication Data is available.
ISBN 0-8487-2596-4
Separations by Bright Arts Co. Pte. Ltd.
Printed in China by Leefung-Asco Printers Ltd.

A Note on Weights and Measures
All recipes include customary U.S., U.K. and metric measurements. Conversions are based on a standard developed for these books and have been rounded off. Actual weights may vary.

contents

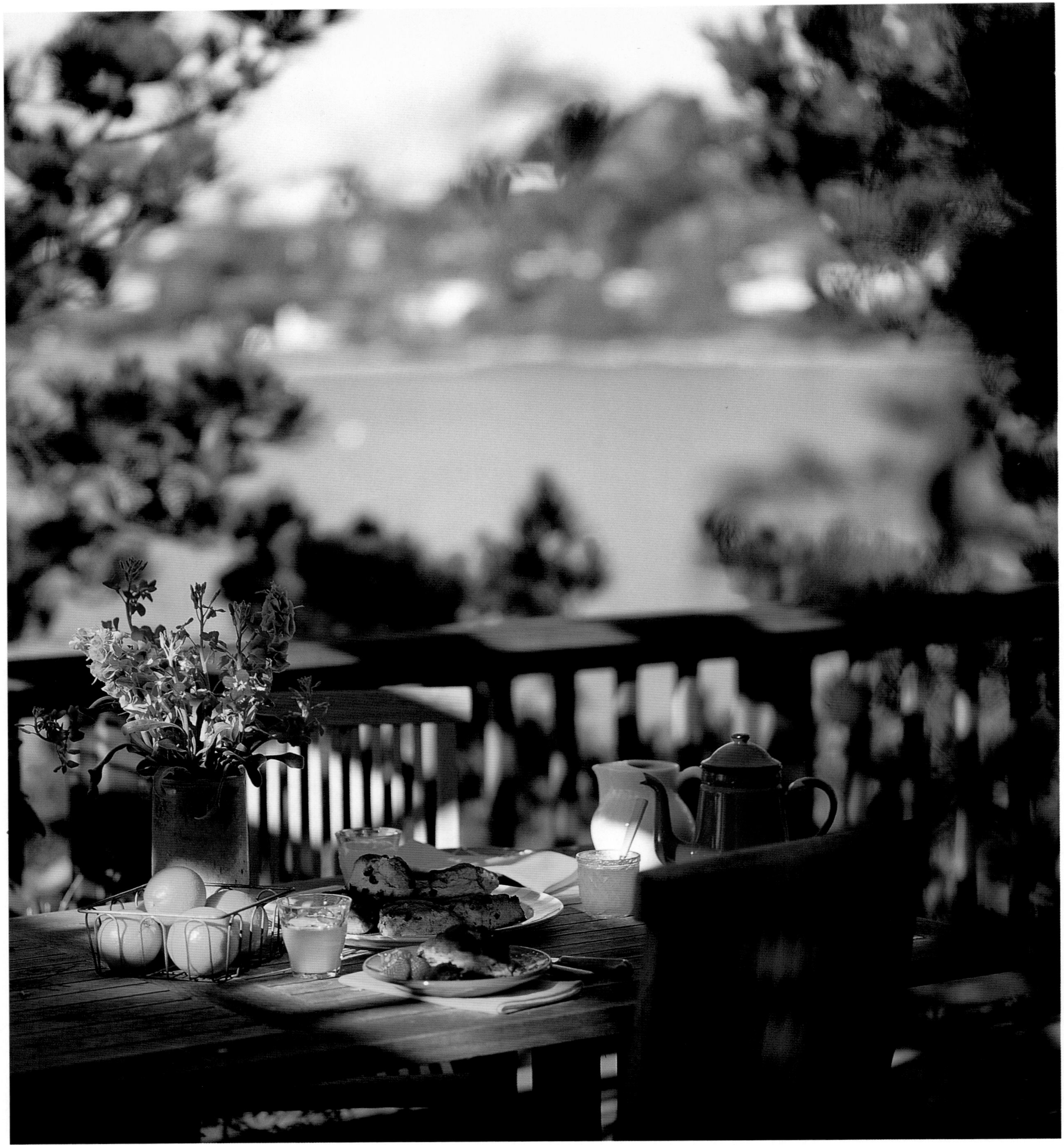

introduction

Outdoor living equals escape. Whether you are vacationing in a cabin in snow country, enjoying the warm, lazy days of summer at the seaside, or headed off to a Saturday afternoon picnic or tailgate party, you are getting away from the demands of everyday life.

Not surprisingly, the combination of fresh air and recreation whet the appetite for good food. Luckily, I have been able to satisfy such cravings at my second home on northern California's Lake Tahoe. I invite my friends and family there, and spoil them with rustic country breakfasts and with bountiful grilled dinners after a day of hiking, swimming, or waterskiing. I gathered those recipes in *Cabin Cooking,* the first book in the Williams-Sonoma Outdoors Series, which was followed by three more titles celebrating good food for the great outdoors. Now, the best of all those recipes are presented here, covering every season and setting, from savory to sweet and everything in between.

Fortunately, you don't have to travel far or have a house on a lake to experience the enjoyment of eating with the outdoors as the backdrop. You can do it in a neighborhood park, at the local beach, or even in front of a warm fire in your apartment. Such experiences are more about a mood than a place—about an appetite that comes from not being clamped to a dining-room chair. Instead of a tablecloth, there's a blanket spread wide. Instead of a carving fork and knife, there's a ladle in a kettle of chowder. Instead of a table, there's your lap.

The recipes in this book have been developed with the idea of making cooking surrounded by nature as easy and as pleasurable as possible. The ingredients are commonplace rather than exotic, and the kitchen equipment does not venture beyond the elementary: a saucepan, a frying pan, an outdoor grill in warm weather, good knives, mixing bowls, wooden spoons. What you assemble from these basic foods and tools are simple seasonal menus: cucumber soup in spring, cherry tomato and corn salad in summer, risotto with greens in autumn, roasted pears in winter.

Use your imagination when serving your meals. Take advantage of a sunny morning or midday or a warm evening and put up a table outdoors—on a porch, under a tree, or near the shore. Shade daytime diners with big umbrellas, and illuminate nighttime meals with lanterns. When the weather is cold, treat yourself to a supper by the hearth, with a roaring fire and a candlelit table. Whether serving indoors or out, use no-nonsense china or enamelware and durable flatware for your place settings and decorate with what nature provides, such as seashells, flowers, and small boughs. Maintain this easygoing style by bringing clams to the table in a tin florist's bucket, wrapping biscuits in a bandana, serving fried potatoes straight from the cast-iron pan in which they were cooked, or arranging lemon squares on a well-cleaned length of driftwood.

Finally, outdoor living also equals relaxed living, a philosophy that reaches from the kitchen, where only easy-to-assemble recipes are prepared, to the dining table, where an informal, leisurely, convivial ambience prevails.

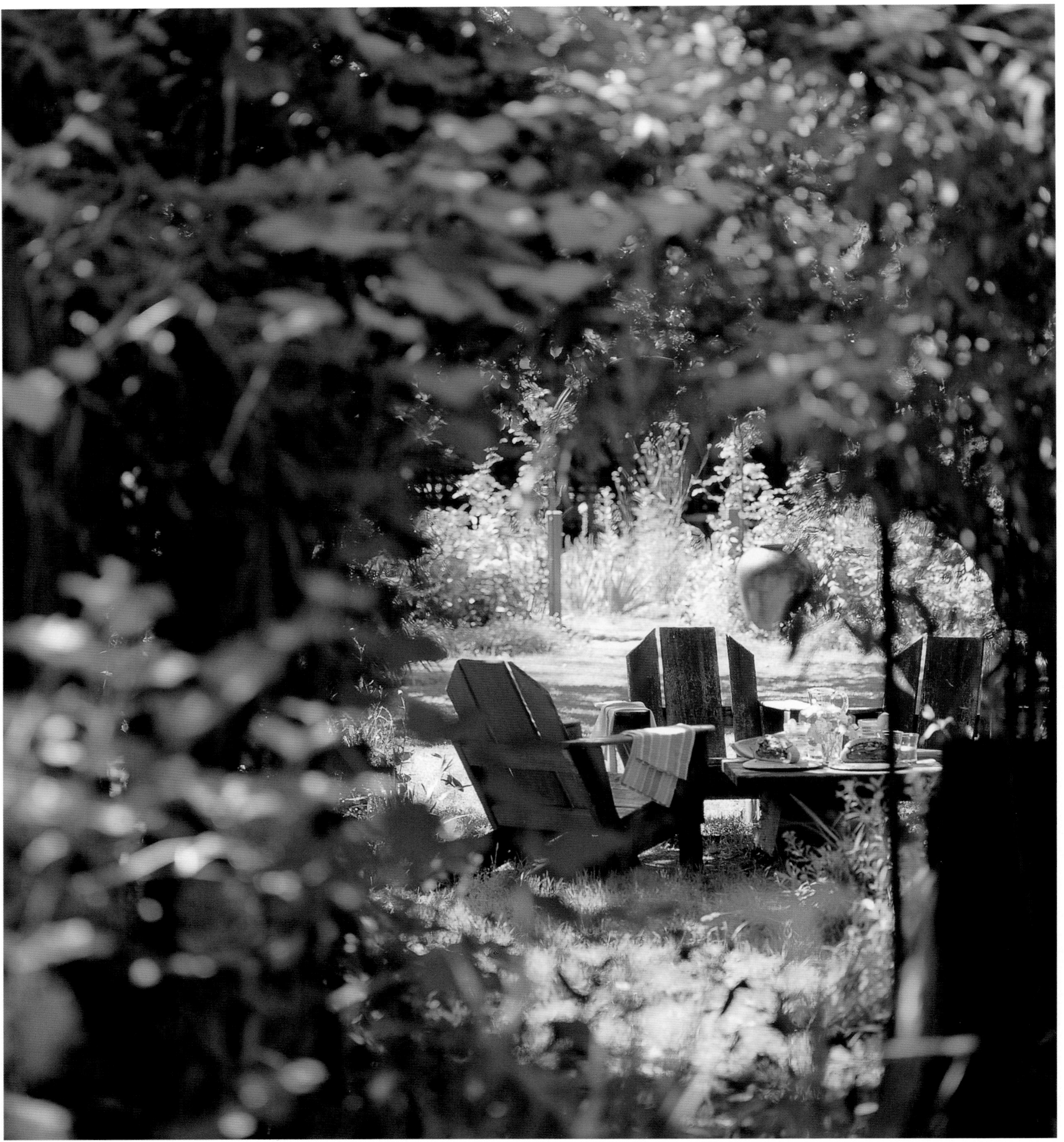

the environment

Nature provides the most alluring setting for any dining experience. Whether you're surrounded by beach, meadow, or your own backyard, or snugly ensconced in a cabin or in front of your fireplace, food tastes better when spiced with fresh air and adventure.

A day at the beach or in the woods—at any time of year—is irresistible. At the beach, the rhythm of the waves; the sweet, salty breeze; the warm sun overhead or the fog rolling in; the sand underfoot: every element coaxes the body into easy relaxation, the mind into serene reverie. In the woods or hills, the call of birds; the crunch of leaves underfoot or the sound of wind through the grasses; the cool, moist air or the subtle scent of wildflowers: all combine to create a sense of well-being. Outdoor meals play an important part in this willing seduction. Your spirit instantly rises when you lift the lid of a picnic basket—or drop the tailgate of your automobile—to reveal the edible treasures you've prepared.

However, you don't need to leave home to enjoy an al fresco meal. Set the table in your backyard or on your deck and rediscover the delights of your own home—your own piece of the outdoors. It's convenient to have the comforts of home close at hand, from your favorite tableware to cushions and blankets, or a vase for freshly cut flowers from your garden, making a home picnic a good idea for any season. Having a kitchen close by also makes it easy to serve foods hot out of the oven or straight from the freezer, increasing your menu choices to include chicken pot pie on a chilly evening or sorbet on a sunny afternoon.

Your menu choices are also increased if you're headed for an extended stay at a cabin or beach house. Whether your getaway is sheltered in the woods, or looks out at the ocean or on a lake or meadow, it brings you blissfully close to nature, while giving you access to a full range of kitchen equipment and appliances.

Spring- and summertime might inspire late, lazy brunches on a lakefront veranda, or sunset dinners overlooking the ocean. During the colder months, in grand lodge and modest cabin alike, the cold, crisp surroundings sharpen your senses. Food looks and smells more seductive, luring you with the promise of warmth, comfort, and fuel for the day's activities. From breakfast breads to steaming oatmeal, chilled soups to hearty overstuffed sandwiches, sizzling steaks to comforting pot pies, and every variety of homey dessert, good food adds another pleasurable dimension to the outdoor experience.

Compose a centerpiece of wildflowers, if local laws allow picking, for an impromptu bouquet. At the beach, build a fire pit from driftwood collected on your wanderings. Come nightfall, breezeproof hurricane lamps provide illumination while underscoring an air of romance.

A Reminder to Tread Lightly

Wherever you enjoy your meal, bear in mind that certain responsibilities accompany its pleasures. Travel on established roads and pathways so that you tread as lightly as possible on the landscape. Collect berries or other edibles only in specially designated areas. At a sandy beach you can build a fire pit, if regulations allow, for cooking or for keeping warm when evening falls, but be sure to put the fire out completely when you leave. Respect the rights of private property owners and take care not to pollute bodies of water with dirty dishes. While observing wildlife, do not approach too closely or disturb habitats; use binoculars for closer viewing. When enjoying meals, clean up thoroughly afterward, taking special care not to leave behind items that might hurt people or wildlife. Cleanup is easy when you bring trash bags to carry away disposables. Acquaint yourself with all local regulations regarding trash disposal, and do your part to help make the area's unique character a lasting legacy. Leaving the site in even better condition than you found it should be your goal.

Your retreat's environment can provide you with a bounty for the table, including fresh, wild berries. Check ahead with area authorities to learn what foods are safe and in season, and what, if any, legal limits there might be on gathering them. Take advantage of a beautiful day or night to eat alfresco, moving a table outdoors, if necessary.

A Note on High-Altitude Cooking

If your retreat is above 3,000 feet (1,000 meters), you'll need to alter some of the recipes in this book to compensate for the effects of reduced air pressure. Only a few adjustments are necessary. When baking, reduce baking powder and soda (bicarbonate of soda) by ⅛–¼ teaspoon per 1 teaspoon, decrease sugar by ½–1 teaspoon per 1 cup (8 oz/250 g), and add 1–2 tablespoons more liquid per 1 cup (8 fl oz/250 ml). Lengthen cooking times by a few minutes for foods that are boiled, and increase baking temperatures by 15–25°F (8–10°C).

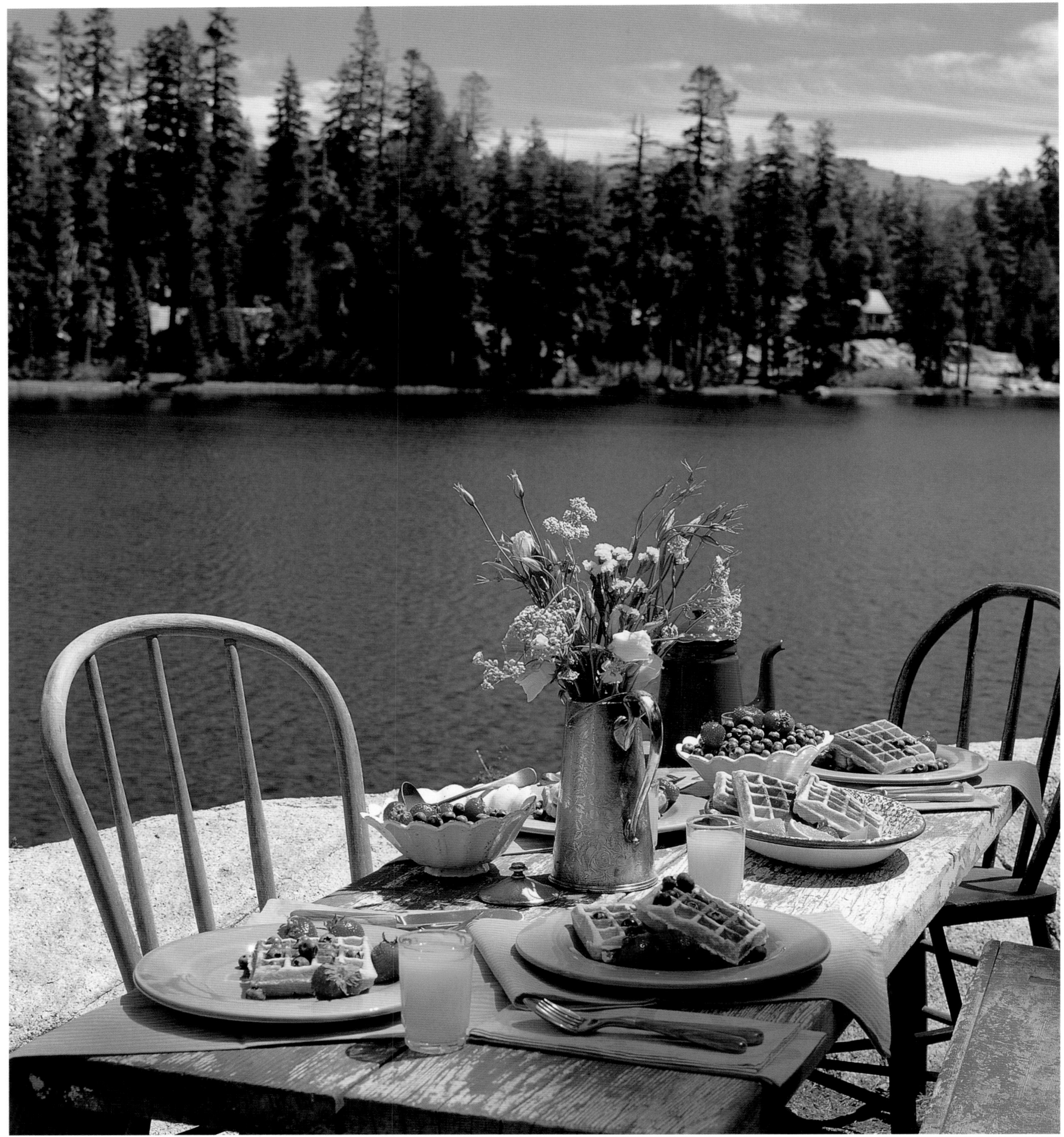

setting the scene

All of your senses—sight, sound, smell, and touch, as well as taste—keenly awaken when you partake of a meal in the outdoors—or with the outdoors as the backdrop. Be aware of them when selecting your location. When you scout the setting to find the best place for a picnic or tailgate, the view is often the most important element. Shifting your position even a few feet can make the difference between a mundane view and an awe-inspiring vista. Think about your physical comfort by picking the softest patch of grass or the smoothest sand. If convenience allows, bring cushions or lightweight folding chairs to make the seating even more comfortable. Whether you're serving a lunch in the hills, a dinner on the deck at dusk, or a brunch beside a window that looks out on a storm-tossed sea, nature can add her distinctive signature to your table. Try decorative items such as pinecones, interesting branches or leaves, shells, wave-polished pebbles, driftwood—and of course, flowers.

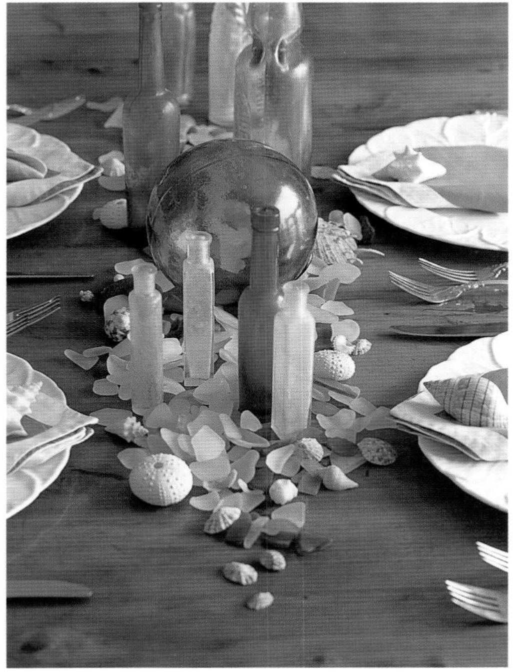

Choosing the Right Tableware

The tableware and accessories you choose for beach house or mountain retreat meals ideally combine both the decorative and the practical. It doesn't matter how elegant or humble your retreat's furnishings and accessories are. Nature is the primary theme, and at every turn your surroundings can provide you with ample inspiration for creating memorable dining experiences. Select colors and patterns that complement the setting. A beach setting might suggest anything from soft blues and greens to hot tropical hues, from solids to sea-inspired motifs. A cabin table might call for the cheerful yellows, pinks, and greens of wildflowers in the spring or the brilliant golds, oranges, and reds of autumn. At the same time, keep in mind that casual seaside or cabin life can subject serving pieces to rough-and-tumble handling. Nonbreakable dishware and easily washable tablecloths and napkins offer years of reliable, easy-care use. Another option is to stock the cabinets with old enamelware from a local antique shop or a favorite set of china that's been retired to the country.

In winter, whether the scene is a cabin dining room, a fireside table for two, or a picnic table in the woods, cold-weather dining calls for coziness. You can easily create that feeling with the tabletop items you choose. Serve breakfast drinks in heavy mugs that will keep coffee and hands warm. Rustic pottery is ideal for lunchtime soups and evening stews. Complement dishware with sturdy cutlery and textured linens. In the evening add candles and a wood fire to light the scene. All of these touches will combine to set a relaxed, convivial tone.

Keep comfort and convenience in mind when putting together your meals. Large totes make it easy to transport containers of food and drink to your picnic spot. For nighttime dining, citronella candles ward off insects while providing a warm glow.

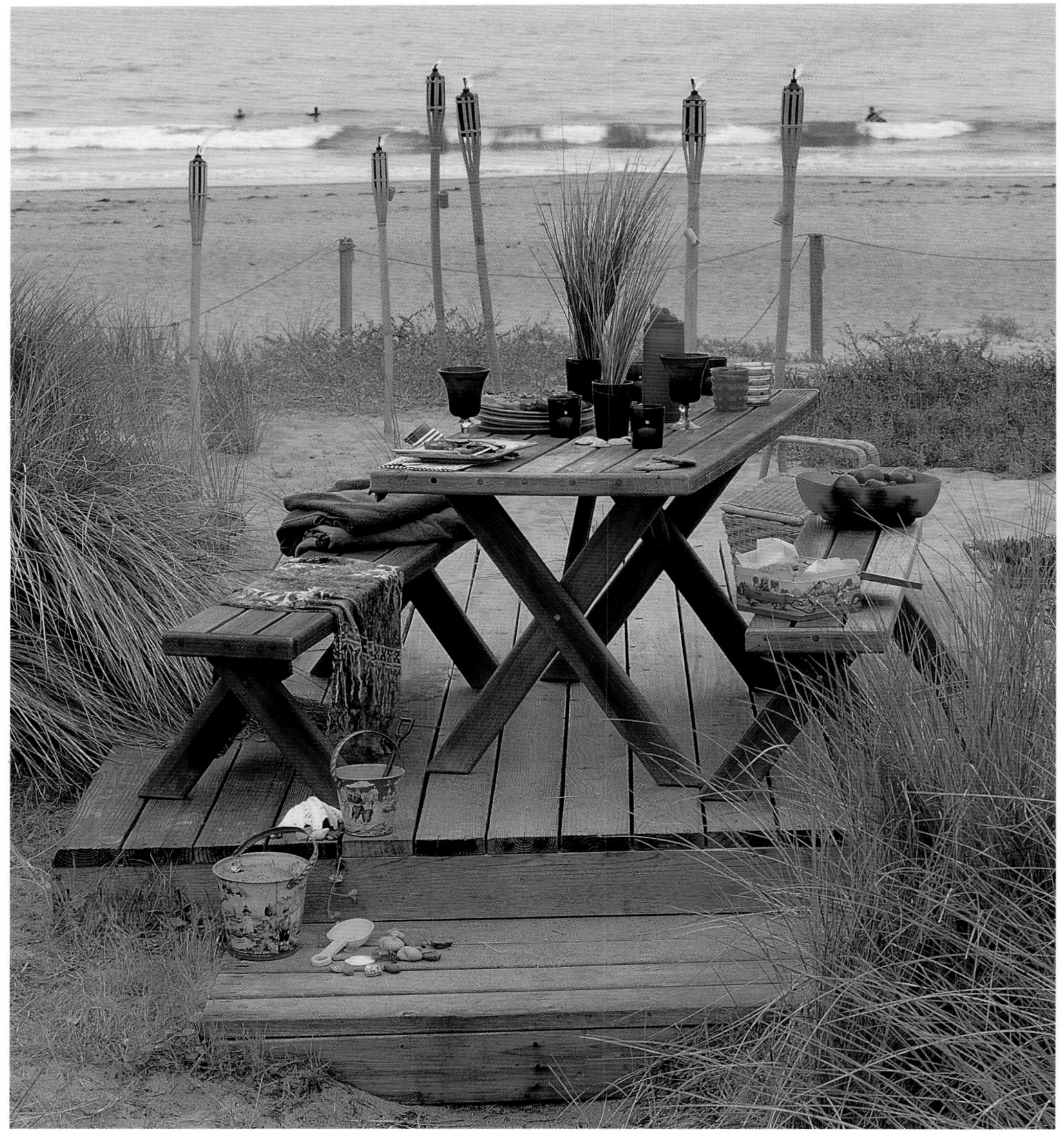

Give comfort it's due by having blankets, throws, or shawls on hand to provide warmth or extra padding for hard benches or ground. Sturdy, lightweight containers are available in all shapes, sizes, and colors; select those that best suit your needs and taste.

Equipment and Packing

A well-stocked kitchen-supply store should carry all the equipment you need for packing your picnic meal. Look for lightweight sealable containers and serving bowls, thermoses, and beverage dispensers. Standard wrapping supplies like waxed paper, plastic wrap, lock-top bags, and heavy-duty foil are indispensable.

Before you pack your basket or hamper, line it with a towel to insulate it and absorb any spillage. Put heavier items and those in rigid containers on the bottom, then place more fragile items on top. Invest, too, in artificial ice to keep beverages cold and perishables fresh. Ideally, dairy products, meats, eggs and mayonnaise should not be left out for more than two hours, or one hour in warm weather.

For serving, bring plates, cutlery, utensils, glasses, and mugs, checking your supplies against those recommended for the recipes. Remember to include plenty of napkins, as well as kitchen towels and trash bags for cleanup.

Many factors will affect the planning of meals for your beach house or cabin, including its distance from home, cooking facilities, and proximity to food markets. You may have to bring equipment or prepared food with you. Make a list of indispensable cooking tools, such as a chef's knife, a paring knife, a saucepan, a heavy frying pan, a spatula, and wooden spoons. Check against an inventory of items on hand at your destination to finalize your list of what you'll need to bring along. For evening meals in the wintertime, consider bringing along a stove-top grill pan, which gives you results reminiscent of outdoor grilling without your having to brave the weather. Alternatively, choose recipes you can transport and assemble easily, paying special attention to keeping perishables safe en route, as described above.

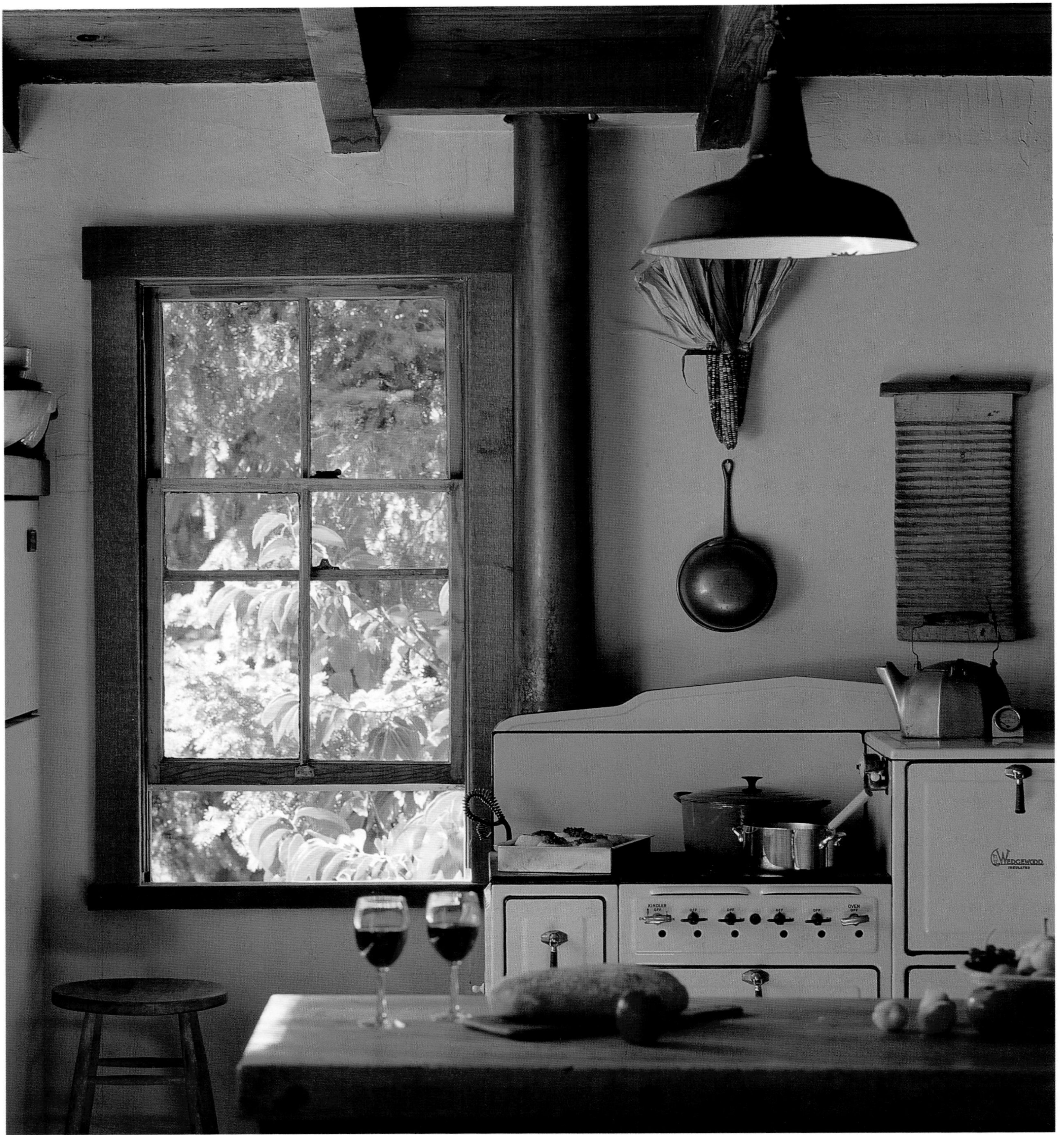
KINDLER
OFF
OFF
OFF
OFF
OFF
OVEN
OFF
WEDGEWOOD
INSULATED

the pantry

The recipes in this book have been developed with goal of making outdoor cooking as easy and pleasurable as possible. Most of the ingredients called for are sold in well-stocked food stores everywhere. An emphasis has been placed on convenience, reducing food preparation time.

A little advance planning will pay off greatly in the ease with which your meals are prepared. Before you go, decide on the recipes you'll cook and then make a list of the ingredients you'll need. When shopping, keep an eye out for high-quality ingredients that will shorten your time in the kitchen, from fresh salsas found in the refrigerated case to preshredded cheeses to scatter atop a pizza. You can even chop vegetables or marinate meat before you leave and pack them in air-tight containers.

Planning a Menu

When choosing your menus, plan to use perishable items such as tender produce, seafood, poultry, and ground meats early in your stay. Reserve hardier ingredients such as root vegetables, apples, citrus fruits, whole cuts of meats, and cured meats for later meals. Consider preparing foods that will provide more than one meal. A turkey breast, for example, once roasted for dinner, will yield leftovers for sandwiches or pot pies.

Stocking the Cabinets

The better stocked your getaway is, the less foodstuffs you'll have to carry with you. If you own the lodge, cabin, or beach house, keep staples on hand. Many pantry items can be stored long-term. Refrigerate preserves, syrups, condiments, and pickles and check expiration dates regularly. Store oils and vinegars, dried beans, pastas, and rice in air-tight containers away from heat and light, and check them regularly for freshness. Alternatively, refrigerate oils as well. Keep dried herbs, breakfast grains, flours, and canned goods in a pantry or cupboard and replace them annually. Items with long shelf lives, such as nuts in their shells, provide nourishing snacks with little effort. In cold weather, basics such as popcorn and hot-drink fixings—tea, coffee, hot chocolate—supply immediate comfort.

Bring along fresh produce to enjoy between meals and to use as colorful centerpieces. A favorite bowl filled with brightly colored cherries, pears, or tangerines; a platter of artichokes; or a couple of festive winter squashes placed on the kitchen table help create an instantly warm, inviting atmosphere.

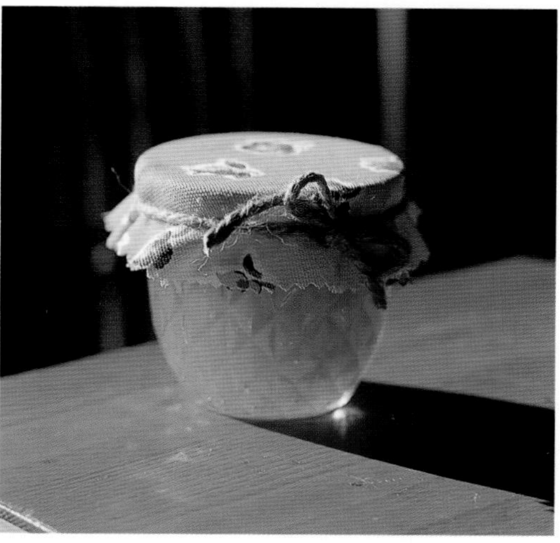

Scour local antique shops for old-fashioned kitchen items, such as cast-iron tea kettles or toast warmers. If you like, store dried goods including beans, flours, and spices in glass or ceramic containers to lengthen their shelf lives.

strawberry lime sparkler

4 cups (1 lb/500 g) strawberries, stems removed

½ cup (4 fl oz/125 ml) lime juice

¾ cup (6 oz/185 g) sugar

1 bottle (24 fl oz/750 ml) sparkling mineral water, chilled

1 bunch fresh mint, stems removed

cracked ice

Pick out 8 of the smallest strawberries and set aside. In a blender, purée the remaining strawberries. Pour the mixture into a sieve set over a large bowl and force through the sieve to remove the seeds. Add the lime juice and sugar and stir well. Cover and refrigerate for 1 hour or up to 1 day.

In a large pitcher, stir together the strawberry mixture and the mineral water. Lightly crush the mint leaves. Pack tall glasses with cracked ice and several mint leaves. Fill with the sparkler and garnish with the reserved strawberries.

serves eight | per serving: calories 104 (kilojoules 437), protein 0 g, carbohydrates 27 g, total fat 0 g, saturated fat 0 g, cholesterol 0 mg, sodium 2 mg, dietary fiber 2 g

apricot-rum funnies

1 ripe banana, cut into 3 or 4 pieces

1½ cups (12 fl oz/375 ml) apricot juice

1 cup (8 fl oz/250 ml) white rum

¼ cup (2 fl oz/60 ml) lemon juice

1 tablespoon grenadine

ice cubes

lemon slices for garnish

In a blender, combine the banana, apricot juice, rum, lemon juice, and grenadine. Fill the blender with ice cubes and blend until smooth, about 30 seconds. Pour into chilled glasses and garnish with lemon slices.

serves six | per serving: calories 146 (kilojoules 613), protein 0 g, carbohydrates 16 g, total fat 0 g, saturated fat 0 g, cholesterol 0 mg, sodium 5 mg, dietary fiber 1 g

champagne cocktail

3 passion fruits

1 teaspoon sugar

1 bottle (24 fl oz/750 ml) champagne or other dry sparkling wine, well chilled

Cut off the top of each passion fruit. Using a small spoon, scoop out the pulp into a sieve placed over a small bowl and push it through the sieve. Stir in the sugar. Put 1 tablespoon of the pulp into the bottom of each of 8 chilled champagne flutes. Pour in the sparkling wine and serve at once.

serves eight | per serving: calories 72 (kilojoules 302), protein 0 g, carbohydrates 3 g, total fat 0 g, saturated fat 0 g, cholesterol 0 mg, sodium 7 mg, dietary fiber 0 g

mixed-berry lemonade

8 lemons

1½ cups (12 oz/375 g) sugar

1 cup (4 oz/125 g) mixed berries

8 cups (64 fl oz/2 l) water

cracked ice

Finely grate enough lemon zest to measure 1 tablespoon and place in a large nonaluminum bowl. Squeeze the juice from the lemons and add to the bowl along with the sugar. Stir until the sugar dissolves. Place the berries in the bottom of a large pitcher. Lightly crush with the back of a spoon, leaving some berries whole. Add the lemon mixture and pour in the water. Stir well and pour over cracked ice in tall chilled glasses.

serves eight to ten | per serving: calories 160 (kilojoules 672), protein 0 g, carbohydrates 42 g, total fat 0 g, saturated fat 0 g, cholesterol 0 mg, sodium 1 mg, dietary fiber 1 g

mango smoothies

2 mangoes, peeled, pitted, and cut into 1-inch (2.5-cm) dice

1 cup (8 oz/250 g) plain yogurt

½ cup (4 fl oz/125 ml) milk

1 banana, coarsely chopped

2 tablespoons lemon juice

1 teaspoon vanilla etract (essence)

Place the mangoes in a plastic bag and freeze until firm, at least 1 hour.

Just before serving, in a blender, combine the frozen mango, yogurt, milk, banana, lemon juice, and vanilla. Blend until very smooth. Pour into chilled glasses and serve immediately.

serves two | per serving: calories 305 (kilojoules 1,281), protein 10 g, carbohydrates 61 g, total fat 5 g, saturated fat 3 g, cholesterol 15 mg, sodium 117 mg, dietary fiber 3 g

ginger iced tea

For a festive touch, wet the rims of tall glasses and dip in a mixture of finely chopped crystallized ginger and sugar.

1 piece fresh ginger, 3 inches (7.5 cm), peeled and coarsely grated

10 cups (2½ qt/2.5 l) water

1 cup (8 oz/250 g) sugar

¼ cup (1 oz/30 g) loose tea leaves such as English Breakfast or Earl Grey

cracked ice

Place the ginger in a large, nonaluminum bowl. Pour in 4 cups (32 fl oz/1 l) of the water, cover, and let stand undisturbed for about 48 hours.

Line a sieve with cheesecloth (muslin) and place over a saucepan. Strain the ginger water through the sieve, then add the sugar to the saucepan. Bring to a boil over high heat, stirring, then reduce the heat to medium and simmer, undisturbed, for 10 minutes. Remove from the heat, stir in the tea, and cover. Let steep for 5 minutes. Strain into a large, heatproof pitcher and pour in the remaining 6 cups (48 fl oz/1.5 l) water. Stir well, cover, and refrigerate until well chilled. Pour over cracked ice in tall glasses.

serves eight | per serving: calories 113 (kilojoules 475), protein 0 g, carbohydrates 29 g, total fat 0 g, saturated fat 0 g, cholesterol 0 mg, sodium 9 mg, dietary fiber 0 g

sun tea with mint cubes

1 small bunch fresh mint

4 cups (32 fl oz/1 l) cold water, plus water for ice cubes

2 tea bags, black, herbal, flavored, or a combination

sugar (optional)

lemon slices

Place a mint leaf in each compartment of 2 ice cube trays. Fill the trays with water, then freeze.

Pour the cold water into a lidded 1-qt (1-l) clear glass container. Place the tea bags in the water, leaving the strings dangling over the side. Cover and set in direct sunlight for at least 1 hour, or for up to 3 hours. Let steep until the tea is a good, strong color.

Remove the mint ice cubes from the trays and place in a large pitcher or individual glasses. Pour in the steeped tea, discarding the bags. Add sugar to taste, if desired, and garnish with lemon slices.

serves four to six | per serving: calories 2 (kilojoules 8), protein 0 g, carbohydrates 1 g, total fat 0 g, saturated fat 0 g, cholesterol 0 mg, sodium 6 mg, dietary fiber 0 g

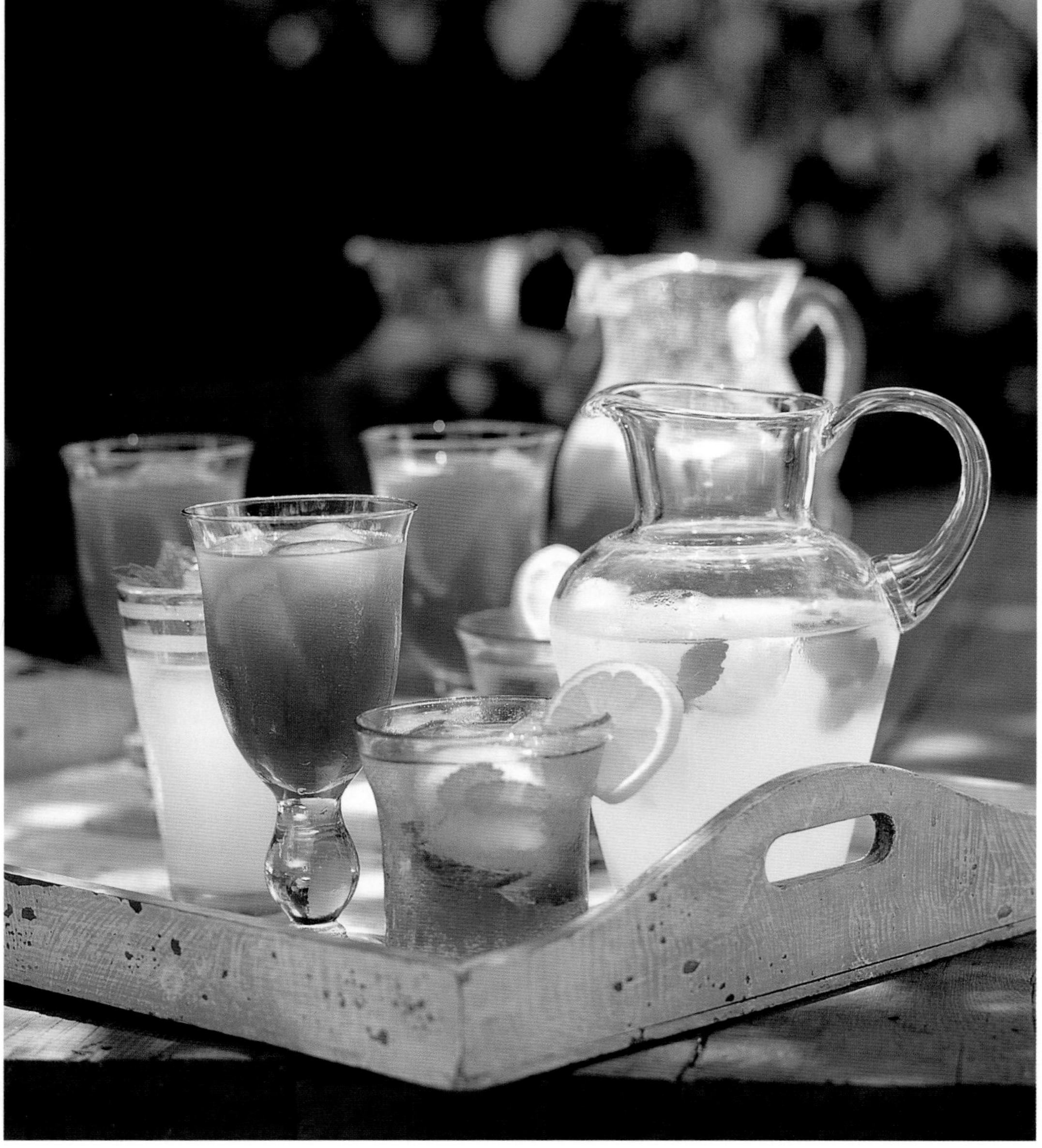

fresh honey lemonade

⅓–½ cup (4–6 oz/125–185 g) honey

1½ cups (12 fl oz/375 ml) steaming hot water

1 cup (8 fl oz/250 ml) lemon juice

ice cubes

fresh mint sprigs (optional)

lemon slices (optional)

In a heatproof 1-qt (1-l) measure or bowl, combine the honey and hot water and stir until the honey is dissolved. Stir in the lemon juice. Let cool for at least 10 minutes or cover and refrigerate until ready to serve.

Pour over ice. If desired, garnish with mint sprigs and lemon slices.

serves two to four | per serving: calories 161 (kilojoules 676), protein 0 g, carbohydrates 44 g, total fat 0 g, saturated fat 0 g, cholesterol 0 mg, sodium 19 mg, dietary fiber 0 g

summer sangria

2 cups (16 fl oz/500 ml) orange juice

⅓ cup (3 oz/90 g) sugar

1 bottle (24 fl oz/750 ml) white wine

½ bottle (12 fl oz/375 ml) red wine

1 cup (8 fl oz/250 ml) sparkling water

ice cubes

2 oranges, thinly sliced

In a large pitcher, stir together the orange juice and sugar until the sugar is dissolved. Add the wines and stir well. If desired, cover and refrigerate for up to 8 hours or until ready to serve.

To serve, add the sparkling water, ice cubes, and orange slices and stir well. Pour into individual glasses.

serves six to eight | per serving: calories 204 (kilojoules 857), protein 1 g, carbohydrates 26 g, total fat 0 g, saturated fat 0 g, cholesterol 0 mg, sodium 8 mg, dietary fiber 1 g

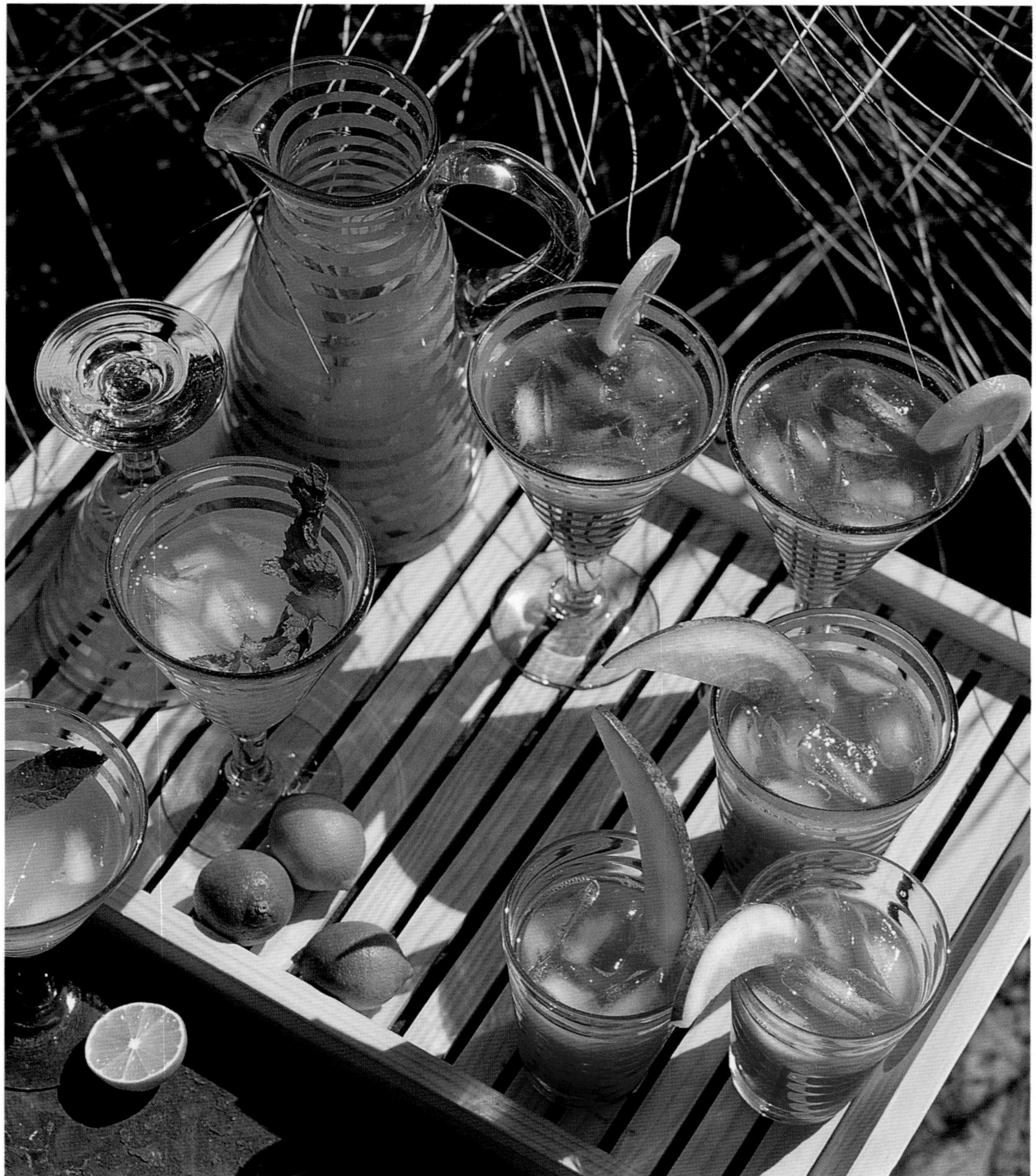

watermelon-and-citrus agua fresca

6 lb (3 kg) watermelon, rind and seeds removed, cut into 1-inch (2.5-cm) chunks

1 cup (8 fl oz/250 ml) orange juice

½ cup (4 fl oz/125 ml) lime juice

¼ cup (2 fl oz/60 ml) lemon juice

1½ cups (12 fl oz/375 ml) cold water

1 tablespoon superfine (castor) sugar

ice cubes

Working in batches if necessary, put the watermelon and citrus juices in a food processor and process until puréed. Place a fine-mesh sieve over a large bowl and pour the purée into the sieve. Using a rubber spatula, press down on the fruit to force the juice into the bowl. Discard the pulp. Stir the water and sugar into the juice. Cover and refrigerate until well chilled. Transfer to a chilled large thermos. Serve over ice.

serves eight | per serving: calories 82 (kilojoules 344), protein 1 g, carbohydrates 19 g, total fat 1 g, saturated fat 0 g, cholesterol 0 mg, sodium 8 mg, dietary fiber 1 g

fresh raspberry spritzers

3 pt (24 oz/750 g) raspberries

1½ cups (10½ oz/330 g) superfine (castor) sugar

2 bottles (24 fl oz/750 ml each) sparkling wine or 6 cups (48 fl oz/1.5 l) sparkling water, well chilled

ice cubes

1 lemon, thinly sliced

Put the raspberries and sugar in a food processor and process until puréed. Place a fine-mesh sieve over a bowl, pour the purée into the sieve, and, using a rubber spatula, press down to force the juice into the bowl. Discard the seeds. Refrigerate the purée until ready to serve. To serve, place 3 tablespoons of the purée into each glass. Add ¾ cup (6 fl oz/180 ml) sparkling wine or water and ice. Garnish with a lemon slice.

serves eight | per serving: calories 309 (kilojoules 1,298), protein 1 g, carbohydrates 50 g, total fat 1 g, saturated fat 0 g, cholesterol 0 mg, sodium 10 mg, dietary fiber 4 g

limeade

1½ cups (12 fl oz/375 ml) lime juice (from 12–15 limes)

6–8 tablespoons (3–4 oz/90–125 g) superfine (castor) sugar

4½ cups (36 fl oz/1.1 l) cold water

18 fresh mint sprigs

ice cubes

In a large pitcher, combine the lime juice and 6 tablespoons sugar, stirring until the sugar dissolves. Stir in the water. Crush the mint sprigs, then stir into the limeade. Taste and add the remaining 2 tablespoons sugar if desired. Cover and refrigerate until well chilled. Transfer to a chilled large thermos. Serve over ice.

serves six | per serving: calories 81 (kilojoules 340), protein 0 g, carbohydrates 22 g, total fat 0 g, saturated fat 0 g, cholesterol 0 mg, sodium 1 mg, dietary fiber 0 g

simple ginger cider with honey

8 cups (64 fl oz/2 l) apple cider

¼ cup (3 oz/90 g) honey

¼ lb (125 g) fresh ginger, peeled and thinly sliced

In a nonaluminum saucepan over low heat, combine the cider, honey, and ginger. Cover and warm, stirring occasionally, for 30 minutes. Transfer to a preheated large thermos. Include the ginger for a more pronounced ginger flavor. Pour into mugs to serve.

serves eight | per serving: calories 158 (kilojoules 664), protein 0 g, carbohydrates 40 g, total fat 0 g, saturated fat 0 g, cholesterol 0 mg, sodium 10 mg, dietary fiber 0 g

cinnamon hot chocolate

8 cups (64 fl oz/2 l) milk

½ lb (250 g) semisweet (plain) or milk chocolate, broken into pieces

8 cinnamon sticks

Put the milk, chocolate, and cinnamon sticks in a saucepan. Warm over medium-low heat, stirring frequently, until the milk is hot and the chocolate has melted completely. Transfer to a preheated large thermos. Include the cinnamon sticks for a more pronounced cinnamon flavor, or rinse off and dry the sticks and pack separately. To serve, pour the hot chocolate into mugs, placing a cinnamon stick in each mug.

serves eight | per serving: calories 285 (kilojoules 1,197), protein 9 g, carbohydrates 30 g, total fat 17 g, saturated fat 10 g, cholesterol 34 mg, sodium 123 mg, dietary fiber 0 g

spicy bloody marys

1 can (46 fl oz/1.4 l) good-quality tomato juice

¾ cup (6 fl oz/180 ml) orange juice

3 tablespoons Worcestershire sauce

2 tablespoons prepared horseradish

2 tablespoons lemon juice

1 teaspoon hot-pepper sauce such as Tabasco

1½ teaspoons celery salt

ice cubes

¾–1 cup (6–8 fl oz/180–250 ml) vodka

6–8 celery stalks, leaves attached

In a large pitcher, stir together the tomato and orange juices, Worcestershire sauce, horseradish, lemon juice, hot-pepper sauce, and celery salt. Cover and refrigerate until well chilled. Transfer to a chilled large thermos. To serve, fill large glasses with ice. Pour 1 shot vodka over the ice in each glass. Add ¾–1 cup (6–8 fl oz/180–250 ml) of the tomato juice mixture. Use a celery stalk to stir each beverage, leaving it in the glass as a garnish.

serves six to eight | per serving: calories 126 (kilojoules 529), protein 2 g, carbohydrates 15 g, total fat 0 g, saturated fat 0 g, cholesterol 0 mg, sodium 990 mg, dietary fiber 2 g

glögg

1 bottle (24 fl oz/750 ml) dry red wine

1¼ cups (10 fl oz/310 ml) brandy

12 whole cloves

6 cardamom pods, lightly crushed

2 cinnamon sticks, broken in half

½ cup (4 oz/125 g) sugar

4 orange zest strips, each ¾ inch (2 cm) wide and 2 inches (5 cm) long

½ cup (3 oz/90 g) raisins

¼ cup (1½ oz/45 g) blanched almonds

In a saucepan over medium heat, combine the wine, brandy, cloves, cardamom pods, and cinnamon sticks. Bring to a simmer and simmer for 15 minutes. Stir in the sugar and orange zest. Divide the raisins and almonds among 4 warmed cups or goblets. Pour in the spiced wine through a sieve and serve.

serves four | per serving: calories 556 (kilojoules 2,335), protein 3 g, carbohydrates 51 g, total fat 6 g, saturated fat 1 g, cholesterol 0 mg, sodium 14 mg, dietary fiber 2 g

snuggler

⅓ cup (3 oz/90 g) plus 1 tablespoon sugar

¼ cup (¾ oz/20 g) unsweetened cocoa powder

4 cups (32 fl oz/1 l) milk

½ cup (4 fl oz/125 ml) heavy (double) cream

¼ cup peppermint schnapps

2 peppermint candies, lightly crushed

In a saucepan over medium heat, combine the ⅓ cup (3 oz/90 g) sugar, the cocoa powder, and milk. Heat, stirring, until steaming; set aside. Meanwhile, whisk the cream with the 1 tablespoon sugar until soft peaks form. Stir the peppermint schnapps into the cocoa. Pour into 4 warmed mugs or goblets and top with whipped cream and crushed candies.

serves four | per serving: calories 353 (kilojoules 1,483), protein 10 g, carbohydrates 37 g, total fat 20 g, saturated fat 12 g, cholesterol 75 mg, sodium 134 mg, dietary fiber 2 g

chai

2 cinnamon sticks, broken in half

8 allspice berries

4 whole cloves

2 peppercorns

4 cups (32 fl oz/1 l) water

16 cardamom pods, lightly crushed

4 slices fresh ginger, lightly crushed

2 tea bags or 1 tablespoon black tea

½ cup (4 fl oz/125 ml) milk, or to taste

3 tablespoons honey, or to taste

With a mortar and pestle, coarsely grind the cinnamon sticks, allspice, cloves, and peppercorns. In a saucepan, combine the ground spices, water, cardamom pods, and ginger. Bring to a boil, reduce heat to medium-low, cover, and simmer for 10 minutes. Set aside, covered, for 10 minutes. Add the tea bags or loose tea in a tea ball to a teapot. Return the spiced water to a boil and pour into the teapot. Let steep for 2–3 minutes, then strain the tea and serve with milk and honey on the side.

serves four | per serving: calories 73 (kilojoules 307), protein 1 g, carbohydrates 16 g, total fat 2 g, saturated fat 1 g, cholesterol 4 mg, sodium 20 mg, dietary fiber 0 g

hot apple cider

4 cups (32 fl oz/1 l) apple cider

3 lemon zest strips, each ¾ inch thick (2 cm) wide and 2 inches (5 cm) long

2 cinnamon sticks, broken in half

6 whole cloves

1 teaspoon allspice berries

4 teaspoons brown sugar

½ cup (4 fl oz/125 ml) heavy (double) cream

2 tablespoons granulated sugar

½ cup (4 fl oz/125 ml) tuaca liqueur or rum

ground cinnamon

In a saucepan over medium-high heat, combine the cider, lemon zest, cinnamon sticks, cloves, allspice, and brown sugar. Bring to a boil, stirring to dissolve the sugar. Reduce to medium-low and simmer for 20 minutes. Meanwhile, whisk the cream with the granulated sugar until soft peaks form. Add 2 tablespoons tuaca or rum to each of 4 warmed mugs. Pour the hot cider through a sieve into the mugs. Top with whipped cream and ground cinnamon and serve.

serves four | per serving: calories 263 (kilojoules 1,105), protein 1 g, carbohydrates 41 g, total fat 11 g, saturated fat 7 g, cholesterol 41 mg, sodium 22 mg, dietary fiber 0 g

hot buttered rum

3 tablespoons brown sugar

1½ tablespoons unsalted butter, at room temperature

⅛ teaspoon each ground nutmeg, cinnamon, and cloves

¾ cup (6 fl oz/180 ml) rum

2 cups (16 fl oz/500 ml) boiling water

4 cinnamon sticks

In a small bowl, stir together the brown sugar, butter, nutmeg, cinnamon, and cloves. Distribute evenly among 4 warmed mugs. Add 3 tablespoons rum to each cup, then fill with the boiling water, stirring well. Garnish with cinnamon sticks.

serves four | per serving: calories 175 (kilojoules 735), protein 0 g, carbohydrates 11 g, total fat 4 g, saturated fat 3 g, cholesterol 12 mg, sodium 5 mg, dietary fiber 0 g

irish coffee

8 teaspoons sugar, or to taste

½ cup (4 fl oz/125 ml) whiskey

2 cups (16 fl oz/500 ml) hot brewed coffee, or as needed

½ cup (4 fl oz/125 ml) heavy (double) cream, lightly beaten to form soft peaks

Place 2 teaspoons sugar in each of 4 medium-sized glass mugs. Add 2 tablespoons whiskey to each mug, then fill with coffee. Holding a spoon rounded side up over each mug, slowly pour the cream over the spoon, floating it on each mug.

serves four | per serving: calories 207 (kilojoules 869), protein 1 g, carbohydrates 10 g, total fat 11 g, saturated fat 7 g, cholesterol 41 mg, sodium 14 mg, dietary fiber 0 g

rich hot chocolate

2 cups (16 fl oz/500 ml) whole or low-fat (2 percent) milk

⅓ cup (2 oz/60 g) semisweet (plain) chocolate chips

1 teaspoon vanilla extract (essence)

In a small saucepan, combine the milk, chocolate chips, and vanilla. Cook over medium heat, stirring once or twice, until the milk is just steaming, 3–5 minutes. Continuing to cook, beat with a wire whisk or a rotary beater until the chocolate is melted and the mixture is frothy. Pour into mugs and serve.

serves two | per serving: calories 288 (kilojoules 1,210), protein 9 g, carbohydrates 30 g, total fat 16 g, saturated fat 10 g, cholesterol 34 mg, sodium 120 mg, dietary fiber 0 g

spiced pinot noir

1 bottle (24 fl oz/750 ml) pinot noir or other dry red wine such as zinfandel or merlot

½ cup (4 oz/125 g) sugar

4 orange zest strips

1 tablespoon whole allspice berries

1 teaspoon whole black peppercorns

In a heavy saucepan, combine the wine, sugar, zest, allspice, and peppercorns. Stir over medium-high heat until the sugar is dissolved and the wine is steaming; do not allow to boil. Reduce the heat to medium-low and cook for about 10 minutes. Remove from the heat and ladle into mugs or heat-proof glasses to serve.

serves four to six | per serving: calories 192 (kilojoules 806), protein 0 g, carbohydrates 26 g, total fat 0 g, saturated fat 0 g, cholesterol 0 mg, sodium 8 mg, dietary fiber 0 g

mulled cider

4 cups (32 fl oz/1 l) pure, unsweetened apple cider

2 cinnamon sticks, broken in half

about 15 whole cloves

6–8 pieces crystallized ginger, 1 oz (30 g) total weight

½ cup (4 fl oz/125 ml) dark rum or bourbon (optional)

1 apple

juice of ½ lemon

In a small, heavy saucepan, combine the cider, cinnamon, cloves, and crystallized ginger. Warm over medium-high heat until the cider is steaming; do not allow to boil. Reduce the heat to medium-low and continue to cook for about 10 minutes. Remove from the heat and, if desired, stir in the rum or bourbon.

Peel and slice the apple, then moisten the slices with lemon juice to keep them from discoloring. Strain the cider into mugs and float 3 apple slices on top of each serving.

serves four | per serving: calories 163 (kilojoules 685), protein 0 g, carbohydrates 41 g, total fat 0 g, saturated fat 0 g, cholesterol 0 mg, sodium 13 mg, dietary fiber 1 g

breakfast & brunch

Raisin-dotted scones baking in an oven, pancakes cooking to a puffy, golden finish on a griddle, strips of bacon sizzling in a frying pan—these are the typical morning sights and scents of a cabin kitchen.

If your day includes a fresh-air activity, first sit down to a stack of oatmeal griddle cakes or cornmeal waffles with blueberry syrup. In fact, tucking into a mushroom-filled omelet, a frittata laced with bacon and potatoes, or some raisin bread French toast may motivate you to hike or swim or ski to work off the calories. Or plan ahead by making the batter for carrot muffins the night before and get out the door in record time.

The day's first meal can also be its most leisurely, enjoyed on a beach-house deck followed by no more than a serious read of the newspaper. An appealing brunch menu on the same deck might include old-fashioned hash with poached eggs, delicate crêpes slathered with strawberry jam, or a hearty serving of Huevos Rancheros crowned with avocado salsa. Share the wealth and invite a few friends to partake of the food and the sunshine.

spring

avocado and crab omelets

Omelets should be served hot out of the pan. Have all the ingredients assembled, the guests seated, and a stack of warmed plates ready before you begin cooking.

1 large avocado, 8–10 oz (250–315 g), halved, pitted, peeled, and finely diced

1 tablespoon lemon juice

½ lb (250 g) cooked lump crabmeat, picked over for shell fragments and flaked

1 tomato, peeled, seeded, and diced

salt and ground pepper to taste

12 eggs

6 tablespoons (3 oz/90 g) unsalted butter

In a bowl, toss the avocado with the lemon juice. Stir in the crabmeat and tomato. Season with salt and pepper.

In a large bowl, whisk 3 of the eggs with salt and pepper until frothy. In a small omelet pan over medium-high heat, melt 2 tablespoons of the butter. When the butter stops bubbling, add the beaten eggs and immediately stir with the back of a fork until they start to thicken, about 10 seconds. Pull the set portion of the eggs back from the edges and tilt the pan to let the uncooked portion run to the sides. Continue cooking, shaking the pan constantly, until almost set, about 20 seconds longer.

Spoon one-fourth of the avocado mixture onto the center of the omelet. Cook until the bottom is browned and the top is set as desired, 30–45 seconds longer.

Hold the pan handle in one hand and tip the pan away from you. Using a fork, fold the top edge of the omelet over onto the center. Quickly flip the pan over so the omelet slides onto a warmed plate, folded in thirds with the seam side down.

Serve at once, then repeat to make 3 more omelets, adding butter to the pan as needed.

serves four | per serving: calories 516 (kilojoules 2,167), protein 32 g, carbohydrates 7 g, total fat 41 g, saturated fat 17 g, cholesterol 741 mg, sodium 357 mg, dietary fiber 1 g

mixed mushroom omelet

This oversized omelet makes a hearty breakfast for two. A nonstick pan will give you the best results; if you have only a regular skillet, use more butter or just scramble the eggs and top them with the mushroom-onion mixture and sour cream.

½ lb (250 g) mixed mushrooms such as button, cremini, shiitake, or chanterelle

1 large portobello mushroom

2 tablespoons unsalted butter

½ yellow onion, sliced

1 teaspoon fresh thyme leaves or ½ teaspoon dried thyme

4 eggs

2 tablespoons warm water

2 tablespoons thinly sliced chives or green (spring) onion tops

salt and ground pepper

¼ cup (2 oz/60 g) sour cream

Wipe the mushroom tops clean with a damp cloth; remove and discard the stems and slice the caps. Cut the portobello slices in half crosswise. Place an 8- to 10-inch (20- to 25-cm) nonstick frying pan over medium-high heat and melt 1 tablespoon of the butter. Add the onion and cook, stirring, until softened, about 7 minutes. Add the mushrooms and thyme and continue to cook, stirring often, until the mushrooms are soft and any liquid has evaporated, about 8 minutes. Remove the mushrooms and onion from the pan and keep warm. Wipe the pan clean and set aside.

In a bowl, beat the eggs with the warm water and chives; season with salt and pepper to taste. Melt the remaining 1 tablespoon butter in the same frying pan over medium-high heat. Pour the egg mixture into the pan. When it begins to set, use a wooden spoon to push the edges gently toward the center, tilting the pan so that the uncooked egg flows underneath. Continue until the eggs are almost set but still slightly moist on top, about 3 minutes.

Spoon the mushroom-onion mixture over half of the omelet; top with the sour cream. Shake the pan to loosen the omelet; if it sticks, loosen the edges with the wooden spoon. Starting with the mushroom-covered side, slide onto a warmed plate. When half of the omelet is on the plate, invert the pan to fold the omelet over the filling. Cut in half and serve at once.

serves two | per serving: calories 380 (kilojoules 1,596), protein 18 g, carbohydrates 16 g, total fat 28 g, saturated fat 14 g, cholesterol 469 mg, sodium 152 mg, dietary fiber 3 g

mountain breakfast scones

To earn their name, these cakelike scones come in mountainous proportions. For smaller scones, cut the dough rectangle in half to form two squares, then cut each square on the diagonal into quarters. Serve the smaller scones with tea, coffee, or hot chocolate in the afternoon.

1½ cups (7½ oz/235 g) all-purpose (plain) flour

3 tablespoons plus 1 teaspoon sugar

2 teaspoons baking powder

pinch of salt

¼ cup (2 oz/60 g) chilled unsalted butter, cut into small pieces

⅓ cup (2 oz/60 g) golden raisins (sultanas)

¾ teaspoon grated orange or lemon zest

⅔ cup (5 fl oz/160 ml) plus 1 tablespoon milk

1 teaspoon ground cinnamon

Preheat the oven to 425°F (220°C). In a bowl, mix together the flour, 3 tablespoons sugar, the baking powder, and the salt. Using 2 knives or a pastry blender, cut in the butter until the mixture resembles coarse meal. Mix in the raisins. Stir the zest into the ⅔ cup (5 fl oz/160 ml) milk. Make a well in the center of the flour mixture and pour the milk mixture into it; mix quickly with a fork until moistened.

Turn the dough out onto a lightly floured work surface and gather together. Knead briefly just until the dough holds together; do not overknead or the scones will be tough. Pat the dough into a rectangle about ½ inch (12 mm) thick, 4 inches (10 cm) wide, and 8 inches (20 cm) long. Starting with a short side, fold the dough in half to make a square. Press the dough lightly so that the top adheres to the bottom. Cut the square on the diagonal into quarters; you will have 4 big triangular scones. Transfer to an ungreased baking sheet, spacing them about 2 inches (5 cm) apart.

In a small bowl, stir together the 1 teaspoon sugar and the cinnamon. Brush the tops of the scones with the 1 tablespoon milk and sprinkle evenly with the cinnamon sugar. Bake until the scones are puffed, but not dry, about 15 minutes. Remove from the oven and let cool on the baking sheet on a rack for about 5 minutes. Serve warm or transfer to the rack and let cool completely.

makes four large scones | per scone: calories 409 (kilojoules 1,718), protein 8 g, carbohydrates 65 g, total fat 14 g, saturated fat 8 g, cholesterol 37 mg, sodium 303 mg, dietary fiber 2 g

overnight carrot muffins

These light, wholesome muffins offer ultra convenience. The batter can be made up to 2 days ahead. Or, if you prefer, bake the muffins right away, decreasing the cooking time by 5 minutes.

2 cups (10 oz/315 g) all-purpose (plain) flour
1 cup (3 oz/90 g) rolled oats
1 cup (7 oz/220 g) firmly packed light brown sugar
2 teaspoons baking soda (bicarbonate of soda)
½ teaspoon salt
½ teaspoon ground allspice
1 cup (6 oz/185 g) raisins
2 eggs
1 cup (8 fl oz/250 ml) buttermilk
½ cup (4 fl oz/125 ml) vegetable oil
1 cup (5 oz/155 g) lightly packed shredded carrots

In a large bowl, stir together the flour, oats, brown sugar, baking soda, salt, and allspice. Add the raisins and toss to coat with the flour mixture. In another bowl, beat the eggs, buttermilk, oil, and carrots until well blended. Pour over the flour-raisin mixture and stir just until blended; do not overmix. Cover tightly and refrigerate overnight, or for up to 2 days.

To bake, preheat the oven to 375°F (190°C). Oil 12 standard muffin pan cups. Spoon the batter into the prepared cups and bake until golden brown and a toothpick inserted in the center of a muffin comes out clean, about 25 minutes. Remove from the oven and let cool in the pan on a rack for about 5 minutes. Serve warm or transfer the muffins to the rack to cool completely.

makes twelve muffins | per muffin: calories 336 (kilojoules 1,411), protein 6 g, carbohydrates 52 g, total fat 12 g, saturated fat 2 g, cholesterol 37 mg, sodium 335 mg, dietary fiber 2 g

scrambled eggs with smoked salmon and chives

Farm-fresh eggs and premium smoked salmon will turn this simple dish into a masterpiece. Serve on a deck overlooking the sea, with toasted bagels and a pitcher of Spicy Bloody Marys (page 26).

15 eggs
½ cup (4 fl oz/125 ml) half-and-half (half cream)
3 oz (90 g) smoked salmon, cut into narrow strips
4 tablespoons (⅓ oz/10 g) snipped fresh chives
½ teaspoon salt
½ teaspoon ground pepper

In a large heatproof bowl, whisk together the eggs and half-and-half until well blended. Set the bowl over (not touching) barely simmering water in a saucepan. Cook, stirring and scraping the bowl sides constantly with a rubber spatula, until the eggs begin to scramble, 12–15 minutes. Stir in the salmon, 3 tablespoons of the chives, the salt, and the pepper. Continue cooking and stirring until the eggs are soft but not runny.

Quickly transfer the eggs to a warmed shallow bowl, sprinkle with the remaining 1 tablespoon chives, and serve immediately.

serves six | per serving: calories 230 (kilojoules 966), protein 19 g, carbohydrates 3 g, total fat 15 g, saturated fat 5 g, cholesterol 542 mg, sodium 642 mg, dietary fiber 0 g

summer

cornmeal waffles with blueberry-orange syrup

The nooks and crannies of these crisp waffles trap a delicious homemade fruit syrup. The waffles can be cooked, cooled, layered with waxed paper in a plastic bag, and frozen for up to 1 month; then just pop the sections into a toaster to reheat.

for the blueberry-orange syrup:

¾ lb (375 g) blueberries (fresh or thawed frozen)

¼ cup (2 oz/60 g) sugar

juice of 1 orange

¼ teaspoon ground cinnamon

for the waffles:

1 cup (5 oz/155 g) all-purpose (plain) flour

1 cup (5 oz/155 g) yellow cornmeal

2 tablespoons sugar

1 tablespoon baking powder

pinch of salt

1½ cups (12 fl oz/375 ml) milk

1 egg, at room temperature, lightly beaten

3 tablespoons unsalted butter, melted, plus butter as needed

To make the syrup, combine the blueberries, sugar, orange juice, and cinnamon in a saucepan. Stir well. Bring to a boil, then reduce the heat to low and simmer, uncovered, until slightly thickened, 8–10 minutes. Remove from the heat and set aside.

To make the waffles, preheat the waffle iron. In a large bowl, stir together the flour, cornmeal, sugar, baking powder, and salt. In another bowl, beat the milk, egg, and 2 tablespoons of the melted butter. Pour into the flour mixture and stir until combined.

Grease the waffle iron with the remaining 1 tablespoon melted butter. Ladle the batter, about ½ cup (4 fl oz/125 ml) at a time, onto the waffle iron and cook according to the manufacturer's directions until golden. Transfer the waffles to a plate; keep warm. Repeat with the remaining batter, adding more butter if needed. Divide the waffles among individual plates, top with the syrup, and serve.

makes eight 6-inch (15-cm) waffles; serves four to six | per waffle: calories 278 (kilojoules 1,168), protein 6 g, carbohydrates 47 g, total fat 6 g, saturated fat 4 g, cholesterol 46 mg, sodium 234 mg, dietary fiber 2 g

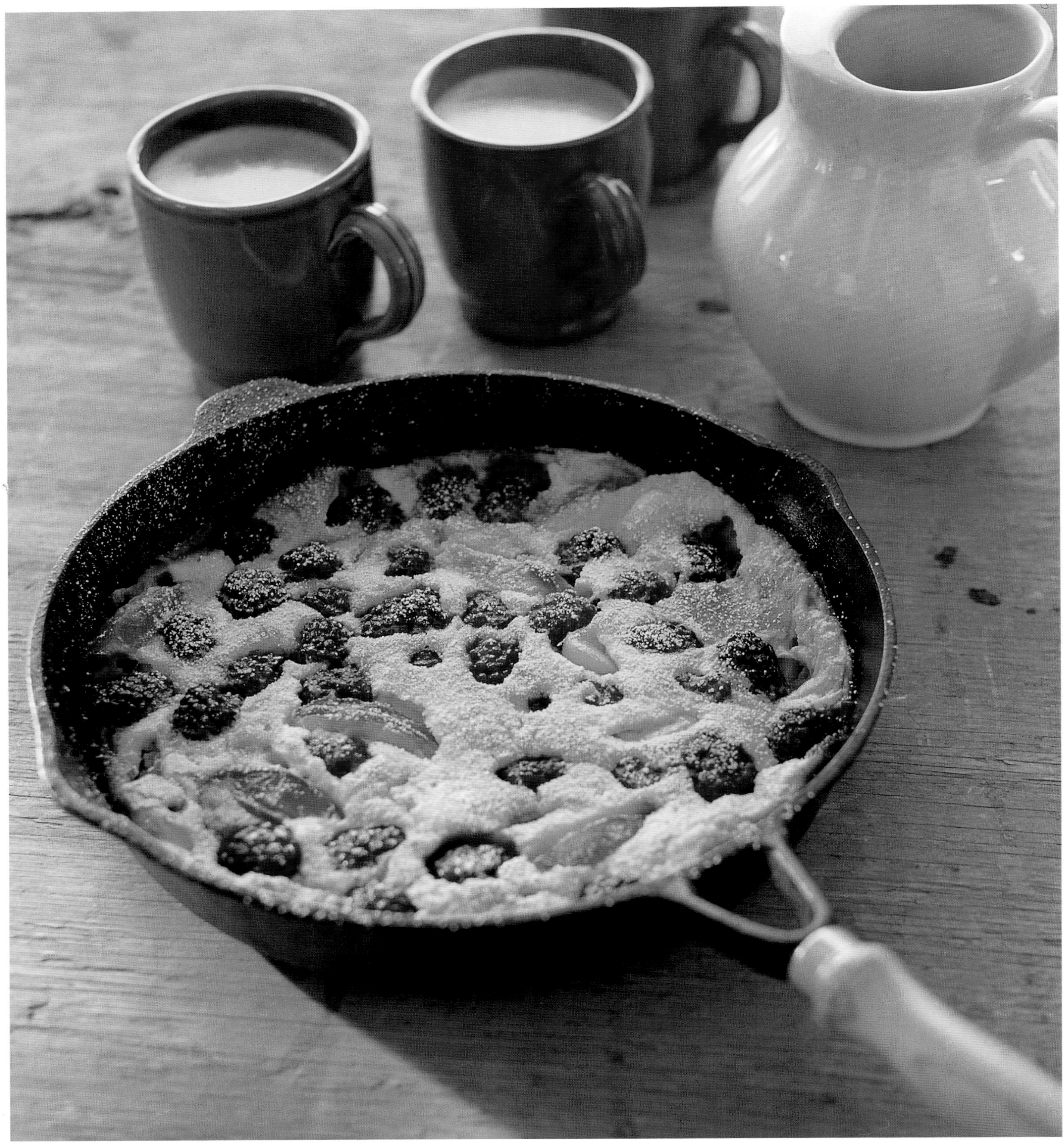

puffed oven pancake with summer fruit

Based on an old recipe for German pancakes, this dish is a one-pan marvel. The batter is baked over sliced peaches or nectarines and berries in a frying pan and dusted with sugar to serve. It's delicious with steaming mugs of coffee or Rich Hot Chocolate (page 29).

⅓ cup (2 oz/60 g) all-purpose (plain) flour

2 tablespoons granulated sugar

⅓ cup (3 oz/80 ml) milk

3 eggs

¼ cup (2 oz/60 g) unsalted butter

2 firm, ripe peaches or nectarines, peeled, if desired, pitted, and sliced

1½ cups (6 oz/185 g) raspberries or blackberries

about 2 tablespoons confectioners' (icing) sugar

lemon wedges (optional)

Preheat the oven to 425°F (220°C). In a bowl, beat together the flour, granulated sugar, milk, and eggs until thoroughly blended. Set aside.

In a 10- to 12-inch (25- to 30-cm) heatproof frying pan over medium-high heat, melt the butter. Add the peaches or nectarines and cook, stirring often, until the fruit is hot and slightly softened, 3–5 minutes, depending on ripeness. Remove from the heat and scatter with the berries.

Pour the egg mixture over the fruit in the pan and immediately put in the oven. Bake until puffed and golden, about 18 minutes.

Remove the pancake from the oven and sift confectioners' sugar over the top. Cut into wedges to serve. If desired, offer lemon wedges on the side.

serves four | per serving: calories 309 (kilojoules 1,298), protein 8 g, carbohydrates 34 g, total fat 16 g, saturated fat 9 g, cholesterol 193 mg, sodium 59 mg, dietary fiber 3 g

summer squash frittata

In this flat, Italian-style omelet, the filling is mixed in with the eggs. If crookneck and pattypan squash are unavailable, substitute 3 medium zucchini.

2 tablespoons olive oil, plus oil as needed

3 small pattypan squashes, diced

2 small yellow crookneck squashes, diced

2 tablespoons chopped fresh oregano or 1 tablespoon dried oregano

salt and ground pepper

6 eggs

2 tablespoons warm water

3 oz (90 g) fontina or Monterey jack cheese, cut into small pieces

In a heatproof 8-inch (20-cm) frying pan over medium-high heat, warm the 2 tablespoons olive oil. Add the diced squashes and cook, stirring occasionally, until softened and lightly browned, about 8 minutes. Stir in the oregano and season to taste with salt and pepper.

Meanwhile, preheat the broiler (grill). In a small bowl, lightly beat the eggs with the warm water, then stir in the cheese. When the squash is ready, spread it in an even layer in the frying pan; if the pan seems dry, add a little more olive oil. Pour in the egg-cheese mixture. When it begins to set, lift the edge with a wooden spoon to let the uncooked eggs flow underneath. Continue to cook until the top of the frittata looks fairly dry, about 4 minutes.

Slip the pan under the broiler, placing it about 6 inches (15 cm) below the heat. Broil (grill) until the top of the frittata is puffed and golden, about 3 minutes. Cut into wedges and serve directly from the pan.

serves four | per serving: calories 298 (kilojoules 1,252), protein 16 g, carbohydrates 6 g, total fat 23 g, saturated fat 8 g, cholesterol 343 mg, sodium 266 mg, dietary fiber 1 g

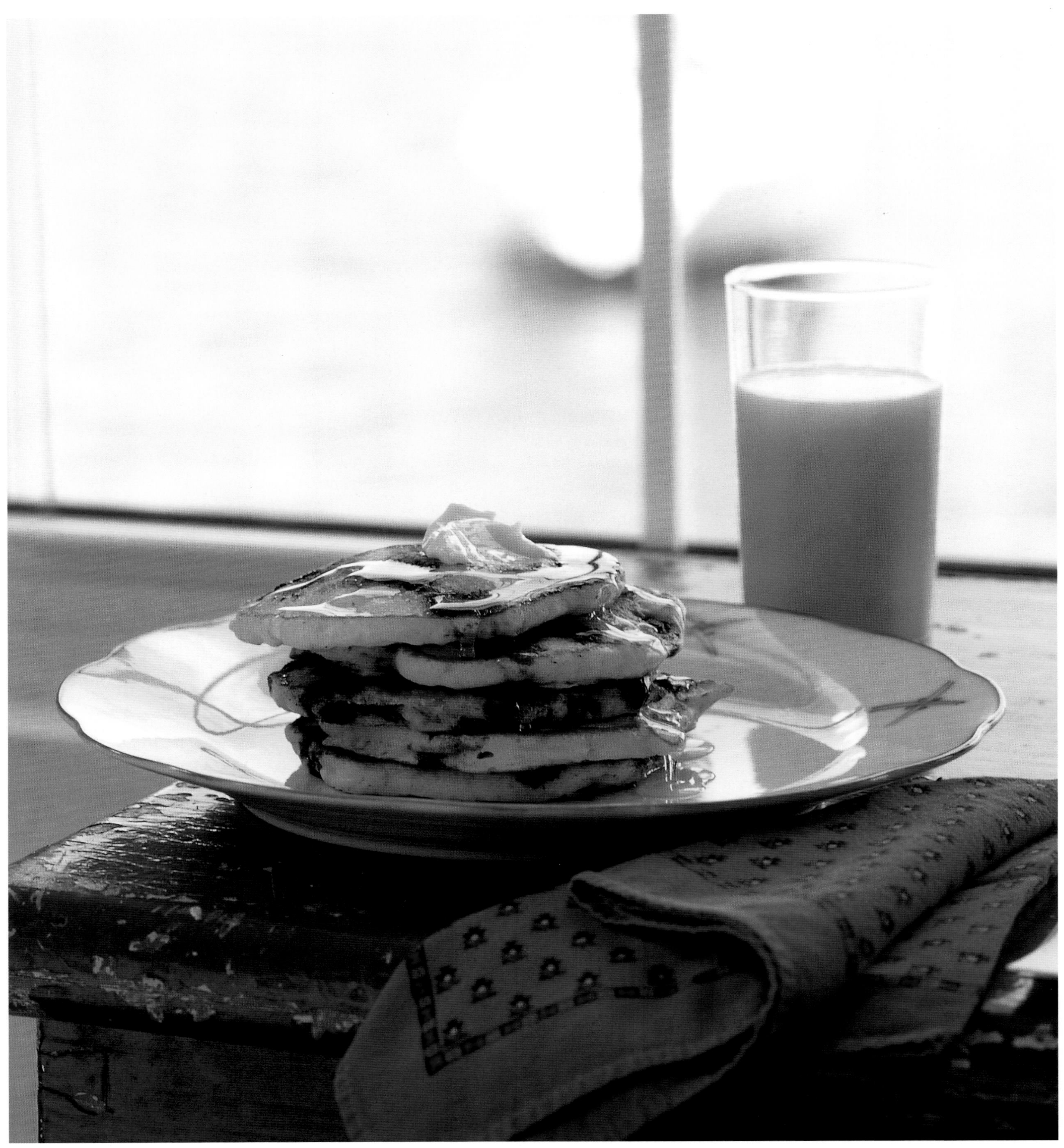

blueberry buttermilk pancakes

For best results, have all the ingredients at room temperature and use a light hand when mixing the batter. For a robust breakfast before a late-morning game of beach volleyball, serve the pancakes with butter and maple syrup or honey and accompany with bacon, smoked sausages, or grilled ham steaks.

2 cups (10 oz/315 g) all-purpose (plain) flour

2 teaspoons baking powder

1 teaspoon baking soda (bicarbonate of soda)

1 teaspoon salt

2 eggs

2 cups (16 fl oz/500 ml) buttermilk

¼ cup (2 oz/60 g) unsalted butter, melted and cooled, plus 1–2 tablespoons

2 cups (8 oz/250 g) small, stemmed blueberries

In a large bowl, sift together the flour, baking powder, baking soda, and salt. In another bowl, beat together the eggs and buttermilk until blended. Pour the wet ingredients into the dry ingredients and mix quickly with a large wooden spoon until a smooth batter forms. Fold in the ¼ cup (2 fl oz/60 ml) melted butter and blueberries.

Preheat a large frying pan or griddle to medium-high heat. Brush well with some of the remaining butter and wipe off any excess with a paper towel. Pour or ladle on about 2 tablespoons of the batter for each pancake, forming circles 4–5 inches (10–13 cm) in diameter. Cook until browned on the bottom and bubbles appear on the surface, about 3 minutes. Using a spatula, flip and cook until lightly browned on the second side, about 3 minutes longer. Transfer to a plate and keep warm. Repeat with the remaining batter, brushing the pan or griddle with more butter as needed.

Divide the pancakes evenly among individual plates and serve with desired toppings (see note).

serves six to eight | per pancake: calories 109 (kilojoules 458), protein 3 g, carbohydrates 14 g, total fat 4 g, saturated fat 2 g, cholesterol 32 mg, sodium 276 mg, dietary fiber 1 g

baked eggs piperade

Piper *is the Basque word for "pepper." Add some finely diced air-cured ham, such as prosciutto, to the pepper mixture just before you pour it into the baking dish for an authentic version of this regional favorite.*

2 tablespoons olive oil

1 onion, finely chopped

1 celery stalk, peeled and finely chopped

1 large red bell pepper (capsicum), seeded and finely diced

1 large yellow bell pepper (capsicum), seeded and finely diced

1 large green bell pepper (capsicum), seeded and finely diced

1 clove garlic, minced

2 tomatoes, peeled, seeded, and chopped

salt and ground pepper to taste

6 eggs

In a large, heavy saucepan over medium-high heat, warm the oil. Add the onion and celery and sauté until slightly softened, about 3 minutes. Add all the bell peppers and sauté until softened, about 5 minutes. Add the garlic and cook for 1 minute longer. Stir in the tomatoes, increase the heat to high, and bring to a boil. Boil rapidly until the liquid given off by the tomatoes reduces and the mixture is slightly thickened, 5–7 minutes. Season well with salt and pepper, then pour into a 2-qt (2-l) baking dish and spread evenly over the bottom. (The recipe can be prepared up to this point 2 days in advance. Cover and refrigerate until ready to cook the eggs.)

Preheat the oven to 375°F (190°C).

Using the back of a large spoon, make 6 evenly spaced indentations in the pepper mixture. Break the eggs, one at a time, into a small saucer and slip an egg into each indentation, being careful not to break the yolks. Sprinkle with salt and pepper.

Bake until the eggs are soft but not tough and the pepper mixture is bubbling, 20–25 minutes. Serve immediately on warmed individual plates.

serves six | per serving: calories 160 (kilojoules 672), protein 8 g, carbohydrates 11 g, total fat 10 g, saturated fat 2 g, cholesterol 213 mg, sodium 76 mg, dietary fiber 3 g

savory bread pudding with goat cheese and ham

Chopped fresh herbs, if available, can be stirred into the beaten egg mixture just before the pudding goes into the oven.

2 tablespoons unsalted butter, at room temperature

24 slices day-old French or Italian bread, ¼ inch (6 mm) thick

¼ lb (125 g) fresh goat cheese, crumbled

1 thick slice boiled ham, about ¼ lb (125 g), finely diced

½ cup (2½ oz/75 g) pitted black olives, preferably Niçoise, coarsely chopped

6 eggs, lightly beaten

2 cups (16 fl oz/500 ml) milk

½ teaspoon salt

¼ teaspoon ground pepper

boiling water, as needed

2 tablespoons grated Parmesan cheese

Preheat the oven to 350°F (180°C). Butter a 2-qt (2-l) baking dish.

Spread a small amount of the butter over one side of each bread slice. Arrange one-third of the bread slices, buttered side up, on the bottom of the prepared baking dish. Scatter half of the goat cheese over the top. Top with half of the ham and half of the olives. Top with half of the remaining bread slices and then layer all of the remaining goat cheese, ham, and olives. Place the remaining bread slices on top.

In a large bowl, whisk together the eggs, milk, salt, and pepper. Ladle or pour the egg mixture over the contents of the baking dish. Cover with aluminum foil. Set the pudding dish in another, larger baking dish and place in the oven. Pour boiling water into the larger baking dish to reach halfway up the sides of the pudding dish.

Bake for 30 minutes. Remove the foil and sprinkle with the Parmesan cheese. Continue to bake until the top is golden brown and the center is set, about 30 minutes longer. Remove from the oven and let cool slightly. Spoon onto individual plates and serve warm.

serves six to eight | per serving: calories 370 (kilojoules 1,554), protein 19 g, carbohydrates 27 g, total fat 20 g, saturated fat 9 g, cholesterol 220 mg, sodium 966 mg, dietary fiber 2 g

upside-down plum coffee cake

This easy, delicious treat is perfect for Sunday brunch at the cabin. Plums are available from May to October, and there are several varieties to choose from. Try Santa Rosa, Black Amber, Laroda, or El Dorado in this dish.

for the topping:

2 tablespoons unsalted butter

½ cup (4 oz/125 g) sugar

½ teaspoon ground cinnamon

4 plums, preferably freestone and about ½ lb (250 g) total weight, halved, pitted, and sliced at least ⅛ inch (3 mm) thick *(see note)*

for the cake:

1½ cups (7½ oz/235 g) all-purpose (plain) flour

1 cup (8 oz/250 g) sugar

2 teaspoons baking powder

¼ teaspoon salt

4 tablespoons (2 oz/60 g) chilled unsalted butter, cut into pieces

1 egg

½ cup (4 fl oz/125 ml) milk

½ teaspoon vanilla extract (essence)

To make the topping, in a 9- or 10-inch (23- or 25-cm) ovenproof nonstick frying pan over medium-high heat, melt the butter. Stir in the sugar and cinnamon and add the plum slices. Cook gently, stirring, until the plums have exuded their juices and the sugar has dissolved, 5–7 minutes. Remove from the heat and strain through a sieve placed over a small bowl. Arrange the plum slices over the bottom of the frying pan, overlapping them in concentric circles. Reserve the juices.

Preheat the oven to 375°F (190°C).

To make the cake, in a large bowl, stir together the flour, sugar, baking powder, and salt. Using 2 knives or your fingertips, cut in the butter until the mixture resembles coarse meal. In a small bowl, using a fork, beat together the egg, milk, and vanilla until blended. Pour into the flour mixture and stir with a wooden spoon just until a smooth batter forms.

Pour the batter over the plums in the frying pan. Bake until a toothpick inserted into the center comes out clean, about 30 minutes. Invert onto a rack, dislodging any slices that adhere to the frying pan and carefully replacing them on the cake. Brush the top of the warm cake with the reserved juices, then let cool. Cut into wedges to serve.

serves eight | per serving: calories 373 (kilojoules 1,567), protein 4 g, carbohydrates 67 g, total fat 10 g, saturated fat 6 g, cholesterol 52 mg, sodium 211 mg, dietary fiber 1 g

raspberry peach muffins

For variety, substitute strawberries or blueberries for the raspberries, and apricots or nectarines for the peaches.

2 cups (10 oz/315 g) all-purpose (plain) flour
½ cup (4 oz/125 g) plus 2 tablespoons sugar
2 teaspoons baking powder
1 teaspoon baking soda (bicarbonate of soda)
¼ teaspoon salt
1 cup (8 fl oz/250 ml) buttermilk
2 eggs
3 tablespoons unsalted butter, melted and cooled
½ cup (2 oz/60 g) raspberries
1 cup (6 oz/185 g) peeled and diced peaches

Preheat the oven to 400°F (200°C). Butter 12 standard muffin-tin cups.

In a large bowl, sift together the flour, ½ cup (4 oz/125 g) sugar, baking powder, baking soda, and salt. In another bowl, whisk together the buttermilk, eggs, and butter until blended.

Make a well in the center of the dry ingredients. Pour in the buttermilk mixture and then stir quickly to form a smooth batter. Do not overmix. Fold in the raspberries and peaches. Spoon into the prepared cups, filling them three-fourths full. Sprinkle the 2 tablespoons sugar evenly over the tops.

Bake until a toothpick inserted into the center of a muffin comes out clean, about 20 minutes. Transfer to a rack to cool for 10 minutes, then turn out onto the rack. Serve hot.

makes twelve muffins | per muffin: calories 190 (kilojoules 798), protein 4 g, carbohydrates 32 g, total fat 5 g, saturated fat 3 g, cholesterol 47 mg, sodium 267 mg, dietary fiber 1 g

frittata with caramelized onions and roasted peppers

A frittata, served at room temperature, is perfect for brunch. It can also be wrapped in foil, packed in a cooler, and toted to the beach for a picnic.

1 large red bell pepper (capsicum)

1 large yellow bell pepper (capsicum)

3 Yukon gold potatoes, about ¾ lb (375 g) total weight

2 tablespoons unsalted butter

2 yellow onions, thinly sliced

¼ teaspoon sugar

pinch of salt, plus ½ teaspoon

6 eggs

¾ teaspoon ground pepper

2 tablespoons grated Parmesan cheese

Preheat the broiler (grill). Cut the bell peppers in half lengthwise and remove the stems, seeds, and ribs. Place the halves, cut sides down, on a baking sheet and broil (grill) until the skins blacken and blister. Remove from the broiler, drape loosely with aluminum foil, let stand for 10 minutes, then peel away the skins and thinly slice; set aside.

Meanwhile, in a saucepan, cook the potatoes in salted water to cover until tender, 30–40 minutes. Drain, peel, let cool, halve lengthwise, and thinly slice.

In a large, heavy frying pan over medium heat, melt the butter. Add the onions, sugar, and the pinch of salt. Cook, stirring often, until the onions are golden brown and lightly caramelized, about 30 minutes.

In a bowl, whisk together the eggs, the ½ teaspoon salt, and the pepper. Arrange the potatoes, overlapping, over the bottom of a large, heavy nonstick frying pan. Scatter over half of the onions and bell peppers. Pour the eggs evenly over the surface, and top with the remaining onions and peppers. Set aside for 20 minutes so that the potatoes absorb some of the eggs.

Place the frying pan over medium-low heat. Cook, shaking the pan often, until the frittata bottom is lightly browned, 10–12 minutes. Slide the frittata onto a large plate, then return it to the pan, browned side up. Cook until lightly browned and set in the center, 2–3 minutes longer. Invert onto a cutting board and sprinkle with the cheese. Let cool to room temperature, then cut into wedges to serve.

serves four to six | per serving: calories 232 (kilojoules 974), protein 11 g, carbohydrates 22 g, total fat 11 g, saturated fat 5 g, cholesterol 269 mg, sodium 614 mg, dietary fiber 3 g

huevos rancheros

for the salsa:

2 large, ripe avocados

4 green (spring) onions, including tender green tops, minced

¼ cup (2 oz/60 g) canned diced green chiles

juice of 2 or 3 limes

3 tablespoons minced fresh cilantro (fresh coriander)

salt

for the huevos rancheros:

2 cans (15 oz/470 g each) black beans, drained and rinsed

warm water as needed

salt and ground pepper

8 eggs

4 green (spring) onions, including tender green tops, thinly sliced

¼ lb (125 g) feta cheese, crumbled

1 tablespoon unsalted butter

4 corn tortillas

To prepare the salsa, pit and peel the avocados. In a bowl, mash the avocados well with a fork. Stir in the green onions, chiles, juice from 2 limes, and minced cilantro. Season to taste with salt and more lime juice, if desired. Cover with plastic wrap and set aside for up to 30 minutes.

Meanwhile, prepare the huevos rancheros: In a small saucepan over medium heat, combine the black beans with a few tablespoons of warm water, just enough to moisten the beans. When the beans are hot, mash lightly with a fork to break them down and thicken them. Season to taste with salt and pepper. Cover the beans and remove from the heat.

Preheat the broiler (grill). In a bowl, beat the eggs with 2 tablespoons warm water. Mix in the green onions and feta cheese. Melt the butter in a large frying pan over medium-high heat. Add the egg-cheese mixture and softly scramble. While the eggs are cooking, place the tortillas on a baking sheet and broil (grill) about 4 inches (10 cm) below the heat, turning once, until just lightly browned, about 3 minutes total.

Place the tortillas on individual plates and spread evenly with the mashed black beans. Top with the scrambled eggs and the salsa, then serve.

serves four | per serving: calories 642 (kilojoules 2,696), protein 29 g, carbohydrates 48 g, total fat 40 g, saturated fat 12 g, cholesterol 458 mg, sodium 931 mg, dietary fiber 10 g

autumn

oatmeal griddle cakes with pecan-maple syrup

Homemade pancakes don't take much longer to make than those prepared from a mix, and they are far tastier and healthier. Top them with nuts, syrup, and yogurt for an unforgettable start to any day.

1 cup (3 oz/90 g) rolled oats
1¾ cups (14 fl oz/430 ml) buttermilk
⅔ cup (3 oz/90 g) chopped pecans
1 cup (8 fl oz/250 ml) pure maple syrup
1 cup (5 oz/155 g) all-purpose (plain) flour
3 tablespoons firmly packed light brown sugar
2 teaspoons baking soda (bicarbonate of soda)
pinch of salt
1 egg, at room temperature, lightly beaten
4 tablespoons (2 oz/60 g) unsalted butter, melted, plus butter as needed
½ cup (4 oz/125 g) low-fat plain or vanilla yogurt

In a large bowl, combine the oats and buttermilk and let stand for about 15 minutes. Meanwhile, in a small saucepan, toast the pecans over medium heat, stirring often, until fragrant and lightly browned, about 5 minutes. Remove from the heat. Pour the maple syrup into the saucepan (the mixture will bubble up); stir well. Cover to keep warm and set aside.

In a small bowl, stir together the flour, brown sugar, baking soda, and salt. Add to the soaked oats, then stir in the egg and 2 tablespoons of the melted butter. Mix well.

In a frying pan over medium-high heat, heat the remaining 2 tablespoons melted butter. Ladle the batter, about ¼ cup (2 fl oz/60 ml) at a time, spaced well apart, into the pan. Cook until the tops are bubbly and the bottoms are golden brown, about 4 minutes. Turn and cook until golden brown on the second side, about 3 minutes longer. Transfer the pancakes to a plate; keep warm. Repeat with the remaining batter, adding more butter if needed.

Divide the pancakes among individual plates and top each serving with some of the pecan-maple syrup and a spoonful of yogurt. Pass the remaining pecan-maple syrup at the table.

makes about twelve pancakes; serves four to six | per pancake: calories 263 (kilojoules 1,105), protein 5 g, carbohydrates 38 g, total fat 10 g, saturated fat 3 g, cholesterol 31 mg, sodium 275 mg, dietary fiber 2 g

raisin bread french toast with sautéed pears

For the best flavor, use Comice or Anjou pears. You can also substitute a good cooking apple. Serve Brown Sugar Bacon (right) alongside to make this a substantial country breakfast.

3 tablespoons unsalted butter

2 firm, ripe pears, cored and cut into chunks (*see note*)

¼ cup (2 fl oz/60 ml) orange juice

6 eggs

½ cup (4 fl oz/125 ml) milk

¼ teaspoon ground cinnamon

¼ teaspoon sugar

pinch of ground nutmeg (optional)

8 slices raisin bread

about 1 cup (8 fl oz/250 ml) maple syrup, warmed

Melt 1 tablespoon of the butter in a large frying pan over medium-high heat. Add the pears and cook, stirring, until just softened, about 3 minutes. Pour in the orange juice, raise the heat to high, and cook, stirring, until the liquid reduces to a glaze and the pears are soft, about 4 minutes. Remove the pears and their sauce from the pan and keep warm while you make the French toast. Wipe the pan clean and set aside.

In a large shallow bowl, beat together the eggs, milk, cinnamon, sugar, and nutmeg, if using. Place 4 slices of the bread in the egg mixture and let soak for about 2 minutes, turning once.

In the same frying pan over medium-high heat, melt 1 tablespoon of the butter. Working with 4 slices at a time, transfer the soaked bread to the pan and cook, turning once, until golden brown, about 4 minutes total. Transfer the French toast to a plate and keep warm. Then soak and cook the remaining 4 bread slices, using the remaining 1 tablespoon butter.

Divide the French toast among warmed individual plates, and top evenly with the pears and their sauce. Pass the warmed maple syrup at the table.

serves four | per serving: calories 613 (kilojoules 2,575), protein 15 g, carbohydrates 97 g, total fat 20 g, saturated fat 9 g, cholesterol 346 mg, sodium 321 mg, dietary fiber 4 g

brown sugar bacon

This recipe has all of two ingredients and is so addictive that you'll wonder why you haven't always made bacon this way. If you don't have a slotted broiler pan, you can fry the bacon in a nonstick frying pan, sprinkling the sugar over it about halfway through cooking.

8 strips thick-cut bacon, about ¾ lb (375 g) total weight

3 tablespoons firmly packed light brown sugar

Preheat the broiler (grill). Line the bottom tray of a slotted broiler pan with aluminum foil.

On a sheet of waxed paper or aluminum foil, arrange the bacon strips side by side. Press the brown sugar through a sieve with the back of a spoon, letting it shower over the bacon strips and distributing it as evenly as possible. Rub a fingertip over each strip to smooth out the sugar and press it into the bacon.

Transfer the strips to the slotted top of the broiler pan, twisting each strip several times to form a corkscrew as you lay it down. The strips can be close together but should not touch.

Broil (grill) 6 inches (15 cm) below the heat until the edges are browned and crisp, 5–7 minutes; watch carefully as the sugar can burn. Turn and broil on the second side until crisp, 2–3 minutes longer. Transfer to paper towels to drain. Serve warm.

serves four | per serving: calories 176 (kilojoules 739), protein 7 g, carbohydrates 10 g, total fat 12 g, saturated fat 4 g, cholesterol 20 mg, sodium 384 mg, dietary fiber 0 g

chorizo and spinach scramble

This version of an old San Francisco dish called Joe's Special is made with spicy Mexican sausage, eggs, and cheese. Hot Italian sausage or regular pork sausage spiked with a little cayenne pepper can be substituted for the chorizo. Serve with Cabin Potatoes (right).

2 tablespoons vegetable oil

¾ lb (375 g) chorizo, thinly sliced *(see note)*

4 green (spring) onions, including tender green tops, sliced

2 bunches fresh spinach, stems removed and leaves chopped, or 1 package (10 oz/315 g) washed spinach leaves, chopped

6 eggs

2 tablespoons warm water

1 cup (4 oz/125 g) shredded Monterey jack cheese

In a large frying pan over medium-high heat, warm the oil. Add the sausage and cook, stirring often, until browned, about 5 minutes. Drain off the fat. Add the green onions and cook until softened, about 2 minutes. Add the chopped spinach in batches, stirring after each addition to wilt the leaves. Once all the spinach has been added and cooked down, pour off any liquid in the bottom of the pan.

In a bowl, beat the eggs with the warm water and cheese. Pour over the spinach-sausage mixture and cook, stirring, until the eggs are softly scrambled. Serve immediately.

serves four | per serving: calories 697 (kilojoules 2,927), protein 41 g, carbohydrates 8 g, total fat 56 g, saturated fat 20 g, cholesterol 424 mg, sodium 1,397 mg, dietary fiber 4 g

cabin potatoes

This potato cake is crisp outside, creamy within, and easy to prepare. If you don't have a nonstick frying pan, simply use a regular one and add more butter to prevent sticking. Though delicious plain, you can top wedges of the potato cake with sour cream and smoked fish, or a dollop of applesauce.

4 large baking potatoes, about 3 lb (1.5 kg) total weight

1 small red onion

salt and ground pepper

4 tablespoons (2 oz/60 g) unsalted butter

Peel, then shred the potatoes. Place in a large bowl. Grate the onion into the potatoes. Season generously with salt and pepper and stir to mix well.

Melt 2 tablespoons of the butter in a 10- to 12-inch (25- to 30-cm) nonstick frying pan over medium-high heat. Add the potato-onion mixture and spread in an even layer, pressing it down to make a cake. Cut a piece of aluminum foil large enough to cover the entire surface and set on the mixture. Place a heatproof plate, top side down, directly on the foil. (It should be just slightly smaller than the pan circumference.) Cook the potatoes, undisturbed, until the bottom is well browned, 12–15 minutes.

Remove the plate and foil. Holding the plate and the pan with hot pads, invert them so that the potato cake turns, browned side up, onto the plate. Return the pan to the heat and melt the remaining 2 tablespoons butter. Slide the potatoes, browned side up, into the pan. Replace the foil and the plate and continue to cook, undisturbed, until well browned on the second side, about 10 minutes longer. Remove from the heat, remove the plate and foil, and slide the potato cake onto a serving plate. Cut into wedges to serve.

serves six | per serving: calories 218 (kilojoules 916), protein 4 g, carbohydrates 34 g, total fat 8 g, saturated fat 5 g, cholesterol 21 mg, sodium 15 mg, dietary fiber 3 g

old-fashioned buttermilk biscuits

Enjoy these delicious biscuits warm from the oven, split open and slathered with butter and honey.

2 cups (10 oz/315 g) all-purpose (plain) flour

2 teaspoons sugar

2 teaspoons baking powder

½ teaspoon baking soda (bicarbonate of soda)

½ teaspoon salt

½ cup (4 oz/125 g) chilled unsalted butter, cut into small pieces

1 cup (8 fl oz/250 ml) buttermilk

Preheat the oven to 425°F (220°C). In a bowl, stir together the flour, sugar, baking powder, baking soda, and salt. Using a pastry blender or 2 knives, cut in the butter until the mixture resembles coarse meal. Pour in the buttermilk and mix quickly with a fork until blended. Turn out onto a lightly floured work surface. Gather the dough together, then knead briefly until it just holds together.

Roll the dough into a circle about 8 inches (20 cm) in diameter or into a rectangle about 8 inches (20 cm) long. Cut into biscuits with a floured 3½-inch (9-cm) cutter or the rim of a large juice glass, or, using a knife, cut the rectangle in half crosswise, then cut each half into 4 pieces.

Arrange the biscuits about 1 inch (2.5 cm) apart on an ungreased large baking sheet. Bake until golden brown and puffy, about 15 minutes. Remove from the oven and let cool on the baking sheet for about 5 minutes. Serve warm.

makes about eight biscuits; serves four to six | per biscuit: calories 257 (kilojoules 1,079), protein 5 g, carbohydrates 31 g, total fat 12 g, saturated fat 8 g, cholesterol 33 mg, sodium 355 mg, dietary fiber 1 g

canadian bacon hash with poached eggs

Canadian bacon makes for a lean and flavorful hash. For extra convenience, boil the potatoes the night before. If poaching eggs seems too complicated, you can top the hash with fried eggs. Accompany with Old-Fashioned Buttermilk Biscuits (left).

3 red potatoes, about 1 lb (500 g) total weight

2 tablespoons unsalted butter

2 tablespoons vegetable oil

½ lb (250 g) sliced Canadian bacon, cut into 1-inch (2.5-cm) pieces

4 green (spring) onions, including tender green tops, thinly sliced

3 stalks celery, thinly sliced

1 red or green bell pepper (capsicum), seeded and diced

½ teaspoon dried thyme

salt and ground pepper

vinegar as needed

4 eggs

chopped fresh parsley (optional)

Place the potatoes in a saucepan and add cold water to cover. Cover and bring to a boil over high heat. Uncover and cook until the potatoes are just tender when pierced, about 20 minutes. Drain the potatoes and let cool (or refrigerate overnight). Peel and cut into 1-inch (2.5-cm) pieces; set aside.

In a large frying pan over medium-high heat, melt the butter in the oil. Add the Canadian bacon and cook, stirring often, until the bacon begins to sizzle and is lightly browned, about 5 minutes. Add the green onions, celery, bell pepper, and thyme and continue to cook, stirring often, until the vegetables have softened, about 4 minutes. Add the potatoes and cook, stirring often, until potatoes are heated through, about 4 minutes (longer if potatoes were refrigerated). Season to taste with salt and pepper.

Meanwhile, fill a sauté pan three-fourths full of water; add several drops of vinegar and bring to a boil. Reduce the heat to a bare simmer. Crack each egg into a small bowl or cup, then slide carefully into the simmering water. Cover and poach the eggs until the whites are firm and the yolk sacs have thin veils of white, 4–6 minutes, depending on your taste.

Spoon the hash onto individual plates and top each serving with a poached egg. Sprinkle with parsley, if desired.

serves four | per serving: calories 381 (kilojoules 1,600), protein 21 g, carbohydrates 25 g, total fat 22 g, saturated fat 7 g, cholesterol 256 mg, sodium 901 mg, dietary fiber 3 g

spiced pumpkin muffins

Serve these moist golden nuggets for breakfast or for a midafternoon snack with Hot Apple Cider (page 28).

2 cups (10 oz/315 g) all-purpose (plain) flour

2 teaspoons baking powder

½ teaspoon baking soda (bicarbonate of soda)

½ teaspoon ground cinnamon

½ teaspoon ground nutmeg

½ teaspoon ground ginger

½ teaspoon ground allspice

¼ teaspoon salt

¼ cup (2 oz/60 g) unsalted butter, at room temperature

½ cup (3½ oz/105 g) plus 2 tablespoons firmly packed dark brown sugar

½ cup (4 oz/125 g) granulated sugar

1 cup (8 oz/250 g) canned pumpkin purée

½ cup (4 fl oz/125 ml) orange juice

1 teaspoon finely chopped orange zest

2 eggs

½ cup (3 oz/90 g) golden raisins (sultanas)

Preheat the oven to 350°F (180°C). Butter a 12-cup muffin tin.

In a medium bowl, stir together the flour, baking powder, baking soda, cinnamon, nutmeg, ginger, allspice, and salt. Set aside.

In a large bowl, using an electric mixer set on medium speed, beat together the butter and brown and granulated sugars until creamy. Reduce the speed to low and add the pumpkin, orange juice and zest, and the eggs. Beat until well blended. Add the flour mixture and beat on low speed just until blended. Do not overmix. Add the raisins and mix just to combine. Divide the mixture evenly among the prepared muffin cups.

Bake until a toothpick inserted into the center of a muffin comes out clean, 20–25 minutes. Transfer to a cooling rack and let cool in the pan for at least 15 minutes, then turn out onto the rack. Serve warm.

makes twelve muffins | per muffin: calories 255 (kilojoules 1,071), protein 4 g, carbohydrates 47 g, total fat 6 g, saturated fat 3 g, cholesterol 48 mg, sodium 199 mg, dietary fiber 1 g

stirred eggs with chives, fontina, and prosciutto

Straining the beaten eggs will ensure a light and fluffy result. Serve these elegant scrambled eggs with warm Spiced Pumpkin Muffins (left) and café au lait. If you're cooking for a crowd, this recipe doubles or triples well, although you will need to use a much larger pan. Cheddar, Swiss, or even goat cheese can be substituted for the fontina, while crisply cooked bacon or pancetta can stand in for the prosciutto.

8 eggs

2 tablespoons milk

salt and ground pepper to taste

1 tablespoon unsalted butter

¼ cup (1 oz/30 g) finely diced fontina cheese

¼ cup (1 oz/30 g) finely shredded prosciutto

1 tablespoon finely chopped fresh chives

In a bowl, whisk the eggs until blended. Pour through a fine-mesh sieve placed over another bowl, making sure that the white stringy part remains in the sieve. Add the milk, salt, and pepper and stir to combine.

In a saucepan over medium heat, melt the butter. Add the eggs and, using a wooden spoon, stir continuously. As the eggs begin to form curds, keep stirring until very creamy, about 3 minutes longer. Add the cheese and prosciutto and continue stirring until the eggs form thicker curds but are still creamy, 2–3 minutes more, or until desired consistency is reached.

Turn the eggs into a warmed shallow bowl and garnish with the chives. Serve immediately.

serves four | per serving: calories 223 (kilojoules 937), protein 17 g, carbohydrates 2 g, total fat 16 g, saturated fat 7 g, cholesterol 448 mg, sodium 318 mg, dietary fiber 0 g

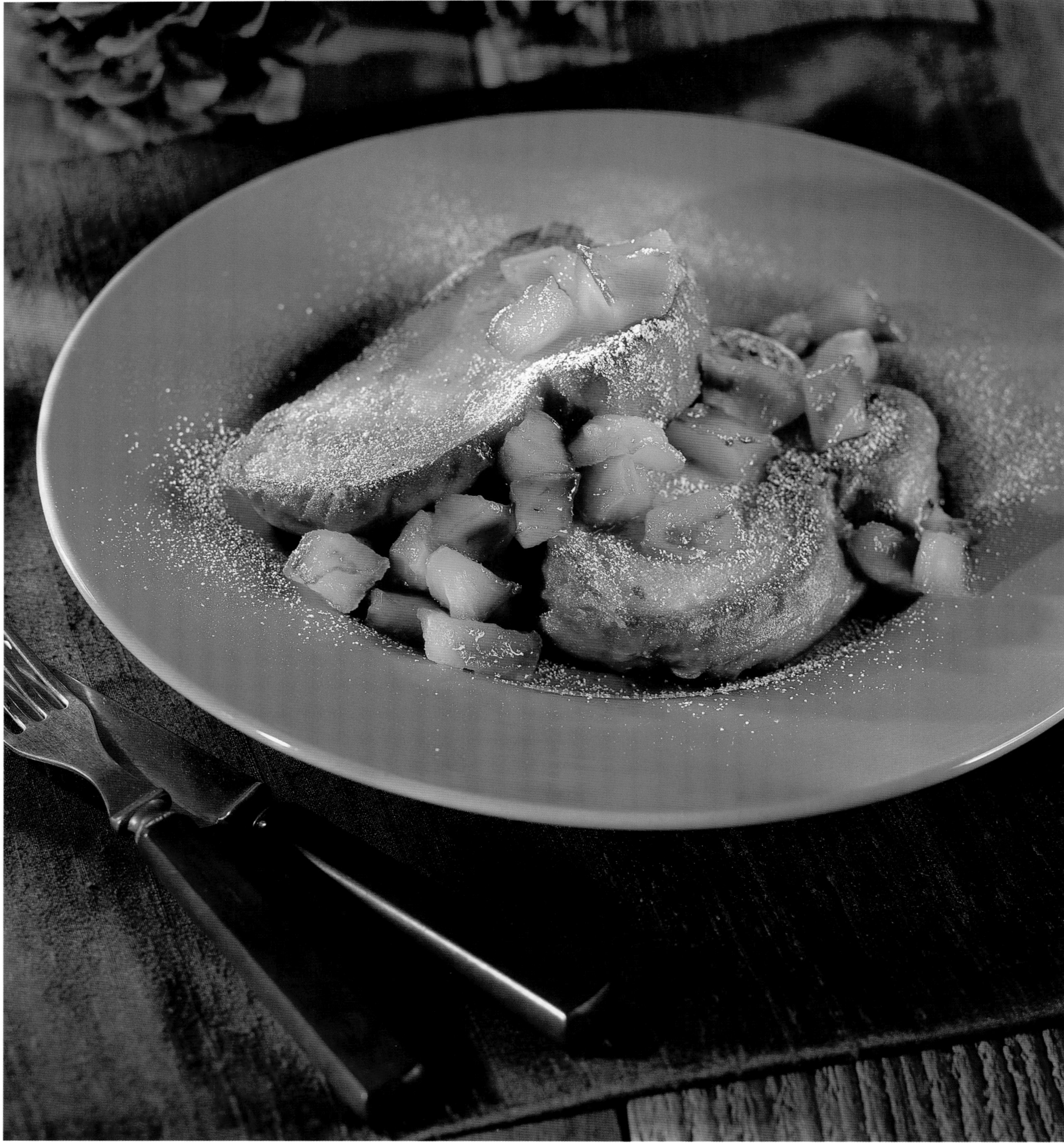

challah french toast with caramelized apples

An old-fashioned cast-iron frying pan—a cabin kitchenware staple—works well for caramelizing the apples. Large, firm pears, preferably Anjou, can be used in place of the apples. Serve the French toast with warm maple syrup or a light dusting of confectioners' (icing) sugar.

for the apples:

3 large cooking apples, such as Rome Beauty or Winesap, 1½–2 lb (750 g–1 kg) total weight, peeled, cored, and finely diced

1 tablespoon lemon juice

½ cup (4 oz/125 g) sugar

1 teaspoon vanilla extract (essence)

2 tablespoons unsalted butter

¼ cup (2 fl oz/60 ml) warm water

for the French toast:

3 tablespoons unsalted butter

2 eggs

2 cups (16 fl oz/500 ml) milk

½ teaspoon vanilla extract (essence)

1 teaspoon sugar

pinch of salt

4 slices challah or brioche, each about 1 inch (2.5 cm) thick

To prepare the apples, place them in a bowl and sprinkle with the lemon juice, sugar, and vanilla. Stir to mix, then set aside, stirring often until they begin to give off juices and the sugar dissolves, about 10 minutes.

In a large, heavy frying pan over medium-high heat, melt the butter. Using a slotted spoon, transfer the apples to the pan. Cook, stirring often, until the apples turn a golden caramel color, 20–25 minutes. Pour in the warm water and stir until glossy. Remove from the heat and cover to keep warm. (The apples can be prepared up to a day ahead. Cover and refrigerate, then reheat gently over low heat.)

To make the French toast, in a large frying pan or on a griddle over medium-high heat, melt the butter. In a large, shallow bowl, whisk together the eggs, milk, vanilla, sugar, and salt. Dip the bread slices briefly into the egg mixture, lift carefully to drain, and place in the frying pan. Cook, turning once, until browned on both sides, 6–7 minutes total.

Transfer to plates, top with the caramelized apples, and serve.

serves two | per serving: calories 1,391 (kilojoules 5,842), protein 31 g, carbohydrates 203 g, total fat 53 g, saturated fat 27 g, cholesterol 406 mg, sodium 1,046 mg, dietary fiber 12 g

oatmeal with dried cherries and almonds

Steel-cut and Irish oats, which have more heft and a nuttier flavor than rolled oats, make a delicious slow-cooked porridge. If you prefer regular rolled oats, use the amount of liquid called for on the package, substitute milk for half of the water, and cook as indicated.

3 cups (24 fl oz/750 ml) water

2 cups (16 fl oz/500 ml) low-fat milk

pinch of salt

⅓ cup (2½ oz/75 g) firmly packed light brown sugar

1 teaspoon vanilla or almond extract (essence)

1 cup (6 oz/185 g) steel-cut or Irish oats *(see note)*

1 cup (6 oz/185 g) dried cherries, coarsely chopped if large

1 tablespoon unsalted butter (optional)

¼ cup (1 oz/30 g) sliced (flaked) almonds

about 1 cup (8 fl oz/250 ml) milk, cream, or buttermilk

In a saucepan over medium-high heat, bring the water, 2 cups (16 fl oz/500 ml) milk, and salt just to a boil. Add the sugar and vanilla or almond extract, stirring until the sugar is dissolved. Stir in the oats and dried cherries. Return to a boil and stir until the mixture starts to look foamy, about 1 minute, then reduce the heat to low and simmer uncovered, stirring often, until the oats are cooked through but still chewy, about 30 minutes. Do not overcook; the oats should still have a little bite.

Stir in the butter, if desired, and let the oatmeal stand, covered, for 5 minutes. Spoon into individual bowls. Sprinkle each serving with sliced almonds, and accompany with milk, cream, or buttermilk.

serves four | per serving: calories 482 (kilojoules 2,024), protein 14 g, carbohydrates 87 g, total fat 11 g, saturated fat 4 g, cholesterol 18 mg, sodium 135 mg, dietary fiber 5 g

winter

breakfast crêpes with strawberry jam

1 cup (5 oz/155 g) unbleached all-purpose (plain) flour

1 tablespoon granulated sugar

1½ cups (12 fl oz/375 ml) milk, plus extra if needed to thin

3 eggs

2 tablespoons unsalted butter, melted, plus about 2 tablespoons unmelted

1 teaspoon vanilla extract (essence)

½ cup (5 oz/155 g) strawberry jam

about 1 tablespoon confectioners' (icing) sugar

In a blender, combine the flour, sugar, 1½ cups (12 fl oz/375 ml) milk, eggs, the 2 tablespoons melted butter, and vanilla. Process until well blended. Pour into a measuring pitcher with a spout, cover, and refrigerate for 2–4 hours. Check the batter before you begin cooking. If it is thick and sluggish, thin with a bit of milk or water to the consistency of heavy (double) cream.

Place an 8- or 9-inch (20- or 23-cm) nonstick frying pan over medium heat and add enough of the 2 tablespoons butter to coat lightly. When hot, pour in 2–3 tablespoon of the batter and tilt the pan, swirling the batter until the pan bottom is evenly covered. Pour any excess batter back into the pitcher. Cook until bubbles appear on the surface, about 1 minute. Flip the crêpe and cook on the second side until just set, 10–20 seconds longer. Turn out onto a plate lined with waxed paper. Cook the remaining batter in the same way, adding butter to the pan as needed and placing waxed paper between the crêpes as they are stacked. You should have about 12 crêpes.

Spread each crêpe evenly with 2 teaspoons of the jam. Fold the crêpe over once and then again so that the crêpe is folded into quarters.

In a large nonstick frying pan over medium heat, melt 1 teaspoon of the butter. Add 4 filled crêpes and sauté, turning once, until browned on both sides, 1–1½ minutes on each side. Transfer to a warmed platter. Repeat with the remaining butter and crêpes.

To serve, arrange 2 or 3 crêpes on each warmed individual plate. Dust with confectioners' sugar. Serve immediately.

serves four to six | per serving: calories 320 (kilojoules 1,344), protein 9 g, carbohydrates 48 g, total fat 11 g, saturated fat 6 g, cholesterol 150 mg, sodium 86 mg, dietary fiber 1 g

apple crumb cake

Homey and delicious, this crowd-pleaser is the perfect anytime snack.

1 cup (8 oz/250 g) unsalted butter, at room temperature, cut into 1-inch (2.5-cm) pieces, plus ⅓ cup (3 oz/90 g), melted

¾ cup (6 oz/185 g) firmly packed dark brown sugar

1¼ cups (10 oz/310 g) granulated sugar

2 teaspoons ground cinnamon

⅛ teaspoon ground ginger

⅛ teaspoon ground nutmeg

⅛ teaspoon ground allspice

4½ cups (22½ oz/695 g) unbleached all-purpose (plain) flour

1 teaspoon salt

1 teaspoon baking powder

1 cup (8 fl oz/250 ml) milk

2 eggs

2 teaspoons vanilla extract (essence)

2 Granny Smith or Fuji apples, peeled, cored, and cut into ½-inch (12-mm) pieces

about 1 teaspoon confectioners' (icing) sugar (optional)

Preheat the oven to 375°F (190°C). Grease a 9-by-13-inch (23-by-33-cm) baking pan with butter.

In a large bowl, combine the 1 cup (8 oz/250 g) cut-up butter, the brown sugar, ½ cup (4 oz/125 g) of the granulated sugar, the cinnamon, ginger, nutmeg, and allspice. Using a pastry blender or 2 knives, cut in the butter until the mixture resembles coarse crumbs. Add 2½ cups (12½ oz/385 g) of the flour and, using your fingers, crumble the mixture together to make large crumb-like pieces. Set aside.

In another large bowl, stir together the remaining 2 cups (10 oz/310 g) flour, the remaining ¾ cup (6 oz/185 g) granulated sugar, the salt, and the baking powder.

In a large measuring pitcher, whisk together the melted butter, milk, eggs, and vanilla. Pour the egg mixture over the flour mixture and stir just to combine. Add the apples and stir again just to combine.

Spoon the batter evenly into the prepared pan, smoothing the top. Sprinkle the brown sugar mixture evenly over the batter, lightly pressing it into the batter.

Bake until the topping is crisp and the cake is springy to the touch, about 45 minutes. Remove from the oven and let cool. Dust with confectioners' sugar, if desired. The cake is best eaten the day it is made.

serves ten | per serving: calories 682 (kilojoules 2,864), protein 9 g, carbohydrates 99 g, total fat 28 g, saturated fat 17 g, cholesterol 115 mg, sodium 322 mg, dietary fiber 2 g

vanilla pear dutch baby

This giant puffed pancake resembles a popover. Serve with crisp bacon, orange juice, and café au lait for a satisfying breakfast at your weekend getaway.

¾ cup (6 fl oz/180 ml) milk

2 eggs

½ cup (2½ oz/75 g) all-purpose (plain) flour

2 tablespoons granulated sugar

1 teaspoon vanilla extract (essence)

1 teaspoon finely chopped orange zest

1 Bosc or Anjou pear, peeled, cored, and finely chopped (about 1 cup/4 oz/125 g)

2 tablespoons unsalted butter

about 1 teaspoon confectioners' (icing) sugar

Preheat the oven to 450°F (230°C). In a blender or in a bowl, combine the milk, eggs, flour, granulated sugar, vanilla, and orange zest. Blend or whisk until smooth. Add the pear pieces and stir to combine.

Put the butter in a 10-inch (25-cm) pie dish or ovenproof frying pan and place in the oven to melt. Remove from the oven and, using a paper towel or pastry brush, brush the inside of the dish or pan to coat it evenly with the butter. Pour in the batter.

Bake for 15 minutes. Reduce the temperature to 350°F (180°C) and bake until the cake is golden brown and well puffed, about 15 minutes more.

Remove from the oven and dust the top generously with the confectioners' sugar. Serve immediately directly from the dish or frying pan.

serves two | per serving: calories 455 (kilojoules 1,911), protein 13 g, carbohydrates 55 g, total fat 20 g, saturated fat 11 g, cholesterol 256 mg, sodium 110 mg, dietary fiber 2 g

bacon and potato frittata

For ease in serving this frittata, use a pizza cutter to cut it into wedges. Accompany with a simple mixed-fruit salad.

6 slices bacon, cut into 1-inch (2.5-cm) pieces

2 tablespoons olive oil

1 lb (500 g) red or white boiling potatoes, peeled and cut into ½-inch (12-mm) dice

1 leek, white and light green parts only, finely chopped

1 bunch spinach, about ½ lb (250 g), tough stems removed

salt and ground pepper to taste

12 eggs

2 tablespoons finely chopped fresh parsley

1½ cups (6 oz/185 g) shredded sharp cheddar cheese

¼ cup (2 fl oz/60 ml) store-bought fresh tomato or tomatillo salsa (optional)

¼ cup (2 fl oz/60 ml) sour cream (optional)

In a 10-inch (25-cm) ovenproof nonstick frying pan over medium-high heat, fry the bacon until crisp, 6–8 minutes. Using a slotted spoon, transfer to paper towels to drain. Pour off the drippings from the pan.

Preheat the oven to 425°F (220°C). Add the olive oil to the same pan and place over medium heat. Add the potatoes and leek and sauté, stirring frequently, until the leek is golden brown and the potatoes are tender inside and crisp on the surface, about 20 minutes. Stir in the spinach, cover, and cook until the spinach is wilted, 2–3 minutes. Season with salt and pepper.

Meanwhile, in a bowl, whisk together the eggs and parsley. Stir in 1¼ cups (5 oz/155 g) of the cheese, the bacon, salt, and pepper.

Using a spatula, flatten the potato mixture in the pan and pour the egg mixture evenly over the top. Reduce the heat to medium-low and cook, stirring occasionally, until the bottom is lightly set and cooked, about 7 minutes. Sprinkle evenly with the remaining ¼ cup (1 oz/30 g) cheese.

Transfer the pan to the oven and bake until the frittata is puffed and brown, 10–15 minutes. Remove from the oven and let cool. Slide onto a round serving platter, cut into wedges, and garnish with the salsa and sour cream, if desired. Serve immediately.

serves six | per serving: calories 402 (kilojoules 1,688), protein 24 g, carbohydrates 16 g, total fat 27 g, saturated fat 11 g, cholesterol 460 mg, sodium 432 mg, dietary fiber 2 g

banana-oatmeal waffles

These flavorful waffles have a moist, cake-like interior. You may find a dusting of confectioners' (icing) sugar is all you need to sweeten them, although maple syrup is always a treat.

1 cup (5 oz/155 g) all-purpose (plain) flour

1 cup (3 oz/90 g) quick-cooking rolled oats or 1 cup (6 oz/185 g) multigrain cereal

2 tablespoons firmly packed brown sugar

1 tablespoon baking powder

½ teaspoon baking soda (bicarbonate of soda)

½ teaspoon ground cinnamon

pinch of ground allspice

pinch of ground nutmeg

½ teaspoon salt

1 cup (8 fl oz/250 ml) sour cream

½ cup (4 fl oz/125 ml) milk

2 eggs

4 tablespoons (2 oz/60 g) unsalted butter, melted

2 ripe bananas, peeled and sliced

vegetable oil for greasing

Preheat the waffle iron according to the manufacturer's directions.

In a large bowl, stir together the flour, oats or cereal, brown sugar, baking powder, baking soda, cinnamon, allspice, nutmeg, and salt.

In a large measuring pitcher, combine the sour cream, milk, eggs, and melted butter and whisk with a fork until well blended. Add the sliced bananas and mash them in well. (An old-fashioned potato masher works well.) Don't worry if the mixture is still a little lumpy. Add the egg mixture to the flour mixture and mix with a fork or a whisk until a smooth batter forms.

Using a paper towel or pastry brush, lightly grease the waffle iron with vegetable oil. Following the manufacturer's directions, ladle in enough batter for 1 waffle (usually about ½ cup/4 fl oz/125 ml), spreading it around evenly as soon as you finish pouring. Close the waffle iron and cook until it opens easily and the waffle is golden brown on the outside and cooked through inside. Transfer to a platter and keep warm while you cook the remaining waffles, regreasing the waffle iron as necessary. Serve hot.

makes about seven waffles | per waffle: calories 344 (kilojoules 1,445), protein 8 g, carbohydrates 38 g, total fat 19 g, saturated fat 10 g, cholesterol 95 mg, sodium 512 mg, dietary fiber 2 g

red flannel hash

Cooking with beets can be messy. You might use gloves when peeling, and place the beets on waxed paper when cutting to make cleanup easy. Be sure to stir the hash and move the mixture around continually after the first 10 minutes of cooking to ensure a brown and crusty result.

2 beets

2½ lb (1.25 kg) white, red, or Yukon gold potatoes, peeled and finely diced

3 cups (about 1¼–1½ lb/625–750 g) finely diced cooked corned beef

½ cup (4 fl oz/125 ml) heavy (double) cream

4 tablespoons (⅓ oz/10 g) finely chopped fresh parsley

1 teaspoon Worcestershire sauce

½ teaspoon salt

¼ teaspoon cayenne pepper

2 tablespoons vegetable oil

2 leeks, white and light green parts only, finely chopped

Preheat the oven to 425°F (220°C).

Trim the beets but do not peel. Place in a small baking pan and add water to a depth of ¼ inch (6 mm). Seal the top with aluminum foil and roast until fork-tender, about 45 minutes. Remove the pan from the oven and, when cool enough to handle, peel and finely dice. Set aside.

Fill a large saucepan three-fourths full of salted water and bring to a boil. Add the potatoes and boil until nearly tender, 7–10 minutes. Drain well and place in a bowl. Add the corned beef, beets, cream, 2 tablespoons of the parsley, the Worcestershire sauce, salt, and cayenne pepper. Stir to mix well.

In a large nonstick frying pan over medium heat, warm the vegetable oil. Add the leeks and sauté, stirring occasionally, until they turn translucent, 4–5 minutes. Add the potato–corned beef mixture and mix well to distribute evenly. Spread the hash evenly in the pan, flattening with a wooden spatula. Cook until a slight crust forms on the bottom, about 10 minutes. Occasionally run the spatula around the edge of the pan to keep the potatoes from sticking. Turn the mixture over and continue cooking, stirring frequently to break up the hash, until crusty and browned, 12–14 minutes longer.

Spoon the hash onto warmed serving plates and garnish with the remaining 2 tablespoons parsley. Serve immediately.

serves eight | per serving: calories 409 (kilojoules 1,718), protein 18 g, carbohydrates 30 g, total fat 24 g, saturated fat 3 g, cholesterol 97 mg, sodium 1,076 mg, dietary fiber 3 g

winter omelet with zucchini, mushrooms, and gruyère

Serve this versatile omelet with citrus fruit or juice for a delightful balance of flavors and colors.

for the filling:

2 tablespoons unsalted butter

1 shallot, minced

1 tablespoon olive oil

½ lb (250 g) fresh mushrooms, brushed clean and thinly sliced

2 zucchini (courgettes), trimmed and julienned

2 tablespoons finely chopped fresh parsley

salt and ground pepper to taste

for the omelets:

12–18 eggs (2 or 3 per person)

salt and ground pepper to taste

6 tablespoons (3 fl oz/90 ml) plain soda water

6 tablespoons (3 oz/90 g) unsalted butter

6 tablespoons (1½ oz/45 g) finely shredded Gruyère cheese

To make the filling, in a frying pan over medium heat, melt the butter. Add the shallot and sauté until softened, about 2 minutes. Increase the heat to medium-high and add the oil. Add the mushrooms and sauté until slightly softened, about 3 minutes. Add the zucchini and continue to sauté until softened, about 3 minutes longer. Add the parsley, salt, and pepper. Remove from the heat and cover to keep warm.

To prepare each omelet, in a bowl, whisk together 2 or 3 eggs, salt, pepper, and 1 tablespoon soda water until smooth. Melt 1 tablespoon of the butter in an 8-inch (20-cm) omelet pan or frying pan, preferably nonstick, over medium heat. When it begins to sizzle, pour in the egg mixture and stir it in the center with a wooden spatula. With the spatula, lift the edges of the egg mixture so the uncooked portion runs to the edge of the pan. Vigorously slide the pan back and forth over the heat until the eggs begin to slip freely in the pan.

When the eggs are lightly cooked but still creamy in the center, spoon one-sixth of the filling over the omelet. Sprinkle 1 tablespoon of the Gruyère cheese over the filling. Shake the pan; if the omelet does not slip easily, carefully loosen the edges with the spatula. Slide the omelet onto a plate and, when halfway out, quickly flip the pan over to fold the omelet in half. Serve immediately. Repeat with the remaining eggs and filling until all the omelets have been made.

serves six | per serving: calories 398 (kilojoules 1,672), protein 22 g, carbohydrates 4 g, total fat 33 g, saturated fat 16 g, cholesterol 687 mg, sodium 217 mg, dietary fiber 0 g

appetizers, soups & salads

When you are in the outdoors, whether holed up in a mountain cabin or picnicking on a sunny beach, sometimes the perfect thing to eat is a little bite. It might be that childhood favorite, a deviled egg, or a spoonful of minty cracked wheat salad you've carried in a hamper. Light chilled soups, poured from a thermos or iced down in a glass jar, cool you off on warm days, while hearty hot soups straight from the stove heat you up in the cold of winter.

These dishes are adaptable and can be served in a variety of ways: three or four appetizers make a meal, soup and salad are a satisfying lunch—a combination of all three inevitably pleases even the fussiest eater. They can also be fancy or homey. Curried Lobster Salad adds a touch of glamour to an oceanside picnic, while potato salad is the ideal comfort food at a tailgate party.

What all the recipes share is their celebration of seasonal fruits and vegetables. Ripe and Kodachrome colored, their appeal is boosted by the flecks of red, green, and orange in a summer avocado-and-vegetable salsa or the winter hues in a salad of oranges, olives, and onions.

spring

chilled artichoke halves with lemon vinaigrette

Artichoke halves make perfect containers for a delicious vinaigrette. These can be made a day ahead and refrigerated until serving.

1 lemon plus 3 lemon slices
3 large artichokes
1 tablespoon olive oil
1 shallot, finely chopped
3 tablespoons lemon juice
1 tablespoon red wine vinegar
1 teaspoon Dijon mustard
1 tablespoon finely chopped fresh chives
1 tablespoon finely chopped fresh flat-leaf (Italian) parsley
½ cup (4 fl oz/125 ml) extra-virgin olive oil
salt and ground pepper

Fill a large bowl three-fourths full with cold water. Halve the lemon and squeeze the juice into the water. Working with 1 artichoke at a time, cut the sharp points off the leaves with kitchen shears. Remove the small dry outer leaves from around the base. Trim the stem 1 inch (2.5 cm) from the base. Immediately place each trimmed artichoke into the lemon water.

Soak all the artichokes in the water for at least 15 minutes to clean them. Drain and place upright in a large saucepan. Add water to a depth of about 4 inches (10 cm). Add the lemon slices and the 1 tablespoon olive oil. Cook over medium heat, partially covered, until the leaves pull off easily, 30–45 minutes. Remove from the pan and let cool.

Meanwhile, in a small bowl, combine the shallot, lemon juice, vinegar, mustard, chives, and parsley. Whisk to combine and slowly whisk in the ½ cup (4 fl oz/125 ml) olive oil until incorporated. Season to taste with salt and pepper. Transfer to a container with a tight-fitting lid.

Cut each artichoke in half. Using a teaspoon, scoop out the prickly choke and discard. Place the artichoke halves in a transportable container and keep chilled until ready to serve.

Just before serving, spoon about 2 tablespoons of the vinaigrette over each artichoke half. Serve chilled or at room temperature.

serves six | per serving: calories 224 (kilojoules 941), protein 3 g, carbohydrates 10 g, total fat 21 g, saturated fat 3 g, cholesterol 0 mg, sodium 98 mg, dietary fiber 4 g

S.PELLE

purée of vegetable soup with lemon and dill

Creamy potatoes, bright orange carrots, yellow summer squash, and green zucchini give this soup color, and dill imparts a fragrant garden freshness. The soup is also excellent chilled.

2 tablespoons olive oil

1 leek, including ½ inch (12 mm) of tender green top, finely chopped

3 White Rose potatoes, about 1 lb (500 g) total weight, peeled and thinly sliced

2 carrots, peeled and thinly sliced

2 crookneck squash, thinly sliced

2 zucchini (courgettes), thinly sliced

6 cups (48 fl oz/1.5 l) chicken broth

2 tablespoons chopped fresh dill

salt and ground white pepper

½ cup (4 fl oz/125 ml) half-and-half (half cream) or milk

1 tablespoon lemon juice

In a soup pot over medium heat, heat the oil. Add the leek and sauté until softened, about 3 minutes. Add the potatoes, carrots, squash, and zucchini and sauté, stirring, until slightly softened, about 3 minutes. Add the broth and dill, reduce the heat to medium-low, and simmer, partially covered, until the vegetables are tender, about 15 minutes longer. Season with salt and pepper.

Working in batches, transfer the soup to a blender or food processor and process to purée. Return the soup to the pot and whisk in the half-and-half or milk and the lemon juice. Taste and adjust the seasonings. Pour into a heated thermos and serve in small, heatproof cups.

serves four to six | per serving: calories 232 (kilojoules 974), protein 7 g, carbohydrates 27 g, total fat 11 g, saturated fat 2 g, cholesterol 9 mg, sodium 1,235 mg, dietary fiber 3 g

asparagus with sun-dried tomato vinaigrette

Roasting the asparagus helps the spears retain their color and texture. For the vinaigrette, use a good-quality Italian Parmesan cheese. Dry Sonoma jack cheese can be substituted. To shave the cheese, draw a sharp vegetable peeler across a block of cheese.

1½ lb (750 g) thin asparagus

¼ cup (2 fl oz/60 ml) water

1 tablespoon olive oil

¼ cup (1¼ oz/37 g) drained, oil-packed sun-dried tomatoes, thinly sliced

2 cloves garlic, coarsely chopped

2 tablespoons balsamic vinegar

2 teaspoons lemon juice

2 tablespoons finely chopped fresh basil

½ cup (4 fl oz/125 ml) extra-virgin olive oil

1 tablespoon grated Parmesan cheese

salt and ground pepper

shavings of Parmesan cheese for garnish *(see note)*

Preheat the oven to 400°F (200°C). Snap off any tough ends of the asparagus stalks. Using a vegetable peeler, peel the outer skin from the bottom 2 inches (5 cm) of each stalk. Place the asparagus in a roasting pan. Add the water and 1 tablespoon oil. Roast until tender when pierced, 10–15 minutes. Drain, transfer to a transportable container, cover, and refrigerate until well chilled, at least 3 hours or for up to 8 hours.

In a food processor with the motor running, add the tomatoes and garlic and process until finely minced. Add the vinegar, lemon juice, and basil and process to combine. With the motor still running, slowly add the ½ cup (4 fl oz/125 ml) oil and process until completely combined. Turn off the motor, add the grated cheese, and pulse just to incorporate. Season to taste with salt and pepper.

Spoon about two-thirds of the dressing onto the chilled asparagus. Reserve the remainder in a container with a tight-fitting lid to serve on the side. Scatter the Parmesan shavings over the asparagus and keep cool until ready to serve. Serve chilled or at room temperature.

serves four to six | per serving: calories 271 (kilojoules 1,138), protein 5 g, carbohydrates 7 g, total fat 27 g, saturated fat 4 g, cholesterol 1 mg, sodium 65 mg, dietary fiber 2 g

raw bar with three dipping sauces

Arrange oysters and clams in large roasting pans filled with shaved ice.

4 dozen oysters on the half shell

8 dozen clams on the half shell

for sauce one:

1 cup (8 oz/250 g) plain yogurt

1 red bell pepper (capsicum), roasted, peeled, and chopped (for method, see Tomato Tart, page 94)

3 or 4 dry-packed sun-dried tomatoes, softened in warm water for 20 minutes and drained

1 tablespoon olive oil

1 tablespoon balsamic vinegar

½ small fresh chile, seeded and minced

1 small clove garlic, minced

for sauce two:

1 cup (6 oz/185 g) peeled and diced papaya

½ cup (3 oz/90 g) peeled and diced mango

1 piece fresh ginger, 2 inches (5 cm) long, peeled and grated

½ small fresh chile, seeded and minced

½ cup (½ oz/15 g) loosely packed fresh mint leaves

2 tablespoons lime juice

for sauce three:

2 tablespoons Southeast Asian fish sauce

2 tablespoons lime juice

2 large wedges ripe tomato

1 tablespoon dark brown sugar

½ cup (2½ oz/75 g) salted roasted peanuts

1 cup (1 oz/30 g) loosely packed fresh cilantro (fresh coriander) leaves

To make each sauce, combine all its ingredients in a food processor or blender and process until smooth. Transfer to separate bowls and chill for at least 2 hours. The sauces can be made up to 1 day in advance.

serves four | per serving: calories 640 (kilojoules 2,688), protein 68 g, carbohydrates 42 g, total fat 22 g, saturated fat 4 g, cholesterol 219 mg, sodium 887 mg, dietary fiber 4 g

deviled eggs

The secret to perfect deviled eggs is in the cooking: don't boil them and don't cook them too long, and you will avoid tough eggs with dreary gray circles around the yolks. For a variation, stir into the yolk mixture 1 teaspoon pesto and ¼ cup (1½ oz/45 g) bay shrimp, or ¼ cup (2 oz/60 g) chopped smoked salmon and 1 teaspoon lemon juice.

6 extra-large eggs, at room temperature

3 tablespoons mayonnaise

¼ teaspoon salt

pinch of dry mustard

ground white pepper

paprika

1 tablespoon finely chopped fresh chives

Place the eggs in a saucepan and cover with cold water. Place over medium-high heat and bring to a rolling boil. Immediately turn off the heat, cover, and let stand for 15 minutes. Transfer the eggs to a strainer and set under cold running water. Crack them all over and peel.

Cut the peeled eggs in half lengthwise. Scoop out the yolks into a small bowl. Mash the yolks with a fork and mix in the mayonnaise, salt, mustard, and pepper to taste until well blended.

Spoon the yolk mixture into the egg white halves and place in a single layer in a storage container. Dust lightly with paprika and sprinkle evenly with the chives. Cover and refrigerate for at least 1 hour or for as long as overnight. Keep chilled until ready to serve.

serves six | per serving: calories 135 (kilojoules 567), protein 7 g, carbohydrates 1 g, total fat 11 g, saturated fat 3 g, cholesterol 249 mg, sodium 202 mg, dietary fiber 0 g

salmon, cream cheese, and cucumber pinwheels

Serve these colorful and sophisticated pinwheels with Deviled Eggs (left). For the cream cheese spread, you can use the suggested herbs or substitute your favorites. The recipe can easily be multiplied to serve a crowd.

2 tablespoons cream cheese, at room temperature

2 teaspoons finely chopped fresh herbs such as chives, dill, burnet, and/or flat-leaf (Italian) parsley

1 flour tortilla, 10 inches (25 cm) in diameter

2 oz (60 g) thinly sliced smoked salmon

1 piece English (hothouse) cucumber, about 6 inches (15 cm) long

In a small bowl, combine the cream cheese and herbs and use a fork to blend well. Set the tortilla on a work surface and spread with the herbed cream cheese all the way to the edges. Cover evenly with the salmon slices.

Draw a sharp vegetable peeler along the cucumber to create 6 thin slices about 6 inches (15 cm) long. Arrange the slices over the salmon.

Tightly roll up the tortilla, trim the ends, cover with plastic wrap, and refrigerate for at least 15 minutes, or for up to 4 hours, to let the ingredients set. Remove the plastic wrap and cut the roll into 8 pinwheel slices.

Transfer to a transportable container and keep chilled until ready to serve.

serves four | per serving: calories 92 (kilojoules 386), protein 5 g, carbohydrates 9 g, total fat 4 g, saturated fat 2 g, cholesterol 11 mg, sodium 199 mg, dietary fiber 1 g

shrimp bisque with chipotle cream

The smoky, earthy flavor of chipotle chiles goes well with this classic bisque. If they are unavailable, use 3 or 4 dry-packed sun-dried tomatoes in their place, proceeding as directed for the chiles.

2 dried chipotle chiles

boiling water, as needed

1½ lb (750 g) shrimp (prawns) in their shells with heads intact

2 yellow onions

1 large tomato, chopped

1 carrot, peeled and chopped

5 cups (40 fl oz/1.25 l) water

1 cup (8 fl oz/250 ml) dry white wine

1 fresh thyme sprig

6–8 peppercorns

¼ cup (2 oz/60 g) white rice

½ teaspoon salt

1½ cups (12 fl oz/375 ml) half-and-half (half cream)

Hungarian hot paprika or cayenne pepper to taste

pinch of coarse salt

¾ cup (6 fl oz/180 ml) sour cream

Place the chipotle chiles in a small bowl and add boiling water to cover. Set aside to soften, about 20 minutes.

Peel and devein the shrimp, reserving the shells and heads. Refrigerate the shrimp meats. Place the shells and heads in a large saucepan. Chop 1 of the onions and add to the saucepan with the tomato, carrot, water, wine, thyme, and peppercorns. Bring to a boil, reduce the heat to low, and simmer for 30 minutes. Strain through a fine-mesh sieve into a clean saucepan.

Finely chop the remaining onion and add it to the stock along with the rice and ½ teaspoon salt. Bring to a boil and cook, uncovered, until the rice is very tender, about 20 minutes. Let cool slightly, then, working in batches, transfer to a blender and purée until smooth. Return the purée to the saucepan. Cut the shrimp meats in half lengthwise, add to the pan, and warm over medium-low heat until cooked through, 2–3 minutes. Pour in the half-and-half and add paprika or cayenne to taste. Heat gently but do not allow to boil.

Drain the chiles, discard the stems and seeds, and place on a cutting board. Sprinkle with the coarse salt and chop to form a thick paste. In a bowl, stir together the chipotle paste and sour cream. Ladle the hot bisque into warmed bowls. Top each with a dollop of the chipotle cream and serve.

serves six | per serving: calories 302 (kilojoules 1,268), protein 23 g, carbohydrates 19 g, total fat 15 g, saturated fat 8 g, cholesterol 175 mg, sodium 393 mg, dietary fiber 2 g

cucumber soup with yogurt cheese and salmon roe

Tiny cubes of peeled and seeded tomato can be used in place of the salmon roe to garnish this low-fat, refreshing soup. Serve as an elegant beginning to a simple meal after a full day at the beach.

for the garnish:

¾ cup (6 oz/185 g) plain yogurt

1 teaspoon grated lemon zest

1 tablespoon snipped fresh chives

salt and ground pepper to taste

for the soup:

2 tablespoons olive oil

1 yellow onion, finely chopped

2 celery stalks, thinly sliced

6 large cucumbers, about 3 lb (1.5 kg) total weight, peeled, halved, seeded, and cut into 1-inch (2.5-cm) lengths

2 cups (16 fl oz/500 ml) chicken broth

salt and ground pepper to taste

2–3 oz (60–90 g) salmon roe

To make the garnish, rinse a double thickness of cheesecloth (muslin), use to line a small sieve, and place over a small bowl. Spoon the yogurt into the sieve, cover, and refrigerate for 24 hours. The liquid will drain off, leaving behind a smooth, creamy "cheese." Discard the liquid and transfer the cheese to a bowl. Stir in the lemon zest and chives and season with salt and pepper. Cover and refrigerate until serving.

To make the soup, in a large, heavy saucepan over medium-high heat, warm the oil. Add the onion and celery and sauté until tender, about 5 minutes. Add the cucumbers, then reduce the heat to low, cover, and cook until tender, about 20 minutes. Pour in the broth and season with salt and pepper. Raise the heat to high and bring to a boil. Remove from the heat, cover, and let cool for 10–15 minutes.

Working in batches, transfer to a blender and blend until very smooth. Transfer to a bowl, cover, and chill well, at least 2 hours. Season with salt and pepper before serving.

Ladle into 4 chilled bowls. Add a dollop of the yogurt cheese and a small spoonful of the salmon roe to each bowl. Serve at once.

serves four | per serving: calories 178 (kilojoules 748), protein 9 g, carbohydrates 15 g, total fat 10 g, saturated fat 1 g, cholesterol 67 mg, sodium 549 mg, dietary fiber 2 g

asian noodle salad with salmon and snow peas

The coolness of citrus and mint enhances the flavor of the noodles and salmon. If Chinese egg noodles are unavailable, you can substitute linguine. The salad can be made a day ahead and refrigerated.

2 carrots, peeled and julienned

½ lb (250 g) snow peas (mangetouts), trimmed and julienned

¾ lb (375 g) salmon fillet

1 lb (500 g) Chinese egg noodles

1 tablespoon plus ¼ cup (2 fl oz/60 ml) canola oil

2 teaspoons Asian sesame oil

¼ cup (2 fl oz/60 ml) rice wine vinegar

1 tablespoon lime juice

1 tablespoon honey

2 cloves garlic, minced

1½ teaspoons peeled and grated fresh ginger

2 tablespoons finely chopped fresh basil, plus sprigs for garnish

2 tablespoons finely chopped fresh mint, plus sprigs for garnish

salt and cracked black pepper

Preheat the oven to 400°F (200°C). Bring a saucepan two-thirds full of water to a boil. Add the carrots and cook for 30 seconds. Using a slotted spoon, scoop out and immerse in a bowl of ice water to stop the cooking. Repeat with the snow peas, cooking them for 1 minute. Set aside.

Remove and discard any errant bones in the salmon. Place the salmon in a small roasting pan and bake until opaque throughout, about 12 minutes. Let cool, then shred into bite-sized pieces.

Bring a large pot of water to a boil. Add the noodles, stir, and cook until barely tender and still firm, about 7 minutes. Drain and rinse under cold running water until cooled. Drain well, place in a large transportable bowl, and toss with the 1 tablespoon canola oil to keep the noodles from sticking together.

In a small bowl, whisk together the ¼ cup (2 fl oz/60 ml) canola oil, the sesame oil, the rice wine vinegar, lime juice, honey, garlic, ginger, chopped basil and mint, and salt and pepper to taste.

Pour the dressing over the noodles and toss to coat. Add the carrots and snow peas and toss again. Carefully toss in the salmon, keeping the pieces intact. Taste and adjust the seasonings. Garnish with mint and basil sprigs. Cover and keep chilled until ready to serve.

serves four to six | per serving: calories 617 (kilojoules 2,591), protein 27 g, carbohydrates 78 g, total fat 21 g, saturated fat 2 g, cholesterol 37 mg, sodium 49 mg, dietary fiber 4 g

cracked wheat and vegetable salad

If you want to substitute bulgur wheat for the cracked wheat, it will need to soak in the hot water for only 20–30 minutes. This salad is good accompanied with grilled shrimp (prawns) or scallops.

1 cup (6 oz/185 g) cracked wheat

1¾ cups (14 fl oz/430 ml) boiling water

1 cup (5 oz/155 g) finely diced English (hothouse) cucumber

½ cup (2½ oz/75 g) finely diced red bell pepper (capsicum)

½ cup (2½ oz/75 g) finely diced, peeled carrot

1 tomato, seeded and finely diced

¾ cup (4 oz/125 g) crumbled feta cheese

¼ cup (⅓ oz/10 g) finely chopped fresh flat-leaf (Italian) parsley

2 tablespoons finely chopped green (spring) onion

2 tablespoons finely chopped fresh mint

6 tablespoons (3 fl oz/90 ml) extra-virgin olive oil

3 tablespoons lemon juice

1 teaspoon Dijon mustard

salt and ground pepper

Place the cracked wheat in a bowl and pour in the boiling water. Let stand until the wheat has absorbed all of the water, about 1 hour. Drain the wheat in a colander, then place in a dry kitchen towel and wring out any remaining water. Transfer to a transportable bowl.

Add the cucumber, bell pepper, and carrot to the cracked wheat. Mix with a fork so that the wheat stays fluffy and is not crushed. Add the tomato, feta, parsley, green onion, and mint. Toss gently to combine.

In a small bowl, combine the oil, lemon juice, mustard, and salt and pepper to taste. Whisk to blend. Pour the dressing over the salad and mix again with the fork. Taste and adjust the seasonings. Cover and keep chilled until ready to serve.

serves four to six | per serving: calories 344 (kilojoules 1,445), protein 8 g, carbohydrates 32 g, total fat 22 g, saturated fat 6 g, cholesterol 20 mg, sodium 294 mg, dietary fiber 8 g

roasted beets with orange vinaigrette

These beets are accented with an orange-flavored vinaigrette and toasted pecans. Walnuts may be substituted. If you want to serve a trio of salads, Green Bean and Sweet Pepper Salad (page 105) and Cracked Wheat and Vegetable Salad (left) make colorful accompaniments.

6 beets, about 2 lb (1 kg), trimmed and scrubbed

¼ cup (1 oz/30 g) coarsely chopped pecans

2 tablespoons orange juice

1 tablespoon balsamic vinegar

1 teaspoon Dijon mustard

¼ cup (2 fl oz/60 ml) olive oil

salt and ground pepper

1 tablespoon chopped fresh chives

Preheat the oven to 425°F (220°C). Place the beets in a roasting pan and pour in water to a depth of ¼ inch (6 mm). Cover the pan with aluminum foil and roast the beets until fork-tender, about 45 minutes. Remove from the oven and let cool.

Reduce the oven temperature to 350°F (180°C). Remove the skins from the beets and cut into ½-inch (12-mm) pieces. Transfer to a transportable bowl, cover, and set aside.

Spread the nuts on a baking sheet and toast in the oven until lightly browned and fragrant, 5–7 minutes. Remove from the oven and set aside.

In a small bowl, whisk together the orange juice, vinegar, and Dijon mustard. Slowly whisk in the olive oil until incorporated. Season to taste with salt and pepper and add the chives.

Pour the dressing over the beets and toss to coat evenly. Sprinkle with the toasted nuts. Cover and keep cool until ready to serve. Serve chilled or at room temperature.

serves six | per serving: calories 161 (kilojoules 676), protein 2 g, carbohydrates 12 g, total fat 12 g, saturated fat 1 g, cholesterol 0 mg, sodium 97 mg, dietary fiber 1 g

summer

grilled vegetable platter with picnic vinaigrette

Grilled seasonal vegetables make a colorful and festive beginning to a picnic. Grilled Marinated Flank Steak (page 202) and Picnic Potato Salad (page 102) would be good choices for the main course.

1 shallot, finely chopped

2 tablespoons red wine vinegar

1 tablespoon lemon juice

1 teaspoon Dijon mustard

6 tablespoons (3 fl oz/90 ml) olive oil, plus oil for brushing

2 tablespoons chopped fresh flat-leaf (Italian) parsley

2 tablespoons chopped fresh basil

salt and ground pepper

2 red bell peppers (capsicums)

2 yellow bell peppers (capsicums)

4 Asian (slender) eggplants (aubergines), cut lengthwise into slices ¼ inch (6 mm) thick

4 zucchini (courgettes), cut lengthwise into slices ¼ inch (6 mm) thick

18 asparagus spears, trimmed and peeled if desired

6 plum (Roma) tomatoes, halved lengthwise

¼ cup (½ oz/15 g) assorted finely chopped fresh herbs such as flat-leaf (Italian) parsley and basil

Prepare a fire in a grill. In a small bowl, combine the shallot, vinegar, lemon juice, and mustard. Whisk in the 6 tablespoons (3 fl oz/90 ml) olive oil, then add the parsley, basil, and salt and pepper to taste. Transfer to a container with a tight-fitting lid.

When the coals are medium-hot, place the peppers on the grill rack and grill, turning, until the skins blacken and blister. Place in a brown paper bag, close tightly, and let stand for 10 minutes. Remove the peppers and peel off the charred skin. Remove the stems, seeds, and ribs. Cut into ½-inch (12-mm) slices. Place in a large storage container.

Lightly brush the eggplant and zucchini slices with olive oil and grill, turning once, until lightly browned, 6–8 minutes total. Place in the storage container. Lightly brush the asparagus and the tomato halves with olive oil. Grill, turning once, until lightly browned, about 5 minutes for the asparagus, 8 minutes for the tomatoes. Add to the container. Drizzle with the vinaigrette and sprinkle with the fresh herbs. Keep chilled until ready to serve.

serves six | per serving: calories 202 (kilojoules 848), protein 4 g, carbohydrates 17 g, total fat 15 g, saturated fat 2 g, cholesterol 0 mg, sodium 39 mg, dietary fiber 4 g

eggplant dip with tomato relish and pita toasts

This portable vegetarian appetizer is perfect for a picnic at the park or beach. Make it at the height of summer, when eggplants and tomatoes are at their peak.

for the dip:

1 leek, including ½ inch (12 mm) of tender green top, finely chopped

3 cloves garlic, minced

2 tablespoons olive oil

2 tablespoons balsamic vinegar

salt and ground pepper

2 large eggplants (aubergines), peeled and coarsely chopped

¼ cup (⅓ oz/10 g) chopped fresh basil

1 teaspoon chopped fresh thyme

1 tablespoon capers, rinsed

for the relish:

2 plum (Roma) tomatoes, peeled, seeded, and finely diced

1 tablespoon olive oil

1 tablespoon balsamic vinegar

salt and ground pepper

for the pita toasts:

2 pita breads, plain or sesame

2 tablespoons olive oil

2 tablespoons grated Parmesan cheese

4–6 fresh basil leaves for garnish

Preheat the oven to 400°F (200°C). To make the dip, lightly coat a large roasting pan with nonstick olive oil cooking spray. In the pan, combine the leek, garlic, oil, 1 tablespoon of the vinegar, and salt and pepper to taste. Add the chopped eggplant and toss to coat with the oil and vinegar. Roast, tossing every 15 minutes, until very soft, 1–1¼ hours.

Meanwhile, prepare the relish: In a small bowl, combine the tomatoes, oil, vinegar, and salt and pepper. Mix well, then taste and adjust the seasonings.

Remove the eggplant mixture from the oven and let cool. Add the remaining 1 tablespoon vinegar and the basil, thyme, and capers. Mix well, then taste and adjust the seasonings.

To make the pita toasts, preheat the broiler (grill). Split each pita in half, then cut each half into 8 triangles. Brush the top of each triangle with oil and then sprinkle with Parmesan cheese. Working in batches, spread the triangles on a baking sheet and toast in the broiler until brown and bubbly, about 3 minutes. Let cool. Repeat with the remaining pita triangles.

Mound the eggplant dip into a transportable serving dish. Garnish with the tomato relish and basil leaves and keep chilled until ready to serve. Transfer the pita toasts to large lock-top plastic bags.

serves four to six | per serving: calories 277 (kilojoules 1,163), protein 6 g, carbohydrates 33 g, total fat 15 g, saturated fat 2 g, cholesterol 2 mg, sodium 258 mg, dietary fiber 4 g

vegetable-avocado salsa with baked tortilla chips

Serve this colorful, spicy dip with Fresh Honey Lemonade or Summer Sangria (both page 24). If you prefer a milder flavor, use a jalapeño chile instead of the serrano. You can also accompany it with blue corn tortilla chips.

for the salsa:

2 large tomatoes, peeled, seeded, and diced

1 yellow bell pepper (capsicum), seeded and diced

1 large carrot, peeled and diced

1 cup (6 oz/185 g) peeled and diced jicama

½ cup (3 oz/90 g) corn kernels (cut from 1 ear of corn)

½ small serrano chile, seeded and finely chopped *(see note)*

2 tablespoons finely chopped fresh cilantro (fresh coriander)

2 tablespoons finely chopped fresh flat-leaf (Italian) parsley

2 tablespoons lime juice

salt and ground pepper

1 avocado, pitted, peeled, and diced

6 corn tortillas, 6 inches (15 cm) in diameter

salt and ground pepper

To make the salsa, combine all the ingredients except the avocado in a bowl. Cover and refrigerate for 1 hour.

Meanwhile, make the chips: Preheat the oven to 400°F (200°C). Cut each tortilla into 6 triangles by first cutting it in half, then cutting each half into thirds. Working in batches, place the triangles on a baking sheet and toast until crisp, 8–10 minutes. Remove from the oven, place the triangles in a bowl, season to taste with salt and pepper, and let cool. Repeat with the remaining tortilla triangles.

Remove the salsa from the refrigerator and spoon into a transportable serving bowl with a lid. Keep chilled until ready to serve. Transfer the chips to large lock-top plastic bags. Pack the avocado separately, and right before serving add to the salsa and mix well to incorporate. Serve with the chips.

serves six to eight | per serving: calories 136 (kilojoules 571), protein 3 g, carbohydrates 22 g, total fat 5 g, saturated fat 1 g, cholesterol 0 mg, sodium 52 mg, dietary fiber 5 g

tomato tart

Experiment with various combinations and colors of tomatoes, if you like.

1 lb (500 g) pizza dough, thawed if frozen

1 red bell pepper (capsicum)

2 tablespoons olive oil, plus oil for brushing

2 yellow onions, finely chopped

3 cloves garlic, minced

3 or 4 tomatoes, about 1½ lb (750 g), peeled, seeded, and chopped

2 teaspoons chopped fresh thyme

salt and ground pepper to taste

1 cup (5 oz/155 g) pitted black olives, preferably oil cured, halved

Lightly butter a 12-inch (30-cm) springform pan. On a lightly floured surface, roll out or stretch the dough into a 15-inch (38-cm) round. Line the prepared pan with the dough and pinch the edges to form a rim. Set aside in a warm place to rise until puffy, about 1 hour.

Meanwhile, preheat the broiler (grill). Cut the bell pepper in half lengthwise and remove the stem, seeds, and ribs. Place, cut sides down, on a baking sheet and broil (grill) until the skin blackens and blisters. Remove from the broiler, drape loosely with aluminum foil, let stand for 10 minutes, then peel away the skin. Cut into long, narrow strips and set aside.

In a saucepan over medium-high heat, warm the 2 tablespoons oil. Add the onions and sauté until tender, about 5 minutes. Add the garlic and sauté for about 1 minute longer. Stir in the tomatoes, thyme, salt, and pepper. Cook, stirring, until thickened, about 20 minutes. Let cool slightly.

Preheat the oven to 450°F (230°C). Spread the tomato mixture evenly in the dough-lined pan. Arrange the pepper strips over the tomatoes. Lightly brush the edges of the tart with olive oil.

Bake the tart until the edges are golden brown and the dough is cooked through, 30–40 minutes, covering the top loosely with foil if it begins to dry out. Transfer the pan to a rack and arrange the olives on top. Brush the tart edges with more olive oil and let cool for about 10 minutes. Carefully remove the pan sides and slide the tart onto a cutting board. Cut into wedges and serve warm.

serves six | per serving: calories 367 (kilojoules 1,541), protein 9 g, carbohydrates 48 g, total fat 18 g, saturated fat 2 g, cholesterol 2 mg, sodium 1,531 mg, dietary fiber 4 g

roasted yellow pepper soup with basil swirl

Serve this simple, richly colored soup with toasted bread and a green salad for a light summer lunch.

for the soup:

6 large yellow bell peppers (capsicums), about 3 lb (1.5 kg) total weight

2 tablespoons plus ⅓ cup (3 fl oz/80 ml) olive oil

1 large yellow onion, finely chopped

1 celery stalk, thinly sliced

2 tablespoons all-purpose (plain) flour

1 lb (500 g) yellow tomatoes, peeled, seeded, and chopped

1¾ cups (14 fl oz/440 ml) chicken broth

salt and ground white pepper to taste

for the basil swirl:

2 cups (2 oz/60 g) loosely packed fresh basil leaves

1 tablespoon lemon juice

¼ cup (2 fl oz/60 ml) ice water

To make the soup, preheat the broiler (grill). Cut the peppers in half lengthwise and remove the stems, seeds, and ribs. Place, cut sides down, on a large baking sheet and broil (grill) until the skins blacken and blister. Remove from the broiler, drape with aluminum foil, let stand for 10 minutes, then peel away the skins. Cut lengthwise into narrow strips.

In a large frying pan over medium-high heat, warm the 2 tablespoons oil. Add the onion and celery and sauté until tender, about 5 minutes. Stir in the flour and cook, stirring, for 3 minutes longer. Add the peppers, tomatoes, and broth, raise the heat to high, and bring to a boil. Season with salt and white pepper. Reduce the heat to medium-high and cook uncovered, stirring often, until slightly thickened, about 15 minutes. Remove from the heat.

Let cool slightly and, working in batches, transfer to a blender. With the motor running, pour in the ⅓ cup (3 fl oz/80 ml) oil. Blend until very smooth, then strain through a fine-mesh sieve placed over a bowl. Cover and chill.

To make the basil swirl, in a blender, combine the basil and lemon juice. With the motor running, slowly pour in the water, blending until smooth.

Ladle the soup into chilled bowls. Working quickly, spoon the basil mixture into a piping bag fitted with a ⅛-inch (3-mm) tip and, starting at the center, pipe a rough spiral onto the surface of each serving. Draw a knife tip from the spiral center to the outside, forming a pattern. Serve at once.

serves six | per serving: calories 247 (kilojoules 1,037), protein 4 g, carbohydrates 21 g, total fat 18 g, saturated fat 2 g, cholesterol 0 mg, sodium 309 mg, dietary fiber 5 g

tomato-basil soup with parmesan cheese

This comforting soup tastes best with fresh ripe tomatoes. You can vary the flavor by substituting fresh dill for the basil. The soup can be made a day ahead and reheated just before pouring into a thermos.

¼ cup (2 fl oz/60 ml) olive oil

1 yellow onion, thinly sliced

1 carrot, peeled and finely chopped

1 celery stalk, finely chopped

1 clove garlic, minced

¼ cup (1½ oz/45 g) all-purpose (plain) flour

6 ripe tomatoes, about 3 lb (1.5 kg) total weight, seeded and coarsely chopped

¼ cup (2 oz/60 g) tomato paste

3 cups (24 fl oz/750 ml) chicken broth

¼ cup (⅓ oz/10 g) finely chopped fresh basil

1 teaspoon sugar

1 cup (8 fl oz/250 ml) milk

salt and ground white pepper

½ cup (¾ oz/20 g) cheese croutons

2 tablespoons grated Parmesan cheese

In a soup pot over medium heat, heat the oil. Add the onion and cook, stirring occasionally, until translucent, about 3 minutes. Add the carrot and celery and cook, stirring occasionally, until the vegetables begin to soften, about 4 minutes. Add the garlic and cook, stirring, until slightly softened, about 1 minute longer.

Sprinkle the flour over the vegetables, reduce the heat to low, and cook, stirring, until incorporated, 1–2 minutes. Add the tomatoes, tomato paste, broth, basil, and sugar, raise the heat to medium-high, and bring to a simmer. Reduce the heat to medium, partially cover, and cook, stirring occasionally, until the vegetables are tender and the flavors are well blended, about 20 minutes.

Working in batches, transfer the soup to a blender or food processor and process to purée, making sure to leave a little texture. Return to the pan and place over medium heat until heated through, 1–2 minutes.

Add the milk, stirring to combine, and season to taste with salt and pepper. Remove from the heat and pour into a heated thermos. Serve in small, heatproof cups, garnished with croutons and a sprinkling of Parmesan cheese.

serves four to six | per serving: calories 291 (kilojoules 1,222), protein 8 g, carbohydrates 31 g, total fat 16 g, saturated fat 3 g, cholesterol 8 mg, sodium 840 mg, dietary fiber 5 g

chilled zucchini-buttermilk soup

The key to the refreshing taste of this soup is first chilling the soup base, then adding the fresh herbs and lemon juice. Try serving the soup before Chopped Salad (page 121).

3 tablespoons olive oil

2 leeks, including ½ inch (12 mm) of tender green tops, finely chopped

6 zucchini (courgettes), about 1½ lb (750 g) total weight, thinly sliced

2 cloves garlic, minced

4 cups (32 fl oz/1 l) chicken broth

3 tablespoons finely chopped fresh basil

2 tablespoons finely chopped fresh chives

1 cup (8 fl oz/250 ml) buttermilk

1 tablespoon lemon juice

salt and ground pepper

In a soup pot over medium heat, warm the oil. Add the leeks and sauté, stirring occasionally, until softened, 5–7 minutes. Add the zucchini and sauté until lightly browned, about 5 minutes longer. Add the garlic and cook, stirring, until softened, about 1 minute.

Pour in the broth, cover, and simmer the soup until the zucchini is tender, about 15 minutes. Working in batches, transfer to a blender or food processor and process to purée. Pour into a bowl, cover, and refrigerate for at least 4 hours or for up to 8 hours. Remove from the refrigerator and add the basil, chives, buttermilk, and lemon juice. Season to taste with salt and pepper.

Pour into a chilled thermos. Serve in small cups.

serves six | per serving: calories 138 (kilojoules 580), protein 5 g, carbohydrates 11 g, total fat 9 g, saturated fat 1 g, cholesterol 2 mg, sodium 721 mg, dietary fiber 1 g

cold curried eggplant soup

Aromatic curry powder adds an appealing bite to the delicate eggplant. Serve chilled and follow with Greek Sandwiches (page 172).

2 tablespoons olive oil

1 yellow onion, chopped

2 teaspoons curry powder

1 large eggplant (aubergine), peeled and cut into ½-inch (12-mm)

4 cups (32 fl oz/1 l) chicken broth

1 lemon slice

½ cup (4 oz/125 g) low-fat plain yogurt

1 tablespoon lemon juice

2 tablespoons finely chopped fresh flat-leaf (Italian) parsley

salt and ground white pepper

In a soup pot over medium heat, warm the oil. Add the onion and sauté, stirring occasionally, until softened, about 5 minutes. Add the curry powder, reduce the heat to low, and cook, stirring constantly, until the curry powder is well blended and very aromatic, about 2 minutes longer.

Add the eggplant, broth, and lemon slice, raise the heat to medium-high, and bring to a boil. Reduce the heat to medium-low, cover, and simmer until the eggplant is soft, about 35 minutes. Remove and discard the lemon slice. Transfer to a blender or food processor and process to purée. Transfer to a bowl and let cool to room temperature.

Stir in the yogurt, lemon juice, parsley, and salt and pepper. Cover and chill for at least 4 hours or for up to 8 hours. Transfer to a chilled thermos and serve in small cups.

serves four to six | per serving: calories 132 (kilojoules 554), protein 5 g, carbohydrates 13 g, total fat 8 g, saturated fat 1 g, cholesterol 1 mg, sodium 823 mg, dietary fiber 3 g

cucumber-avocado soup with tomato salsa

A cool, creamy uncooked purée of cucumber and avocado is accented by a spicy salsa. A purchased fresh tomato or tomatillo salsa, available in the refrigerator cases of most food stores, works well, or substitute a favorite recipe of your own. Serve with Grilled Vegetable Sandwiches (page 160).

1 large ripe avocado, pitted, peeled, and cut into pieces

1 large English (hothouse) cucumber, cut into pieces

1½ cups (12 fl oz/375 ml) chicken broth

5 tablespoons fresh tomato or tomatillo salsa *(see note)*

3 tablespoons lemon juice

½ cup (4 oz/125 g) sour cream

¼ cup (¾ oz/20 g) finely sliced green (spring) onions

salt and ground pepper

In a food processor, combine the avocado and cucumber and process until smooth. Add the chicken broth, 3 tablespoons of the salsa, the lemon juice, the sour cream, and the green onions and process until combined. Season to taste with salt and pepper. Transfer to a bowl, cover, and chill for at least 2 hours or for up to 8 hours.

Transfer to a chilled thermos. Serve in small cups or bowls. Garnish each portion with a dollop of the remaining 2 tablespoons salsa.

serves four to six | per serving: calories 156 (kilojoules 655), protein 3 g, carbohydrates 9 g, total fat 13 g, saturated fat 4 g, cholesterol 10 mg, sodium 481 mg, dietary fiber 2 g

tortilla soup with lime

If you can't find canned hominy, substitute fresh or thawed frozen corn kernels and add them with the tomatoes.

6 corn tortillas

salt

6 cups (48 fl oz/1.5 l) chicken broth

1 can (15 oz/470 g) yellow hominy, drained and rinsed (see note)

½ cup (2½ oz/75 g) finely chopped red onion

½ teaspoon ground cumin

½ teaspoon dried oregano

2 firm, ripe plum (Roma) tomatoes, seeded and diced

juice of 2 limes

2 ripe avocados, pitted, peeled, and cubed

sprigs of fresh cilantro (fresh coriander)

about ¼ cup (2 oz/60 g) sour cream or nonfat plain yogurt

Preheat the oven to 350°F (180°C). Dip each tortilla into a bowl of cold water, then sprinkle with salt. Stack the tortillas and cut into thin strips, then cut the strips in half crosswise. Scatter the tortilla strips on a large baking sheet and bake until crisp, about 15 minutes.

Meanwhile, in a large saucepan, combine the broth, hominy, onion, cumin, and oregano. Bring to a boil, then reduce the heat to low and simmer, covered, until the onion is tender, about 15 minutes. Add the tomatoes and lime juice, return the soup to a boil, and then remove from the heat.

Remove the tortilla strips from the oven. Ladle the soup into warmed individual bowls and top each portion with some of the hot strips. Accompany with the avocado cubes, cilantro sprigs, and sour cream or yogurt in small serving bowls.

serves four | per serving: calories 414 (kilojoules 1,739), protein 10 g, carbohydrates 45 g, total fat 23 g, saturated fat 5 g, cholesterol 6 mg, sodium 1,806 mg, dietary fiber 7 g

cherry tomato and corn salad

Vine-ripened cherry tomatoes and fragrant herbs complement the sweet fresh corn in this quintessential summer salad. It makes a good accompaniment to Grilled Marinated Flank Steak (page 202).

3 cups (18 oz/560 g) fresh white or yellow corn kernels (cut from about 6 ears of cooked corn)

20 yellow or red cherry tomatoes, quartered

2 tablespoons finely chopped fresh basil

1 tablespoon finely chopped fresh flat-leaf (Italian) parsley

1 tablespoon extra-virgin olive oil

1 teaspoon red wine vinegar

salt and ground pepper

In a transportable bowl, combine the corn, tomatoes, basil, and parsley. Add the olive oil, vinegar, and salt and pepper to taste. Stir to combine. Taste and adjust the seasonings. Cover until ready to serve.

Serve at room temperature.

serves four to six | per serving: calories 121 (kilojoules 508), protein 4 g, carbohydrates 21 g, total fat 4 g, saturated fat 1 g, cholesterol 0 mg, sodium 19 mg, dietary fiber 4 g

picnic potato salad

The skins are left on the potatoes to give this salad extra color and texture. To spark up the flavor, you can add 2 tablespoons pickle relish or chopped red onion. This salad, along with Cherry Tomato and Corn Salad (left), pairs well with cold Lemon-Garlic Herbed Chicken (page 155) or your favorite sandwich.

3 lb (1.5 kg) new potatoes, red-skinned, tan-skinned, or Yellow Finn

¾ cup (6 oz/185 g) sour cream

¾ cup (6 fl oz/180 ml) mayonnaise

2 celery stalks, finely diced

2 tablespoons chopped green (spring) onion

2 teaspoons celery seeds

¼ cup (⅓ oz/10 g) chopped fresh flat-leaf (Italian) parsley, plus sprigs for garnish

2 hard-boiled eggs, coarsely chopped

1 teaspoon dry mustard

salt and ground white pepper

Place the potatoes in a large pot with water to cover. Bring to a boil, reduce the heat to medium, and cook, uncovered, until tender but slightly resistant when pierced, about 30 minutes. Drain and let cool. Do not peel. Cut into 1½-inch (4-cm) pieces and place in a bowl.

In a small bowl, combine the sour cream, mayonnaise, celery, green onion, celery seeds, chopped parsley, eggs, mustard, and salt and pepper to taste. Mix well.

Pour the dressing over the potatoes and toss to coat. Taste and adjust the seasonings. Cover and refrigerate for at least 1 hour or for up to 8 hours.

Transfer the salad to a transportable serving bowl and garnish with parsley sprigs. Cover and keep chilled until ready to serve.

serves six to eight | per serving: calories 407 (kilojoules 1,709), protein 7 g, carbohydrates 38 g, total fat 26 g, saturated fat 6 g, cholesterol 85 mg, sodium 191 mg, dietary fiber 4 g

curried lobster salad

For a shortcut, buy 1 pound (500 g) cooked lobster meat. Shaved coconut, which comes in thick curls, is available in most health-food stores and specialty markets.

3 live lobsters, 1½ lb (750 g) each
2 celery stalks, thinly sliced
⅓ cup (3 oz/90 g) plain yogurt
¼ cup (2 fl oz/60 ml) mayonnaise
1 tablespoon lemon juice
1 teaspoon mild curry powder
pinch of cayenne pepper
salt and ground black pepper
⅓ cup (1½ oz/45 g) shaved unsweetened dried coconut
vegetable oil for frying
8 green (spring) onions, including tender green tops, cut into 2-inch (5-cm) julienne

Bring a large pot three-fourths full of salted water to a boil. Add the lobsters, bring back to a boil, and cook until the shells turn bright red, about 10 minutes. Drain well and let cool.

Working with 1 lobster at a time, twist off the "arms" and break off the claws. Bend the "thumb" of each claw down until it cracks. Using a lobster cracker or mallet, crack the claw shells and extract the meat with a small fork. Crack the "arms" and extract the meat. Using your hands, break the lobster in half at the point where the body meets the tail. Squeeze the sides of the tail together so that the shell underside cracks. With the underside facing you, and one hand on each side of the shell, press open the tail, exposing the meat. Extract it with the fork. Repeat with the remaining lobsters. Cut the meat into ½-inch (12-mm) pieces. Let cool completely. In a bowl, combine the lobster meat, celery, yogurt, mayonnaise, lemon juice, curry powder, cayenne pepper, and salt and black pepper to taste. Mix well.

In a small, dry frying pan over medium-low heat, toast the coconut, stirring often, until golden brown, about 3 minutes. Set aside and let cool.

In a heavy saucepan, pour in oil to a depth of ½ inch (12 mm) and heat until hot (about 350°F/180°C). Add one-third of the green onions and fry until browned around the edges, about 1 minute. Using a slotted spoon, transfer to paper towels to drain. Repeat with the remaining green onions.

To serve, divide the lobster mixture evenly among chilled plates. Sprinkle with the coconut and green onions and serve immediately.

serves four to six | per serving: calories 294 (kilojoules 1,235), protein 21 g, carbohydrates 7 g, total fat 21 g, saturated fat 7 g, cholesterol 72 mg, sodium 438 mg, dietary fiber 2 g

green bean and sweet pepper salad

A citrus-flavored dressing accentuates the sweetness of green beans and bell peppers. You can also add other vegetables, such as sliced carrots, mushrooms, or jicama. Serve alongside an Italian Hero Sandwich (page 153) or Roast Beef and Spicy Slaw Sandwiches (page 189).

1 lb (500 g) green beans, trimmed
1 yellow bell pepper (capsicum), seeded and julienned
1 red bell pepper (capsicum), seeded and julienned
¼ cup (2 fl oz/60 ml) lemon juice
1 teaspoon Dijon mustard
1 tablespoon finely chopped fresh chives
1 tablespoon finely chopped fresh flat-leaf (Italian) parsley
½ cup (4 fl oz/125 ml) extra-virgin olive oil
salt and ground pepper

Bring a saucepan two-thirds full of water to a boil. Add the beans and cook until tender-crisp, 7–10 minutes. Drain and immerse in a bowl of ice water to stop the cooking. Drain well and transfer to a transportable bowl. Add the bell peppers.

In a small bowl, combine the lemon juice, mustard, chives, and parsley. Whisk in the oil until incorporated. Season to taste with salt and pepper.

Pour the dressing over the vegetables and toss to combine. Taste and adjust the seasonings. Cover and keep chilled until ready to serve.

serves four to six | per serving: calories 229 (kilojoules 962), protein 2 g, carbohydrates 8 g, total fat 23 g, saturated fat 3 g, cholesterol 0 mg, sodium 32 mg, dietary fiber 2 g

fruit salad with toasted coconut

This fruit salad is excellent served alone or with a big dollop of your favorite yogurt spooned on each portion. Try flavors like piña colada, vanilla, or pineapple to enhance the flavors of the fruit.

½ cup (2 oz/60 g) shredded coconut

1 ripe pineapple, peeled, cored, and cut into ½-inch (12-mm) chunks

1 ripe papaya, peeled, seeded, and cut into ½-inch (12-mm) chunks

1 ripe cantaloupe, peeled, seeded, and cut into ½-inch (12-mm) chunks

1 ripe mango, peeled, pitted, and cut into ½-inch (12-mm) chunks

6 fresh mint leaves

Preheat the oven to 350°F (180°C). Spread the coconut on a baking pan and toast in the oven until golden, about 5 minutes. Set aside to cool.

In a large transportable bowl, combine all the fruit. Cover and keep chilled until ready to serve. Just before serving, sprinkle with the toasted coconut and spoon onto small plates. Garnish with the mint leaves.

serves six | per serving: calories 157 (kilojoules 659), protein 2 g, carbohydrates 33 g, total fat 4 g, saturated fat 3 g, cholesterol 0 mg, sodium 35 mg, dietary fiber 3 g

tropical fruit with honey-lime dressing

This mix of exotic fruits makes a wonderful first-course dinner salad.

for the honey-lime dressing:

2 tablespoons lime juice

1 tablespoon honey

1 teaspoon Dijon mustard

¼ teaspoon salt

⅛ teaspoon ground white pepper

¼ cup (2 fl oz/60 ml) vegetable oil

for the salad:

1 cantaloupe

1 small papaya

2 mangoes

2 kiwifruits

zest of 1 lemon, cut into long julienne

zest of 1 lime, cut into long julienne

To make the dressing, in a small bowl, whisk together the lime juice, honey, mustard, salt, and white pepper until the honey dissolves. Slowly add the oil, whisking constantly, until the dressing is thick and emulsified. You should have about ½ cup (4 fl oz/125 ml). Cover and chill until serving.

To make the salad, halve and seed the cantaloupe and the papaya. Using a melon baller, form attractive rounds of the flesh of each. Alternatively, peel and cut the flesh into small cubes. Peel the mangoes and cut the flesh into 1-inch (2.5-cm) cubes. Peel the kiwifruits, cut in half lengthwise, and slice thickly. Combine all the fruits in a large bowl, cover, and chill well, at least 2 hours.

Just before serving, pour the dressing over the fruit and stir gently to coat. Spoon into a chilled glass bowl, garnish with the lemon and lime julienne, and serve immediately.

serves six | per serving: calories 205 (kilojoules 861), protein 2 g, carbohydrates 31 g, total fat 10 g, saturated fat 1 g, cholesterol 0 mg, sodium 129 mg, dietary fiber 3 g

couscous salad

1 eggplant (aubergine), about 1 lb (500 g), trimmed and quartered lengthwise

salt for sprinkling and to taste, plus ½ teaspoon

4 tablespoons (2 fl oz/60 ml) olive oil

ground pepper to taste, plus ¼ teaspoon

2 cups (16 fl oz/500 ml) tomato juice

1¼ cups (10 oz/315 g) instant couscous (1 box)

2 tablespoons red wine vinegar

¼ cup (2 fl oz/60 ml) extra-virgin olive oil

25 small cherry tomatoes, about ½ lb (250 g), stems removed and halved

2 cups (14 oz/440 g) rinsed and drained canned chickpeas (garbanzo beans)

2 tablespoons finely chopped fresh parsley

8–10 crisp romaine (cos) lettuce leaves

Liberally sprinkle the exposed flesh of the eggplant with salt. Set aside to drain on paper towels for 30 minutes. Rinse and pat dry. Brush with 2 tablespoons of the olive oil and season with salt and pepper.

In a large, heavy nonstick frying pan over medium-high heat, cook the eggplant, turning often, until well browned and soft, about 12 minutes. Transfer to paper towels to drain and let cool.

In a large saucepan over high heat, combine the tomato juice, the remaining 2 tablespoons olive oil, the ½ teaspoon salt, and the ¼ teaspoon pepper. Bring to a boil, stir in the couscous, remove from the heat, cover, and set aside for 5 minutes until the liquid is absorbed. Remove the lid, fluff with a fork, and transfer to a large bowl to cool.

Meanwhile, make a simple vinaigrette: Place the vinegar in a small bowl and slowly whisk in the extra-virgin olive oil until an emulsion forms.

Cut the eggplant crosswise into slices about ½ inch (12 mm) thick and add to the couscous. Add the tomatoes, chickpeas, and vinaigrette. Mix well and season with salt and pepper. (The salad can be made to this point up to 2 hours in advance. Cover and keep at room temperature.)

Stir in the parsley. Make a bed of the lettuce leaves on a serving platter. Mound the salad in the center and serve at once.

serves six | per serving: calories 491 (kilojoules 2,062), protein 14 g, carbohydrates 65 g, total fat 21 g, saturated fat 3 g, cholesterol 0 mg, sodium 555 mg, dietary fiber 6 g

stuffed cherry tomatoes with crab and tarragon

24 cherry tomatoes, about ¾ lb (375 g) total weight

½ lb (250 g) cooked lump crabmeat, picked over for shell fragments and flaked

1 tablespoon lemon juice

2 teaspoons finely chopped fresh tarragon, plus 24 whole leaves

1–2 tablespoons mayonnaise

several drops of Tabasco or other hot-pepper sauce, or to taste

salt and ground pepper to taste

Cut a slice ¼ inch (6 mm) thick off the top of each tomato and discard the tops. Using a small melon baller, scoop out the seeds of each tomato. Sprinkle the insides with salt and invert onto a baking sheet lined with paper towels. Set aside for 30 minutes to drain.

In a small bowl, mix together the crab, lemon juice, and chopped tarragon. Stir in enough mayonnaise to bind the mixture. Season with hot-pepper sauce, salt, and pepper. Cover and chill thoroughly.

Fill each tomato with a heaping teaspoonful of the crab mixture, mounding the top, and garnish with a tarragon leaf. Serve chilled.

serves four to six | per piece: calories 19 (kilojoules 80), protein 2 g, carbohydrates 1 g, total fat 1 g, saturated fat 0 g, cholesterol 10 mg, sodium 33 mg, dietary fiber 0 g

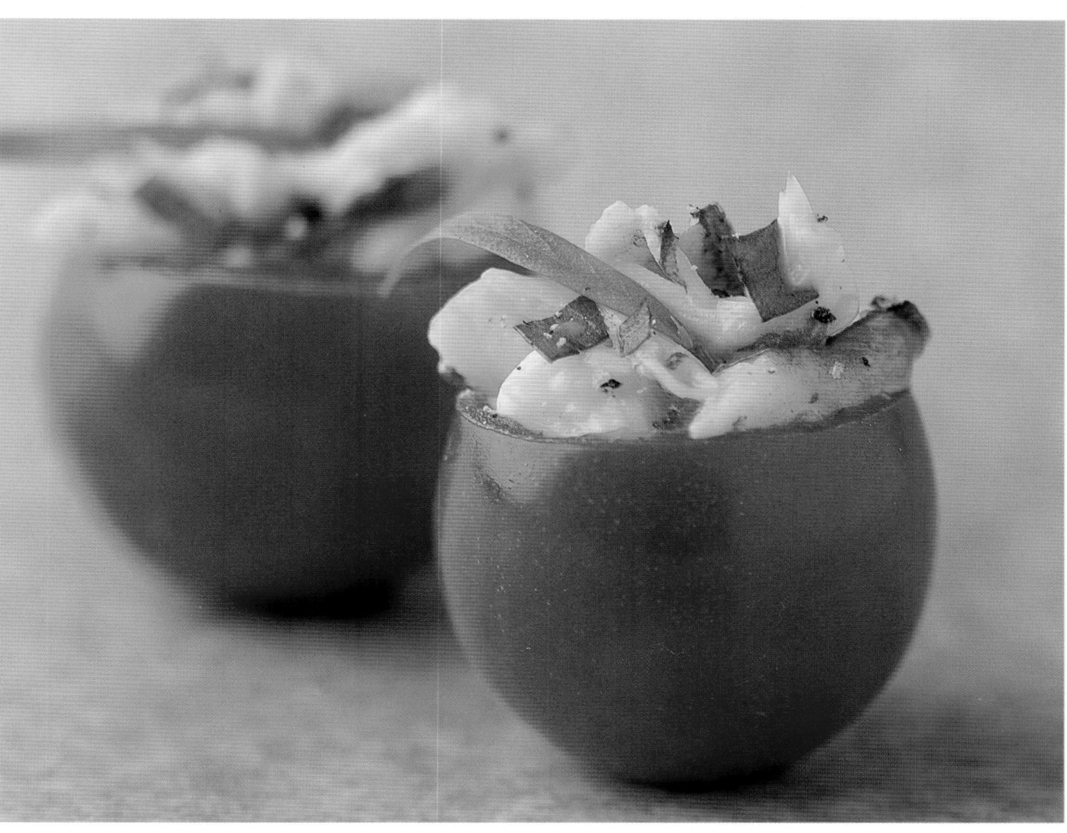

summer celebration pasta salad

Light pasta salads are always appreciated on hot summer days. To make a more substantial main-course salad, add 1 pound (500 g) cooked shrimp (prawns), cubed or shredded chicken, or bay scallops. For additional color, add julienned carrot and zucchini (courgette).

1 teaspoon salt

1 lb (500 g) fusilli or penne

1 tablespoon plus ⅓ cup (3 fl oz/80 ml) extra-virgin olive oil

2 lb (1 kg) ripe tomatoes, peeled, seeded, and coarsely chopped

5 cloves garlic, minced

½ cup (¾ oz/20 g) coarsely chopped fresh basil

¼ cup (⅓ oz/10 g) finely chopped fresh flat-leaf (Italian) parsley

3 tablespoons red wine vinegar

1 lb (500 g) fresh mozzarella cheese, cut into 1-inch (2.5-cm) cubes

½ cup (2 oz/60 g) grated Parmesan cheese

salt and ground pepper

Bring a large pot two-thirds full of water to a boil over high heat and add the salt. Add the pasta, stir well, and cook until al dente (tender but firm to the bite), 7–10 minutes or according to the package directions. Drain, place in a transportable bowl, and mix in the 1 tablespoon olive oil to keep the pasta from sticking together.

In a bowl, combine the tomatoes, garlic, basil, parsley, ⅓ cup (3 fl oz/80 ml) olive oil, vinegar, mozzarella and Parmesan cheeses, and salt and pepper to taste. Stir to mix well. Taste and adjust the seasonings.

Pour the sauce over the pasta and mix well to distribute evenly. Cover and keep chilled until ready to serve.

serves four to six | per serving: calories 838 (kilojoules 3,520), protein 34 g, carbohydrates 81 g, total fat 42 g, saturated fat 5 g, cholesterol 73 mg, sodium 608 mg, dietary fiber 5 g

pasta salad with grilled tuna and roasted tomatoes

Serve this lunch salad to a hungry crowd just back from the beach. The ingredients can be prepared ahead of time and tossed with the dressing just before serving.

8 plum tomatoes, about 1¼ lb (625 g) total weight, halved lengthwise

2 tablespoons plus ½ cup (4 fl oz/125 ml) olive oil

salt and ground pepper to taste

1 lb (500 g) pasta shells

2 lb (1 kg) tuna fillets, about ¾ inch (2 cm) thick

1 cup (1 oz/30 g) loosely packed fresh basil leaves

3 tablespoons red wine vinegar

1 lb (500 g) fresh mozzarella cheese, finely diced

¼ cup (⅓ oz/10 g) chopped fresh parsley

Preheat the oven to 450°F (230°C). Prepare a hot fire in a grill.

Place the tomatoes on a baking sheet and toss with 1 tablespoon of the oil. Arrange them, cut sides up, on the sheet and sprinkle with salt. Roast until tender, about 20 minutes. Let cool, then cut in half crosswise.

Meanwhile, bring a large pot three-fourths full of salted water to a boil. Add the pasta and cook until al dente (tender but firm to the bite), about 10 minutes. Drain, rinse under cold running water, and drain again. Set aside.

Coat both sides of the tuna with 1 tablespoon of the oil. Season well with salt and pepper. Place on the grill rack and grill until lightly browned, about 3 minutes. Turn and cook until done to your taste, 3–4 minutes for medium. Transfer to a cutting board, let cool, and cut into ¾-inch (2-cm) cubes.

In a food processor or blender, combine the basil leaves and the remaining ½ cup (4 fl oz/125 ml) oil. Pulse or blend until chopped to a coarse purée. Add the vinegar and season with salt and pepper. Pulse or blend until combined.

In a large bowl, combine the pasta, tomatoes, tuna, mozzarella, parsley, and basil dressing. Toss gently and serve.

serves eight | per serving: calories 700 (kilojoules 2,940), protein 44 g, carbohydrates 48 g, total fat 36 g, saturated fat 4 g, cholesterol 83 mg, sodium 289 mg, dietary fiber 2 g

salade niçoise

In this version of salade niçoise all of the ingredients are combined and mixed with a lemony dressing that can be prepared hours ahead. It is hearty enough to serve as a main course along with a loaf of crusty French bread.

1 lb (500 g) new potatoes, red-skinned, tan-skinned, or Yellow Finn

1 lb (500 g) green beans, trimmed and cut into 2-inch (5-cm) pieces

2 cans (12 oz/375 g each) white-meat tuna packed in water, drained and broken into chunks

1 small red bell pepper (capsicum), seeded and julienned

1 small red onion, thinly sliced and cut into ½-inch (12-mm) pieces

8 cherry tomatoes, quartered

½ cup (2½ oz/75 g) pitted Niçoise olives

2 tablespoons drained capers

6 tablespoons finely chopped fresh basil

salt and ground pepper to taste

⅓ cup (3 fl oz/80 ml) lemon juice

1 teaspoon Dijon mustard

2 cloves garlic, minced

⅔ cup (5 fl oz/160 ml) extra-virgin olive oil

2 hard-boiled eggs, quartered

Place the potatoes in a saucepan with water to cover. Bring to a boil, reduce the heat to medium, and cook, uncovered, until tender but slightly resistant when pierced, 20–30 minutes. Drain, let cool, and cut into bite-sized pieces. Place in a large bowl.

Bring a saucepan three-fourths full of salted water to a boil. Immerse the green beans in the water and cook until tender but slightly resistant when pierced, 5–7 minutes. Drain and immerse in a bowl of ice water to stop the cooking. Drain well and add to the bowl with the potatoes. Add the tuna, bell pepper, red onion, tomatoes, olives, capers, 2 tablespoons of the basil, and pepper to taste and stir to combine.

In a small bowl, combine the lemon juice, mustard, garlic, and 2 tablespoons of the basil. Slowly whisk in the olive oil. Season with salt and pepper.

Combine enough dressing with the salad to moisten it. Toss gently. Arrange in a large, shallow transportable bowl. Place the egg quarters around the edges. Sprinkle the remaining 2 tablespoons basil on top. Cover and keep chilled until ready to serve. Serve any remaining dressing on the side.

serves six | per serving: calories 526 (kilojoules 2,209), protein 34 g, carbohydrates 24 g, total fat 34 g, saturated fat 5 g, cholesterol 115 mg, sodium 739 mg, dietary fiber 4 g

autumn

pork brochettes with peanut sauce

The Indonesian satay, a skewer of delectable meat or chicken, is the inspiration for these piquant brochettes. You can bring the marinated skewers to a picnic or tailgate party, ready to be grilled at the last minute, or grill them ahead and serve them chilled. Either way, they are a great beginning to a party.

½ cup (4 fl oz/125 ml) orange juice

2 tablespoons lime juice

2 tablespoons vegetable oil

1 teaspoon chopped fresh oregano

1 teaspoon finely chopped fresh cilantro (fresh coriander)

½ teaspoon ground cumin

salt and ground pepper

1 lb (500 g) pork tenderloin, cut into 1-inch (2.5-cm) pieces

for the sauce:

½ cup (4 oz/125 g) chunky peanut butter

¾ cup (6 fl oz/180 ml) coconut milk

1 tablespoon soy sauce

1 tablespoon honey

2 teaspoons peeled and minced fresh ginger

2 cloves garlic, minced

In a bowl, combine the orange juice, lime juice, oil, oregano, cilantro, cumin, and salt and pepper to taste. Whisk until blended. Thread the pork onto wooden or metal skewers and arrange in a shallow nonaluminum dish. (If using wooden skewers, first soak in water for at least 15 minutes.) Reserve 3 tablespoons of the marinade and pour the remainder over the skewered pork. Cover and refrigerate for at least 6 hours or for up to 12 hours.

Meanwhile make the sauce: In a bowl, whisk together all the ingredients. Transfer to a small transportable container.

Prepare a fire in a grill. When the coals are medium-hot, place the skewers on the grill rack and brush with the remaining 3 tablespoons marinade. Grill until well browned, 5–7 minutes on each side. Remove from the grill and arrange on a large plate or transfer to a transportable container. Serve with the peanut sauce.

serves four to six | per serving: calories 401 (kilojoules 1,684), protein 25 g, carbohydrates 13 g, total fat 29 g, saturated fat 11 g, cholesterol 57 mg, sodium 361 mg, dietary fiber 2 g

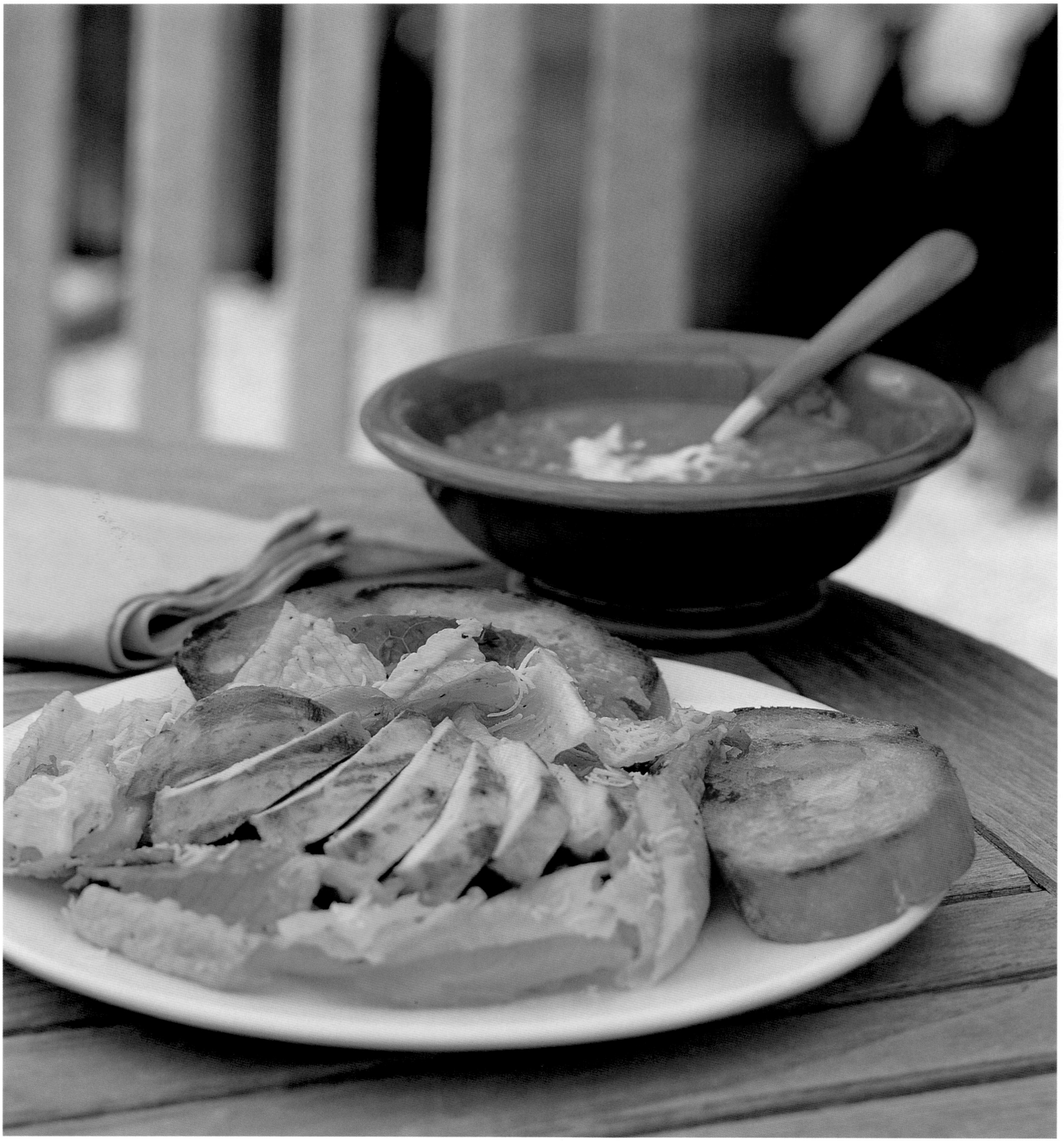

chicken caesar salad

This Caesar features an eggless dressing, perfect for a warm-weather lunch by the lake. If you prefer, grill the bruschetta and the chicken over hot coals. If desired, accompany with Spiced Lentil and Rice Soup (right).

4 skinless, boneless chicken breast halves, about 1½ lb (750 g) total weight

½ cup (4 oz/125 ml) lemon juice

1½ tablespoons Worcestershire sauce

1 tablespoon Dijon mustard

8 tablespoons (4 fl oz/125 ml) extra-virgin olive oil

8 slices crusty Italian or sourdough bread

1 or 2 cloves garlic

1 head romaine (cos) lettuce, leaves separated and torn into pieces

¾ cup (3 oz/90 g) grated Parmesan or aged Asiago cheese

1 anchovy fillet in olive oil (optional)

ground pepper

Place the chicken breasts in a nonaluminum container. In a small bowl, whisk together the lemon juice, Worcestershire sauce, and mustard. Whisk in 2 tablespoons of the olive oil. Pour half of this mixture over the chicken breasts, turn to coat well, then cover and marinate for up to 1 hour at room temperature or up to 4 hours in the refrigerator. Cover the remaining mixture and set aside.

Preheat the broiler (grill). Arrange the bread slices on a broiler pan and broil (grill) about 4 inches (10 cm) below the heat, turning once, until golden brown on both sides, about 4 minutes total. Remove from the broiler and immediately brush one side of each slice with some of the remaining olive oil, then rub the same side with a garlic clove. Set the bruschetta aside. Place the chicken breasts on the same broiler pan and broil, turning once, until golden brown on the outside and no longer pink in the center when cut, about 15 minutes total. Remove from the broiler and slice each breast crosswise into strips, keeping the slices together.

Place the lettuce in a large bowl. Add the cheese and toss lightly. Whisk the remaining olive oil with the reserved lemon juice–mustard mixture. If desired, mash the anchovy fillet into the dressing. Pour over the lettuce, season liberally with pepper, and toss well. Divide the salad among individual plates. Top each portion with a sliced chicken breast and garnish with 2 bruschetta slices, then serve.

serves four | per serving: calories 654 (kilojoules 2,747), protein 54 g, carbohydrates 27 g, total fat 36 g, saturated fat 9 g, cholesterol 116 mg, sodium 871 mg, dietary fiber 4 g

spiced lentil and rice soup

Lentils, which don't have to be presoaked, cook relatively fast, making this a quick-to-fix soup.

about 1¾ cups (12 oz/375 g) dried brown lentils

2 tablespoons vegetable oil

1 large yellow or red onion, chopped

2 large carrots, chopped

½ cup (3½ oz/105 g) long-grain white rice

1½ tablespoons good-quality curry powder

8 cups (64 fl oz/2 l) chicken or vegetable broth, plus broth as needed

salt and ground pepper

½ cup (4 oz/125 g) plain nonfat yogurt

½ teaspoon ground cumin

Rinse the lentils in a fine-mesh sieve and discard any stones or debris.

In a deep, heavy pot, warm the oil over medium-high heat. Add the onion and carrots and cook, stirring, until the onion is soft, about 5 minutes. Stir in the rice, curry powder, and lentils. Stir until the mixture is fragrant and the beans and rice are coated with oil, about 2 minutes. Add the 8 cups (64 fl oz/2 l) broth, cover, and bring to a boil. Stir again, then reduce the heat to low, and simmer, covered, until the lentils and rice are cooked through, about 30 minutes.

Remove from the heat and let stand for about 10 minutes before serving. Season well with salt and pepper. (Or let cool, covered, and refrigerate for up to 24 hours. Reheat before serving; if the soup becomes too thick, thin first with a little more broth.)

In a small bowl, blend the yogurt and cumin. Ladle the soup into bowls and drizzle a little yogurt on top of each portion.

serves six | per serving: calories 386 (kilojoules 1,621), protein 22 g, carbohydrates 57 g, total fat 8 g, saturated fat 1 g, cholesterol 0 mg, sodium 1,373 mg, dietary fiber 9 g

coleslaw with cider dressing

This sweet-and-sour cabbage salad makes an excellent companion for any sandwich. It's also good with Grilled Marinated Flank Steak (page 202). If you like caraway seeds, add ½ teaspoon for a slightly pungent accent.

4 cups (12 oz/375 g) shredded green cabbage

2 cups (6 oz/185 g) shredded red cabbage

1 carrot, peeled and shredded

¾ cup (6 fl oz/180 ml) mayonnaise

½ cup (4 oz/125 g) sour cream

1½ tablespoons sugar

3 tablespoons cider vinegar

2 tablespoons finely chopped fresh flat-leaf (Italian) parsley

2 cloves garlic, minced

salt and ground pepper

In a large transportable bowl, combine the shredded cabbages and carrot. In another bowl combine the remaining ingredients, including salt and pepper to taste. Whisk until smooth.

Pour the dressing over the vegetables and toss well. Taste and adjust the seasonings. Cover and refrigerate until the flavors are blended, at least 2 hours or for up to 8 hours. Keep chilled until ready to serve.

serves six | per serving: calories 279 (kilojoules 1,172), protein 2 g, carbohydrates 11 g, total fat 26 g, saturated fat 6 g, cholesterol 25 mg, sodium 185 mg, dietary fiber 2 g

greek rice salad

Rice is the basis for a filling lunch salad that's easy to take on a picnic. Make it a day ahead so the flavors have a chance to develop.

3 cups (24 fl oz/750 ml) water

½ teaspoon salt

1½ cups (10½ oz/330 g) long-grain white rice

¾ cup (6 fl oz/180 ml) lemon juice

1 tablespoon Dijon mustard

½ cup (4 fl oz/125 ml) extra-virgin olive oil

2 tablespoons chopped fresh oregano or 1 tablespoon dried oregano

6 oz (185 g) feta cheese, crumbled

6 oz (185 g) Kalamata or other brine-cured olives, halved and pitted

about 1 lb (500 g) red or yellow cherry tomatoes, cut in half if large

1 cucumber, peeled, seeded, and diced

½ cup (½ oz/15 g) packed fresh mint leaves or parsley leaves, coarsely chopped

In a saucepan, combine the water and salt and bring to a boil. Add the rice, reduce the heat to low, cover, and simmer until the rice is tender and the water is absorbed, about 20 minutes.

Meanwhile, in a large salad bowl, whisk together the lemon juice and mustard. Add the oil, whisking constantly until blended. Stir in the oregano. Add the feta, olives, tomatoes, and cucumber and toss well to coat. Set aside.

When the rice is done, place it in a fine-mesh sieve and rinse with cold running water until cool. Drain well, shaking out the excess water. Add to the salad bowl and toss gently to combine. Add the mint or parsley and toss again. Serve or cover and refrigerate for up to 24 hours.

serves four to six | per serving: calories 629 (kilojoules 2,642), protein 10 g, carbohydrates 62 g, total fat 38 g, saturated fat 9 g, cholesterol 30 mg, sodium 1,219 mg, dietary fiber 2 g

spinach salad with pears, gorgonzola, and walnuts

Pears and toasted walnuts add a crunchy dimension to the pungent greens in this autumn tossed salad. Be sure to select a quality Gorgonzola that will crumble easily.

3 tablespoons sherry wine vinegar

1 tablespoon lemon juice

1 teaspoon honey Dijon mustard

½ cup (4 fl oz/125 ml) olive oil

½ cup (2 oz/60 g) chopped walnuts

¾ lb (375 g) spinach, stems removed, torn into bite-sized pieces

2 heads Belgian endive (chicory/witloof), cored and thinly sliced

1 firm but ripe pear, peeled, cored, and sliced

½ cup (2½ oz/75 g) crumbled Gorgonzola cheese

Preheat the oven to 350°F (180°C).

In a small bowl, whisk together the vinegar, lemon juice, and mustard. Slowly whisk in the olive oil until incorporated. Taste and adjust the seasonings. Transfer to a container with a tight-fitting lid.

Spread the walnuts on a baking sheet and toast in the oven until lightly browned and fragrant, 7–10 minutes.

In a transportable bowl, combine the spinach, endive, pear slices, and toasted walnuts. Sprinkle with the Gorgonzola.

Cover and keep chilled until ready to serve. To serve, drizzle the vinaigrette over the salad and toss to mix well.

serves four to six | per serving: calories 350 (kilojoules 1,470), protein 6 g, carbohydrates 10 g, total fat 33 g, saturated fat 7 g, cholesterol 12 mg, sodium 261 mg, dietary fiber 3 g

chopped salad

Full of crunchy vegetables and chopped chicken, this salad can be served as part of a salad buffet or as a main course. For the vinaigrette, you can substitute ranch or blue cheese dressing.

2 skinless, boneless chicken breast halves, about 5 oz (155 g) each

1 head iceberg lettuce, cored and finely shredded

½ jicama, peeled and finely diced

½ cup (2½ oz/75 g) diced red bell pepper (capsicum)

½ cup (2½ oz/75 g) peeled, seeded, and finely diced cucumber

1 celery stalk, finely diced

1 carrot, peeled and finely diced

1 cup (6 oz/185 g) drained canned chickpeas (garbanzo beans), coarsely chopped

2 tablespoons red wine vinegar

1 tablespoon lemon juice

1 teaspoon Dijon mustard

1 shallot, finely chopped

6 tablespoons (3 fl oz/90 ml) extra-virgin olive oil

2 tablespoons finely chopped fresh flat-leaf (Italian) parsley

salt and ground pepper

Place the chicken in a sauté pan and add water to cover. Place over medium-high heat and bring to a simmer. Reduce the heat to low and simmer, uncovered, until the chicken is no longer pink in the center when cut into with a knife, 10–12 minutes. Remove from the heat and set aside to cool in the liquid.

In a large transportable bowl, combine the lettuce, jicama, bell pepper, cucumber, celery, carrot, and chickpeas. Toss well. Drain the chicken and finely chop. Add to the vegetables and toss to combine. Cover and keep chilled until ready to serve.

In a small bowl, combine the vinegar, lemon juice, mustard, and shallot. Slowly whisk in the olive oil until incorporated. Add the parsley and season to taste with salt and pepper. Taste and adjust the seasonings. Transfer to a container with a tight-fitting lid.

To serve, pour the dressing over the salad and toss to coat.

serves four to six | per serving: calories 314 (kilojoules 1,319), protein 19 g, carbohydrates 20 g, total fat 19 g, saturated fat 3 g, cholesterol 35 mg, sodium 158 mg, dietary fiber 7 g

chinese shredded chicken salad

You can make this crunchy salad of cucumbers and carrots up to 4 hours ahead of serving. Begin with Cold Curried Eggplant Soup (page 98) and offer Plum-Almond Tart (page 256) for dessert.

4 skinless, boneless chicken breast halves, about 5 oz (155 g) each

¼ cup (2 fl oz/60 ml) soy sauce

¼ cup (2 fl oz/60 ml) unseasoned rice wine vinegar

1 clove garlic, minced

1 tablespoon peanut butter

pinch of sugar

pinch of Chinese hot mustard

¼ cup (2 fl oz/60 ml) Asian sesame oil

1 tablespoon chile oil

1 tablespoon canola oil

1 tablespoon sesame seeds

1 English (hothouse) cucumber, julienned

2 carrots, peeled and julienned

2 green (spring) onions, including tender green tops, thinly sliced on the diagonal

2 tablespoons finely chopped fresh cilantro (fresh coriander)

Place the chicken in a sauté pan and add water to cover. Place over medium-high heat and bring to a simmer. Reduce the heat to low and simmer, uncovered, until the chicken is no longer pink in the center when cut into with a knife, 10–12 minutes. Remove from the heat and set aside to cool in the liquid.

In a bowl, combine the soy sauce, vinegar, garlic, peanut butter, sugar, and hot mustard. Whisk to mix well. Slowly whisk in the oils until completely incorporated. Taste and adjust the seasonings.

Place the sesame seeds in a frying pan over high heat. Toast, shaking the pan, until light brown, about 2 minutes. Immediately remove from the pan.

Drain the chicken. Shred by tearing the meat into long, thin pieces. In a transportable bowl, combine the chicken, cucumber, carrots, green onions, and 1 tablespoon of the cilantro. Pour over the dressing and mix well. Taste and adjust the seasonings. Garnish with the sesame seeds and the remaining 1 tablespoon cilantro. Cover and keep chilled until ready to serve.

serves six to eight | per serving: calories 242 (kilojoules 1,016), protein 22 g, carbohydrates 6 g, total fat 15 g, saturated fat 2 g, cholesterol 50 mg, sodium 664 mg, dietary fiber 2 g

warm cannellini salad with tuna and sage

Beans and tuna—two ingredients that keep indefinitely when canned—are combined in a rustic salad with Tuscan overtones. Offer the salad with toasted slices of crusty bread and a crisp white wine.

juice of 2 large lemons

2 teaspoons Dijon mustard

½ small red onion, finely chopped

4 celery stalks, halved lengthwise and thinly sliced

1 can (6 oz/185 g) chunk white tuna packed in spring water, drained

¼ cup (2 fl oz/60 ml) extra-virgin olive oil

2 heaping tablespoons chopped fresh sage or 2½ teaspoons dried sage

2 cans (15 oz/470 g each) cannellini beans, drained and well rinsed

salt and ground pepper

In a large bowl, stir together the lemon juice and mustard until the mustard dissolves completely. Add the onion and celery and mix well. Gently stir in the tuna.

In a large frying pan over medium heat, warm the oil and sage until the oil is hot and the sage starts to sizzle. Add the beans and cook, stirring once or twice, until hot, about 3 minutes. Add to the bowl with the tuna and stir to coat. Season to taste with salt and pepper. Serve warm.

serves four | per serving: calories 347 (kilojoules 1,457), protein 22 g, carbohydrates 29 g, total fat 16 g, saturated fat 2 g, cholesterol 17 mg, sodium 508 mg, dietary fiber 9 g

cheese toasts with celery root–carrot salad

Because carrots and celery root last so long in the refrigerator, this is a good choice to serve at the end of a week's stay at a cabin.

¼ cup (2 fl oz/60 ml) sherry wine vinegar or red wine vinegar

1 tablespoon Dijon mustard

⅓ cup (3 fl oz/80 ml) extra-virgin olive oil

4 large carrots, about 1½ lb (750 g) total weight, shredded

1 celery root (celeriac)

salt and ground pepper

chopped fresh tarragon, chervil, or parsley (optional)

4 large slices coarse country bread, each about ½ inch (12 mm) thick

1 cup (4 oz/125 g) shredded Gruyère cheese

Preheat the broiler (grill). In a small bowl, whisk together the vinegar and mustard. Pour in the oil, whisking constantly, until blended. Set aside.

Place the shredded carrots in a serving bowl. Using a large, sharp knife, cut off the peel from the celery root and trim away any brown spots. Cut the celery root into quarters and shred. Add to the bowl with the carrots and pour in the dressing. Toss well. Season to taste with salt and pepper and toss in the herbs, if using. Set aside.

Arrange the bread slices on a broiler (grill) pan and broil (grill) until golden on one side, about 2 minutes. Turn and top evenly with the cheese. Broil until the cheese melts, about 2 minutes. Transfer to individual plates and top with some of the salad. Serve the remaining salad on the side.

serves four | per serving: calories 474 (kilojoules 1,991), protein 14 g, carbohydrates 42 g, total fat 29 g, saturated fat 8 g, cholesterol 31 mg, sodium 518 mg, dietary fiber 6 g

winter

three-onion soup with gruyère croutons

The key here is to caramelize the onions and leeks slowly, which gives this soup an especially rich flavor. This typical bistro dish makes a substantial luncheon main course with an accompanying plate of Shredded Root Vegetable Salad (page 132).

3 tablespoons olive oil

2 large red onions, thinly sliced

2 yellow onions, thinly sliced

4 leeks, white part only, thinly sliced

¼ teaspoon sugar

7 cups (56 fl oz/1.75 l) chicken or beef broth

½ cup (4 fl oz/125 ml) dry white wine

2 cloves garlic, minced

1 bay leaf

¼ teaspoon dried thyme

salt and ground pepper to taste

12 baguette slices, each ¼ inch (6 mm) thick

¾ cup (3 oz/90 g) shredded Gruyère cheese

2 tablespoons finely chopped fresh parsley

In a large nonaluminum pot over medium heat, warm the olive oil. Add the red and yellow onions and sauté until wilted, about 15 minutes. Add the leeks and sugar and continue cooking, stirring frequently, until caramelized, 30–45 minutes.

Add the broth, wine, garlic, and bay leaf. Cover partially and simmer until thickened slightly, about 30 minutes. Discard the bay leaf. Add the thyme, salt, and pepper.

Meanwhile, preheat the broiler (grill). Arrange the bread slices on a baking sheet and broil (grill) until golden, 1½–2 minutes. Watch carefully to prevent burning.

Ladle the soup into individual flameproof soup bowls placed on a baking sheet. Place 2 or 3 bread slices on top of each serving and sprinkle evenly with the cheese. Broil until melted and golden. Remove from the broiler, sprinkle a little parsley over the tops, and serve immediately.

serves four to six | per serving: calories 389 (kilojoules 1,634), protein 14 g, carbohydrates 45 g, total fat 18 g, saturated fat 5 g, cholesterol 19 mg, sodium 1,672 mg, dietary fiber 5 g

sicilian orange, olive, and onion salad

Sicily, land of citrus fruit and olives, is the inspiration for this unusual salad. Blood oranges or tangerines would be welcome substitutions.

for the dressing:

1 teaspoon Dijon mustard

½ teaspoon salt

¼ teaspoon ground pepper

1 tablespoon balsamic vinegar

1 tablespoon orange juice

about ½ cup (4 fl oz/125 ml) extra-virgin olive oil

for the salad:

2 navel oranges

1 small red onion, halved and thinly sliced

12 oil-cured black olives, halved, pitted, and cut into thin slivers

8 cups (½ lb/250 g) loosely packed assorted young lettuce leaves

To make the dressing, in a salad bowl, whisk together the mustard, salt, pepper, vinegar, and orange juice until the salt dissolves. Slowly add the oil, whisking constantly until thickened and emulsified. Add just enough to make the dressing shiny. You should have ½ cup (4 fl oz/125 ml) dressing.

To make the salad, cut a slice off the top and bottom of each orange to expose the flesh. Place the orange upright on a cutting board and thickly slice off the peel in strips, cutting around the contour of the fruit to expose the flesh. Cut along both sides of each section to free the sections from the membranes.

Add the onion slices to the salad bowl and toss to separate and to coat with the dressing. Add the orange sections and the olives and toss again. Pile the lettuce greens on top. Toss the salad one more time just before serving.

serves six | per serving: calories 215 (kilojoules 903), protein 2 g, carbohydrates 9 g, total fat 21 g, saturated fat 3 g, cholesterol 0 mg, sodium 386 mg, dietary fiber 2 g

black bean chili

2 cups (14 oz/440 g) dried black beans

3 tablespoons vegetable oil

3 yellow onions, finely chopped

5 cloves garlic, minced

¼ cup (2 oz/60 g) good-quality chile powder

4 teaspoons dried oregano

4 teaspoons ground cumin

1 teaspoon ground coriander

1 tablespoon paprika

¼ teaspoon cayenne pepper

3 cups (24 fl oz/750 ml) vegetable broth

1½ cups (9 oz/280 g) canned diced tomatoes with juice

½–1 canned chipotle chile or 1 small seeded jalapeño chile, minced

3 cups (24 fl oz/750 ml) water

1 tablespoon rice vinegar or white wine vinegar

3 tablespoons finely chopped fresh cilantro (fresh coriander)

salt to taste

for the garnish:

½ cup (2 oz/60 g) diced Muenster cheese

½ cup (4 fl oz/125 ml) sour cream

6–8 fresh cilantro (fresh coriander) sprigs

Pick over the beans, discarding any stones or misshapen beans. Rinse and drain. Place in a bowl, add plenty of water to cover, and let stand for at least 4 hours or for up to overnight. Drain and set aside.

In a heavy pot over medium heat, warm the vegetable oil. Add the onions and sauté until softened, about 5 minutes. Add the garlic, chile powder, oregano, cumin, coriander, paprika, and cayenne pepper and stir to combine. Cook, stirring occasionally, about 5 minutes.

Add the broth, tomatoes, chile, water, and reserved beans and bring to a boil. Reduce the heat to low, cover partially, and cook for 45 minutes. Uncover and continue to cook until the beans are tender, about 45 minutes longer. If the chili is too soupy, using a potato masher, mash some of the beans to help thicken the mixture. When the beans are ready, add the vinegar and chopped cilantro and stir to combine. Season with salt.

To serve, divide the Muenster cheese among warmed bowls and ladle in the chili. Garnish each serving with sour cream and cilantro.

serves six to eight | per serving: calories 393 (kilojoules 1,651), protein 17 g, carbohydrates 52 g, total fat 15 g, saturated fat 5 g, cholesterol 15 mg, sodium 661 mg, dietary fiber 12 g

vegetable soup with aioli

for the aioli:

1 head garlic

1 tablespoon olive oil

¼ cup (2 fl oz/60 ml) mayonnaise

1 teaspoon lemon juice

salt to taste

pinch of cayenne pepper

2 tablespoons olive oil

2 leeks, white and light green parts only, finely chopped

3 carrots, peeled and diced

1 red or white rose potato, about ½ lb (250 g), peeled and diced

3 zucchini (courgettes), diced

6 fresh mushrooms, diced

½ small cabbage, shredded

7 cups (56 fl oz/1.75 l) chicken broth

½ cup (3 oz/90 g) canned crushed tomatoes

1 clove garlic, minced

¼ teaspoon dried thyme

¼ teaspoon dried oregano

salt and ground pepper to taste

½ cup (1¾ oz/50 g) dried egg noodles

3 tablespoons finely chopped fresh parsley

To make the aioli, preheat the oven to 425°F (220°C). Cut off the top fourth of the garlic head and then score around its perimeter. Sprinkle with the 1 tablespoon olive oil. Wrap tightly in aluminum foil and place in a small baking dish. Bake until soft when pierced, 45–60 minutes. Let cool, then squeeze the soft pulp into a small bowl and mash. Add the mayonnaise, lemon juice, salt, and cayenne pepper. Mix well. Cover and refrigerate.

In a large, heavy pot over medium heat, warm the 2 tablespoons olive oil. Add the leeks and sauté until they begin to soften but not color, 3–5 minutes. Add the carrots, potato, zucchini, and mushrooms and sauté until slightly softened, about 3 minutes. Add the cabbage and sauté just until softened, about 2 minutes more. Add the broth, tomatoes, garlic, thyme, oregano, salt, and pepper and bring to a boil. Reduce the heat to medium-low and simmer, uncovered, until the vegetables are tender, 20–25 minutes.

Meanwhile, bring a pot three-fourths full of salted water to a boil. Add the noodles and cook until al dente (tender yet firm to the bite), about 8 minutes, or according to the package directions. Add to the soup and stir well.

Ladle into warmed bowls and top each bowl with a dollop of the aioli. Garnish with the parsley and serve immediately.

serves six to eight | per serving: calories 247 (kilojoules 1,037), protein 7 g, carbohydrates 27 g, total fat 14 g, saturated fat 2 g, cholesterol 11 mg, sodium 1,123 mg, dietary fiber 4 g

german potato salad

Select a creamy-style potato like the red rose or white rose or even a Yukon gold for this hearty salad. Idaho or russet potatoes lack the correct texture. Serve the salad alongside your favorite sandwich or on its own with a glass of full-bodied Zinfandel.

2 lb (1 kg) creamy-style potatoes *(see note)*, unpeeled

6 slices bacon, cut into 1-inch (2.5-cm) pieces

6 tablespoons (3 fl oz/90 ml) olive oil

1 yellow onion, thinly sliced

1 tablespoon sugar

2 teaspoons all-purpose (plain) flour

salt and ground pepper to taste

½ cup (4 fl oz/125 ml) water

¼ cup (2 fl oz/60 ml) cider vinegar

¼ cup (⅓ oz/10 g) minced fresh parsley, plus 2 tablespoons chopped

Bring a large saucepan three-fourths full of water to a boil over high heat. Add the potatoes, reduce the heat to medium-high, and cook, uncovered, until tender but still slightly resistant when pierced with a fork, 25–30 minutes. Drain and let cool slightly, then peel and cut into slices ½–1 inch (12 mm–2.5 cm) thick. Place in a serving bowl.

In a frying pan over medium-high heat, fry the bacon until crisp and brown, 6–8 minutes. Using a slotted spoon, transfer to paper towels to drain, then add to the potatoes. Pour off the drippings from the pan. Return the pan to medium heat and warm the olive oil. Add the onion and sauté until soft and lightly browned, 5–7 minutes. Add the sugar, flour, salt, pepper, and water and continue cooking until the dressing begins to thicken, 3–5 minutes. Add the vinegar and the ¼ cup (⅓ oz/10 g) minced parsley and cook for 1 minute longer. Taste and adjust the seasonings. Pour the dressing over the potatoes and toss gently to combine.

Garnish with the chopped parsley and serve immediately.

serves four to six | per serving: calories 359 (kilojoules 1,508), protein 6 g, carbohydrates 40 g, total fat 20 g, saturated fat 4 g, cholesterol 6 mg, sodium 130 mg, dietary fiber 3 g

hearty lentil soup

For a vegetarian version, omit the turkey and substitute vegetable broth for the chicken broth. The flavor will be different but not diminished.

2 tablespoons olive oil

1 large yellow onion, finely chopped

3 carrots, peeled and finely chopped

2 celery stalks, finely chopped

3 cloves garlic, minced

2 cups (14 oz/440 g) brown lentils, picked over and rinsed

1½ cups (9 oz/280 g) coarsely chopped honey-roasted turkey

8–9 cups (64–72 fl oz/2–2.25 l) chicken broth

2 cups (12 oz/375 g) canned diced tomatoes with juice

4 tablespoons (⅓ oz/10 g) finely chopped fresh parsley

½ teaspoon dried thyme

1 tablespoon balsamic vinegar

salt and ground pepper to taste

for the garnish:

¼ cup (⅓ oz/10 g) finely chopped fresh parsley

sour cream (optional)

croutons (optional)

In a 6-qt (6-l) soup pot over medium heat, warm the olive oil. Add the onion and sauté until slightly softened, about 3 minutes. Add the carrots and celery and continue to sauté until slightly softened, about 5 minutes. Add the garlic and sauté for about 1 minute longer. Add the lentils, ½ cup (3 oz/90 g) of the chopped turkey, 8 cups (64 fl oz/2 l) of the broth, the tomatoes, 2 tablespoons of the parsley, and the thyme and bring to a simmer. Reduce the heat to medium-low and cook, uncovered, stirring occasionally, until the lentils are tender, about 30 minutes. (Test for tenderness by pushing them with the back of a wooden spoon; if they break up easily, they are cooked.) Remove from the heat and let cool slightly.

Working in batches, purée the soup in a blender, making sure to retain some texture. If the soup seems too thick, add another cup (8 fl oz/250 ml) broth or water to thin to desired consistency. Return to the pan over medium heat. Add the remaining 1 cup (6 oz/190 g) turkey, remaining 2 tablespoons parsley, the vinegar, salt, and pepper. Simmer for 5 minutes to blend the flavors. Taste and adjust the seasonings.

Ladle into warmed bowls. Garnish with the ¼ cup (⅓ oz/10 g) parsley and with sour cream and croutons, if using. Serve at once.

serves eight | per serving: calories 297 (kilojoules 1,247), protein 23 g, carbohydrates 39 g, total fat 6 g, saturated fat 1 g, cholesterol 14 mg, sodium 1,545 mg, dietary fiber 8 g

grapefruit, fennel, and mushroom salad

Winter's bounty is celebrated in this flavorful salad. Serve before Hearty Lentil Soup (page 131) with a basket of warm sourdough bread.

for the dressing:

1 shallot, finely chopped

juice of ½ pink grapefruit

1 tablespoon balsamic vinegar

½ cup (4 fl oz/125 ml) olive oil

salt and ground pepper to taste

1 large pink grapefruit

1 fennel bulb

2 heads butter (Boston) lettuce, leaves separated and torn into bite-sized pieces

4 fresh white mushrooms, brushed clean and thinly sliced

To make the dressing, in a small bowl, whisk together the shallot, grapefruit juice, and vinegar. Slowly add the oil, whisking constantly until fully incorporated. Season with salt and pepper. Set aside.

Using a small knife, cut a slice off the top and bottom of the grapefruit to expose the fruit. Place upright on a cutting board and slice off the peel in strips, cutting around the contour of the grapefruit to expose the flesh. Holding it over a bowl, cut along either side of each section, letting the section drop into the bowl. Remove any seeds and discard. Cut the sections in 1-inch (2.5-cm) pieces. Cut off the stems and feathery tops and any bruised outer stalks from the fennel bulb. Thinly slice lengthwise.

Arrange the butter lettuce in a shallow salad bowl. Place the grapefruit pieces, fennel, and mushrooms on top in an attractive pattern. At the table, drizzle with the dressing, toss, and serve.

serves four to six | per serving: calories 241 (kilojoules 1,012), protein 2 g, carbohydrates 11 g, total fat 22 g, saturated fat 3 g, cholesterol 0 mg, sodium 66 mg, dietary fiber 2 g

shredded root vegetable salad

This light and refreshing salad can be served as is or dressed up with crumbled goat cheese. Serve with Chicken and Jack Cheese Quesadillas (page 211) or Flank Steak Sandwiches (page 213).

for the dressing:

1 shallot, finely chopped

3 tablespoons red wine vinegar

½ cup (4 fl oz/125 ml) plus 1 tablespoon olive oil

2 teaspoons Dijon mustard

2 tablespoons chopped fresh parsley

salt and ground pepper to taste

8 carrots, peeled and shredded

4 small or 3 large beets, peeled and shredded

8–10 romaine (cos) lettuce leaves

16–20 cherry tomatoes

2 tablespoons finely chopped fresh parsley

To make the dressing, in a small bowl, whisk together the shallot, vinegar, olive oil, mustard, parsley, salt, and pepper.

In a bowl, combine the carrots with ¼ cup (2 fl oz/60 ml) of the dressing and let marinate for 15 minutes. In another bowl, combine the beets with the remaining dressing and let marinate for 15 minutes.

Arrange the lettuce leaves on a large serving platter or individual plates. Arrange the carrots and the beets in 2 separate mounds on the lettuce. Garnish with the cherry tomatoes, arranging them around the edges. Sprinkle with the parsley and serve.

serves six | per serving: calories 253 (kilojoules 1,063), protein 2 g, carbohydrates 16 g, total fat 21 g, saturated fat 3 g, cholesterol 0 mg, sodium 109 mg, dietary fiber 4 g

tomato-rice soup

For this warming recipe, select a good-quality canned diced tomato for the best results. You can vary the flavor to your taste with herbs and spices such as tarragon, basil, or curry powder.

2 tablespoons olive oil

1 yellow onion, very thinly sliced

1 carrot, peeled and very finely chopped

1 celery stalk, very finely chopped

¼ cup (1¾ oz/50 g) long-grain rice

1 clove garlic, minced

2 tablespoons all-purpose (plain) flour

3 cups (24 fl oz/750 ml) chicken broth

1 can (28 oz/875 g) diced tomatoes with juice

¼ cup (2 oz/60 g) tomato paste

½–1 teaspoon sugar

1½ cups (12 fl oz/375 ml) milk

salt and white pepper to taste

grated Parmesan cheese (optional)

In a large, heavy saucepan over medium heat, warm the oil. Add the onion and sauté until translucent, 3–4 minutes. Add the carrot and celery and sauté until the vegetables begin to soften, 4–5 minutes longer. Add the rice and garlic and cook, stirring, until coated with the oil, about 1 minute.

Sprinkle the flour over the vegetables, reduce the heat to low, and continue to cook, stirring constantly, until the flour is incorporated, 1–2 minutes. Add the broth, tomatoes, tomato paste, and ½–1 teaspoon sugar, depending on the tartness of the tomatoes. Raise the heat to medium-high and bring to a simmer. Cover partially, reduce the heat to medium, and cook, stirring occasionally, until the vegetables and rice are cooked through and the flavors are blended, about 20 minutes. Remove from the heat and let cool slightly.

Working in batches, purée the soup in a blender, making sure to retain some texture. Return to the pan over medium heat. Add the milk, salt, and pepper and stir to combine. Heat to warm the soup through. Taste and adjust the seasonings.

Ladle into warmed soup bowls and sprinkle with the Parmesan cheese, if desired. Serve at once.

serves four to six | per serving: calories 223 (kilojoules 937), protein 7 g, carbohydrates 29 g, total fat 10 g, saturated fat 3 g, cholesterol 10 mg, sodium 998 mg, dietary fiber 3 g

main courses

Outdooor living usually calls for main courses that are familiar, homey, soulful—the dishes that nearly everyone craves. You might never think of serving reuben sandwiches in your dining room, but when you are staring out at snow-capped mountains from the back porch, they taste incredible.

This, too, is the time to put your grill to work, whether it is a hibachi or a kettle barbecue, a fancy gas grill or a no-frills grate over a beach campfire. Out come the swordfish steaks, ancho-rubbed flank steaks, meaty slabs of eggplant (aubergine), and lemon-marinated chicken. If you fish, you probably practice catch and release, but grilled farm-raised trout can taste just as wild with a parsley-caper green sauce. And at your next tailgate party, offer classic grilled hamburgers and healthful grilled vegetable sandwiches to please every palate.

When the meal and its service are casual, swap knife-and-fork dishes for stews, chile, pot pies, polenta, or hefty sandwiches. In winter in the mountains, return fondue to its traditional après-ski role, setting up the pot in front of the fire-place. In summer at the beach, bake a pizza indoors and then line up chairs or stools along the veranda banister with its view of the sand and sea.

spring

fusilli primavera

The best produce of spring and summer is the inspiration for this sauce. If you cannot find a red bell pepper, leave it out rather than use a green bell pepper.

1 lb (500 g) fusilli or other bite-sized pasta shape

about ¾ lb (375 g) asparagus

½ cup (4 fl oz/120 ml) extra-virgin olive oil

3 green (spring) onions, including tender green tops, thinly sliced

1 red bell pepper (capsicum), seeded and diced

2 yellow crookneck squash or zucchini (courgettes), diced

¼ cup (⅓ oz/10 g) packed shredded fresh basil leaves or chopped fresh parsley

1½ teaspoons chopped fresh thyme or ¾ teaspoon dried thyme

grated zest of 1 large lemon

ground pepper

about ½ cup (2 oz/60 g) grated Parmesan cheese

Bring a large pot two-thirds full of salted water to a boil over high heat. Add the pasta, stir well, and cook until al dente (tender but firm to the bite), about 12 minutes or according to the package directions.

Meanwhile, trim any tough ends from the asparagus and discard. Cut the asparagus on the diagonal into 1-inch (2.5-cm) lengths; set aside. In a large frying pan, warm ¼ cup (2 fl oz/60 ml) of the oil over medium-high heat. Add the green onions and red pepper and cook, stirring, until the pepper is softened, about 3 minutes. Add the squash or zucchini and the asparagus and cook, stirring often, until the vegetables are tender-crisp, about 7 minutes. Remove from the heat and stir in the basil or parsley, thyme, and lemon zest.

Drain the pasta and return to the pot. Add the vegetables and the remaining ¼ cup (2 fl oz/60 ml) oil. Season well with pepper and toss until warmed through. Serve at once with the grated Parmesan cheese.

serves four | per serving: calories 754 (kilojoules 3,167), protein 23 g, carbohydrates 93 g, total fat 34 g, saturated fat 7 g, cholesterol 10 mg, sodium 627 mg, dietary fiber 4 g

grilled swordfish steaks with ginger-orange butter

A compound butter is a great way to dress up any grilled fish. Try creating your own butter using fresh herbs or other citrus fruits such as lemon or lime.

for the butter:

¼ cup (2 oz/60 g) unsalted butter, at room temperature

1 tablespoon orange juice

1 piece fresh ginger, 3 inches (7.5 cm) long, peeled and grated

1 teaspoon finely grated orange zest

¼ teaspoon salt

¼ teaspoon white pepper

1 tablespoon snipped fresh chives

for the fish:

4 swordfish steaks, each about 6 oz (185 g) and 1 inch (2.5 cm) thick

salt and ground pepper to taste

¼ cup (2 fl oz/60 ml) orange juice

2 tablespoons olive oil

To make the butter, in a food processor, combine the butter, orange juice, ginger, orange zest, salt, and white pepper and process until blended. Add the chives and process briefly to mix. Alternatively, mix together in a small bowl with a wooden spoon. Place the butter on a piece of plastic wrap and shape into a cylinder 4 inches (10 cm) long. Wrap securely and refrigerate until serving. (The butter can be made and refrigerated up to 2 days in advance or frozen for up to 2 months.)

Season the fish with salt and pepper. Place in a nonreactive baking dish and pour the orange juice and olive oil over the top. Cover and refrigerate for 1 hour, turning several times.

Prepare a hot fire in a grill, or preheat the broiler (grill). Remove the fish from the marinade and pat dry with paper towels. Place on the grill rack or under the broiler 5–6 inches (13–15 cm) from the heat source. Grill or broil, turning once, until lightly browned and opaque throughout, about 5 minutes on each side.

Transfer the fish steaks to warmed individual plates. Cut the butter into 4 equal pieces and place on the steaks. Serve at once.

serves four | per serving: calories 307 (kilojoules 1,289), protein 30 g, carbohydrates 2 g, total fat 19 g, saturated fat 9 g, cholesterol 90 mg, sodium 282 mg, dietary fiber 0 g

seafood quiche

The rich flavors of lobster, crab, and shrimp are balanced by the pleasing bitterness of watercress in this attractive, portable dish.

for the filling:

½ lb (250 g) cooked lobster meat, cut into 1-inch (2.5-cm) pieces

½ lb (250 g) cooked lump crabmeat, picked over for shell fragments

½ lb (250 g) cooked shrimp (prawns), peeled and deveined

2 tablespoons vodka

1 tablespoon lemon juice

⅛ teaspoon cayenne pepper

4 eggs

1 cup (8 fl oz/250 ml) heavy (double) cream

½ cup (2 oz/60 g) grated Parmesan cheese

½ teaspoon salt

1 cup (1½ oz/45 g) tightly packed watercress leaves

1 tablespoon Dijon mustard

for the pastry:

1 cup (5 oz/155 g) all-purpose (plain) flour

½ cup (2½ oz/75 g) yellow cornmeal

1 teaspoon salt

¾ cup (6 oz/185 g) chilled unsalted butter, cut into small pieces

3 tablespoons ice water, or more if needed

To begin the filling, in a bowl, combine the lobster, crab, and shrimp. Sprinkle with the vodka, lemon juice, and cayenne and toss gently. Cover and refrigerate until ready to assemble the quiche.

To make the pastry, in a bowl, stir together the flour, cornmeal, and salt. Using 2 knives or a pastry blender, cut in the butter until the mixture resembles coarse crumbs. Stirring and tossing with a fork, sprinkle with enough ice water to moisten lightly. Gather the dough into a ball.

On a lightly floured surface, roll out the dough into a 12-inch (30-cm) round. Transfer to a 9-inch (23-cm) deep-dish pie pan. Trim the edges and flute attractively. Chill for 10 minutes. Preheat the oven to 375°F (190°C).

Finish the filling: In a bowl, whisk together the eggs, cream, cheese, and salt. Drain any liquid from the seafood into the egg mixture, whisk again, and stir in the watercress. Brush the bottom of the pastry shell with the mustard. Top with the seafood and then the egg mixture.

Bake until the filling is just set, about 25 minutes. Transfer to a rack. Serve warm or at room temperature.

serves six to eight | per serving: calories 595 (kilojoules 2,499), protein 31 g, carbohydrates 26 g, total fat 39 g, saturated fat 23 g, cholesterol 347 mg, sodium 1,042 mg, dietary fiber 1 g

lake fish with tart green sauce

You can use any lean freshwater fish for this recipe, including bass, trout, pike, or perch.

2 green (spring) onions, including tender green tops, finely chopped

2 cups (2 oz/60 g) parsley leaves, finely chopped

⅓ cup (2½ oz/75 g) capers, rinsed and chopped

1 large clove garlic, minced

½ cup (4 fl oz/125 ml) extra-virgin olive oil, plus oil as needed

¼ cup (2 fl oz/60 ml) lemon juice

4–6 fish fillets, about 6 oz (185 g) each *(see note)*

salt and ground pepper

Preheat the broiler (grill) or prepare a fire in a grill. In a small bowl, stir together the green onions, parsley, capers, garlic, ½ cup (4 fl oz/125 ml) olive oil, and lemon juice. Set aside. The sauce can be made up to 4 hours ahead, covered, and refrigerated until ready to use.

Brush each fillet with olive oil and sprinkle with salt and pepper. If using a broiler, preheat the broiler pan and brush the pan rack with olive oil. If using a grill, oil a piece of double aluminum foil just large enough to hold the fillets in a single layer. Place the fillets, skin sides down (if there is skin), on the rack in the broiler pan or on the foil on the grill rack. Cover, if grilling, and cook, without turning, until the fish is just opaque throughout, about 6 minutes. Transfer the fish to plates and top each serving with a few spoonfuls of the sauce. Pass additional sauce at the table.

serves four to six | per serving: calories 448 (kilojoules 1,882), protein 33 g, carbohydrates 3 g, total fat 34 g, saturated fat 5 g, cholesterol 116 mg, sodium 512 mg, dietary fiber 1 g

panfried trout with creamy slaw

Fresh trout is dredged in cornmeal, fried in classic streamside fashion, and served with a cool, creamy coleslaw. A food processor fitted with the shredding disk is easiest for shredding the vegetables, although the large holes of a cheese grater will work just fine.

for the slaw:

½ cup (4 oz/125 g) plain nonfat yogurt

¼ cup (2 oz/60 g) mayonnaise

¼ cup (2 fl oz/60 ml) cider vinegar

2 teaspoons cumin seeds

1 small head green cabbage, cored and shredded

2 large carrots, shredded

4 green (spring) onions, including tender green tops, thinly sliced

salt and ground pepper

for the trout:

4 dressed bone-in or boneless trout with heads intact, 6–8 oz (185–250 g) each

½ cup (4 fl oz/125 ml) milk

½ cup (2½ oz/75 g) yellow cornmeal

salt and ground pepper

2 tablespoons unsalted butter

2 tablespoons vegetable oil

To prepare the slaw, in a large salad bowl, whisk together the yogurt, mayonnaise, and vinegar until smooth. Stir in the cumin seeds. Add the cabbage, carrots, and green onions and toss well. Season to taste with salt and pepper. Set aside. The slaw may be made up to 8 hours ahead, covered, and refrigerated until ready to serve.

To prepare the trout, rinse the fish and pat dry inside and out with paper towels. Pour the milk into a pie pan; spread the cornmeal on a plate. Dip both sides of each fish into the milk, letting the excess drip off, then roll in cornmeal to coat, shaking off the excess. Set the fish, without touching each other, on waxed paper or another plate. Sprinkle with salt and pepper.

In a wide, heavy frying pan, melt the butter in the oil over medium-high heat. Add the fish and cook until crisp and browned on one side, 4–5 minutes. Using a large spatula, gently turn and cook until the second side is crisp and the flesh is just opaque throughout (gently open the cavity to check), 5–6 minutes longer. Serve hot with the slaw alongside.

serves four | per serving: calories 512 (kilojoules 2,150), protein 27 g, carbohydrates 31 g, total fat 32 g, saturated fat 8 g, cholesterol 85 mg, sodium 209 mg, dietary fiber 6 g

smoked turkey reuben sandwiches

Named after a sandwich originated at Reuben's in New York City many years ago, this American classic is updated here with smoked turkey in place of the usual corned beef. Serve with Shredded Root Vegetable Salad (page 132) and some kosher dill pickles on the side.

for the dressing:

½ cup (4 fl oz/125 ml) mayonnaise

¼ cup (2 fl oz/60 ml) bottled chile sauce

1½ tablespoons sweet green pickle relish

8 slices rye bread

¼ cup (2 oz/60 g) unsalted butter, at room temperature

½ lb (250 g) Swiss cheese, grated

¼ lb (125 g) sliced smoked turkey

1 cup (6 oz/185 g) well-drained uncooked sauerkraut

To make the dressing, in a small bowl, stir together the mayonnaise, chile sauce, and pickle relish until well mixed. Set aside.

Lay the bread slices on a large work surface and spread one side of each slice evenly with the butter. Turn the slices over and spread the other side of each slice evenly with the dressing.

Sprinkle a bit of cheese on 4 of the dressing-spread bread slices, then lay the turkey slices over the cheese, dividing them evenly. Make sure the turkey does not hang over the edge, trimming if necessary. Spread the sauerkraut evenly atop the turkey, and then distribute the remaining grated cheese evenly over the sauerkraut. Top with the remaining slices of bread, buttered sides out, and press down firmly to compact the sandwiches.

Place a large nonstick frying pan or a griddle over medium-high heat. Using a wooden spatula, carefully lift the sandwiches from the work surface and place in the hot pan or on the griddle. Grill, occasionally pressing down gently on top of each sandwich with the spatula, until the underside is golden, 4–5 minutes. Carefully turn the sandwiches over and cook, again pressing down on them, until the second side is golden and the cheese has melted, 3–4 minutes longer. Turn over one more time and cook for 2–3 minutes longer.

Transfer to individual plates and serve immediately.

serves four | per serving: calories 742 (kilojoules 3,116), protein 28 g, carbohydrates 42 g, total fat 52 g, saturated fat 21 g, cholesterol 114 mg, sodium 1,438 mg, dietary fiber 5 g

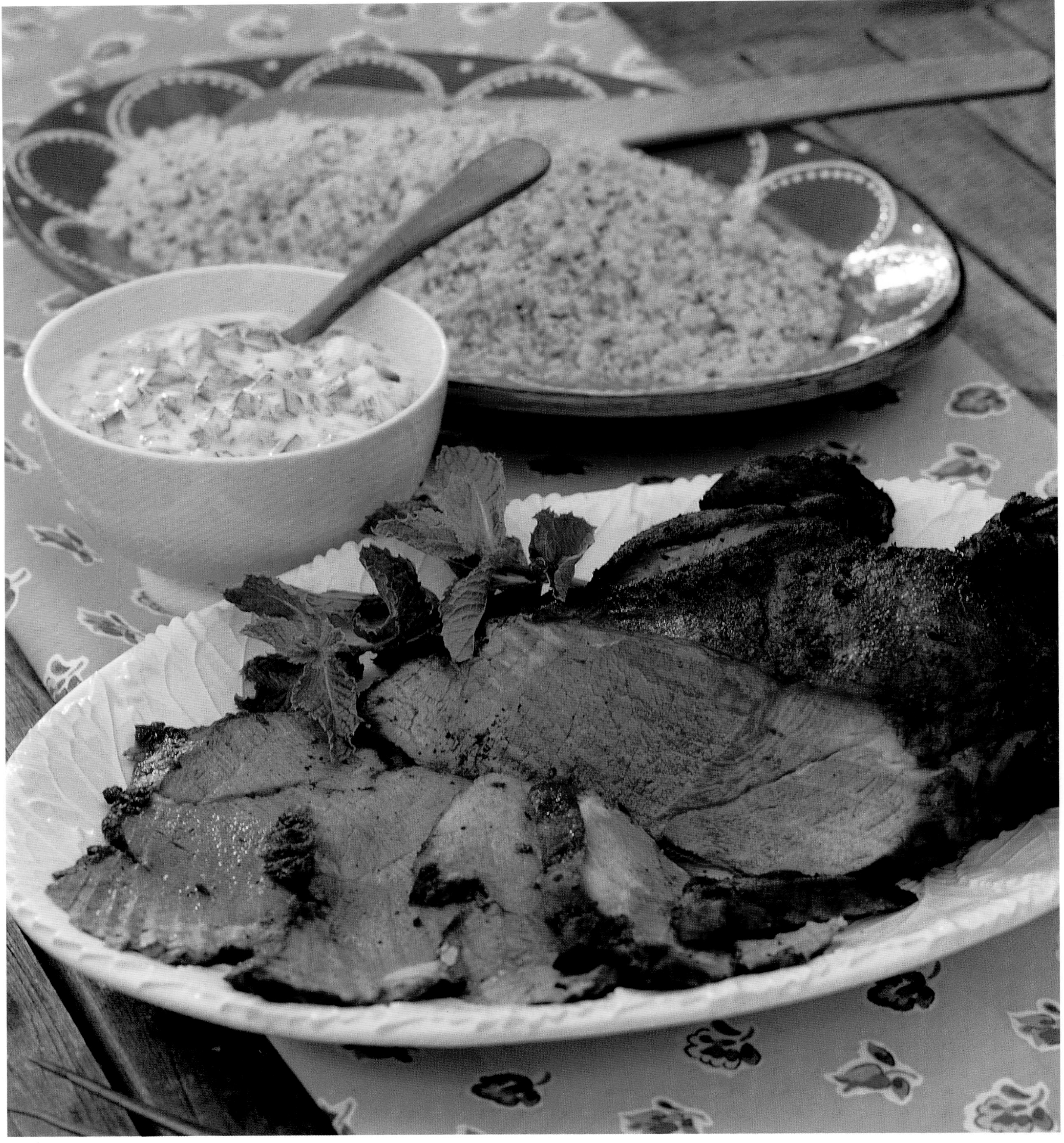

grilled leg of lamb with mint raita

A boneless leg of lamb is ideal for spring grilling. If you can't find a leg, substitute six lamb shoulder chops.

for the lamb:

2 cloves garlic, minced

1 tablespoon paprika

2 teaspoons ground cumin

1 teaspoon ground coriander

½ teaspoon vegetable oil

2 teaspoons red wine vinegar

1 teaspoon water

1 butterflied leg of lamb, 2½–3 lb (1.25–1.5 kg)

for the raita:

1 cup (8 oz/250 g) plain nonfat yogurt

1 large ripe tomato, seeded and diced

½ small cucumber, peeled, seeded, and diced

¼ cup (⅓ oz/10 g) coarsely chopped fresh mint, cilantro (fresh coriander), or parsley

juice of 1 lime

To prepare the lamb, in the bottom of a large nonaluminum bowl, stir together the garlic, paprika, cumin, coriander, oil, vinegar, and water to form a paste. Spoon about half of the mixture onto the underside (the side without fat) of the butterflied leg and spread in an even layer. Place the meat, fat side down, in the remaining spice rub in the bowl and move around to coat with the spices. Cover the bowl tightly and refrigerate for at least 4 hours or for up to 24 hours.

Prepare a fire in a grill. When the coals are hot, lift the meat from the bowl and place, fat side down, on the grill rack. Cook, turning once, until both sides are well browned and the meat is pink when cut into with a knife, or until an instant-read thermometer inserted into the thickest part of the leg registers 130–135°F (54–57°C) for medium-rare, 25–30 minutes total.

Meanwhile, make the raita: In a small bowl, stir together the yogurt, tomato, cucumber, chopped herb, and lime juice until smooth.

When the meat is cooked, transfer to a cutting board and let rest for 5 minutes. Thinly slice across the grain and arrange on a serving platter. Pass the raita at the table.

serves six | per serving: calories 443 (kilojoules 1,861), protein 42 g, carbohydrates 7 g, total fat 26 g, saturated fat 11 g, cholesterol 144 mg, sodium 137 mg, dietary fiber 1 g

cold poached salmon with cucumber-avocado relish

A rich, crunchy relish is the perfect complement for poached salmon. Serve with Asparagus with Sun-Dried Tomato Vinaigrette (page 78).

1 English (hothouse) cucumber, seeded and finely diced

1 small, ripe avocado, pitted, peeled, and finely diced

2 tablespoons chopped fresh dill

2 tablespoons olive oil

2 tablespoons unseasoned rice wine vinegar

1 tablespoon lemon juice

½ teaspoon sugar

salt to taste

2 lb (1 kg) salmon fillet, or 4 pieces salmon fillet, ½ lb (250 g) each

In a bowl, combine the cucumber, avocado, dill, oil, vinegar, lemon juice, sugar, and salt. Stir to mix well. Set aside.

Remove and discard any errant bones in the salmon. Place in a sauté pan and add water to cover. Place over medium heat and bring to a simmer. Poach until the flesh is firm and flaky, 7–10 minutes, depending on the thickness of the fillet or pieces; allow 10 minutes per 1 inch (2.5 cm) measured at the thickest part. Remove from the heat and set aside to cool in the liquid. When cool, drain and transfer to a transportable container. Cut into 4 pieces if using a whole fillet. Cover and refrigerate until well chilled, about 4 hours.

Spoon the relish over the salmon and keep chilled until ready to serve.

serves four | per serving: calories 454 (kilojoules 1,907), protein 46 g, carbohydrates 5 g, total fat 27 g, saturated fat 4 g, cholesterol 125 mg, sodium 108 mg, dietary fiber 1 g

soft-shell crab sandwiches

In spring, blue crabs shed their hard, brittle shells and begin to grow new ones. If caught in this transitional state, they are referred to as soft-shell crabs and can be eaten in their entirety.

for the pesto mayonnaise:

1 cup (1½ oz/45 g) tightly packed fresh basil leaves

5 cloves garlic, coarsely chopped

½ cup (2½ oz/75 g) pine nuts, toasted

¾ cup (6 fl oz/180 ml) olive oil

1 cup (8 fl oz/250 ml) mayonnaise

salt and ground pepper to taste

for the soft-shell crabs:

12 small soft-shell crabs

1 cup (5 oz/155 g) all-purpose (plain) flour

1 teaspoon salt

½ teaspoon ground pepper

¼ teaspoon paprika

6 tablespoons (3 oz/90 g) unsalted butter

for the sandwiches:

6 large rolls, preferably brioche, split and toasted

2 large tomatoes, peeled, seeded, and cut into ¼-inch (6-mm) dice

6 large lettuce leaves

salt and ground pepper to taste

To make the mayonnaise, in a food processor or blender, combine the basil, garlic, and pine nuts. Process briefly to mix. With the motor running, slowly pour in the oil and process until thick, about 30 seconds. Transfer to a bowl and stir in the mayonnaise. Season with salt and pepper. Cover and refrigerate until ready to assemble the sandwiches.

First, clean the soft-shell crabs: Working with one at a time, turn it on its back and lift up and snap off the apron. Lift the flaps on either end of the body and pull out and discard the spongy gill tissue. Snip away the eyes, then discard the bile sac near the top of the legs. Dry thoroughly.

In a shallow bowl, combine the flour, salt, pepper, and paprika. Coat the crabs lightly in the mixture, tapping off any excess. In a large frying pan over medium-high heat, melt half of the butter until sizzling. Add 6 crabs and cook, turning once, until browned, about 3 minutes on each side. Keep warm on a plate. Repeat with the remaining butter and crabs.

Liberally spread the cut sides of the rolls with the mayonnaise. Place 2 crabs on the bottom of each roll and top with the tomato and lettuce. Season with salt and pepper, place the tops on, and serve immediately.

serves six | per serving: calories 1,090 (kilojoules 4,578), protein 28 g, carbohydrates 66 g, total fat 82 g, saturated fat 18 g, cholesterol 214 mg, sodium 1,516 mg, dietary fiber 5 g

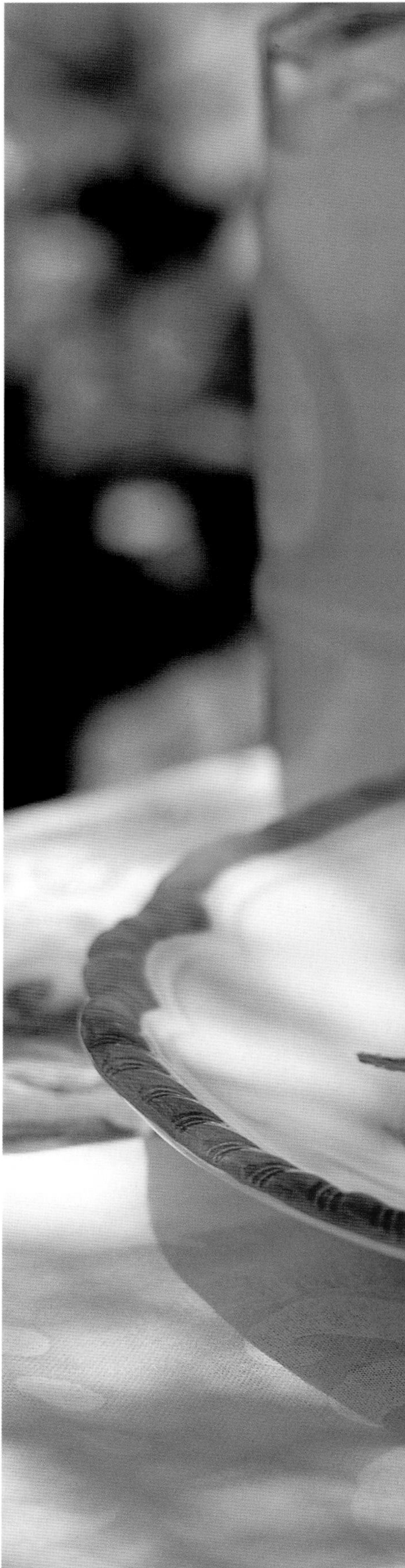

cumin-rubbed lamb skewers with roasted peppers

Toast and grind whole cumin seeds to give the lamb the full effect of this pungent spice. Serve with couscous tossed with an assortment of finely chopped fresh herbs and sautéed cherry tomatoes.

2 lb (1 kg) lean lamb, preferably cut from the leg

2 tablespoons ground cumin

2 teaspoons salt

½ teaspoon ground pepper

4 tablespoons (2 fl oz/60 ml) olive oil

2 red bell peppers (capsicums)

2 yellow bell peppers (capsicums)

16 mushrooms, about ½ lb (250 g) total weight, brushed clean, stems trimmed, and caps halved

Cut the lamb into sixteen 2½–3-inch (6–7.5-cm) cubes. Place in a large bowl and sprinkle with the cumin, salt, and pepper. Using your hands, rub the cumin mixture into the lamb cubes. Add 2 tablespoons of the olive oil, toss well to coat, cover, and refrigerate for 12–24 hours.

Preheat the broiler (grill). Cut the bell peppers in half lengthwise and discard the stems, seeds, and ribs. Place, cut sides down, on a baking sheet and broil (grill) until the skins blacken and blister. Remove from the broiler, drape loosely with aluminum foil, let stand for 10 minutes, then peel away the skins. Cut lengthwise into wide strips; you will need 32 strips.

Prepare a medium-hot fire in a grill, or leave the broiler on.

Thread the lamb cubes onto 8 long metal skewers, dividing the meat evenly and alternating them with the pepper strips and mushroom halves.

Brush the skewers with the remaining 2 tablespoons olive oil. Place on the grill rack or under a broiler about 6 inches (15 cm) from the heat source. Grill or broil, turning often, until the lamb is well browned and firm to the touch, 12–15 minutes for medium. Transfer to individual plates and serve at once.

serves four | per serving: calories 475 (kilojoules 1,995), protein 51 g, carbohydrates 9 g, total fat 26 g, saturated fat 6 g, cholesterol 152 mg, sodium 1,290 mg, dietary fiber 2 g

italian hero sandwich

This is the sandwich to make when you want a real attention grabber. At a good Italian delicatessen, you'll be able to find the peppers and sliced meats, as well as a crusty loaf that will hold all the fixings.

¼ cup (2 fl oz/60 ml) red wine vinegar

1 teaspoon dried oregano

½ teaspoon dry mustard

salt and ground pepper

½ cup (4 fl oz/125 ml) extra-virgin olive oil

1 loaf Italian bread with sesame seeds, about 24 inches (60 cm) long, cut in half lengthwise

½ cup (2½ oz/75 g) seeded and chopped pepperoncini

½ cup (2½ oz/75 g) seeded and chopped cherry peppers

2 cups (6 oz/185 g) finely shredded iceberg lettuce

4 tomatoes, thinly sliced

5 oz (155 g) thinly sliced salami

5 oz (155 g) thinly sliced cappicola

5 oz (155 g) thinly sliced salami cotto

5 oz (155 g) thinly sliced mortadella

5 oz (155 g) thinly sliced provolone cheese

In a small bowl, combine the vinegar, oregano, mustard, and salt and pepper to taste. Stir to mix well. Whisk in the olive oil until incorporated.

On a work surface, lay out 3 long pieces of plastic wrap, placing them side by side and slightly overlapping. Place the bottom half of the loaf over the wrap. Spread the pepperoncini and cherry peppers over the bread. Scatter evenly with the lettuce and layer with the tomatoes. Drizzle with a few tablespoons of the dressing. Layer the meats, one at a time, over the tomatoes, making sure to distribute them evenly. Top with a layer of cheese.

Drizzle the remaining dressing over the cut side of the top of the loaf. Place on the layered sandwich and enclose in the plastic. Refrigerate for at least 1 hour or for up to 4 hours to develop the flavors.

To serve, unwrap the sandwich and slice into large pieces about 3–4 inches (7.5–10 cm) wide.

serves six to eight | per serving: calories 688 (kilojoules 2,890), protein 27 g, carbohydrates 41 g, total fat 47 g, saturated fat 15 g, cholesterol 73 mg, sodium 1,897 mg, dietary fiber 3 g

lime-and-coconut-soaked chicken with cilantro

The tropical flavors of lime and coconut add an extra exotic touch to this simple dish. If you like, add one lemongrass stalk (tender base only), chopped, and/or one 2-inch (5-cm) piece fresh ginger, peeled and grated, to the marinade. Serve the skewers on a bed of rice or couscous.

1¾ cups (14 fl oz/430 ml) canned coconut milk

⅓ cup (3 fl oz/80 ml) lime juice

1½ lb (750 g) boneless, skinless chicken breasts, cut into 1-inch (2.5-cm) cubes

salt and ground pepper to taste

2 tablespoons finely chopped fresh cilantro (fresh coriander)

In a large bowl, stir together the coconut milk and lime juice. Add the chicken, turn to coat, and refrigerate for 4 hours or for up to overnight.

Prepare a medium-hot fire in a grill, or preheat the broiler (grill).

Remove the chicken from the marinade and pat dry with paper towels. Thread the cubes of chicken onto 4 long metal skewers. Season well with salt and pepper. Place the skewers on the grill rack or under the broiler about 5–6 inches (13–15 cm) from the heat source. Grill or broil, turning often, until lightly browned and no longer pink in the center when cut into with a sharp knife, 7–10 minutes.

Remove from the grill or broiler, sprinkle with the cilantro, and serve immediately.

serves four | per serving: calories 216 (kilojouoles 907), protein 40 g, carbohydrates 1 g, total fat 5 g, saturated fat 3 g, cholesterol 99 mg, sodium 113 mg, dietary fiber 0 g

grilled eggplant caprese

Adding grilled eggplant slices and a side of toasted bread to the classic caprese trio—mozzarella, basil, and ripe tomatoes—makes it a complete summer lunch. If whole-milk mozzarella is unavailable, substitute thin rounds of goat cheese or sprinkle the vegetables with feta.

2 large eggplants (aubergines), thinly sliced

about ⅓ cup (3 fl oz/80 ml) extra-virgin olive oil

1 loaf coarse country bread, sliced

8 oz (250 g) fresh whole-milk mozzarella cheese, thinly sliced *(see note)*

1 lb (500 g) ripe tomatoes, thinly sliced

about 24 large fresh basil leaves

3 tablespoons balsamic vinegar

salt and ground pepper

Prepare a fire in a grill or preheat the broiler (grill).

If using a grill, when the coals are hot, brush one side of each eggplant slice with olive oil and place, oiled side down, on the grill rack. Cook the slices until well browned on one side, brush with more olive oil, turn, and cook until well browned on the second side, about 10 minutes total.

If using a broiler, brush a baking sheet lightly with oil. Brush one side of each eggplant slice with olive oil and place, oiled side up, on the sheet. Broil (grill) about 4 inches (10 cm) below the heat until well browned on top, then turn, brush with oil, and broil until well browned on the second side, about 10 minutes total.

Remove the eggplant from the grill or broiler and let cool. Repeat the procedure with the bread slices and oil, brushing each side with oil and grilling or broiling until golden brown on both sides, about 5 minutes total.

When the eggplant is cool, arrange on a platter with the cheese and tomato slices. Stack the basil leaves and roll them up like a cigar; cut crosswise into thin shreds. Scatter the basil over the vegetables and cheese, then drizzle with the balsamic vinegar. Season to taste with salt and pepper. Offer the toasted bread alongside.

serves four | per serving: calories 696 (kilojoules 2,923), protein 24 g, carbohydrates 74 g, total fat 35 g, saturated fat 11 g, cholesterol 44 mg, sodium 892 mg, dietary fiber 8 g

the ultimate blt

Not much beats an old standby made with the best ingredients possible. Basil substitutes for lettuce; its sharp herbal taste is the perfect balance to the sweet bacon. If basil is unavailable, use good-quality lettuce.

8 slices Brown Sugar Bacon (page 53)

8 slices coarse country bread

1 cup (4 oz/125 g) grated Vermont or other sharp cheddar cheese

3 tablespoons mayonnaise

1 large ripe red or yellow tomato, cored and sliced

32 fresh basil leaves *(see note)*

Preheat the broiler (grill). Place a double piece of aluminum foil large enough to hold all the bread slices on a broiler pan and arrange the bread slices on top. Toast the bread until golden on one side, about 2 minutes. Turn and top 4 of the slices with the cheese, dividing it evenly. Continue to toast until the cheese is melted and the other 4 slices are golden on the second side, about 2 minutes. Remove from the broiler.

Spread the plain bread slices with the mayonnaise. Place 2 strips of bacon, broken in half, atop each slice. Cover with the tomato slices, then the basil leaves, distributing them as evenly as possible. Invert the slices with melted cheese onto the slices with the basil. Cut the sandwiches in half and serve immediately.

serves four | per sandwich: calories 538 (kilojoules 2,260), protein 20 g, carbohydrates 43 g, total fat 32 g, saturated fat 12 g, cholesterol 56 mg, sodium 974 mg, dietary fiber 3 g

grilled vegetable sandwiches

The key to making these luscious Mediterranean sandwiches is to grill the vegetables ahead and assemble them just before going on a picnic. Make sure to use a good-quality pesto from a well-stocked food store or delicatessen. For a large group, offer Grilled Chicken Sandwiches with Olive Mayonnaise (right) as well.

2 red bell peppers (capsicums)

1 large eggplant (aubergine), cut lengthwise into slices ½ inch (12 mm) thick

3 zucchini (courgettes), cut lengthwise into slices ½ inch (12 mm) thick

6 large sourdough or French rolls, cut in half

¾ cup (6 fl oz/180 ml) pesto

1 lb (500 g) fresh mozzarella cheese, cut into ½-inch (12-mm) slices

salt and ground pepper

Prepare a fire in a grill. When the coals are medium-hot, place the peppers on the grill rack and grill, turning, until the skins blacken and blister. Remove from the grill, place in a brown paper bag, close tightly, and let stand for 10 minutes.

Lightly coat the eggplant and zucchini with nonstick olive oil cooking spray. Grill, turning once, until the vegetables are soft and grill marks appear, 6–8 minutes total. Transfer to a platter.

Remove the peppers from the bag, drain, and peel off the charred skin. Remove the stems, seeds, and ribs. Cut the peppers into ½-inch (12-mm) slices. Cut the eggplant and zucchini slices to fit on the rolls.

Spread the bottom half of each roll with 1 tablespoon of the pesto. Top with the eggplant, then layer with the slices of zucchini, peppers, and cheese. Sprinkle with salt and pepper to taste. Spread the top half of each roll with another tablespoon of pesto, then place the top on each sandwich.

Secure with toothpicks and cut in half, if desired. Transfer to a transportable container and keep chilled until ready to serve.

serves six | per serving: calories 654 (kilojoules 2,747), protein 26 g, carbohydrates 60 g, total fat 34 g, saturated fat 3 g, cholesterol 58 mg, sodium 798 mg, dietary fiber 5 g

grilled chicken sandwiches with olive mayonnaise

Enjoy this elegant version of a plain chicken sandwich (photo right) hot off the grill or cold. You'll find olive paste in a well-stocked food store or an Italian delicatessen. Serve with Picnic Potato Salad (page 102) or Coleslaw with Cider Dressing (page 118).

2 tablespoons lemon juice

1½ tablespoons Dijon mustard

6 skinless, boneless chicken breast halves, about 5 oz (155 g) each

¾ cup (6 fl oz/180 ml) mayonnaise

3 tablespoons olive paste

2 red bell peppers (capsicums)

6 seeded sourdough French rolls, cut in half

1 bunch arugula (rocket), stems removed

In a small bowl, combine the lemon juice and mustard. Arrange the chicken breasts in a nonaluminum dish and spoon over the marinade. Cover and refrigerate for at least 15 minutes or for up to 4 hours. In another small bowl, blend together the mayonnaise and olive paste, cover, and refrigerate.

Prepare a fire in a grill. When the coals are medium-hot, place the peppers on the grill rack and grill, turning, until the skins blacken and blister. Remove from the grill, place in a brown paper bag, close tightly, and let stand for 10 minutes.

Meanwhile, remove the chicken from the marinade, letting the excess drip off, and place on the grill rack. Grill, turning once, until no longer pink in the center when cut into with a knife, 10–14 minutes total. Remove from the grill and let cool for about 5 minutes.

Remove the peppers from the bag, drain, and peel off the charred skin. Remove the stems, seeds, and ribs. Cut into ½-inch (12-mm) slices.

Cut the chicken on the diagonal into thin slices. Spread about 1 tablespoon olive mayonnaise on the bottom of each roll. Top with the arugula and then the chicken slices, overlapping them slightly. Top with the bell pepper strips. Spread the top half of each roll with another tablespoon of olive mayonnaise, then place the top on each sandwich. Secure with toothpicks, cut in half if desired, and wrap in aluminum foil. Serve warm or chilled.

serves six | per serving: calories 673 (kilojoules 2,827), protein 50 g, carbohydrates 40 g, total fat 34 g, saturated fat 5 g, cholesterol 125 mg, sodium 1,162 mg, dietary fiber 3 g

seared scallops with saffron creamed corn

Present this elegant main course on large decorative plates that set off the unique color of saffron.

1 cup (8 fl oz/250 ml) heavy (double) cream
pinch of saffron threads
2 tablespoons olive oil
1 large carrot, peeled and finely chopped
1 yellow onion, finely chopped
1 celery stalk, halved lengthwise and thinly sliced
6 cups (2¼ lb/1.1 kg) corn kernels (from about 8 ears)
salt and ground pepper to taste
2 tablespoons unsalted butter
2 tablespoons vegetable oil
18 sea scallops, about 1½ lb (750 g) total weight
1 tablespoon finely chopped fresh parsley

In a small saucepan over medium-high heat, combine the cream and the saffron. Bring just to a boil, remove from the heat, cover, and let stand for 10 minutes. Stir well to infuse the cream with the saffron.

In a large, heavy frying pan over medium-high heat, warm the olive oil. Add the carrot, onion, and celery and sauté until softened, 5–7 minutes. Stir in the corn and cook, stirring occasionally, until just beginning to soften, about 5 minutes. Pour in the cream mixture and season well with salt and pepper. Cook, stirring often, until the cream thickens slightly and the corn is tender, about 10 minutes longer. (The recipe can be made up to this point 1 day in advance. Cover and refrigerate.)

Just before serving, in a large frying pan over high heat, melt the butter with the vegetable oil. Season the scallops with salt and pepper and, working in batches if necessary, place in the pan in a single layer. Do not crowd the pan. Cook, turning once, until browned on the outside and just opaque in the center, about 2 minutes on each side.

Reheat the corn if necessary, then taste and adjust the seasonings. Divide the corn evenly among warmed individual plates. Top with the scallops, sprinkle with the parsley, and serve at once.

serves six | per serving: calories 516 (kilojoules 2,167), protein 26 g, carbohydrates 41 g, total fat 30 g, saturated fat 13 g, cholesterol 102 mg, sodium 237 mg, dietary fiber 7 g

ancho chile–rubbed flank steaks

Quick and easy to grill, flank steak is perfect for the beach house. Ancho chiles are dark red and have an earthy, slightly sweet flavor. They are not blisteringly hot. Marinate the steak overnight for a more intense flavor.

4 ancho chiles
2 cloves garlic
2 teaspoons coarse salt
1 teaspoon ground pepper
1 teaspoon ground cumin
½ teaspoon ground cinnamon
2 beef flank steaks, about 1¼ lb (625 g) each
1 bunch fresh cilantro (fresh coriander), stems removed

Prepare a hot fire in a grill, or preheat the broiler (grill).

In a cast-iron frying pan over medium-high heat, toast the anchos, turning often, until fragrant and pliable, 5–7 minutes. Transfer to a cutting board and discard the stems and seeds. Top the anchos with the garlic, coarse salt, pepper, cumin, and cinnamon. Chop repeatedly with a large knife until you have a cohesive mixture. Rub all over the flank steaks.

Place the steaks on the grill rack or under the broiler 4–6 inches (10–15 cm) from the heat source. Grill or broil, turning once, 4–5 minutes on each side for medium-rare. Transfer to a cutting board, let stand for 5 minutes, then cut into thin slices against the grain.

Place the cilantro leaves in the center of a large plate and fan the sliced steaks around the edge. Serve immediately.

serves six | per serving: calories 322 (kilojoules 1,352), protein 37 g, carbohydrates 2 g, total fat 17 g, saturated fat 7 g, cholesterol 94 mg, sodium 608 mg, dietary fiber 1 g

summer squash stuffed with lamb

Stuffed vegetables are easy to make ahead and then bake at the last minute. Try ground (minced) beef, veal, or turkey in place of the lamb.

3 yellow summer squashes

3 zucchini (courgettes)

ice water, to cover

3 tablespoons olive oil

1 large yellow onion, finely chopped

1 clove garlic, minced

1½ lb (750 g) ground (minced) lean lamb

2 tomatoes, peeled, seeded, and coarsely chopped

1 tablespoon tomato paste

1 teaspoon finely chopped fresh thyme

salt and ground pepper to taste

½ cup (1 oz/30 g) fresh bread crumbs

Bring a large pot three-fourths full of salted water to a boil. Halve the squashes and zucchini lengthwise. Using a small spoon, scoop out the seeds and enough flesh to form a shell ¼ inch (6 mm) thick. Add the shells to the boiling water. Boil until barely tender but not limp, about 1 minute. Using a slotted spoon, transfer the shells to a bowl of ice water. Let cool completely, then transfer to paper towels to drain.

In a large frying pan over medium-high heat, warm 2 tablespoons of the oil. Add the onion and sauté until tender, about 5 minutes. Add the garlic and sauté for about 1 minute longer. Stir in the lamb, tomatoes, tomato paste, thyme, salt, and pepper. Cook, stirring often, until the mixture thickens and the liquid has almost evaporated, about 15 minutes. Season again with salt and pepper. (The recipe can be prepared up to this point several hours in advance. Refrigerate the shells and the filling separately.)

Preheat an oven to 375°F (190°C). Line a large baking sheet with heavy-duty aluminum foil and lightly oil the foil.

Fill the shells with equal amounts of the lamb mixture and place on the prepared baking sheet. Sprinkle the bread crumbs evenly over the tops and drizzle with the remaining 1 tablespoon oil.

Bake until heated through and browned on top, 12–15 minutes. Serve hot.

serves six | per serving: calories 293 (kilojoules 1,231), protein 25 g, carbohydrates 15 g, total fat 15 g, saturated fat 4 g, cholesterol 75 mg, sodium 134 mg, dietary fiber 3 g

new england stove-top clambake

Here is an easy way to re-create a traditional Native American feast.

2 lb (1 kg) well-rinsed seaweed or corn husks, soaked in cold water for 1 hour and drained

3 celery stalks, coarsely chopped

12–18 small red potatoes

salt and ground pepper to taste

1 chicken, about 3½ lb (1.75 kg), cut into 6 serving pieces

1½ lb (750 g) kielbasa or similar smoked pork sausage, cut into 6 equal pieces

6 small yellow onions

6 small lobsters, scrubbed clean

6 ears of corn, shucked

4 dozen soft-shell clams such as steamers or razor clams

2 dozen mussels, well scrubbed and debearded

1 cup (8 oz/250 g) unsalted butter, melted

2 lemons, cut into wedges

Line the bottom of a very large stockpot with the seaweed or corn husks. Add the celery and cold water to cover (about 6 cups/48 fl oz/1.5 l). Bring to a boil over medium-high heat. Add the potatoes, then reduce the heat to medium, season with salt and pepper, and cook for 15 minutes.

Meanwhile, cut 6 pieces of cheesecloth (muslin) each 18 by 36 inches (45 by 90 cm). Divide the chicken and sausage evenly among the cheesecloth pieces and wrap well. Place the onions and then the chicken-sausage packets on top of the potatoes, season with salt and pepper, cover, and cook for 15 minutes. Add the lobsters and corn, again season with salt and pepper, re-cover, and cook for 8 minutes. Place the clams and mussels in the pot, discarding any that do not close to the touch, and cover. Cook until the shells open, about 10 minutes.

Uncover and discard any clams and mussels that did not open. Ladle the clams and mussels into large bowls and spoon over some of the cooking liquid from the pot. Serve as a first course. Serve the potatoes, onions, chicken, sausage, lobster, and corn on large individual plates as the main course. Accompany with the melted butter and lemon wedges.

serves six | per serving: calories 1,610 (kilojoules 6,762), protein 100 g, carbohydrates 97 g, total fat 94 g, saturated fat 39 g, cholesterol 413 mg, sodium 1,953 mg, dietary fiber 12 g

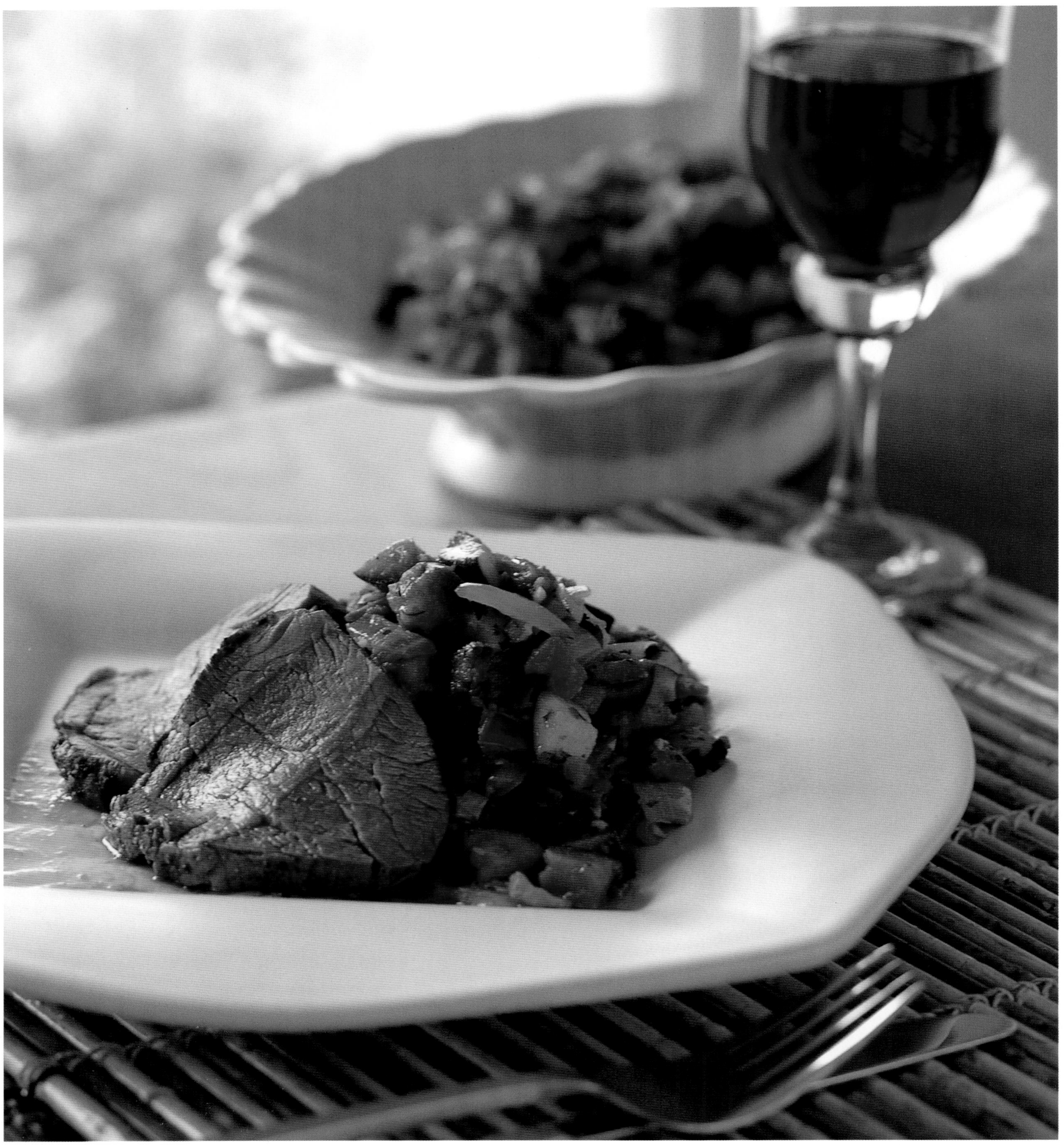

beef tenderloin with quick ratatouille

The ratatouille can be served at room temperature. A golden brown–topped potato gratin makes a perfect side dish.

9 tablespoons (4½ fl oz/140 ml) olive oil

2 yellow onions, coarsely chopped

6 cloves garlic, minced

2 zucchini (courgettes), quartered lengthwise, seeded, and cut into chunks

1 large eggplant (aubergine), cut into cubes

2 fresh tomatoes, seeded and chopped

1 can (15 oz/470 g) crushed tomatoes in thick purée

⅓ cup (½ oz/15 g) finely chopped fresh parsley

2 tablespoons chopped fresh thyme

salt and ground pepper to taste

1 beef tenderloin, 2½ lb (1.25 kg), tied with string

In a large, heavy, wide pot over medium-high heat, warm 1 tablespoon of the oil. Add the onions and garlic and cook, stirring often, until the onions are tender, about 5 minutes. Transfer to a plate.

Heat 7 tablespoons (3½ fl oz/105 ml) of the oil in the same pot over medium-high heat. Add the zucchini and eggplant and cook, stirring often, until golden, about 10 minutes. Add the onion mixture, the fresh and canned tomatoes, the parsley, and the thyme. Season with salt and pepper. Simmer, stirring often, until slightly thickened and pulpy, about 10 minutes. Season again with salt and pepper.

Meanwhile, preheat the oven to 400°F (200°C). Put the tenderloin in a roasting pan and coat with the remaining 1 tablespoon oil. Season with salt and pepper.

Roast the tenderloin until an instant-read thermometer inserted into the thickest part registers 130°F (54°C) for medium-rare, 30–35 minutes, or until done to your liking. Transfer to a warm spot, cover loosely with aluminum foil, and let stand for 10 minutes.

Cut into slices against the grain. Arrange several slices, overlapping, on warmed plates. Spoon a small amount of the ratatouille on the side.

serves six | per serving: calories 634 (kilojoules 2,663), protein 36 g, carbohydrates 22 g, total fat 45 g, saturated fat 13 g, cholesterol 109 mg, sodium 201 mg, dietary fiber 4 g

grilled pork medallions with curried peach salsa

This salsa is also delicious with grilled chicken. To peel a peach, immerse in boiling water for about 30 seconds, then remove, let cool, and slip off the skin.

2 tablespoons soy sauce

2 tablespoons red wine vinegar

2 tablespoons olive oil

1 tablespoon chopped fresh thyme

1½ lb (750 g) pork tenderloin, cut crosswise into slices 2 inches (5 cm) thick and lightly pounded

salt and ground pepper to taste

for the salsa:

2 tablespoons unsalted butter

1 small yellow onion, finely chopped

1 celery stalk, finely chopped

2 teaspoons mild curry powder, or more to taste

½ cup (4 fl oz/125 ml) water

6 small peaches, peeled, pitted, and cut into ½-inch (12-mm) dice

1 small red bell pepper (capsicum), seeded and cut into ¼-inch (6-mm) dice

½ cup (¾ oz/20 g) finely chopped fresh cilantro (fresh coriander)

salt and ground pepper to taste

In a small bowl, stir together the soy sauce, vinegar, oil, and thyme. Place the pork medallions in a shallow nonreactive dish and pour over the soy mixture. Cover and refrigerate, turning often, for 3 hours or up to overnight.

Meanwhile, make the salsa: In a small saucepan over medium-high heat, melt the butter. Add the onion and celery and sauté until softened, about 5 minutes. Stir in the curry powder and cook, stirring often, until well blended, about 2 minutes longer. Remove from the heat and pour in the water. Stir well to blend, cover, and let cool to room temperature.

In a bowl, combine the peaches, bell pepper, and curry mixture. Stir well, cover, and refrigerate. Just before serving, stir in the cilantro and season with salt and pepper.

Prepare a medium-hot fire in a grill, or preheat the broiler (grill). Remove the pork from the marinade and pat dry. Season with salt and pepper. Place on the grill rack or under the broiler 4–6 inches (10–15 cm) from the heat source. Grill or broil, turning once, until lightly browned on the outside and slightly pink when cut into the center, about 5 minutes on each side.

Transfer to warmed individual plates. Pass the salsa at the table.

serves four | per serving: calories 398 (kilojoules 1,672), protein 36 g, carbohydrates 21 g, total fat 19 g, saturated fat 7 g, cholesterol 123 mg, sodium 343 mg, dietary fiber 4 g

fish cakes with coriander

A quick tomato sauce or spicy tomato salsa, tartar sauce, or lemon wedges would complement these fish cakes.

2 tablespoons olive oil

½ cup (2½ oz/75 g) finely chopped red bell pepper (capsicum)

½ cup (2½ oz/75 g) finely chopped green bell pepper (capsicum)

1 yellow onion, finely chopped

1 tablespoon finely chopped fresh thyme

salt to taste, plus 1 teaspoon

ground pepper to taste, plus ½ teaspoon

2 lb (1 kg) cod fillets, trimmed of skin and any errant bones removed, cut into large pieces

1 cup (2 oz/60 g) fresh bread crumbs

2 tablespoons coriander seeds

vegetable oil for frying

1 cup (5 oz/155 g) all-purpose (plain) flour

In a small saucepan over medium-high heat, warm the olive oil. Add the bell peppers and onion and sauté until softened, 7–10 minutes. Stir in the thyme and season to taste with salt and pepper. Let cool.

Line a baking sheet with waxed paper. In a food processor, working in batches, process the cod until ground, 20–30 seconds per batch. Transfer to a bowl. Add the pepper mixture, bread crumbs, 1 teaspoon salt, and ½ teaspoon pepper. Stir just until the mixture holds together loosely. Divide into 12 equal portions and form into cakes about 2½ inches (6 cm) in diameter. Place on the prepared baking sheet, cover tightly, and refrigerate for at least 2 hours or for up to 12 hours.

In a small, dry frying pan over medium heat, toast the coriander seeds, shaking the pan often, until fragrant and lightly browned, 3–5 minutes. Let cool slightly, then crush lightly.

In a large, heavy frying pan over medium-high heat, pour in oil to a depth of ¼ inch (6 mm). Heat until hot but not smoking. Dredge the cakes in the flour and tap off excess. Working in batches, fry, turning once, until golden brown and firm to the touch, 3–5 minutes on each side. Transfer to paper towels to drain and season with salt and pepper; keep warm.

Sprinkle the cakes with the coriander seeds and serve immediately.

serves six | per serving: calories 483 (kilojoules 2,029), protein 33 g, carbohydrates 42 g, total fat 21 g, saturated fat 3 g, cholesterol 65 mg, sodium 563 mg, dietary fiber 6 g

perfect grilled hamburgers

The best-quality meat is mixed with icy water and sweet tomato-chile sauce to create a juicy burger embellished with a dollop of olive paste. The burgers should be served right after grilling, so make sure to transport the meat in a cooler and take along a spatula.

2 lb (1 kg) ground (minced) sirloin

¼ cup (2 fl oz/60 ml) ice water

¼ cup (2 fl oz/60 ml) chile sauce

6 onion rolls, cut in half

6 tablespoons (3 oz/90 g) olive paste

6 iceberg or red romaine (cos) lettuce leaves

6 thick tomato slices

Dijon mustard to taste

pickle relish to taste

In a bowl, thoroughly mix the ground sirloin with the ice water and chile sauce. Shape into 6 thick patties. Cover and refrigerate until ready to grill.

Prepare a fire in a grill. When the coals are medium-hot, place the onion rolls on the grill rack, cut sides down, and toast until lightly browned, about 2 minutes. Transfer to a platter.

Place the patties on the grill rack and grill until grill marks appear on the first side, 3–4 minutes. Turn and grill on the second side, 4–6 minutes longer for medium-rare. Remove from the grill and set on the bottoms of the rolls. Top each burger with 1 tablespoon olive paste, a lettuce leaf, and a tomato slice, then with the top half of the roll. Serve immediately with the mustard and relish on the side.

serves six | per serving: calories 533 (kilojoules 2,239), protein 34 g, carbohydrates 35 g, total fat 28 g, saturated fat 9 g, cholesterol 95 mg, sodium 1,059 mg, dietary fiber 1 g

blt wraps with tahini sauce

These are the perfect sandwiches to tote on a boat for a portable lunch. Lavash, Armenian cracker bread available in both soft and crisp forms, is available in Middle Eastern markets and in well-stocked food stores. If unavailable, use pita bread split in half horizontally.

½ cup (5 oz/155 g) tahini (sesame paste)

2 tablespoons olive oil

2 tablespoons soy sauce

2 tablespoons white wine vinegar or rice vinegar

¼ teaspoon red pepper flakes

¼ lb (125 g) thinly sliced bacon

2 large soft lavash, each about 16 inches (40 cm) in diameter

2 large tomatoes, thinly sliced

1 large head romaine (cos) lettuce, leaves separated and cut into coarse strips

In a small bowl, stir together the tahini, oil, soy sauce, vinegar, and pepper flakes until smooth.

In a large frying pan over medium-high heat, fry the bacon until browned and crisp, about 5 minutes. Transfer to paper towels to drain.

Cut each bread round into quarters. Spread each quarter with an equal amount of the tahini mixture. Break the bacon into large pieces and scatter over the quarters. Top with the tomato slices and then the lettuce strips. Working with 1 quarter at a time, fold the point about one-third of the way toward the rounded edge, then roll up left to right into a tight log. Wrap each quarter securely in parchment (baking) or waxed paper. Cut off any excess paper. The wraps are now ready to be "peeled" and eaten.

serves four | per serving: calories 625 (kilojoules 2,625), protein 24 g, carbohydrates 70 g, total fat 30 g, saturated fat 5 g, cholesterol 7 mg, sodium 867 mg, dietary fiber 12 g

greek sandwiches

You can fill the pita pockets in advance or take the filling and pita breads to a picnic and assemble just before serving. Accompany these vegetarian sandwiches with Coleslaw with Cider Dressing (page 118).

2 tablespoons red wine vinegar

2 tablespoons lemon juice

2 tablespoons finely chopped fresh flat-leaf (Italian) parsley

1 teaspoon dried oregano

½ teaspoon dry mustard

salt and ground pepper

½ cup (4 fl oz/125 ml) extra-virgin olive oil

30 cherry tomatoes, quartered

1 English (hothouse) cucumber, coarsely chopped

½ small red onion, finely chopped

1½ cups (7½ oz/235 g) crumbled feta cheese

¾ cup (3½ oz/105 g) coarsely chopped, pitted Kalamata olives

6 sandwich-size pita breads

In a small bowl, combine the vinegar, lemon juice, parsley, oregano, mustard, and salt and pepper to taste. Slowly whisk in the olive oil until incorporated.

In a bowl, combine the tomatoes, cucumber, red onion, cheese, and olives. Pour over the dressing and toss to coat well. Taste and adjust the seasonings.

Carefully split each pita bread along the edge to open halfway. Using a large spoon, stuff the pita breads with the filling, dividing it evenly. Arrange in a transportable container, cover, and keep chilled until ready to serve.

serves six | per serving: calories 494 (kilojoules 2,075), protein 11 g, carbohydrates 43 g, total fat 32 g, saturated fat 9 g, cholesterol 32 m

ratatouille tart

Simple, portable, yet elegant, this tart is an ideal way to prepare summer's bounty.

for the dough:

1 cup (5 oz/155 g) all-purpose (plain) flour

pinch of salt

6 tablespoons (3 oz/90 g) frozen unsalted butter, cut into pieces

¼ cup (2 fl oz/60 ml) ice water

1 small eggplant (aubergine), about 1¼ lb (625 g), peeled and finely diced

6 tablespoons (3 fl oz/90 ml) olive oil

2 shallots, finely chopped

½ lb (250 g) white mushrooms, sliced

1 small red bell pepper (capsicum), seeded and diced

2 cloves garlic, minced

salt and ground pepper

3 eggs, beaten

1 cup (8 oz/250 ml) crushed tomatoes

2 tablespoons finely chopped fresh flat-leaf (Italian) parsley

¼ cup (⅓ oz/10 g) chopped fresh basil

1 teaspoon chopped fresh thyme

5 tablespoons grated Parmesan cheese

3 tablespoons Dijon mustard

5 tablespoons shredded Gruyère cheese

6 cherry tomatoes, halved

Preheat the oven to 375°F (190°C).

To make the dough, in a food processor, combine the flour and salt and process to blend. Add the butter and process until the mixture resembles coarse meal, 5–10 seconds. With the motor running, add the water until the dough just comes together.

On a floured work surface, press the dough into a disk. Roll out to fit an 11-inch (28-cm) tart pan with a removable bottom. Trim even with the rim. Place on a baking sheet. Prick the bottom and sides with a fork, line with waxed paper, and fill with pie weights. Bake for 20–25 minutes. Let cool. Remove the paper and weights.

Place the eggplant in a colander, sprinkle with salt, and let stand for 15 minutes. Rinse and pat dry. In a frying pan over medium heat, heat the oil. Add the shallots and sauté until soft, 3 minutes. Add the eggplant, mushrooms, and red pepper and sauté, stirring, until soft, 7–10 minutes. Add the garlic and cook for 1 minute. Season with salt and pepper. Transfer to a bowl.

In small bowl, stir together the eggs, crushed tomatoes, herbs, 2 tablespoons of the Parmesan cheese, and the eggplant mixture to make the filling.

Spread the mustard over the baked pastry shell. Sprinkle with the Gruyère. Return to the oven and bake until the cheese just begins to melt, 5–7 minutes.

Remove from the oven. Pour in the filling. Arrange the cherry tomatoes around the outside of the tart. Sprinkle the remaining 3 tablespoons Parmesan cheese over the top. Bake until just set, 25–30 minutes. Let cool, then remove the sides and transfer to a plate. Serve warm or at room temperature cut into wedges.

serves six | per serving: calories 440 (kilojoules 1,848), protein 11 g, carbohydrates 30 g, total fat 31 g, saturated fat 11 g, cholesterol 146 mg, sodium 359 mg, dietary fiber 3 g

grilled flank steak with tomato-corn relish

A no-fail choice for the barbecue, flank steak is fast and easy to cook. If you don't have balsamic vinegar, substitute red wine mixed with 1 tablespoon brown sugar.

½ cup (4 fl oz/125 ml) plus 1 tablespoon balsamic vinegar

4 tablespoons (2 fl oz/60 ml) olive oil

2 cloves garlic, minced

1 tablespoon chopped fresh rosemary or 1 tablespoon dried rosemary

1 flank steak, about 1½ lb (750 g)

8 green (spring) onions

3 ears of corn, husks and silks removed

1 lb (500 g) firm, ripe plum (Roma) tomatoes, cored, halved lengthwise, and seeded

salt

In a nonaluminum container, combine the ½ cup (4 fl oz/125 ml) balsamic vinegar, 2 tablespoons of the oil, the garlic, and the rosemary. Add the steak and turn to coat well. Cover tightly and refrigerate for at least 8 hours or for up to 24 hours.

Prepare a fire in a grill. Remove the steak from the refrigerator and let come to room temperature. Leaving the green onions whole, brush all the vegetables lightly with 1 tablespoon of the olive oil.

When the coals are hot, place the vegetables on the grill. Grill, turning, until the green onions are slightly charred, about 3 minutes; the tomatoes are softened and slightly charred, about 4 minutes; and the corn is blackened in spots and the kernels are tender, about 12 minutes. Set aside.

Place the steak on the grill rack. Grill, turning once, until well browned on both sides and medium-rare in the center, about 10 minutes total, depending on the thickness of the steak.

While the steak is cooking, cut the corn kernels off the cobs. Coarsely chop the tomatoes and thinly slice the onions. Place the vegetables in a bowl and drizzle with the 1 tablespoon balsamic vinegar and the remaining 1 tablespoon olive oil. Season to taste with salt and mix well. Remove the steak from the grill and slice thinly across the grain. Serve with the tomato-corn relish.

serves six | per serving: calories 334 (kilojoules 1,403), protein 25 g, carbohydrates 19 g, total fat 18 g, saturated fat 5 g, cholesterol 57 mg, sodium 89 mg, dietary fiber 4 g

tandoori-style grilled chicken legs

You can re-create the intense flavor of Indian chicken baked in a clay oven by soaking whole legs in a spicy yogurt marinade and grilling them on a covered barbecue or under a broiler. Serve with basmati rice and with sliced cucumbers and tomatoes drizzled with vinegar and oil.

½ cup (4 fl oz/125 ml) lime juice

1 hot green chile such as jalapeño or serrano, seeded, or 1 teaspoon red pepper flakes

1½ teaspoons paprika

1 teaspoon cumin seeds

1 teaspoon ground turmeric

2 cloves garlic

1 piece fresh ginger, about 2 inches (5 cm), peeled

1 cup (8 oz/250 g) plain low-fat or nonfat yogurt

6 whole chicken legs, 2½ lb (1.25 kg) total weight

sprigs of fresh cilantro (fresh coriander), optional

In a blender or food processor, combine the lime juice, chile or red pepper flakes, paprika, cumin seeds, turmeric, garlic, ginger, and yogurt. Process until smooth.

Using a sharp knife, cut a few diagonal slashes along the top side of each chicken leg down to the bone (this helps the meat absorb the marinade). Place the legs in a nonaluminum container or in a large lock-top plastic bag. Add the yogurt mixture, turn a few times to coat, then cover the container or seal the bag and refrigerate for at least 4 hours or for up to 24 hours.

Prepare a fire in a grill or preheat the broiler (grill).

If using a grill, when the coals are hot, lift the chicken from the marinade, letting the excess drain off. Place, skin sides down, on the grill rack. Cover the grill and open the vents. Grill the chicken, turning once, until the exterior is crisp and the meat is no longer pink near the bone when cut, about 35 minutes total. If using a broiler, place the chicken on a broiler pan and broil (grill) about 6 inches (15 cm) below the heat, turning once, for about 30 minutes total.

Remove the chicken from the grill or broiler and arrange on a serving platter or individual plates. Garnish with cilantro sprigs, if desired.

serves six | per serving: calories 234 (kilojoules 983), protein 25 g, carbohydrates 3 g, total fat 13 g, saturated fat 4 g, cholesterol 87 mg, sodium 96 mg, dietary fiber 0 g

red snapper ceviche with tomatillos and chiles

For the best results, use the freshest snapper available. If tomatillos are unavailable, use seeded green tomatoes in their place.

1 lb (500 g) skinless red snapper fillet, cut into ½-inch (12-mm) dice

¾ cup (6 fl oz/180 ml) lime juice (from 6–8 limes)

4 or 5 small tomatillos, about ½ lb (250 g) total weight, husks removed and cut into ¼-inch (6-mm) dice

1 firm but ripe tomato, seeded and cut into ¼-inch (6-mm) dice

1 small jalapeño chile, seeded and minced

1 small clove garlic, minced

½ small white onion, cut into ¼-inch (6-mm) dice

¼ cup (2 fl oz/60 ml) olive oil

½ cup (¾ oz/20 g) finely chopped fresh cilantro (fresh coriander)

salt and ground pepper to taste

8 large butter (Boston) or green-leaf lettuce leaves

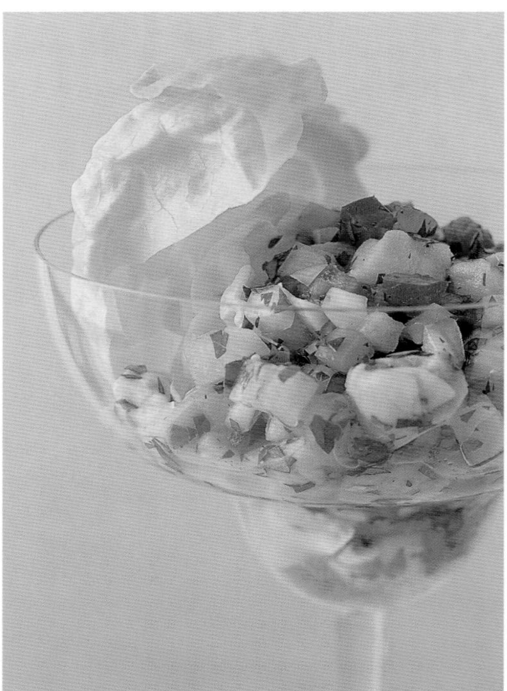

In a large nonaluminum bowl, combine the snapper and the lime juice, turning to coat. Cover and refrigerate for 4–6 hours.

Add the tomatillos, tomato, jalapeño, garlic, and onion to the fish and mix gently to combine. Stir in the oil and cilantro. Season with salt and pepper.

Line a chilled shallow bowl with the lettuce leaves. Using a slotted spoon, transfer the ceviche to the center. Serve immediately.

serves four to six | per serving: calories 214 (kilojoules 899), protein 20 g, carbohydrates 6 g, total fat 12 g, saturated fat 2 g, cholesterol 34 mg, sodium 66 mg, dietary fiber 1 g

stuffed summer sandwich

If you prefer a vegetarian version of this portable sandwich, replace the ham with sliced mozzarella, Monterey jack cheese, or grilled eggplant. The loaf can be covered in plastic wrap, refrigerated overnight, and sliced just before serving.

2 large red bell peppers (capsicums)

1 round loaf sourdough or coarse country bread

1 can (6 oz/185 g) pitted black olives, drained

1 clove garlic

2 tablespoons olive oil

½ lb (250 g) thinly sliced baked ham or prosciutto

1 large ripe tomato, thinly sliced

1 cup (1 oz/30 g) packed fresh basil leaves or 4–6 leaves of red-leaf lettuce

Preheat the broiler (grill). Cut the bell peppers into quarters and remove the stems, seeds, and ribs. Place the quarters, cut sides down, on a baking sheet and broil (grill) about 4 inches (10 cm) below the heat until the skins blacken and blister. Transfer to a paper bag and seal; let steam until cool enough to handle. Peel off and discard the skins. Set the peppers aside.

Place the bread on a cutting board and, with the tip of a serrated knife, cut a large circle in the top about ½ inch (12 mm) deep and 1 inch (2.5 cm) from the edge. Pull out the circle of crust; remove all of the bread attached to it to make a lid. Pull out all of the bread from the interior of the loaf, leaving a shell ½ inch (12 mm) thick. Set the bread shell and lid aside. (Reserve the pulled-out bread for another use.)

In a blender or food processor, combine the olives, garlic, and olive oil; process until fairly smooth. Using a rubber spatula, spread the olive paste around the inside of the bread shell and on the underside of the bread lid. (Alternatively, mince the olives and garlic, place in a small bowl and stir in the olive oil to make a coarse paste. Spread the olive paste on the bottom of the bread shell.) Line the bread shell with half of the ham or prosciutto. Top with half of the roasted pepper quarters, then half of the tomato slices, and a few basil leaves or 2 or 3 lettuce leaves. Use just enough to cover the filling without overlapping too much. Repeat the layers, ending with basil or lettuce. Replace the bread lid and press down lightly to compact the layers. Cut into wedges and serve.

serves six | per serving: calories 366 (kilojoules 1,537), protein 16 g, carbohydrates 45 g, total fat 13 g, saturated fat 3 g, cholesterol 22 mg, sodium 1,280 mg, dietary fiber 4 g

jambalaya

Frozen cooked crayfish are found in well-stocked food stores; if they are unavailable, omit them and increase the shrimp to 1½ pounds (750 g).

2 tablespoons vegetable oil, or as needed

¾ lb (375 g) andouille sausage or similar smoked spicy sausage, thinly sliced

1 large yellow onion, finely chopped

2 celery stalks, thinly sliced

2 green bell peppers (capsicums), seeded and finely chopped

3 cloves garlic, minced

1 teaspoon dried oregano

1 teaspoon dried thyme

1 teaspoon paprika

¼ teaspoon cayenne pepper

2 bay leaves

salt and ground pepper to taste

2 cups (14 oz/440 g) long-grain white rice

3⅓ cups (27 fl oz/830 ml) chicken broth

1 can (15 oz/470 g) crushed tomatoes in thick purée

1 lb (500 g) shrimp (prawns), peeled and deveined

1 lb (500 g) cooked crayfish *(see note)*

3 green (spring) onions, including tender green tops, chopped

In a large pot over medium-high heat, warm the 2 tablespoons oil. Add the sausage and cook, stirring often, until golden brown, about 5 minutes. Using a slotted spoon, transfer to a plate. Pour off all but 2 tablespoons fat from the pot; if less remains, add enough oil to make 2 tablespoons.

Return the pot to medium-high heat and add the onion, celery, bell peppers, and garlic. Cover and cook, stirring often, until the vegetables start to soften, about 5 minutes. Stir in the oregano, thyme, paprika, cayenne, and bay leaves. Season with salt and pepper. Add the rice and cook, stirring, for 1 minute. Add the broth and tomatoes, cover, and bring to a boil. Reduce the heat to low and simmer until the rice is almost done, about 15 minutes.

Raise the heat to medium and stir in the reserved sausage and the shrimp. Set the crayfish on top. Bring back to a simmer, cover, and cook for 3 minutes. Remove from the heat and let stand, covered, until the rice and shrimp are just done, about 5 minutes. Then uncover, remove the crayfish, and stir in the green onions. Spoon into a warmed serving dish, arrange the crayfish on top, and serve.

serves six | per serving: calories 705 (kilojoules 2,961), protein 49 g, carbohydrates 65 g, total fat 26 g, saturated fat 7 g, cholesterol 275 mg, sodium 1,562 mg, dietary fiber 2 g

panfried tuna with black bean salsa

Goya brand canned black beans are best for the salsa, as they are firm and hold their shape better than most other brands. If the salsa needs more heat, reserve seeds from the chile and add to taste before serving.

for the black bean salsa:

2 cans (15 oz/470 g each) black beans, drained and rinsed *(see note)*

3 tomatoes, seeded and finely diced

1 red onion, finely chopped

½ cup (¾ oz/20 g) finely chopped fresh cilantro (fresh coriander)

¼ cup (⅓ oz/10 g) finely chopped fresh parsley

1 jalapeño chile, seeded and minced

½ cup (4 fl oz/125 ml) tomato juice

3½ tablespoons lime juice (about 2 limes)

salt and ground pepper

6 tuna steaks, each about 6 oz (185 g) and 1 inch (2.5 cm) thick

¼ cup (2 fl oz/60 ml) olive oil

salt and ground pepper to taste

To make the salsa, in a large bowl, combine the beans, tomatoes, onion, cilantro, parsley, chile, tomato juice, and lime juice. Stir well and season with salt and pepper. Cover and chill for about 15 minutes.

Preheat a large frying pan or stove-top grill pan over medium-high heat. Coat the tuna with the oil and season to taste with salt and pepper. Place the tuna in the pan and cook until golden brown on the underside, about 2½ minutes. Turn and cook until golden brown on the second side and done to your liking, about 2½ minutes longer for medium-rare.

Transfer to warmed individual plates and serve immediately. Pass the salsa at the table.

serves six | per serving: calories 412 (kilojoules 1,730), protein 42 g, carbohydrates 21 g, total fat 17 g, saturated fat 3 g, cholesterol 58 mg, sodium 373 mg, dietary fiber 6 g

jerked chicken grilled under a brick

There is a wide range given here for the chiles. In Jamaica, where jerk originated, most cooks would use the maximum amount. The minimum amount is tame but still spicy. Weighting the chicken pieces as they grill helps them cook evenly and keeps them moist.

4–8 very hot fresh chiles such as Scotch bonnet or habanero, seeded *(see note)*

4 green (spring) onions, including tender green tops, chopped

juice of 1 orange

juice of 2 limes

2 tablespoons mixed dried herbs such as thyme, rosemary, and oregano, in any combination

1 tablespoon distilled white or cider vinegar

1 tablespoon ground allspice

1 tablespoon ground coriander

1 tablespoon dry hot mustard

1 tablespoon coarse salt

1 tablespoon ground pepper

6 chicken legs (thigh and drumstick), about ½ lb (250 g) each

Prepare a medium-hot fire in a grill. Wrap 6 bricks or flat rocks in aluminum foil.

In a food processor or blender, combine the chiles, green onions, orange juice, lime juice, dried herbs, vinegar, allspice, coriander, mustard, salt, and pepper. Process to a paste. Smear the chicken pieces with the paste.

Place the chicken pieces on the grill rack 5–6 inches (13–15 cm) from the fire and top each piece with a brick. (The fire must not be too hot or the outside of the chicken will be charred and the inside will remain raw.) Grill until nicely browned on the underside, about 15 minutes. Remove the bricks, turn the pieces over, and replace the bricks. Continue to grill until nicely browned on the second side and no longer pink in the center when cut into with a knife, about 15 minutes longer.

Transfer to a large platter and serve warm or at room temperature.

serves six | per serving: calories 289 (kilojoules 1,214), protein 30 g, carbohydrates 6 g, total fat 16 g, saturated fat 4 g, cholesterol 103 mg, sodium 838 mg, dietary fiber 1 g

autumn

beef stew with caramelized onions and amber lager

The ingredients here are basic, but the flavor is rich and complex. Like most stews, it tastes even better reheated the second day. Serve each portion over rice, mashed potatoes, or parsleyed egg noodles, and offer a steamed green vegetable alongside.

¼ cup (2 fl oz/60 ml) vegetable oil

2½ lb (1.25 kg) beef stew meat, preferably chuck, cut into 1-inch (2.5-cm) chunks

1½ lb (750 g) yellow onions, sliced

1 tablespoon unsalted butter

2 teaspoons sugar

2 tablespoons all-purpose (plain) flour

1½ teaspoons dried thyme

3 carrots, sliced

1 bottle (12 fl oz/375 ml) good-quality amber lager or pale ale

1 cup (8 fl oz/250 ml) beef or chicken broth

1 tablespoon tomato paste

salt and ground pepper

In a large, heavy pot, warm the oil over high heat until hot but not smoking. Working in batches, brown the meat well on all sides, 5–7 minutes. Adjust the heat as necessary to keep the meat from scorching. Transfer the browned meat to a plate and repeat until all the meat is browned.

Add the onions and butter to the pot and stir over high heat until the onions start to soften, about 5 minutes. Reduce the heat to medium and sprinkle in the sugar. Continue to cook the onions, stirring occasionally, until golden brown, about 15 minutes. Add the flour, thyme, and carrots and raise the heat to high. Stir for 1 minute, then pour in the lager or ale, letting it come to a vigorous boil. Stir in the broth and tomato paste and return to a boil.

Return the meat and any accumulated juices on the plate to the pot, let the liquid come just to a boil, then reduce the heat to low, cover, and simmer until the meat is tender when pierced and the sauce is slightly thickened, 1½–2 hours. Season to taste with salt and pepper. Serve on warmed plates.

serves four to six | per serving: calories 801 (kilojoules 3,364), protein 42 g, carbohydrates 24 g, total fat 59 g, saturated fat 21 g, cholesterol 170 mg, sodium 365 mg, dietary fiber 4 g

Wilson

counselor

READ THE THIRD COLUMN ON EACH PAGE
WHEN WORKING WITH **INDIVIDUALS**

SUPPORT. You don't know which of the friends and acquaintances on this list you will eventually be contacting; nor can you predict what a personal 'kick' they may get out of helping you.

ASSURANCE. This is completely normal and completely mistaken. We will show you, by the time you need to decide how to use this list, exactly how you can let your friends and acquaintances help you,—without imposing on them or downgrading yourself in their eyes, in the slightest.

REASSURANCE. Relax! Some of them are kicking themselves today, for not having kept in better touch with you, too. It's a two-way street.

CAUTIONING. You are to meet people in a purely friendly fashion, as one with a lot of enthusiasm about some things, who is trying to learn more. Say nothing *at this point* about your eventual interest in job-hunting.

instructor

READ THE FOURTH COLUMN ON EACH PAGE
WHEN WORKING WITH **GROUPS**, WORKSHOPS, CONFERENCES, ETC.

THE PROGRAM ELEMENTS IN THIS FIRST COLUMN HELP THE STUDENT IDENTIFY HIS/HER PRIMARY **FUNCTIONAL GOAL** (WHAT)

student

THE PROGRAM ELEMENTS IN THIS SECOND COLUMN HELP THE STUDENT IDENTIFY HIS/HER PRIMARY **ORGANIZATIONAL GOAL** (WHERE)

you would most like to live. In person, wherever possible. By letter, where face-to-face contact is not immediately possible.

(More about this, after the exercise on Targeting, when we discuss making your own Personal Economic Survey.)

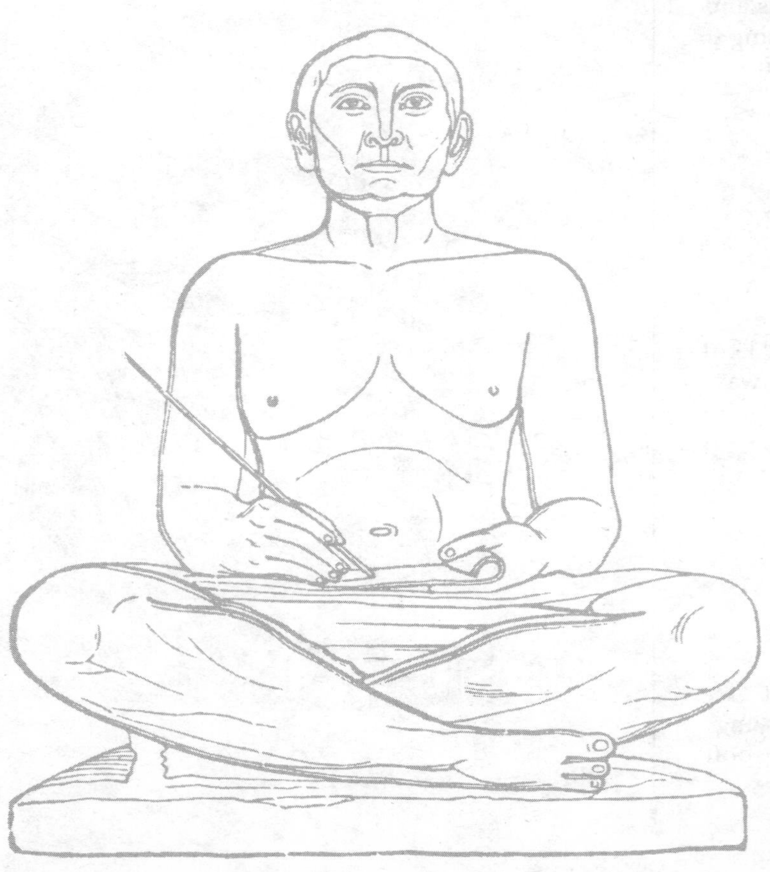

c. Other homework: catching up on any assignments from previous class sessions not done on time.

d. Reading in Parachute, chapter six.

e. Other reading, as earlier assigned. Ask students if anyone has come across some book he/she thinks is particularly valuable, which they would like to recommend to the rest of the class.

3. **CLASSROOM EXERCISES**

a. Much of the time will have been spent in students' recounting experiences from their Practice Field Survey. Do not attempt to shut off this discussion prematurely. It is *very valuable.*

b. So far as Contacts are concerned, you may want to choose some institutions (and positions within those institutions) at random, and let the class play the game of seeing who within the class knows someone who might be able to get a personal introduction to the subject who was chosen at random. (e.g., Dean of Students, University of Texas, Austin; etc.) Must be played with the whole class.

It is sometimes useful to allow this to be a homework exercise, and see if someone within the total class can locate someone they know who knows someone else who could introduce the class (if need be) to whatever person the class pulls out of a hat (so to speak).

FIFTH CLASS SESSION

SOME SUGGESTED PROGRAM ELEMENTS

1. **LOOKING BACK**

a. Ask how many started on their contacts list (show of hands). It is useful at this point, if the class is relatively manageable in size, to go around the room asking for actual total numbers on their Contact List so far, and put these numbers (but *not* the students' names) up on a blackboard, or sheet of newsprint. Then ask for any reflections, learnings, or questions, students might have as a result of this process, so far.

b. [If the students had, as homework, tried to find a contact who knew some institutional representative whom they chose, check to see how

student

THE PROGRAM ELEMENTS IN THIS FIRST COLUMN HELP THE STUDENT IDENTIFY HIS/HER PRIMARY **FUNCTIONAL GOAL** (WHAT)

THE PROGRAM ELEMENTS IN THIS SECOND COLUMN HELP THE STUDENT IDENTIFY HIS/HER PRIMARY **ORGANIZATIONAL GOAL** (WHERE)

Goal:
To begin to plan how to identify places where you might like to work.
To prepare yourself to make an organized effort to learn more about each of them.
To work toward identifying that one place (or places) where you would be happiest, as you set about accomplishing your goals.

8. First Step in Targeting

Organize a file folder entitled "Potential Organizational Targets" (the word *Target* implies something aimed at, chosen by you. If you prefer some other word such as 'Landing-Place', or whatever, by all means, substitute it.).

Into this file go *all* organizations or people in organizations that have ever interested you. As you go on in this course, you will gradually evolve *your own personal criteria*— in accordance with your skills, interests, values and goals—which will then enable you *at that time* to screen out many organizations as not of major interest.

For now you include *any* organization, etc.—
a) about which you have good feelings; OR

Avoid:
If you are inclined toward self-employment, thinking you don't need to do targeting. (You still need to collect names of people who are doing what you would like to do; as well as names of potential clients, etc.)

counselor

READ THE THIRD COLUMN ON EACH PAGE
WHEN WORKING WITH **INDIVIDUALS**

instructor

READ THE FOURTH COLUMN ON EACH PAGE
WHEN WORKING WITH **GROUPS**, WORKSHOPS, CONFERENCES, ETC.

this search went; assuming that it went well, draw the moral from it: how easy it is to meet people *if* you start with your own contacts. It's a very small world, indeed.]

c. Ask how they did on locating their geographical preferences (show of hands for those who completed this).

d. List some of their preferred places on the blackboard or on newsprint; have them discuss the factors which made them choose those particular places. (This can be done in small groups, if preferred.)

e. Discuss their outside reading. Any significant learnings, any books they wish to recommend to others (why?). List all such suggestions up on the blackboard or on newsprint, so everyone can copy down.

DEFINITION OF "TARGET". Any organization which seems attractive enough to you, to warrant further investigation to see whether you want to eventually mount a carefully organized approach to one key man in it.

CLARIFICATION. Any favorable interest
no matter why
no matter what form: agencies, institutions, or whatever
currently or at any time in the past
no matter where located
–in any organization which seems attractive to you purely for your own reasons.

GIVING EXAMPLES. You just might be a hi-fi enthusiast who has learned through experience that the ABC Company produces top-notch equipment, and is in your judgment leading the field. You might even have corresponded with some of its officials, and been favorably impressed with their friendliness

2. **LOOKING AHEAD**

a. Discuss *Targeting* at length, including its rationale, Appendix G. Have discussion. A classroom exercise is also provided (below) and if it is used, it ought to be used at this point. Then point out, when the class is reassembled, that targeting is (like their contacts list) to be *a continuing ongoing assignment,* on which they are to keep working, each week from now on.

Goal:
To free up your imagination to think of some places where you might be happiest working, that would not otherwise have occurred to you.

Goal:
To begin making an organized effort to learn more about each of them.

THE PROGRAM ELEMENTS IN THIS FIRST COLUMN HELP THE STUDENT IDENTIFY HIS/HER PRIMARY **FUNCTIONAL GOAL** (WHAT)

student

THE PROGRAM ELEMENTS IN THIS SECOND COLUMN HELP THE STUDENT IDENTIFY HIS/HER PRIMARY **ORGANIZATIONAL GOAL** (WHERE)

b) which you admire; OR

c) which you have had some favorable experience with, at some time;

d) which is doing something constructive about a subject or subjects that interest you.

1. Go back and try to recall any such group. Put its name, address and anything you know about it, on a file card; and then drop it in this file of POTs; or else give it a file of its own.

2. For the present, each time you read in the papers or magazines about some company or other group doing something which you find both fascinating and admirable, *clip every such article,* and start a Potential Organization Target file on it. Do not hesitate, also, to get in touch with the people named in such articles, if only to say that you like what they are doing, *and would appreciate hearing more about their activities and philosophy.* You will be happily surprised at their responses, and at the speed with which your folder on each such organization begins to grow.

Please read Appendix G at this point.

Avoid:
Reading articles about people or places you admire, sighing, and throwing the articles away.

Goal:
To fix your own standards in your mind as to what kinds of people you most prefer to be surrounded by, since
[1] Almost all jobs

9. People-Environments

Identify
and discuss
the types of men and women
you like;
and

Error:
Feeling that what you do is the only important thing, and how you work with people is utterly irrelevant.

counselor

READ THE THIRD COLUMN ON EACH PAGE
WHEN WORKING WITH **INDIVIDUALS**

and expertise. Or, as another example, you just might be an avid amateur environmentalist who has been silently cheering your old State Environmentalist on, in his battles against polluting-corporations; if so, his name goes in your Potential Organizational Targets File.

REITERATION. Cut out any article about any company or group that genuinely *interests you. You* are the sole judge; if it interests you, and you admire them, cut it out. If it doesn't interest you, *don't* cut it out.

REMINDING. When you begin your Personal Economic Survey of your prime geographical target area, as we will shortly tell you to do, remember that every economic entity you come across, *that interests you,* is to go without fail into your Potential Organizational Targets files. Put down its name, address, any literature you pick up about it, any observations made by you or others. Trust *nothing* to memory or chance.

INFORMATION. As Holland says (see the column to the right), jobs *are* people environments. Cf. also page 87 in *Parachute.*

instructor

READ THE FOURTH COLUMN ON EACH PAGE
WHEN WORKING WITH **GROUPS**, WORKSHOPS, CONFERENCES, ETC.

b. Discuss people-environments. [For *your own* background reading on this subject you may want to read *Making Vocational Choices: a theory of careers* by John L. Holland (Englewood Cliffs, New Jersey, Prentice-Hall, Inc., 1973), which we wholeheartily recommend. It is crucially important, however, that you do not 'throw' these theories into this discussion prematurely. *First,* let the students make their own self-discoveries.

student

THE PROGRAM ELEMENTS IN THIS FIRST COLUMN HELP THE STUDENT IDENTIFY HIS/HER PRIMARY **FUNCTIONAL GOAL** (WHAT)

THE PROGRAM ELEMENTS IN THIS SECOND COLUMN HELP THE STUDENT IDENTIFY HIS/HER PRIMARY **ORGANIZATIONAL GOAL** (WHERE)

are people environments; and [2] Knowing which people-environments you prefer, offers you leads as to the kind of job you should aim for; and [3] Other things being equal, you will probably always do your best work when you are not surrounded by people who bug you.

the types of men and women you dislike; aiding yourself in this exercise, by thinking of the specific people you know or have known in your life.
Also
please state the reasons for your feelings, pro or con. Do not overlook people you have met during this course in your Practice Field Survey, and will meet during your Personal Economic Survey.

Error:
Feeling that you ought to be able to work with any kind of person, and that therefore whom you prefer to be with is utterly irrelevant.

10. Your Philosophy of Life

Goal:
To begin to surface your value system, which is one important determinant of what you will, and will not, enjoy doing.

Write a brief character study of yourself, emphasizing your philosophy of life, your views on business, social and public ethics, and your opinion of such matters as the rule of law in daily activities, the importance of goals in life, etc.

Error:
Feeling that your values and ethics are going to have to be subordinated to success.

counselor

READ THE THIRD COLUMN ON EACH PAGE
WHEN WORKING WITH **INDIVIDUALS**

REASSURANCE. As we go about our daily life, in our family, on the street, patronizing stores, or attending school, etc. we do indeed have to rub shoulders with, and learn how to get along with, all sorts and conditions of men and women. Our skill in being a human being is dependent on our learning how to get along with everybody. But, when we are thinking about what work we want to do with the heart of each day, and with the heart of who we are, we are talking about something altogether different. This can become a very intimate relationship—and it is worthwhile thinking hard about the *kind* of person you want to be with That Much Time.

DEFINITIONS. Whole life planning is incomplete without your values and ethical system being surfaced and counted as an important element in whatever decisions you make. Moreover, you *must* know what values are important to you, *before* you decide to work in a particular milieu or organization, for then you will know what to look for.

instructor

READ THE FOURTH COLUMN ON EACH PAGE
WHEN WORKING WITH **GROUPS**, WORKSHOPS, CONFERENCES, ETC.

That is the principle to be observed throughout this whole course.] One way of getting into this subject is to use the classroom exercise below. Then discuss. Then make this a homework assignment, to be completed before the next class session.

c. Discuss and assign the program element YOUR PHILOSOPHY OF LIFE, to be completed before the next class session.

student

THE PROGRAM ELEMENTS IN THIS FIRST COLUMN HELP THE STUDENT IDENTIFY HIS/HER PRIMARY **FUNCTIONAL GOAL** (WHAT)

job (job), ***n.*** [ME. *gobbe*, a lump, portion; orig., mouthful < Celt. *gob*, *gop*, the mouth]. 1. a piece of work; definite piece of work, as in one's trade, or done by agreement for pay. 2. anything one has to do; task; chore; duty. 3. the thing or material being worked on. 4. a thing done supposedly in the public interest but actually for private gain; dishonest piece of official business. 5. a position of employment; situation; work. 6. [Colloq.], a criminal act or deed, as a theft, etc. 7. [Colloq.], any happening, affair, etc. *adj.* hired or done by the job: see also **job lot.**

THE PROGRAM ELEMENTS IN THIS SECOND COLUMN HELP THE STUDENT IDENTIFY HIS/HER PRIMARY **ORGANIZATIONAL GOAL** (WHERE)

spec·i·fi·ca·tion (spes'ə-fi-kā'shən), ***n.*** [ML. *specificatio*], 1. a specifying; detailed mention or definition. 2. *usually pl.* a detailed description of the parts of a whole; statement or enumeration of particulars, as to size, quality, performance, terms, etc.: as, here are the *specifications* for the new building. 3. something specified; specified item, etc. Abbreviated **spec.**

counselor

READ THE THIRD COLUMN ON EACH PAGE
WHEN WORKING WITH **INDIVIDUALS**

instructor

READ THE FOURTH COLUMN ON EACH PAGE
WHEN WORKING WITH **GROUPS**, WORKSHOPS, CONFERENCES, ETC.

d. Remind them of their Contacts list, and of the importance of:

(1) Adding some more names of people they already know, each week.

(2) Making a conscious effort to meet people each week, and to add those names to their Contacts list. Ask each student to try for three new people by next class session, please.

e. Remind them to keep up with their reading. Give them the page numbers in *Parachute* related to this week's assignment (88–90; 95).

3. CLASSROOM EXERCISES

a. Targeting. Divide the class into small groups (5—8 members) and have them discuss all the various organizations they have known—directly, through their friends, their families, seen portrayed in movies, etc. Questions to be discussed: What turns you off about organizations? What turns you on? When you see a group or organization you like or even admire, what strikes you about it?

After discussing this for some time, introduce a new question into the small groups: what particular organizations, group activities, or individuals do *you* especially feel are admirable?

Suggested time: 30—90 minutes.

When the groups reconvene as a class, share the results; then suggest that by next class session every student have the names of three individuals, activities, or groups that he or she admires.

b. People Environments. Break into small groups (5—8 members) and discuss the *kinds* of people that just turn you off (needless to say, the class should not mention names) and *why*. Discuss the kinds of people, then, that you really enjoy. And why? No attempt should be made necessarily to reach consensus; it is sufficient if even *one* member of the class feels *that way*. The purpose of this exercise is to encourage each class member to surface his or her feelings.

When the group reconvenes, ask each member to draw up his or her own complete list, according to the directions of THE PEOPLE ENVIRONMENTS exercise, before the next class session, at which time it will be discussed.

student

THE PROGRAM ELEMENTS IN THIS FIRST COLUMN HELP THE STUDENT IDENTIFY HIS/HER PRIMARY **FUNCTIONAL GOAL** (WHAT)

THE PROGRAM ELEMENTS IN THIS SECOND COLUMN HELP THE STUDENT IDENTIFY HIS/HER PRIMARY **ORGANIZATIONAL GOAL** (WHERE)

counselor

READ THE THIRD COLUMN ON EACH PAGE
WHEN WORKING WITH **INDIVIDUALS**

instructor

READ THE FOURTH COLUMN ON EACH PAGE
WHEN WORKING WITH **GROUPS**, WORKSHOPS, CONFERENCES, ETC.

c. Philosophy of Life. Divide the class into trios, and number the students in each trio, A, B, and C. The exercise is that one is to play reporter, and 'interview' the second as to his/her philosophy of life. Each 'interview' is to last seven minutes. Then another 'interview' is to be done, etc. Suggested rotation: A interviews B, C interviews A, B interviews C.

When the groups reassemble as a class, have them discuss the *elements* which they now think should be included in anybody's philosophy of life. List these on a blackboard or sheet of newsprint. Ask the class to copy them, for their homework guidance when they write up their own individual philosophy, before the next class session.

SIXTH CLASS SESSION

SOME SUGGESTED PROGRAM ELEMENTS

1. **LOOKING BACK**

a. Check on completion of the homework assignments to date, viz.,
BEGINNING FILES ON TARGETING
PEOPLE ENVIRONMENTS
PHILOSOPHY OF LIFE
CONTACTS LIST
READING

b. Treat all of these in the usual manner, i.e., how many completed each assignment (show of hands), buddy system to help any who are falling hopelessly behind, discussion of any questions that arose as a result of the homework, discussion of insights learned.

c. Also, in the case of Targeting, make a special point of emphasizing the uniqueness of the individual. Part of the task of the class is to value and protect the right of each individual to choose what interests him or her the most.

d. *Optional, for college students:* If the majority of the class has finished writing up the type of people they enjoy being with, you might

student

THE PROGRAM ELEMENTS IN THIS FIRST COLUMN HELP THE STUDENT IDENTIFY HIS/HER PRIMARY **FUNCTIONAL GOAL** (WHAT)

THE PROGRAM ELEMENTS IN THIS SECOND COLUMN HELP THE STUDENT IDENTIFY HIS/HER PRIMARY **ORGANIZATIONAL GOAL** (WHERE)

Goal:
To prepare you to be able to spell out to your Ultimate Prime Targets (i.e., prospective employers) *your* specific requirements for doing your creative, productive best.

11. Your Ideal Job Specifications

Begin drawing up a list of your own ideal job specifications. Dare to dream! The list *must* include:
1. *All* specific long and short-range interests.
2. All your desires concerning future working responsibilities, independence or lack of it.
3. Your desires concerning future working conditions.
4. And future working circumstances, opportunities, and goals.

Putting all of this together, we ask you to describe tentatively, in one well-thought-out paragraph, the type of job you feel you could be happiest and most productive in. Then: discuss your present abilities in this area.

See Appendix H.

Error:
Thinking that 'what you want' is irrelevant, since you are supposedly at the mercy of 'what's out there'.

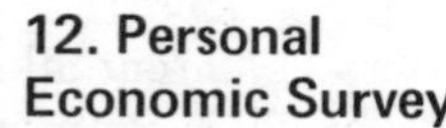

12. Personal Economic Survey

It is now necessary for you to research the economy of your chosen geographical area, placing top priority of time and effort on your *first* choice, while applying the same procedures with progressively lower priority to your second and third choices.

In each case, mark out *your prime geographical target area.* Procure a good large-scale map of your preferred area and even more

counselor

READ THE THIRD COLUMN ON EACH PAGE WHEN WORKING WITH **INDIVIDUALS**

instructor

READ THE FOURTH COLUMN ON EACH PAGE WHEN WORKING WITH **GROUPS**, WORKSHOPS, CONFERENCES, ETC.

now present to them something of Holland's typologies (of people environments), viz., Realistic, Investigative, Artistic, Social, Enterprising, and Conventional, and suggest that they now look at the type of people they prefer in terms of such environment-typologies, to see if each student discerns any patterns among the people s/he prefers. If any are intrigued by this, suggest they go read in Holland for homework. (Tell them to beware, however, of letting ANY typology become a limiting parameter for their own desires and dreams of Possibilities.)

DEFINITION. What-you-believe helps to determine what happens. Cf. the driver who sees a green light ahead, and debates whether or not he will reach it before it turns red. What he decides to believe, will help to determine what happens. So we say here: dare to dream.

2. **LOOKING AHEAD**

a. **IDEAL JOB SPECIFICATIONS.** Explain this program element, together with its rationale, at length. (Appendix H.) An exercise to help the students get into this is described below, and you may want to use this *first* before explaining this homework assignment. The assignment is to be completed before the next class-session.

TEACHING–BY CONTRAST. By means of targeting, the personal economic survey, and so on, we are here (as elsewhere) of course reversing the usual order of things.

Traditional wisdom holds that, in job-hunting 'personnel procedures', the organization should investigate the individual, to see if s/he is good enough to warrant her/him being considered for the great favor of hiring her/him–in some capacity dictated by the organization.

b. **PERSONAL ECONOMIC SURVEY.** Present and discuss this program element, as an on-going homework assignment which they are to *begin* this week–though (like Contact Lists and Targeting) it is going to take a much longer time to complete. The rationale for this Survey is found, of course, under the Program Element "Practice Field Survey", which was a dress-rehearsal for this. The same methodology (Appendix E) applies, also–with additional suggestions in the Program Element column, to the left, on these pages.

student

THE PROGRAM ELEMENTS IN THIS FIRST COLUMN HELP THE STUDENT IDENTIFY HIS/HER PRIMARY **FUNCTIONAL GOAL** (WHAT)

THE PROGRAM ELEMENTS IN THIS SECOND COLUMN HELP THE STUDENT IDENTIFY HIS/HER PRIMARY **ORGANIZATIONAL GOAL** (WHERE)

Goal:
To make a preliminary study of your geographical preference area, in order to gain *a good background* against which more pointed targeting (so to speak) can later be conducted, intensively and in depth.

To become the best informed individual on your chosen geographical area—as quickly as you can.

To learn how to do this whole process, so that you can do it again as often as you wish, for the rest of your life.

To ensure that you consider the total picture of the community, thus avoiding impetuous, ill-advised decisions.

Goal:
To be sure that all options are considered.

detailed maps of various sections within it, if such are available (ask the Chamber of Commerce there).

Choose a section where you think you might want to live (or, if it is your present community that you chose as your first choice, then start with where you already live—assuming you wish to remain there). Stick a large pin in that spot.

Decide how many miles maximum you would care to commute from there, to work, each day. Add one half again, as a safety factor to allow for possible changes in your plans later. Then cut a piece of string, of a length equalling that total mileage—calibrated to the same scale as the map. Tie one end of the string to the pin, and the other end to a red map crayon (or some other writing instrument). Swing the crayon, on the map, all the way around the pin. The resultant circle is your prime geographical target area.

It is now your job to gather every bit of intelligence available on every economic entity operating within that circle—and as quickly as you can. This means not only the obvious kinds of organizations, but also the variety of human activities that take place within such entities as: local governmental agencies, educational institutions, professional and other associations, private entrepreneurial kinds of operations.

You want particularly to learn about the different *types* of organizations or operations in your prime geographical target area.

counselor

READ THE THIRD COLUMN ON EACH PAGE
WHEN WORKING WITH **INDIVIDUALS**

We, however, are showing you that—contrariwise—the individual should investigate the organizations, in order to determine whether or not any of them is good enough to warrant her/his considering letting *them* join her/him, in a capacity dictated by the individual and her / his unique talents, interests, and goals.

[If any student, at this point, laughs nervously and asks, "Really?", just answer "Yes," firmly. S/he will discover soon enough for her/himself the fact that this really does work.]

TEACHING. The uniqueness of each individual must be safeguarded at all points in this process. The places that interest others may utterly turn you off. The places that interest you might not be of interest to others. No matter: each of you is unique, and it is the places that interest *you* for whatever reason, that you must pursue. What others may, or may not, think is irrelevant.

THE PROGRAM ELEMENTS IN THIS FIRST COLUMN HELP THE STUDENT IDENTIFY HIS/HER PRIMARY **FUNCTIONAL GOAL** (WHAT)

Goal:
To discover information, as one way to narrow down the field of 'targets' that will need intensive investigation, later.

Goal:
To learn how, and where, to look for clues of places that may have problems, for which your talents are needed (assuming that the problems are of interest to you and they are places where you would be interested in working).

student

THE PROGRAM ELEMENTS IN THIS SECOND COLUMN HELP THE STUDENT IDENTIFY HIS/HER PRIMARY **ORGANIZATIONAL GOAL** (WHERE)

How do you gather such information? Ferret it out from all available information sources:

(1) *Directories* of business firms in the area, of R&D firms, of government agencies, of educational institutions, of not-for-profit institutions, of associations, etc. These are available from Chambers of Commerce locally, from city, state and county government agencies, from private firms, from Planning Boards, from Economic Development agencies, from trade and professional associations, Boards of Trade, etc. Ask the local librarian there for help.

(2) *The Yellow Pages* of the telephone book (to gain an idea of the scope and range of the economic activities in your chosen area).

(3) The leading local *newspaper(s)* in your chosen area (if you live elsewhere, subscribe by mail to them).

You will not be looking so much at the front page news, as at the Business news pages, for clues and leads as to interesting activities in town, etc. You will inevitably learn vital facts about local expansion plans of certain organizations, plans to introduce new type activities which might well be of vital interest (later) to you, etc., etc.

This kind of information can be gathered *even at a distance* from your first geographical preference; indeed you will be surprised at *how much* you can gather at a distance. Nevertheless, we *urge* you to make every

counselor

READ THE THIRD COLUMN ON EACH PAGE
WHEN WORKING WITH **INDIVIDUALS**

instructor

READ THE FOURTH COLUMN ON EACH PAGE
WHEN WORKING WITH **GROUPS**, WORKSHOPS, CONFERENCES, ETC.

THE PROGRAM ELEMENTS IN THIS FIRST COLUMN HELP THE STUDENT IDENTIFY HIS/HER PRIMARY **FUNCTIONAL GOAL** (WHAT)

Goal:
To discover more Contacts and Targets, for your growing files.

student

THE PROGRAM ELEMENTS IN THIS SECOND COLUMN HELP THE STUDENT IDENTIFY HIS/HER PRIMARY **ORGANIZATIONAL GOAL** (WHERE)

effort to visit at least your *top* geographical preference whenever possible, before you get started on your actual job search campaign later. Nothing can be so useful to you as your own personal on-site reconnaissance mission. For details, see Appendix E, Section II. Your Practice Field Survey was preparation for this personal economic survey; go about it in the same way.

Additional suggestions: talk to

a banker (at headquarters in town, not at a branch office)

the reporter on the local paper (the business editor especially)

professors at any nearby colleges, particularly in the business department

the mayor, plus city and county department heads

the heads of Rotary, Kiwanis, and the Lions

ordinary citizens.

Keep careful records of your Survey! Identify *information sources* in your geographical area, that you may want to come back to, later.

Keep files of *Contacts* (individuals) and *Potential Targets* (organizations).

If your job hunt is a year or two off, use your vacation, etc. to visit your (future) home town.

Error:
coming across in your interviews of people 'on-site' as one who is looking for a job. *Avoid this at all costs.*

counselor

READ THE THIRD COLUMN ON EACH PAGE
WHEN WORKING WITH **INDIVIDUALS**

RE-EMPHASIZING. You are trying to learn everything you need to know in order to be able to make intelligent decisions about your life, and effective plans, *later.* Do not hesitate to explain this to those *you* choose to interview.

If job-offers result anyway (as they often do), play it cool. You are:
(1) Pleased
(2) Interested
(3) Going to consider it when the time for such decisions comes.
(4) Definitely going to keep in touch, to let him/her know how your survey progresses.

Then, *do* keep in touch. Give him/her further opportunities to see for him/herself just how bright and extraordinary you are.

instructor

READ THE FOURTH COLUMN ON EACH PAGE
WHEN WORKING WITH **GROUPS**, WORKSHOPS, CONFERENCES, ETC.

Goal:
To further refine and define *your* SPECIFIC requirements for doing your creative, productive best.

THE PROGRAM ELEMENTS IN THIS FIRST COLUMN HELP THE STUDENT IDENTIFY HIS/HER PRIMARY **FUNCTIONAL GOAL** (WHAT)

student

THE PROGRAM ELEMENTS IN THIS SECOND COLUMN HELP THE STUDENT IDENTIFY HIS/HER PRIMARY **ORGANIZATIONAL GOAL** (WHERE)

As you go about your Personal Economic Survey of your prime geographical target area, keep rewriting your Ideal Job Specifications list, adding to it, refining it, etc.

counselor

READ THE THIRD COLUMN ON EACH PAGE
WHEN WORKING WITH **INDIVIDUALS**

instructor

READ THE FOURTH COLUMN ON EACH PAGE
WHEN WORKING WITH **GROUPS**, WORKSHOPS, CONFERENCES, ETC.

c. CONTACTS, TARGETING AND READING are continuing homework assignments, naturally. They should however be emphasized–lest the students forget about them.

3. **CLASSROOM EXERCISES**

a. IDEAL JOB SPECIFICATIONS. An interesting way to get into this subject is for the instructor to bring a number of pages of classified ads from the local (or nearest urban) newspaper. Sunday urban papers (the New York Times, The Washington Post, the Los Angeles Times, etc.) are particularly useful.

Break the class into small groups (5–8 members) and supply them with copies of the classified ads. Tell them they are to spend 10–15 minutes *by themselves* studying the classified ads, to see what kinds of descriptions are given of jobs. e.g.,

"Will be responsible on an individual project basis to provide acceptable and workable solutions in a short period of time to complex problems". Or:

"Non-smoker preferred." Or:

"Must be willing to travel." etc.

Ask each student, while s/he is studying these ads, to circle any *factor* or *element* in an ad that s/he likes (regardless of whether or not s/he likes the whole job and the whole ad). Ask each student to put an X beside any factor s/he particularly dislikes.

After this individual study period, each small group is to begin talking with each other about their circles and their "X"s, together with the reasons Why.

Each group should have a convener or leader, plus someone else who acts as scribe. Large sheets of newsprint should be available to each small group, and on this should be written the learnings of that group. When the discussion of the ads is completed, the question to be faced is: now what does this tell you about the elements you would like to see in an ideal ad–just made for you? ("You may never, of course, see such an ad; but suppose you did?") Put these elements down on the newsprint.

When the small groups reconvene, have each group report to the class

student

THE PROGRAM ELEMENTS IN THIS FIRST COLUMN HELP THE STUDENT IDENTIFY HIS/HER PRIMARY **FUNCTIONAL GOAL** (WHAT)

i·den·ti·fy (ī-den′tə-fī′), ***v.t.*** **[IDENTIFIED (-fīd′), IDENTIFYING], [ML. **identificare;* see IDENTICAL & -FY], 1. to make identical; consider or treat as the same: as, *identify* your interests with ours. 2. to show to be a certain person or thing; fix the identity of; show to be the same as something or someone assumed, described, or claimed. 3. to join or associate closely: as, he has become *identified* with the labor movement. 4. in *psychoanalysis,* to make identification of (oneself) with someone else: often used absolutely.**

THE PROGRAM ELEMENTS IN THIS SECOND COLUMN HELP THE STUDENT IDENTIFY HIS/HER PRIMARY **ORGANIZATIONAL GOAL** (WHERE)

skill (skil), *n.* [ME., discernment, reason; ON. *skil,* distinction, etc., akin to *skilja,* to cut apart, separate, etc.; IE. base **sqel-,* to cut (cf. SHIELD, SHILLING); basic sense "ability to separate," hence "discernment"], 1. great ability or proficiency; expertness: as, his *skill* in mathematics is well known. 2. an art, craft, or science, especially one involving the use of the hands or body; hence, 3. ability in such an art, craft, or science. 4. [Obs.], knowledge; understanding; judgment. *v.i.* [Archaic], to matter, avail, or make a difference: as, what *skills* it that we suffer? —*SYN.* see **art.**

counselor

READ THE THIRD COLUMN ON EACH PAGE
WHEN WORKING WITH **INDIVIDUALS**

instructor

READ THE FOURTH COLUMN ON EACH PAGE
WHEN WORKING WITH **GROUPS**, WORKSHOPS, CONFERENCES, ETC.

their self-discoveries, putting up the sheets of newsprint so that all the class can share—and learn.

THEN describe to the class the Program Element IDEAL JOB SPECIFICATIONS, and ask each of the class members to keep these factors in mind (discovered through their analysis of the classified ads) when they come to write down their own job specifications. Give the rationale for the Ideal Job Specifications at this point.

b. PERSONAL ECONOMIC SURVEY.

(1) If the members of the class are currently employed, or have had some work experience (i.e., are beyond college) divide the class into pairs. In each pair, A and B, begin by *pretending* A is interested in B's organization and employer. B of course knows what A needs to know in order to make an intelligent decision about B's organization and employer. Assume, however, that B is under some private pledge not to reveal any of this information directly to A. He (or she) *is* permitted, however, to tell A *where* and *how* to go about, as an outsider, learning this information. So, during this exercise, B is to tell A this; then they are to reverse roles, pretending that B is interested in A's employer, and A is to tell B how to get the information s/he would need about A's organization.

(2) If the class members are still in school and have allegedly had no significant work history as yet, let them still break into pairs and discuss this question: what information would you need to know about any organization in order to make an intelligent decision about whether it interested you or not. After considerable time devoted to the discussion of that question, *then and only then* get into a discussion of *how* would you go about getting that information? If preferred, this can be done in somewhat larger groups (5–8 class members in each) instead of in pairs.

Also, if preferred, the instructor can (prior to the class session) take sheets of newsprint (one sheet for *each* small group) and divide them in half, in the following manner:

student

THE PROGRAM ELEMENTS IN THIS FIRST COLUMN HELP THE STUDENT IDENTIFY HIS/HER PRIMARY **FUNCTIONAL GOAL** (WHAT)

THE PROGRAM ELEMENTS IN THIS SECOND COLUMN HELP THE STUDENT IDENTIFY HIS/HER PRIMARY **ORGANIZATIONAL GOAL** (WHERE)

bunch (bunch), *n.* [ME. *bunche, bonch,* a hump; akin to MLG. *bunk,* D. *bonk,* Norw. *bunka,* a hump, heap, bunch], 1. a cluster or tuft of things growing together: as, a *bunch* of grapes. 2. a collection of things of the same kind fastened or grouped together, or regarded as belonging together: as, a *bunch* of keys. Abbreviated **bch.** 3. [Rare], a hump. 4. [Colloq.], a group (of people). *v.t. & v.i.* 1. to form or collect into a bunch

clus·ter (klus'tẽr), *n.* [ME.; AS. *clyster, cluster* (akin to north G. dial. *kluster*) with *clys-, clus-* for Gmc. **klut,* base of *clot*], 1. a number of things of the same sort gathered together or growing together; bunch. 2. a number of persons, animals, or things grouped together. *v.i. & v.t.* to gather or grow in a cluster or clusters.

Vital Facts Which Would/Will Be Helpful in Deciding Whether To Investigate an Organizational Target Further	How I Can Go About Gathering Information About These Facts

One sheet should then be given to each small group convener, and when the small-group discussion is ended, these sheets are to be posted at the front of the room. Have additional blank sheets, for groups to pick up if they run out of space; they can always make lines on the second sheet, for themselves.

If all of these exercises are concluded, and class time still remains in this sixth session, you may want to get into the beginning of explaining SKILL-IDENTIFICATION—in order that, next session, you can break into trios without any further delay.

Of course, as we explained in the Second Class Session material, p. 21, you may already have gotten into this explanation at that point, especially if you are dealing with students who are all in mid-life. In which case, continue.

SEVENTH CLASS SESSION

SOME SUGGESTED PROGRAM ELEMENTS

1. **LOOKING BACK**

   a. Homework to be completed by now.

   IDEAL JOB SPECIFICATIONS: check to see how many (show of hands) completed this assignment. Ask for any surprise learnings or insights that came out of the exercise. Invite volunteers to read theirs aloud.

student

THE PROGRAM ELEMENTS IN THIS FIRST COLUMN HELP THE STUDENT IDENTIFY HIS/HER PRIMARY **FUNCTIONAL GOAL** (WHAT)

THE PROGRAM ELEMENTS IN THIS SECOND COLUMN HELP THE STUDENT IDENTIFY HIS/HER PRIMARY **ORGANIZATIONAL GOAL** (WHERE)

Goal:
To identify, out of your work-autobiography, the goodly *number and* perhaps rather surprising (to you) *variety* of marketable skills and qualities that you have.

To break them down into any

13. Skills Identification

The Personal Economic Survey, if thoroughly conducted on-site at your prime geographical target area(s), will convince you that you are not really ready to 'go for broke' quite yet. You will readily perceive how necessary it is for you to have more information about your self and your objectives, before you will know *exactly* what to look for.

Hence we return to your work-autobiography, as though to a gold-mine. Our intention is to

b. Ongoing assignments.

(1) PERSONAL ECONOMIC SURVEY. Has anyone thus far done anything on this? Ask. (Show of hands.) Any learnings? Any stumbling blocks? Any problems?

(2) CONTACTS LIST. Seek to find out how many in the class by this time have over 200 names on their list. Over 300? 400? 500? If people seem to be having trouble getting names, go back over the Contacts List *instructions,* to be sure they understand the list includes *anyone* they know, slightly or well.

(3) TARGETING. "Did anyone in the class read a newspaper or magazine during the past week?" (Show of hands) "Did anyone see any organization or individual that they admired, while reading?" (Show of hands) "Did they cut it out and put it in their targets file?" "Did anyone follow up on such an interest, by writing the organization or individual for further information?" "Or simply to tell the individual how much they admired what they read about him or her?" End this by encouraging the students to do these things, during the coming week. Read. Clip. Follow up. Whether the target is in their chosen geographical preference areas, or not. But most ESPECIALLY if it is.

(4) READING. "Any books, chapters or articles to recommend to the rest of the class?" "Any unusual insights?" "Any helpful ideas you read, that you would like to share with the rest of the class?"

2. LOOKING AHEAD

The homework will be all of the on-going assignments, as above, plus doing skills-identification on their work-autobiography, which will be begun in class now.

3. CLASSROOM EXERCISE

It is assumed each student will have brought her/his work-autobiography with him or her.

The instructor should introduce the subject by covering all the material under SKILLS IDENTIFICATION in this manual—most specifically including Appendix I, in the back of this manual.

essential sub-components.

To examine them in order to establish their validity.

To help you assess their relative value to *you.*

To show you your uniqueness as an individual, which consists (in part) in the fact that only you have these same skills in this exceptional *balance* and *blend.*

student

THE PROGRAM ELEMENTS IN THIS FIRST COLUMN HELP THE STUDENT IDENTIFY HIS/HER PRIMARY **FUNCTIONAL GOAL** (WHAT)

'mine' it for every single skill that you have ever used and demonstrated, at any time in your life. The more thoroughly you do this process, the more you will discover the uniqueness that is You. And therefore the more you will know what the most appropriate job objectives, *for you,* are.

In order to do Skill Identification, it is necessary to have the following:

1. The detailed *work-autobiography,* 50–200 pages or more, which you prepared at the beginning of this course.
2. Some *understanding* of the principle of skill identification, which (hopefully) you picked up earlier, in the Exercises in Appendix C.
3. A *basic vocabulary* in skill identification, in order to prime the pump of *your own* creative (verbal) imagination. This sample vocabulary, along with some Exercises to practice upon, will be found in Appendix I.
4. *Time* subsequently spent going over your work-autobiography, page by page, writing down the skills—in your own words—that you see being used.

Goal:
To increase your self-confidence about your future.
"I can do it, because I did do it."

THE PROGRAM ELEMENTS IN THIS SECOND COLUMN HELP THE STUDENT IDENTIFY HIS/HER PRIMARY **ORGANIZATIONAL GOAL** (WHERE)

Error:
Thinking you need to use (or stay within) the language of the Dictionary of Occupational Titles (people, data, things scales).

counselor

READ THE THIRD COLUMN ON EACH PAGE
WHEN WORKING WITH **INDIVIDUALS**

UNDERLINING. You are to put *your own* labels on your skills, using your own language. You can range as far afield as you wish, and be as creative as you want to be. There is no prescribed formula here, and no prescribed language.

It is preferable to avoid the D.O.T. language when you first start. You may, or may not, want to use it in order to find additional skill-identifications, after your own creative juices have had their field day.

instructor

READ THE FOURTH COLUMN ON EACH PAGE
WHEN WORKING WITH **GROUPS**, WORKSHOPS, CONFERENCES, ETC.

Discuss. Ask if there are any questions. Then do the exercise in Appendix I, III. or any other like it that the instructor cares to substitute. Let volunteers from the class give what skills they see. NOTE WHO IS ANSWERING AT THIS POINT; they will likely be the students who are grasping this process the fastest, and they should be (each of them) put into separate trios (as below), so that each trio has at least one person in it who is catching on fast to this process, and can help others.

Divide the class into trios (3 class members in each group). Let us call the members in each trio, A, B and C. First A and B are to play 'instructor' to C, letting C read off a page or so from his or her work-autobiography, saying what skills s/he sees; and then A and B are to add their own perception of the skills C missed. After five to ten minutes, the roles are to be changed, and B & C are to play 'instructor' to A in the same manner; then C & A are to play instructor to B. This process is to be repeated, continuously revolving between C, A, & B with about 1–10 minutes for each 'segment', as long as class time permits.

student

THE PROGRAM ELEMENTS IN THIS FIRST COLUMN HELP THE STUDENT IDENTIFY HIS/HER PRIMARY **FUNCTIONAL GOAL** (WHAT)

THE PROGRAM ELEMENTS IN THIS SECOND COLUMN HELP THE STUDENT IDENTIFY HIS/HER PRIMARY **ORGANIZATIONAL GOAL** (WHERE)

5. Then getting *someone else* (preferably someone experienced in skill-identification) to go over *your* skills-identification list, to see what ones you missed (few if any of us can do our own skills-identification all by ourselves, because of the screening element in human nature which we alluded to earlier, in "A Summary of Professional Skills" page 182). When all of this is completed you may end up with a list of anywhere between 200-500 skills, or more; though many of these will be duplications—the same skill described in different places in different words, perhaps.

Goal:
To build your self-confidence still further, as you see the *number*, the *range*, and the *depth*, of the transferable, marketable skills *you already possess.*

Since all the requirements, listed above, are at hand, we ask you now to:

a. Practice on the exercises in Appendix I, page 204.

b. Then, begin the skills-identification in your own work-autobiography, page by page, paragraph by paragraph, sentence by sentence.

Goal:
To make the list as broad and comprehensive as possible.

c. When you have done your best, then share it with someone: mate, friend, instructor, or with a small group, in order to pull out additional skills from your autobiography, that you may have missed.

Goal:
To stimulate your own insights, at an even higher level now, as you make this list your own, and to teach that *you* are in full command throughout.

d. When this is completed, read over all the skill-identifications to be sure you can "own" them all; revise, if you wish:

(1) Add any you care to.
(2) Strike out any that you believe, in retrospect, are completely in error. Do not, however, strike out any, simply because you have an overwhelming fit of false modesty, or self-doubt at this point.
(3) Describe any skill more accurately, in your own words, if you can.

counselor

READ THE THIRD COLUMN ON EACH PAGE
WHEN WORKING WITH **INDIVIDUALS**

instructor

READ THE FOURTH COLUMN ON EACH PAGE
WHEN WORKING WITH **GROUPS**, WORKSHOPS, CONFERENCES, ETC.

THE EIGHTH CLASS SESSION
SOME SUGGESTED PROGRAM ELEMENTS

The eighth class session is entirely devoted to continuing the work in trios. However, the membership in the trios should be *rearranged* at this session—putting fast and slow students together in each trio, on the basis of the instructor's observation (during the seventh class session) as to who were the fast learners of this particular process, and who were slower. [If there is someone who is agonizingly slow, pair him or her with *two* fast learners *of this process,* this time around.]

The homework assignment will be: to finish up the skills-identification on their work-autobiography.

> N.B. Where circumstances permit it may be advantageous to meet *all day* as a class (say, on a Saturday or Sunday) and combine the Seventh and Eighth Sessions into one, in order to get the skills-identification done more quickly. We would suggest 9–4, or 10–5, with an hour out for lunch.

IT MUST BE POINTED OUT TO THE CLASS THAT IT WILL BE IMPOSSIBLE TO GO ON TO THE NEXT EXERCISE (CLUSTERING) UNTIL *EACH* STUDENT HAS *COMPLETED* THE SKILLS-IDENTIFICATION, FOR EVERY SINGLE PAGE IN HIS/HER WORK-AUTOBIOGRAPHY. IT IS THEREFORE CRUCIAL THAT EVERYONE COMPLETE THIS HOMEWORK ASSIGNMENT PRIOR TO THE NEXT CLASS SESSION.

It may, accordingly, be necessary to skip a week (in the class meetings) in order to allow the class to complete this work at home. If, by the end of the eighth session (or by the end of the all day session, if one is held) it becomes apparent that *some* students still have a great deal of work to do on the skills-identification, then this step (skipping next week's class, in order to give everyone a chance to catch up) should be taken *without hesitation.*

Goal:
To prepare for clustering, by putting the identifications into easier form for you to use,
AND
To increase your familiarity with the skills, as you go back over all of the old old material once again.
AND
To increase your self-confidence further, as you see the cumulative impressiveness of all your skills *which you have successfully demonstrated in action.*
AND
To aid you in further memorization and *complete internalizing* of these convincing truths about yourself, as you *connect* the skills with the exact moment in time (in your autobiography) when each skill appeared.

student

THE PROGRAM ELEMENTS IN THIS FIRST COLUMN HELP THE STUDENT IDENTIFY HIS/HER PRIMARY **FUNCTIONAL GOAL** (WHAT)

14. Skills Lists

Then please copy all of your skills onto 8½x11" sheets, double-spaced, one entry to a line, DIVIDED INTO TWO LISTS:

First, *your skills.*
Second, *your personal traits or qualities.*

(The difference between the two lists, is explained in the Counselor's column, to the right.)

When copying, there are two rules for you to follow:

1. *Exact* duplicate names for your skills should not be repeated; but *similar* identifications—even of the same skill—*must* be listed.

2. List them in the order they occur, beginning from the beginning, and do not try *in any way* to organize, combine, categorize, or summarize them—nor any other form of arranging . . . *at this point* in the process. When you are done with the listing, check and double-check your original identifications, to be sure there were no inadvertent omissions made, during the copying.

When done, take the second list (the Traits list) and set it aside, for use later. Take the first list, of Skills, in hand, for it is to be your working tool, in our next Exercise.

THE PROGRAM ELEMENTS IN THIS SECOND COLUMN HELP THE STUDENT IDENTIFY HIS/HER PRIMARY **ORGANIZATIONAL GOAL** (WHERE)

Error:
Not dividing skill identifications into two separate lists, as requested.

Error:
Putting down exact duplications.

Error:
Trying to organize these lists in any way, as you are copying.

Error:
Leaving out too many skill identifications just because they seem similar to some other; trying to whittle down the list too much.

counselor

READ THE THIRD COLUMN ON EACH PAGE
WHEN WORKING WITH **INDIVIDUALS**

DEFINITIONS. The difference between skills, vs. traits, vastly oversimplified, is:
(1) *Skills* are functions, or action-oriented statements, usually with a subject or object, expressed or implied: e.g., *project* management. Skills are easily translated into sentences. e.g., I managed a project.
(2) *Traits* are qualities which characterize all that a person does, and usually have no subject or object: e.g., integrity, competitive spirit, etc. They are usually impossible to translate into a sentence, without adding verbs or other thoughts.

WARNING. Premature categorizing will inevitably result in
a. eliminating important stuff, and
b. setting erroneous ways of looking at this stuff, into concrete.

instructor

READ THE FOURTH COLUMN ON EACH PAGE
WHEN WORKING WITH **GROUPS**, WORKSHOPS, CONFERENCES, ETC.

NINTH CLASS SESSION
SOME SUGGESTED PROGRAM ELEMENTS

1. LOOKING BACK

a. *Homework to be completed by now:*

SKILLS-IDENTIFICATION. Ask for a show of hands as to how many have completed it. If *any* have not, serious consideration should be given at that point to this problem. You may want to devote this class-session to working on Skills-Identification further (in trios), with two students who have finished theirs working with one who has not, in each trio. [If this class session *is* devoted to trios, you will of course have to abridge subsequent lesson plans as contained in this manual.]

b. *Ongoing assignments*

(1) PERSONAL ECONOMIC SURVEY
(2) CONTACTS LIST
(3) TARGETING
(4) READING

Ask what the class have been able to do in each of these areas, *if anything* (they may have been too busy working on skills-identification; if so, bravo! On the other hand, some of the faster students may have *also* done something in these areas; and that information is useful as a reminder to the rest of the class that contacts, targeting, reading, and surveying are part of a continuing process, that they need to work at).

2. LOOKING AHEAD

The homework will be: complete the clustering of their skills, which will be begun in class today. If any time is left over, after that, then they are to work on their talking papers.

Goal:
To start putting the pieces back together, by identifying the 'basic building blocks' of your skills, in order to determine what your precise strengths are, and what you have to offer.
And:
To help you see how strong you are, in a whole variety of those clusters or basic building blocks.
And:
To prepare you for writing helpful 'talking papers'.
And:
To enable you to continue adding to these clusters as a part of your whole life planning, for the rest of your life, once you grasp how this process is done.

student

THE PROGRAM ELEMENTS IN THIS FIRST COLUMN HELP THE STUDENT IDENTIFY HIS/HER PRIMARY **FUNCTIONAL GOAL** (WHAT)

15. Clustering of Your Skills

(May also be called 'functional analysis of your transferable skills')

We ask you now to take your skills list and go through a process of arranging these skills into what we might call families, or building blocks, or clusters—that is to say, a series of groupings, each of which has a common theme. Detailed instructions on how to do this Clustering, are to be found in Appendix J. We ask you to work your way through that Appendix, at this point, and then to set about doing the Clustering of your identifiable Skills list. This will take some time and hard thought on your part, but it is crucial to the building of your definition of your own personal primary functional goal.

Do it now, please.

Check over your clustering, when the process is all done:

a. Change any subject headings that you wish.
b. Regroup them into different or smaller clusters, wherever you wish.
c. Add any skills or qualities to any cluster, that you feel should be there, in retrospect.

THE PROGRAM ELEMENTS IN THIS SECOND COLUMN HELP THE STUDENT IDENTIFY HIS/HER PRIMARY **ORGANIZATIONAL GOAL** (WHERE)

Error:
Feeling that there is some 'right' way of doing the clustering, which you may not tumble to.

counselor

READ THE THIRD COLUMN ON EACH PAGE
WHEN WORKING WITH **INDIVIDUALS**

REASSURANCE. You cluster according to your own preferences. There are no categories that you have to fit into, no system that you must embrace at this point.

We are looking for your uniqueness as an individual and part of that uniqueness is expressed not only in the skills and personal traits that you possess, but also in the way that you blend them together. How you perceive them, how you cluster them, is a part of your uniqueness.

If you have no clue whatsoever as to how to go about it, then some of the suggestions in Appendix J may serve as *starters* for you. But, after that, you can go in any direction you want; and you can even go back later, and revise the clusters if—as you get into this process—you begin to perceive more persuasive ways (to YOU) of arranging your skills.

instructor

READ THE FOURTH COLUMN ON EACH PAGE
WHEN WORKING WITH **GROUPS**, WORKSHOPS, CONFERENCES, ETC.

3. **CLASSROOM EXERCISES**

a. Explain the Program Element CLUSTERING OF YOUR SKILLS, together with Appendix J—*in detail and at length.*

b. Questions and discussion from the class.

c. Divide the class into trios again—hopefully different trios from before, and—if you have gotten to know the class well by now, be sure to place students in trios *by assignment,* so that there are good 'mixes' —i.e., students who pick up the process faster, paired off (or trio-d off) with students who pick it up somewhat slower.

d. Each trio should decide for itself *how* it wants to operate. A logical order of things would be as follows:

(1) The three members of each trio checking each other to be sure that all three understand how to begin. (Appendix J, III.A. and B.) It should be emphasized each one *must* be working from the LIST OF SKILLS that s/he made after his/her skills-identification was all completed, not from the list of Personal Traits, which s/he separated out after the Skills-Identification was complete, and certainly not from the work-autobiography directly.

(2) Each of the members of the trio then spending time working by him/herself on their first cluster. Time: 15—30 minutes.

(3) A & B then sitting on either side of C, to check out how s/he is doing—looking over his/her shoulder at his/her skills list to be sure s/he didn't miss any *for that particular cluster.* A & B can only make *suggestions* here. C's judgment, after listening to the suggestions, is final and determinative *for C.*

(4) Reversing step "(3)", with B & C now sitting on either side of A, to check out how s/he is doing.

(5) Reversing step "(3)", now, with A & C sitting on either side of B.

(6) Going back to their individual work for another 15—30 minutes, then repeating steps "(3)"–"(5)".

(7) Repeating "(6)" for the remainder of the class time.

student

THE PROGRAM ELEMENTS IN THIS FIRST COLUMN HELP THE STUDENT IDENTIFY HIS/HER PRIMARY **FUNCTIONAL GOAL** (WHAT)

THE PROGRAM ELEMENTS IN THIS SECOND COLUMN HELP THE STUDENT IDENTIFY HIS/HER PRIMARY **ORGANIZATIONAL GOAL** (WHERE)

Goal:
To break out your each and every asset, separately and completely, in order—

- a –To aid you in making your selection later of those 'building blocks' in which you feel most confident, and which you most enjoy using.
- b –To enable you to develop and master, for life, an absolutely overpowering presentation of your strengths in each cluster or building block, for your use whenever you wish.
- c –To enable you, most particularly, to be prepared to handle yourself in interviews, for the rest of your life, with an unshakeable confidence—since you will know how each skill

16. Talking Papers

Now, take each 'family', cluster, or 'building block' of your skills, in turn, and write a *separate* one or two page (at the very most) Talking Paper (or: Briefing Card) for *each* cluster.

The guidelines for these Talking Papers are as follows:

1. Each Talking Paper is not to be a polished speech, but is rather to be an automatic memory aid—designed to help you to have all the facts clearly marshalled and organized in your mind, regarding each of your skill 'clusters' or 'building blocks'. You do not, therefore, have to spell out everything in detail; but you *do* have to put down enough to insure that you will never forget any fact or experience which could be helpful to you, were you asked (as well you may be) by some prospective employer (or client, if you're dreaming of running your own show) to make a complete presentation to him or her on this particular subject (i.e., your skills in this cluster) during an interview, or elsewhere.

2. So, start with your first cluster category. Read it over. Get it firmly in mind, especially its subject heading. Now, with a fresh sheet of paper in your typewriter (or under your pen) go back through your entire work-autobiography, re-reading it *from the one particular point-of-view of this cluster.* And every experience, training, or whatever, that you have had which is related to and suppor-

Error:
Trying to cut corners (time-wise and work-wise) at this point.

counselor

READ THE THIRD COLUMN ON EACH PAGE
WHEN WORKING WITH **INDIVIDUALS**

EXHORTATION. Don't do it. The throat you cut will be your own.

instructor

READ THE FOURTH COLUMN ON EACH PAGE
WHEN WORKING WITH **GROUPS**, WORKSHOPS, CONFERENCES, ETC.

e. If the class is long, there should of course be an intermission (coffee-break or whatever) at one or two points in this long (and exciting/tiring) process.

f. Ten minutes before the end of the class, explain the Talking Papers assignment—in case any student finishes the clustering at home early on, and wants to begin writing his/her Talking Papers. Emphasize that no Talking Papers can be written until the clustering is completed.

that you claim is related to a true experience of your own, and can handle any objections that any interviewer might throw at you.

• d —To enable you especially to answer such interviewers' questions as: "Exactly what do you know about this subject?" "What has your education and training in it been, and how useful was it?" And: "Can you tell me in detail some of your more significant personal achievements in it?" "What do you think you can accomplish with this particular asset in my organization?" "Why are you so interested in applying it here?"

student

THE PROGRAM ELEMENTS IN THIS FIRST COLUMN HELP THE STUDENT IDENTIFY HIS/HER PRIMARY **FUNCTIONAL GOAL** (WHAT)

tive of this cluster, should get jotted down on that fresh sheet of paper.

a. Be sure to emphasize your successful achievements in this particular cluster while typing your notes (or writing them).

b. Include percentages, dollar figures, and other statistics which measure achievements in your Talking Paper notes, whenever possible.

c. Ignore chronology and time breaks; your object is simply to get everything down that you have ever done, in this particular skill area, regardless of when you did it.

d. Use any system of short-hand that you wish to, so long as your Talking Paper is complete, and *readily intelligible* to You.

3. When you have finished one cluster category to your satisfaction, *forget it* as completely as you can, and take the next cluster—along with a fresh sheet of paper in your typewriter. Read the work-autobiography again, *now with only this cluster in mind,* and proceed as in "2." above. *Give it your best effort, as though it were the only cluster of skills that you possessed.*

a. Do not try to short-circuit this process, in order to save time. The repetition of going back and forth over your work-autobiography may *seem* wasteful at first; but upon reflection, it will occur to you that you are more than indelibly memorizing all your experiences; you are doing something much more profound: internalizing a new concept of yourself.

THE PROGRAM ELEMENTS IN THIS SECOND COLUMN HELP THE STUDENT IDENTIFY HIS/HER PRIMARY **ORGANIZATIONAL GOAL** (WHERE)

Error: Writing this as though it were a series of polished papers to be read by others.

Error: Writing a Talking Paper so illegibly or shorthandedly that even *You* can't figure out later what it says.

Error: Making the Talking Papers interdependent upon each other, so that you can only understand one if you have seen some of the others.

counselor

READ THE THIRD COLUMN ON EACH PAGE
WHEN WORKING WITH **INDIVIDUALS**

UNDERLINING. These papers are for your eyes alone, so you can use whatever form of communication is most helpful to you. The language can be informal, and the thoughts summarized—just as long as You remember all the key points.

These are aids to your memory, more than anything else.

CLARIFICATION. In putting together your Talking Paper for each cluster, you are basically trying to answer just two questions:
1. What do you know about this?
2. What have you done in it?

instructor

READ THE FOURTH COLUMN ON EACH PAGE
WHEN WORKING WITH **GROUPS**, WORKSHOPS, CONFERENCES, ETC.

student

THE PROGRAM ELEMENTS IN THIS FIRST COLUMN HELP THE STUDENT IDENTIFY HIS/HER PRIMARY **FUNCTIONAL GOAL** (WHAT)

THE PROGRAM ELEMENTS IN THIS SECOND COLUMN HELP THE STUDENT IDENTIFY HIS/HER PRIMARY **ORGANIZATIONAL GOAL** (WHERE)

b. You will note overlap and repetition, as you copy down experiences you have used in a previous Talking Paper. Do not try to avoid this, by some alleged time-saving device such as cross-referencing or whatever. All supporting detail for each cluster *must* be included. Each talking paper must be able to stand alone, in your notes and more importantly, in your mind. This is crucial to your future decisions; and should you decide to work for another, this will be essential to your interviews. You never know when this may be the *only* thing you're asked about.

4. When this cluster is done, try to forget it as much as possible, and go on to the next cluster; repeat this process, until every cluster has been covered, with a Talking Paper/Briefing Notes.

5. The next step is to practice each Talking Paper at home. You are not trying to memorize each paper but only to master it; though it will not hurt to commit a few key phrases and statistics to memory (underline them) if you wish.

a. Ask your partner or mate or a friend to critique you on both subject matter and delivery.

b. Or, critique yourself on your oral presentation of each Talking Paper by using a mirror and/or a tape recorder.

Remember, you are trying to answer the typical kinds of questions an interviewer might throw at you:

Goal:
To master each subject (i.e., each cluster of your skills) so fully, that you are completely at ease, as well as flexible, in discussing it; and able to field any and all questions on it, handily, under any circumstances.

Error:
Trying to cut corners in order to save time.

Error:
Trying to avoid overlap and repetition between the Papers.

Error:
Failing to practice your Talking Papers orally.

Error:
Failing to critique your Talking Papers delivery (by your mate or by yourself).

counselor

READ THE THIRD COLUMN ON EACH PAGE
WHEN WORKING WITH **INDIVIDUALS**

instructor

READ THE FOURTH COLUMN ON EACH PAGE
WHEN WORKING WITH **GROUPS**, WORKSHOPS, CONFERENCES, ETC.

NOT TO BE TAUGHT TO OTHERS UNTIL THE INSTRUCTOR HAS FIRST TAKEN THE COURSE HIM (HER) SELF.

student

THE PROGRAM ELEMENTS IN THIS FIRST COLUMN HELP THE STUDENT IDENTIFY HIS/HER PRIMARY **FUNCTIONAL GOAL** (WHAT)

THE PROGRAM ELEMENTS IN THIS SECOND COLUMN HELP THE STUDENT IDENTIFY HIS/HER PRIMARY **ORGANIZATIONAL GOAL** (WHERE)

Goal:
Also, to familiarize yourself with each of your skill clusters, or building blocks, one last time before you choose which of these clusters are most important to you.

"Exactly what do you know about this subject?" "What has your education and training in it been, and how useful was it?" "Can you tell me in complete detail some of your more significant personal achievements in it?" "What do you think you can accomplish with this particular asset, in my organization?" "Why are you interested in applying it here?" You should know the answers to these from your Talking Papers, and practice them. This kind of preparation is necessary even if you never intend to work for anybody else. You *may* still have to convince your prospective customers or clients; and you *surely* must convince yourself, of your skill strengths & experience.

Do it now, please.

Error:
Failing to realize how crucial this preparation may be for your future job-search.

Error:
Thinking that because you may end up as your own employer, you don't need these Talking Papers.

Goal:
To reduce the number of your cluster categories to a manageable number, and in descending order of your own preference, as a prelude to deciding which ones will form

17. Your Top Ten Clusters

We ask you now to assemble all your Talking Papers as if they were a deck of cards. Then take the time to place them in descending order of your own preference, keeping in mind *with equal weight,* two criteria:

1. "In my own heart of hearts, in which of all these cluster categories am I truly most competent?"
2. (With equal weight) "Which one do I really most *enjoy* performing?"

Three alternative methods for doing this prioritizing of your clusters, are described in Appendix K, page 220.

Error:
Trying to prioritize your clusters without having first written your Talking Papers.

counselor

READ THE THIRD COLUMN ON EACH PAGE
WHEN WORKING WITH **INDIVIDUALS**

instructor

READ THE FOURTH COLUMN ON EACH PAGE
WHEN WORKING WITH **GROUPS**, WORKSHOPS, CONFERENCES, ETC.

TENTH CLASS SESSION
SOME SUGGESTED PROGRAM ELEMENTS

1. **LOOKING BACK**

a. Homework to be completed by now.

CLUSTERING OF YOUR SKILLS. Check to see what the class has done about this (show of hands). How many have completed theirs? (If absolutely nobody has, you will then have to decide whether you want to turn this tenth session into just a repetition of the ninth lesson plan (which see); or whether you want to trust that they will get it done during the week anyway. And press on, now.

b. Ongoing assignments. Ask if anyone got so far as to begin working on their Talking Papers? (Show of hands) Any problems? Discuss. (The discussion will be helpful to the rest of the class who may eventually encounter the same problems, otherwise.)

Ask if anyone has had any problems (or victories) with the other ongoing assignments: Personal Economic Survey, Contacts List, Targeting, and Reading. Devote a brief time at best, to this.

DIRECTIONS; WARNING. You cannot fully *feel* the strength of each cluster (or its weakness in your value hierarchy) until you have first written a Talking Paper on it.

EXHORTATION. If you allow what you think you know about 'the marketplace' to influence your decisions at this point, you will

2. **LOOKING AHEAD**

The assignments are:
THE TALKING PAPERS & TOP TEN CLUSTERS
WHAT YOU WOULD LIKE TO ACCOMPLISH
HOW MUCH ARE YOU WORTH?
WHAT NEEDS DOING

Explain each of these Program Elements as contained in this manual to the left, and also in Appendices K (for Top Ten Clusters) and L (for How Much Are You Worth?). The exercises following are designed to then start the class in the homework assignments during class time.

a basis for your Ideal Job Description, and which other ones will be committed to your Asset Inventory, for future reference and use.

student

THE PROGRAM ELEMENTS IN THIS FIRST COLUMN HELP THE STUDENT IDENTIFY HIS/HER PRIMARY **FUNCTIONAL GOAL** (WHAT)

THE PROGRAM ELEMENTS IN THIS SECOND COLUMN HELP THE STUDENT IDENTIFY HIS/HER PRIMARY **ORGANIZATIONAL GOAL** (WHERE)

When your Talking Papers are all arranged in order of preference, your first choice being on top, etc., then please number them—a large #1 at the top of the first Talking Paper, a large #2 at the top of the second Talking Paper, etc. When they are all numbered, please copy the cluster title for each of 'your Top Ten' onto a separate piece of paper. A sample form is found in Appendix K.

Error:
Guessing which clusters might be more 'marketable', and allowing such guesses to influence your choice of priorities.

Goal:
To help you begin to surface your Ultimate Life Goal—what you most want to accomplish with your life before you die.

18. What You Would Like to Accomplish

The next decision you need to make, is: What would you most like to accomplish in the next ten or twenty years—in terms of:

a. productive, enjoyable work?
b. further development of your own skills and capacities?
c. caring for your family? or loved one?

Write as short or long an essay on this subject as you wish.

Do it now, please.

counselor

READ THE THIRD COLUMN ON EACH PAGE
WHEN WORKING WITH **INDIVIDUALS**

abort this entire process—and, what is infinitely more important, you will end up cheating Yourself.

CLARIFICATION. "Enjoy" = get the biggest bang out of doing.

UNDERLINING. The most crucial ones, for the later analysis, and the most important are the first five or six.

STIMULATING YOUR IMAGINATION. Imagine it is ten or twenty years from now, and you see your old instructor in this course (or a friend) once again. S/he asks you, after greetings are exchanged, to tell her/him exactly what you have achieved in these three areas (to the left). Imagine your life has succeeded spectacularly in the intervening years. What would you like to be able to say?

instructor

READ THE FOURTH COLUMN ON EACH PAGE
WHEN WORKING WITH **GROUPS**, WORKSHOPS, CONFERENCES, ETC.

3. CLASSROOM EXERCISES

a. WHAT YOU WOULD LIKE TO ACCOMPLISH. Divide the class into small groups (5–8 members in each small group) and have them discuss these three questions, in turn (spending about 15–25 minutes on each question, *before* proceeding to the next):

(1) If you were given ten million dollars, as a restricted gift, which you could only spend upon yourself (you could not give it away), and as a consequence you did not *have* to work, what would you do with your time

(a) At first?
(b) Later on?

If you were, later on, given another $10,000,000, and you were required to give the money away, what kinds of causes, organizations, charities, etc. would you then give it to?

(2) If you had to write a movie scenario for the life of someone exactly like you, whose life went exactly as yours has up to this point, what would you *then* portray happening to him/her during the next ten years? during the next ten years after that?

(3) What would you hope would happen to you in the next ten or twenty years, in the way of work, in the way of developing your skills,

student

THE PROGRAM ELEMENTS IN THIS FIRST COLUMN HELP THE STUDENT IDENTIFY HIS/HER PRIMARY **FUNCTIONAL GOAL** (WHAT)

THE PROGRAM ELEMENTS IN THIS SECOND COLUMN HELP THE STUDENT IDENTIFY HIS/HER PRIMARY **ORGANIZATIONAL GOAL** (WHERE)

Goal:
To know what your bargaining parameters will be (including your bottom limit) during salary negotiations later.
Also:
To gain some idea of the level at which you will need to be conducting your job search within your Ultimate Target organizations.

19. How Much Are You Worth?

You need to deal also with your decisions about that subject called money, remuneration, bread, or whatever. (Write this out, please.)

1. *What is your rock-bottom, barebones budget for just one year?* That is to say, if worst came to absolute worst, what is the least amount on which you could keep yourself and your loved one(s) operating, decently but frugally, for just twelve months?

(Assume you had no provision for the future, such as savings, to draw upon during this period; and disregard any 'outside income' such as your mate's earnings, inheritances, dividends from stocks, rent from properties, retirement pay, or any other income which really ought not to have to bear the burden of your daily living.)

(It may be that you do not have the slightest intention of ever having to scrimp by on so little, but even so it *is* essential for you to know what a pure subsistence budget for you would look like, just in case.)

Error:
Not knowing what your bargaining parameters are, so that you later inadvertently settle for something below what you can actually live on.

in the way of caring for your family? How does this differ (if it does) from your answers to (1) and (2) above? And if it does, why?

b. Have each small group subsequently report back to the larger class the *variety* of answers which that group turned up (without necessarily attaching the answers to *particular* persons within that group).

c. HOW MUCH ARE YOU WORTH? Have each student work individually on the questions given in the Program Element HOW MUCH ARE YOU WORTH? by him/herself for twenty minutes. Then divide the class into trios, and discuss. Instruct the trios before they go off that they are *particularly* to check out students who are evaluating themselves at too low an economic level (a student may *choose* the subsistence route ultimately, but our hope is that s/he will choose it because of his/her philosophy about life-style, as one of *two possible alternatives* s/he *could* legitimately opt for; rather than choosing subsistence because s/he feels that's all s/he *is* worth).

Have each trio then discuss their philosophy about money, and their feelings about their own present life-style. Is it too rich? Is it too poor? (according to *their* lights; no one else's.)

student

THE PROGRAM ELEMENTS IN THIS FIRST COLUMN HELP THE STUDENT IDENTIFY HIS/HER PRIMARY **FUNCTIONAL GOAL** (WHAT)

THE PROGRAM ELEMENTS IN THIS SECOND COLUMN HELP THE STUDENT IDENTIFY HIS/HER PRIMARY **ORGANIZATIONAL GOAL** (WHERE)

2. *On the other hand, what do you think your peak salary should be, and when (at what age) do you feel you should (and hopefully, will) attain it?* This is under ideal conditions, of course.

3. Having thus established your economic floor and ceiling, the next logical question deals with the inbetween. *How much do you really believe your talents and services should be worth now (right now)—assuming you could operate at your most productive and enjoyable level?*

Error:
Not knowing what you are really worth, and so, later convincing an interviewer you don't know what things cost.

Goal:
To get you to start high enough, so that you will be able to be at your own productive best—working with those who are your peers in ability.

4. Taking all of the foregoing into account, *if you were to seek another job in the near future (or your first job), what starting salary would you* like *to ask for?*

5. And: *what amount would you reasonably expect to get?* If it is different from your answer to 4 above, please discuss your reasons for this.

(Appendix L may help you in thinking through your answers to these questions.)

Error:
Being overcome by modesty, and putting your sights too low, even for planning purposes at this stage of the game.

Goal:
To help surface whatever your *real* interests might be, for the future, without running into your mental limits concerning your

20. What Needs Doing?

In preparation for your ultimate decision about *what* you want to do the most, please describe, briefly or at length, as you please, *what specific significant accomplishments* BY OTHERS *would you most like to see brought to fruition during your lifetime?*

counselor

READ THE THIRD COLUMN ON EACH PAGE
WHEN WORKING WITH **INDIVIDUALS**

instructor

READ THE FOURTH COLUMN ON EACH PAGE
WHEN WORKING WITH **GROUPS**, WORKSHOPS, CONFERENCES, ETC.

GUIDELINES FROM EXPERIENCE. If you have no idea whatsoever what your talents are worth on the current market, you may wish to know that of all those who have taken this course (i.e., completed this process successfully) over fifteen years, some have started as high as $45,000 per year; but the average has been $14,000. $20,000 has proved in the past to be the magic barrier (like the sound barrier) for *most* students, though not all. This however will change upward, as inflation continues.

HELPING YOU GET RID OF MENTAL BARRIERS. We learned long ago that asking students pointblank to list all the many kinds of activities which could possibly interest them, produced only blank stares or hesitant, incomplete answers—at best. But coming at this subject by asking what you want to see *others* get done, and then asking "would you

d. WHAT NEEDS DOING? Divide the class into small groups (5–8 people in each). Have them *brainstorm* the question: What accomplishments would you like to see *others* bring to fruition, within *your* lifetime? What problems of this country or the world would you like to see solved?

Brainstorming means that ideas must be made as suggestions, and copied down on sheets of newsprint, as fast as possible—*without any criticism or evaluation* as the suggestions are being made. Class members

own ability to participate.
And:
To help nail down any hidden goals you may have for your life.
And:
To help you see that *a job* is "an attempt to answer some problem or need".

student

THE PROGRAM ELEMENTS IN THIS FIRST COLUMN HELP THE STUDENT IDENTIFY HIS/HER PRIMARY **FUNCTIONAL GOAL** (WHAT)

What major (or minor) problems of this country or the world would you like to see solved before you die? After each accomplishment that you list, please state: would *you* like to assist and participate in achieving it *if you could?* Why? Or if not, why not?

Some students prefer to get at the above question by raising it in its negative form; i.e., what *bugs* you about the world today, and what would you like to see done about it?

THE PROGRAM ELEMENTS IN THIS SECOND COLUMN HELP THE STUDENT IDENTIFY HIS/HER PRIMARY **ORGANIZATIONAL GOAL** (WHERE)

Error
When discussing whether you would like to assist, or not, allowing what you think you 'know for a fact' as to reasons why you couldn't even hope to be involved, to ultimately influence your answer.

Error:
Prematurely disqualifying yourself because of your feeling that you would not be accepted into the effort, for any of the usual boneheaded 'personnel' reasons.

counselor

READ THE THIRD COLUMN ON EACH PAGE
WHEN WORKING WITH **INDIVIDUALS**

like to be involved in *that?*" seems to get around this kind of mental block. Maybe you can be, and maybe you can't; we can decide that *later.* But, for now: dare to dream.

PRACTICAL AIDS. Indicate the *degree* of your interest: contributing a few dollars a year, actively following their accomplishments in articles, news and books, or helping to solve it yourself (do you *want* to; not, at this stage, *can* you).

instructor

READ THE FOURTH COLUMN ON EACH PAGE
WHEN WORKING WITH **GROUPS**, WORKSHOPS, CONFERENCES, ETC.

can 'piggyback' on ideas, making suggestions that are variations on previous ideas, or further developments of them. But no comments such as "I disagree" or "I don't think that's a very good idea" are permitted.

When the creative juices have come to an end, go back over the ideas on the board and by a show of hands within the group see how many believe each idea, in turn, is important to solve. Have each member of the group copy down, on *his/her own sheet* of 8½ x 11" paper, any issue or accomplishment that he/she votes for.

Then go around the circle (in the group) and have each person read off one item from his/her own personal list, and say whether or not s/he would like to be involved in helping accomplish This, or solve This, *in any way*—by contributing money to it, by volunteering for it, by making it a part of their life's work—whatever.

When the class reconvenes as a whole, ask for sample concerns that were raised in each group. Then suggest to the class that they go back and look at their earlier exercise of WHAT YOU WOULD LIKE TO ACCOMPLISH, to see where they stated they would give their $10,000,000 away to—to see if *this* suggests any issues or concerns that they omitted in this present exercise. Upon this note, the session is ended.

It is crucial that the Talking Papers and Top Ten Clusters be done before this next assignment; therefore it may be necessary to let an extra week go by before this next class session. One of the best ways of testing this is simply to ask the class if they think they can get the Talking Papers, and the subsequent clustering of those Talking Papers (or prioritizing of them) done within the time before the next class session. If they say No, then we advise you to give them an extra week, and postpone next week's class session.

student

THE PROGRAM ELEMENTS IN THIS FIRST COLUMN HELP THE STUDENT IDENTIFY HIS/HER PRIMARY **FUNCTIONAL GOAL** (WHAT)

THE PROGRAM ELEMENTS IN THIS SECOND COLUMN HELP THE STUDENT IDENTIFY HIS/HER PRIMARY **ORGANIZATIONAL GOAL** (WHERE)

Goal:
To define where, at the present time, you see your life ultimately going; even though your vision about this is subject to change, later.

21. Your Ultimate Life Goal

In the light now of your careful review of the answers you gave to all of the foregoing exercises, write out just exactly *what you most want to accomplish with your life before you die.* (Some students find it useful to imagine they are writing their obituary as they *wish* it might appear, at the end of their lives.)

Error:
Thinking that goals 'lock you in' to some path, when you want to remain flexible.

Goal:
To define precisely how, where, with whom and through the use of exactly which of your greatest skills,

22. Your Immediate Job Objective

Here is where all the work you have done thus far on identifying your primary functional goal, on the one hand, and on identifying your primary organizational goal on the other hand, is drawn together, to form your specific immediate objective—your first planned step, after all this work, towards the eventual attainment of your Ultimate Life Goal.

counselor

READ THE THIRD COLUMN ON EACH PAGE WHEN WORKING WITH **INDIVIDUALS**

instructor

READ THE FOURTH COLUMN ON EACH PAGE WHEN WORKING WITH **GROUPS**, WORKSHOPS, CONFERENCES, ETC.

ELEVENTH CLASS SESSION

SOME SUGGESTED PROGRAM ELEMENTS

1. **LOOKING BACK**

a. Homework to be completed by now.

TALKING PAPERS & TOP TEN CLUSTERS. Ask for show of hands as to how many completed these. If few, ask how many of their talking papers they did get done (you might put the numbers—*without* any names of students—up on the blackboard or on a sheet of newsprint, in order to get the overall picture clearly). If the numbers are all small, you've got a problem. (See the paragraph in the box, page 91.)

b. Ongoing homework assignments.

PERSONAL ECONOMIC SURVEY, CONTACTS LIST, TARGETING, READING. Any new developments, learnings, surprises, problems encountered, or whatever? (Give the students time to think and answer, before hurrying on.)

EXPLANATION. Goals can always be adapted, changed or completely discarded as time goes on. This is only a statement of how you see the future Now—at this moment. And—incidentally—people get much more locked into inflexible postures when they have no goals.

2. **LOOKING AHEAD**

a. Your homework assignment is to write out your Ultimate Life Goal, and then—since you now have put together a comprehensive information data-bank about yourself, your assignment is to put it all in some kind of synthesis via YOUR IMMEDIATE JOB OBJECTIVE.

The order in which you should explain YOUR IMMEDIATE JOB OBJECTIVE is, first, the Program Element columns (to the left), then the section on "Job Titles", with diagram, and the rest of Appendix M. Or, if you prefer, weave back and forth between these elements—just so you get them all in, in some kind of *logical* order. Ask then for questions, please.

In *Parachute*, students must read chapter Seven, before the next class.

strongest personal qualities and other personal assets you intend to begin working step by logical step towards reaching your Ultimate Life Goal, using your own list of Top Ten Skills (clusters) as your basic working material.

student

THE PROGRAM ELEMENTS IN THIS FIRST COLUMN HELP THE STUDENT IDENTIFY HIS/HER PRIMARY **FUNCTIONAL GOAL** (WHAT)

THE PROGRAM ELEMENTS IN THIS SECOND COLUMN HELP THE STUDENT IDENTIFY HIS/HER PRIMARY **ORGANIZATIONAL GOAL** (WHERE)

The heart of the exercise is taking your top ten skill choices, and analyzing each in turn to identify your functional and organizational goals which—when combined together—form your Objective.

But this analysis of your top ten skill choices *must* be done in the light of everything you have already learned, or articulated, about Yourself in this course.

Accordingly, we ask you to do the following, step-by-step procedure:

1. Begin by taking the time (several hours if necessary) to review, read and reflect upon *everything* you have written thus far in this program. You will want to pay *especial* attention to the following Program Elements:

   a. Your Future Accomplishments - what you said you wanted to accomplish in the next ten years.

   b. What Needs Doing, or What Bugs You in the World - what you said you would like to see others accomplish, especially the things in which you would like to participate, or assist, during your lifetime.

   c. Your Ultimate Life Goal - what you said you want to accomplish with your life, before you die.

But *all* of the other exercises—Ideal Job Specifications, Your Preferred People Environments, Your Ideal Starting Salary, etc. should also be read, reviewed and reflected upon. Nothing you have written should be omitted in your review at this point.

2. Your next step will be to analyze your top ten skills (clusters), but this analysis must proceed now *in the light of* all that you have just reviewed. If your memory is super-excellent, you may be able to keep all of this juggled in your head. If your memory is normal, we would advise you to use some chart, such as that which you will find on page 224 in this manual. (In its present size, it may not be completely useful—so we suggest you reproduce it on a large piece of paper, such as shelf-paper.) It gives you a framework that ensures you will keep everything in front of you, as you analyze your top ten skills.

3. Write out *the full-name* or cluster of your top ten (not just the heading or title), in order. (*Occasionally,* where you feel your eleventh and twelfth skills are integrally related to the top ten, you *may* want to add them to your list at this point.)

Error:
Trying to assemble your job objective without first having done all the assignments which form 'the ingredients' for this synthesis.

Error:
trying to analyze your top ten skill clusters all by themselves, apart from all the other decisions you have made in this course.

Error:
Writing out only the most abbreviated descriptions of each cluster.

counselor

READ THE THIRD COLUMN ON EACH PAGE
WHEN WORKING WITH **INDIVIDUALS**

WARNING. This is a synthesis of a number of diverse elements, and therefore it is crucial that you should have all the elements at hand before you attempt this synthesis. Otherwise, it's like trying to make bread without having all the ingredients—like flour, or milk, or yeast. You'll get a very different product, as a result. So here. This is a comprehensive information system about You as an individual, and you need all the elements of that information system gathered here, for this exercise.

MOTIVATION. The strength and ultimate success of your forthcoming active search campaign will largely depend upon the thoroughness and accuracy of your analysis in this section of your program—and this in turn depends, of course, upon how diligently you did the earlier parts of the program, which furnish the raw materials for your analysis now.

instructor

READ THE FOURTH COLUMN ON EACH PAGE
WHEN WORKING WITH **GROUPS**, WORKSHOPS, CONFERENCES, ETC.

3. CLASSROOM EXERCISES

a. ULTIMATE LIFE GOAL. Divide the class into small groups (5—8 members in each group) and have them discuss "What I Most Want to Accomplish with My Life Before I Die". Or, let each of them individually write out an imaginary "dream" obituary for themselves (time: 20 minutes), and then convene into small groups, to read the 'obits' aloud and discuss what strikes the other members of the group about each 'obit', in turn.

(If the creative juices are stymied by this assignment, let them write up 'a bad obituary' (what they hope *won't* be said) for themselves; and then, after writing it, write up one which is just the reverse of the bad one. This will, hopefully, get the creative imagination going in each student. Then discuss in small groups.)

b. YOUR IMMEDIATE JOB OBJECTIVE. The instructor might want to have large sheets of shelf-paper (or newsprint) available for each student, and let him/her copy the diagram on page 224 in this manual, considerably enlarged, onto that sheet of shelf-paper or newsprint.

Have each individual, then, spend some time individually copying into the circles of that diagram the various decisions that s/he has already made, in this course. (The circle on Ultimate Life Goal will, of course, stay blank until the homework assignment on that subject is completed.)

Encourage each individual to begin to draw arrows on his or her diagram then, where s/he sees connections or relationships between various circles or elements.

It may be desirable to have all of this take place in Trios, so that anybody who doesn't know where to look for this material in his/her previous course work, etc. will have some help.

Ask each student to remember their trio, and begin with that same trio the next session.

student

THE PROGRAM ELEMENTS IN THIS FIRST COLUMN HELP THE STUDENT IDENTIFY HIS/HER PRIMARY **FUNCTIONAL GOAL** (WHAT)

THE PROGRAM ELEMENTS IN THIS SECOND COLUMN HELP THE STUDENT IDENTIFY HIS/HER PRIMARY **ORGANIZATIONAL GOAL** (WHERE)

Goal:
To identify the one specific skill (cluster) you most want to stress, in combination with any other, and supported by your other choices of skills (clusters).

4. Go down the list, beginning with the top skill (cluster), and analyze each (cluster) in turn. The questions you will want to raise about each skill (cluster), as you go, include the following:

a. Is this skill (cluster) able to stand–alone, or in combination with one or more of the other top ten–as your primary functional goal, stated either as a job title (very rarely) or in descriptive terms? Cf. Appendix M for examples.

b. Or is this skill (cluster) one which belongs in a secondary, rather than primary, role functionally, because it is:

(1) An overly-general skill (cluster) which can be used in almost any organization or occupation, and therefore must be temporarily set aside, to be employed in a strong supporting role later (though it may, even at this point, give definition of the *level* that you should be shooting for).

(2) Too specialized and particular a skill, and not one you would want as your primary functional goal–perhaps because it is too narrow, or at too low a level; though, again, it may be useful in a secondary supporting role later?

c. Or, is this skill (cluster) a kind of 'odd man out'–because it doesn't really fit with any of the other top ten?

Error:
Leaping too soon to seize upon a cluster as your functional or organizational objective, without first looking at all of your top ten clusters–in order to get the overall picture.

Goal:
To help you see that your uniqueness as an individual consists not in any one skill that you may possess, but in the BLEND of them all; and to help you see that this blend

a – expands the scope of your job objective considerably;

b –increases the challenge and interest of any job you might define as a result; and

c –raises the income that you may consequently ask for.

Having made the above decisions about that skill (cluster) from a *functional* point of view, what does it now seem to you to say about your primary *organizational* goal–that place or places (identified usually in descriptive terms which *could* fit a number of targets) in which you would most prefer to do what you want to do–either as an employee, or as self-employed? Cf. Appendix M for examples.

We recommend you write down your thoughts about each of your top ten, as you analyze them in turn the first time around.

5. Note the affinities and relationships that exist among your top ten skills (clusters)–draw lines between them, if that helps you to visualize them better. Which skills (clusters) seem to be intimately related to one another, so that those two (or three, or whatever) almost seem to form one super-cluster? Look also at the surrounding circles on the chart you have drawn, and study the other raw materials you have so vividly summarized there. Do any of these, also, seem related to particular skills (clusters)–elaborating upon them, or focussing them, or whatever? Again, draw lines on the chart to link them up, and demonstrate visually this relationship. You are, of course, applying the clustering technique once again. But this represents your Final Clustering, as you seek to reduce the basic number of your 'building blocks' down to an ever more readily

Error:
Not seeking linkages and larger clusters.

counselor

READ THE THIRD COLUMN ON EACH PAGE
WHEN WORKING WITH **INDIVIDUALS**

MAKING ALTERNATIVES CLEAR. You can describe your functional goal either:

a) as *a job title.* This is used very rarely. Cf. the rationale, in the back of this manual. But it is *sometimes* advisable if it accurately and universally described precisely what you want to do, enjoy doing, and do well. e.g., Director of Plant and Engineering Services.

b) in *descriptive terms.* See Appendix M for examples. You can leave this decision until you finish your job objective analysis.

Your organizational goal can be stated with equal clarity and success in either of two ways, also:

a) Rarely, by naming a specific organization, or division thereof. A big gamble!

b) Most often, a set of targets described in detail but not by name (cf. Appendix M).

UNDERLINING. This whole process is a clustering one, and if done with thoroughness, becomes synergistic (the result is more than the sum of its parts).

instructor

READ THE FOURTH COLUMN ON EACH PAGE
WHEN WORKING WITH **GROUPS**, WORKSHOPS, CONFERENCES, ETC.

(Ask each student to fold the shelf-paper or newsprint sheet so that it tucks inside their notebook, and caution them to be SURE to bring that paper or sheet with them the next session.)

c. **OPTIONAL EXERCISE.** You may want to ask for volunteers among the class members who will make it their business to go visit either the federal/state, or private employment agencies, before the next class session.

These volunteers should be students who are rather well aware of what their immediate job objective is to be.

They are to pick any agencies they wish (with the proviso that they are not to visit any which serve up a 'registration form' that is really a contract obligating the student to pay a fee in advance for services; if this happens, tell them—as soon as they read it, and before they sign it—to walk out of there).

They are to present their objective simply and honestly and request the agency's suggestions as to the kinds of places where they might go.

They are to be honest about their background and qualifications, and if the agency asks if they have ever done 'this' before, they are to admit 'no' *if* the answer in truth *is* 'no'. Etc.

After they get out, they are to write down the general outline of the whole procedure and interview they ran into for reporting next session.

manageable figure, while—in the process of combining or clustering them—you gain a strengthening kind of synergistic effect, so that (hopefully) the whole will be more than the sum of its parts.

6. If you have been able to fill in the chart so as to take a stab at your primary functional goal, and some guess as to how you might define your primary organizational goal, you are then (and only then) ready to try the first tentative draft of your Specific Immediate Objective. There are several suggestions you might wish to keep in mind, while doing so:

a. Six lines should probably be the maximum length for your work objective, *if* you have a ¾" margin on both sides of 8½x11 paper.

b. Your objective should *blend,* insofar as possible, *selections* from all the pertinent clusters in your top ten, arranged in this order: primary *functional* goal (or blend), primary *organizational* goal, *strong* supporting skills, and then *secondary* supporting skills. See Appendix M for examples.

c. Its form should be succinct and compact, in *some such* structure as the following:
Post as (OR Challenging) ______________________________ post
in my own organization/shop OR
with (leading) ______________________ firm/institution/organization
(seeking to ______________________________)
where/in which/requiring ______________________________
unique ______________________________ knowledge,
(broad) experience ______________________________,
(proven/demonstrated) skills in ______________________________
____
____
____
which can be (fully) used/utilized to (the fullest) advantage (preferably where strong background/interest in ______________________________
can also be additional assets).

This form, of course, is only a suggestion, though it has proved over the years to be one which enables all relevant information to be included, in a briefer format than any other.

Error: Making your objective so long, that it no longer performs its assigned function of being a 'precis' or summary.

7. Where a student enjoys a strong combination of functional skills which are equally appropriate to two different fields in which s/he is almost *equally interested,* it is perfectly feasible and legitimate to write up *two* different objectives, rearranging the skills in their order of appropriate priority,—so long as you stay *honest* by keeping within the skill- and desire-definitions which you have labored so hard to establish in this course. (It would not, of course, be kosher to

counselor

READ THE THIRD COLUMN ON EACH PAGE
WHEN WORKING WITH **INDIVIDUALS**

instructor

READ THE FOURTH COLUMN ON EACH PAGE
WHEN WORKING WITH **GROUPS**, WORKSHOPS, CONFERENCES, ETC.

tar·get (tär′git), *n.* [ME.; OFr. *targette*, dim. of *targe*, a shield; see TARGE], 1. originally, a small shield, especially a round one. 2. a round, flat .le. 6. something resembling a target in shape or use, as the sliding sight on a surveyor's leveling rod, a disk-shaped signal on a railroad switch, the metallic surface (in an X-ray tube) upon which the stream of cathode rays impinge and from which X rays emanate, etc. Abbreviated **t.**

Goal:
To continue altering your view of yourself: you are no longer one who has come out of your previous field. You *are* already in the field that you are now aiming at, because you *already* possess all the functional skills necessary. You can pick up "the job content skills" rather quickly.
Also:
To teach you that how you see yourself is determinative of how others see you.

attempt to alter your record just to make a few Brownie points somewhere.) A second objective can also be perfectly proper if you want to aim your functional skills at a different kind of organization; in this case you would simply change that one part of your objective, leaving the rest as it was in your first objective.

8. Rewrite your Objective as often as you need to, until *you* are totally satisfied with it. You are the ultimate judge, and you alone. Though you are encouraged, of course, to bounce it off the sympathetic ears of your mate, loved one, or friend.

9. Start adapting your thinking about yourself to the world (fields of interest) that you are proposing to enter.

   a. View yourself as one *who already is* what you are claiming to be, in your Objective. Your relationship to others already in this field is that of a peer; you are not in any way subordinate to them.

   b. Learn how your new peers think and act in *your* field. Go to the library and read interviews (in periodicals and elsewhere) which your peers have given in the past. Pay particular attention to their courtesies and customs as well as their language.

   c. If there are books in this field, and you have not already read them, get at it! If there are journals or periodicals, subscribe! And look up back issues in the library, so as to familiarize yourself quickly with what has been happening in this field. Be willing to spend quite a bit of time on this!

Error:
Feeling that the objective you want so much to aim at, requires you to exaggerate or falsify your past experience to look like more than you've really had.

Error:
Still thinking of yourself as 'student', 'engineer', 'military man', 'clergyman', 'housewife' or whatever you were before you took this course.

counselor

READ THE THIRD COLUMN ON EACH PAGE
WHEN WORKING WITH **INDIVIDUALS**

RE-EDUCATION. You already *are* whatever it is you are aiming at, in your immediate objective, because you have the equipment the job requires, based on your past use of functional skills, and you are problem-oriented (pp. 118-119 in *Parachute*) and therefore a problem-solver, which not only puts you equal to your peers in your new field but even ahead of many of them.

instructor

READ THE FOURTH COLUMN ON EACH PAGE
WHEN WORKING WITH **GROUPS**, WORKSHOPS, CONFERENCES, ETC.

Twelfth Class Session

TWELFTH CLASS SESSION
SOME SUGGESTED PROGRAM ELEMENTS

1. LOOKING BACK

a. Homework to be completed by now. If the ULTIMATE LIFE GOAL exercise and YOUR IMMEDIATE JOB OBJECTIVE are done by this session, fine. (Ask for a show of hands.) It is permissible to have the OBJECTIVE continue as homework until next time. Ask, however, what problems are being encountered; and let other members of the class, where possible, answer such questions.

Goal:
To cut your big research job (of the hundreds of organizations active in your general field) down to size, and to learn how to keep cutting it down further.

Goal:
To identify those organizations or group activities which you want to investigate further.

Goal:
To learn how to gather information about them and their problems, so that you can draw up a logical plan of approach to those few places that you decide you would like to work with.

THE PROGRAM ELEMENTS IN THIS FIRST COLUMN HELP THE STUDENT IDENTIFY HIS/HER PRIMARY **FUNCTIONAL GOAL** (WHAT)

student

THE PROGRAM ELEMENTS IN THIS SECOND COLUMN HELP THE STUDENT IDENTIFY HIS/HER PRIMARY **ORGANIZATIONAL GOAL** (WHERE)

23. Systematic Targeting

Under "First Step in Targeting" earlier in this course, you began to accumulate information about a number of *Potential Organizational Targets,* in order to learn whether or not they merited further investigation for *your* purposes.

Now that you have finished your Specific Immediate Objective, it is time to go back over these P.O.T.s and separate them into two categories:

1. Those which failed your tests or criteria: throw away the info on them, or transfer to a "General Interest File" for possible future reference.

2. Those which merit closer examination for your purposes. *Promote* these to "Live Organizational Targets".

LIVE ORGANIZATIONAL TARGETS

1. *Definition:* these are the group activities which you will actively investigate further until you know enough about them to decide whether or not they should be included in your final category (as explained below) of Ultimate Organizational Targets.

2. *Mechanics:* a combination of 5 by 8 file cards, backed up by file folders, has proved most useful to students in the past. On each card put the essential details about a group activity or organization that interests you. Key the cards to back-up file folders, in

counselor

READ THE THIRD COLUMN ON EACH PAGE
WHEN WORKING WITH **INDIVIDUALS**

DEFINITION. This whole process of targeting is necessary, regardless of what kind of work you are aiming toward.

If you want to be self-employed, then 'targets' are places which might buy from you.

If you want to be a consultant, then 'targets' are places which might need your services.

If you want to work for someone, then of course 'targets' are for you places where you might enjoy working, because they are pursuing your interests and fit your ideal job specifications perhaps.

DIRECTIONS. Information which might go on each file card, for each organization or group activity:
Name, address, phone for headquarters; names and titles of top executives; brief sketch, activities and purpose; major products or services; territories covered or publics served; principal customers; last year's volume; number of employees; and any other information that is of interest to you, according to your own criteria.

instructor

READ THE FOURTH COLUMN ON EACH PAGE
WHEN WORKING WITH **GROUPS**, WORKSHOPS, CONFERENCES, ETC.

b. On-going homework assignments.
PERSONAL ECONOMIC SURVEY
CONTACTS LIST
TARGETING
READING
have probably been slumbering during this period, what with the pressure put upon the students to concentrate on the skills-identification, listing, clustering, talking papers, prioritizing, and specific objective exercises. However, some members of the class *may* have gotten so caught up in some of these other processes that they haven't been able to resist giving time to them. If so, ask them to share their learnings, surprises, problems, etc. with the class. If other members of the class can handle any problems that are arising—for some—fine!

2. **LOOKING AHEAD**

a. Any homework previously assigned, such as YOUR IMMEDIATE JOB OBJECTIVE ought to be completed, if it has not been already, by the next class session.

b. Present to the class, as an ongoing assignment, the Program Element SYSTEMATIC TARGETING (to the left). After you have explained it in detail, illustrate it with the material in Appendix N, in the back of this manual. For homework, each student is to spend two—four hours working on Targeting, either within or outside of his/her prime geographical preference area. This may involve writing to various information sources within that geographical area (if it is at some distance), or visiting some information sources—e.g., the Chamber of Commerce, and other places designated in Appendix E—if the prime geographical area is nearby. It may involve actively reading magazines and newspapers and trade periodicals in his/her chosen field to see what group activities look interesting,,, etc. A checklist (of the actual steps taken) should be kept, together with an account of how much time was devoted to each step in this Targeting process.

Goal:
To continue to cast a very wide net indeed, so that no intriguing possibility can escape your attention, even as—at the same time—you continue to narrow down the field.

THE PROGRAM ELEMENTS IN THIS FIRST COLUMN HELP THE STUDENT IDENTIFY HIS/HER PRIMARY **FUNCTIONAL GOAL** (WHAT)

student

THE PROGRAM ELEMENTS IN THIS SECOND COLUMN HELP THE STUDENT IDENTIFY HIS/HER PRIMARY **ORGANIZATIONAL GOAL** (WHERE)

which you can keep more lengthy background items: annual reports, magazine clippings, brochures, etc.

3. *Scope of your research:* big business corporations (keep one card and folder for *each* division or department within it, that interests you); small business firms; not-for-profit institutions of all kinds; foundations; professional societies; voluntary associations; federal/state/local government agencies; educational institutions; study groups; entrepreneurial activities or avenues of self-employment that interest you.

4. *Casual information gathering:* Continue to clip every item about any form of activity which concerns itself with whatever really interests you, as each item happens to come your way in newspapers, magazines, journals, etc.; add to the appropriate folder.

5. *Active systematic information gathering:* For these Live Organizational Targets of yours, begin seeking out every bit of additional information you can possibly discover about each one. The principle is unvarying: no matter what field you are interested in, there are masses of information available on it, *if only* you will look for them.

6. *Side benefit: contacts:* An invaluable side benefit as you actively seek information is that you will inevitably be making additional knowledgeable friendly contacts, who could be helpful to you in various says (potential clients, referrals, etc.) later. Every single such name should be going onto your contacts list.

Error:
Trying to keep this sort of information just in your head, without going to the trouble of setting up files, etc. (Inevitably thus overlooking some intriguing possibilities.)

Error:
Introducing yourself as a jobseeker.

Error:
Feeling that there is no way that you as an individual can get the information you need or want.

counselor

READ THE THIRD COLUMN ON EACH PAGE
WHEN WORKING WITH **INDIVIDUALS**

PRACTICAL AIDS. There are many ways and many places where the information you need, can be found:

1. Writing or telephoning the activity or organization and asking for a copy of their latest brochure, booklet, annual report and anything else they have for public distribution.
2. Visiting their headquarters and asking to be shown around as *an interested citizen* who wants to know more about what they're doing.
3. Asking your friends what they happen to know about the activity or organization, and/or if they can get additional information for you.
4. Asking your friendly librarian how to use all the major reference works such as Standard & Poor, Thomas, etc. Explain exactly what you are trying to do and ask what other material there is.
5. Find if there is a professional society, a consortium, or any other voluntary association in this field.

instructor

READ THE FOURTH COLUMN ON EACH PAGE
WHEN WORKING WITH **GROUPS**, WORKSHOPS, CONFERENCES, ETC.

c. Present to the class, as an assignment for next time, the Program Element YOUR PERSONAL OPERATIONS PLAN, page 114. But see page 113.

3. CLASSROOM EXERCISES

a. If the class didn't get very far with YOUR IMMEDIATE JOB OBJECTIVE, you may want them to begin with the same trios that the Eleventh Session ended with, and continue working with their large pieces of shelf-paper, aiding each other to analyze clusters, etc. (A & B work on C's analysis for awhile; then B & C work on A's; then C & A work on B's, and so on—in rotation, for 10—15 minutes before rotating.

(You may want to begin the class session with this exercise, and save the "Looking Back" and "Looking Ahead" for later, just to vary the class routine.)

b. SYSTEMATIC TARGETING. As an introduction to this subject, you may want to let one member of the class say what his or her field is (in their Immediate Job Objective) and see what possibilities the other members of the whole class can suggest that s/he ought to investigate. Continue this 'game' for some time, to get an idea across to the class of the breadth and variety of possibilities. This may also generate some contacts or leads for various class members.

If, at the end of the Eleventh Class Session, you solicited any volunteers to go visit employment agencies (federal-state and private) in town, this is the point at which they ought to give their report on what sort of experiences they had, as they investigated their particular field, or interest with those agencies.

The contrast, then, between what the class can suggest (uneducated amateurs!) and what the employment agencies suggested (personnel experts!) should be discussed. Were any helpful individuals discovered

student

THE PROGRAM ELEMENTS IN THIS FIRST COLUMN HELP THE STUDENT IDENTIFY HIS/HER PRIMARY **FUNCTIONAL GOAL** (WHAT)

THE PROGRAM ELEMENTS IN THIS SECOND COLUMN HELP THE STUDENT IDENTIFY HIS/HER PRIMARY **ORGANIZATIONAL GOAL** (WHERE)

ULTIMATE ORGANIZATIONAL TARGETS

1. *Definition:* these are the group activities which are still of extreme interest to you after completing the two screening processes described above. (Potential & Live).

2. *Mechanics:* Transfer the cards and file folders of activities which have failed to pass your personal criteria, to the "General Interest" files, as before. The cards and folders remaining are by definition your U.O.T.s.

3. *Scope:* As a result of all the separate decisions you have made thus far, and in the light of all the background information you have obtained through your surveys and investigations, you should begin to have a very clear idea of precisely what you are looking for in your Ultimate Organizational Targets. There are two possible ends to this process:

a. *One* Ultimate Organizational Target only, because among all those you are investigating one activity stands head and shoulders above everything else in terms of *your* interest. This decision to select only one is rarely taken. (Only once in all the fifteen year history of this program; though the student was successful in getting hired there, while his instructor's hair turned white.)

b. *Several* Ultimate Organizational Targets, preserving several attractive options (to You)

Error: Narrowing your possibilities too quickly, out of a desire to cut corners, save time, or from a general sense of impending impending doom if this isn't resolved immediately (spelled: "p-a-n-i-c").

counselor

READ THE THIRD COLUMN ON EACH PAGE
WHEN WORKING WITH **INDIVIDUALS**

6. Bankers, stockbrokers may know about the activity.

7. Also professors of the appropriate discipline at a nearby college or university.

8. Also local, state, and federal government agencies.

9. The local newspaper editor.

In addition, ask local people *how* they go about gathering information on something, whatever the subject (ask the newspaper editor, ask local consumer groups, environmental protection agencies, social change groups, etc.). You will learn *very* quickly.

instructor

READ THE FOURTH COLUMN ON EACH PAGE
WHEN WORKING WITH **GROUPS**, WORKSHOPS, CONFERENCES, ETC.

at any of the agencies? If so, by what criteria were they evaluated as helpful—by the class member(s) who went there? What were the characteristics of an *un*helpful agency counselor?

What should become clear is that there is all the difference in the world between the traditional 'personnel/employment agency system' (which starts with the job, and tries to fit the job-hunter to THAT) and Targeting, which starts with the job-hunter, and asks that the jobs accommodate themselves to him/her.

THE PROGRAM ELEMENTS IN THIS FIRST COLUMN HELP THE STUDENT IDENTIFY HIS/HER PRIMARY **FUNCTIONAL GOAL** (WHAT)

Goal:
To aid you in developing a number of attractive alternatives, instead of being pinned down to just one possible future.

Goal:
To discover common ground (or, hopefully, mutual enthusiasms) which you and your ultimate individual targets share.

student

THE PROGRAM ELEMENTS IN THIS SECOND COLUMN HELP THE STUDENT IDENTIFY HIS/HER PRIMARY **ORGANIZATIONAL GOAL** (WHERE)

in order to avoid disappointment for reasons beyond your control. Also in order to (hopefully) have several attractive offers, in the end, to compare against each other.

ULTIMATE INDIVIDUAL TARGETS

1. *Definition:* the end result of all your investigations, surveys and targeting, is your correct identification of an Ultimate Individual Target in *each* of your Ultimate Organizational Targets; that is to say, the one official in each such activity or organization who

a. shares your major enthusiasm or interest;

b. has primary responsibility for the activity which you are eager to undertake for that organization;

c. has sufficient authority to hire you, employ you as consultant, or buy your product or services.

2. *Identifying him or her:* it is important to analyze and investigate each Ultimate Organizational Target carefully enough so that you can, in the end, identify your Ultimate Individual Target by his (or her) properly-spelled name (in full), and his (or her) title.

3. *Investigating him or her:* you investigate him or her just as you did your Ultimate Organizational Target. One helpful device, at this point, is to set yourself the task of writing up a complete resume *on* him or her. You will discover that the more senior or

Error:
Choosing an organizational or individual target because you feel you'd have a 'good chance with him' (or her) when in reality s/he really doesn't interest you.

Error:
Latching on to someone who is devoid of authority.

Error:
Feeling there is no way you can possibly identify him (or her.

counselor

READ THE THIRD COLUMN ON EACH PAGE
WHEN WORKING WITH **INDIVIDUALS**

instructor

READ THE FOURTH COLUMN ON EACH PAGE
WHEN WORKING WITH **GROUPS**, WORKSHOPS, CONFERENCES, ETC.

PRACTICAL AIDS. Experience has proved there are three avenues of approach to this task:

a. Start by identifying precisely that department, staff section, group, or other organizational entity, which is in fact already active in the functional area that interests you most (or would be charged with such activity, most logically, if it were to be introduced as a new function or position). Then find out who is

THE PROGRAM ELEMENTS IN THIS FIRST COLUMN HELP THE STUDENT IDENTIFY HIS/HER PRIMARY **FUNCTIONAL GOAL** (WHAT)

student

THE PROGRAM ELEMENTS IN THIS SECOND COLUMN HELP THE STUDENT IDENTIFY HIS/HER PRIMARY **ORGANIZATIONAL GOAL** (WHERE)

important the person you are aiming at, the more information there is about him/her in the public domain. Try:

a. Your friendly reference librarian, asking for guidance in using the directories on outstanding individuals (Who's Who in Industry, Who's Who in America, etc.)

b. Call his/her organization and ask for any publicity or press release on him/her, any speeches he/she has given, any biographical information, etc. If a large organization, route your request to the public relations department.

c. If during your personal economic survey you developed a friendship with a newspaper editor or reporter, ask what they have on him/her in 'the morgue' as it is called there.

What you are looking for, in all of this investigation, is *common ground* between the two of you:

same military background?
same college background?
same geographical background?
same avocation? sports? church?
same professional memberships?
mutual friends? (here is where your contacts may be handy)
same travel? (where)
SOME SHARED INTEREST.

Beyond this, you want to research, if you can:

details of his/her operation;
what his/her department does;

counselor

READ THE THIRD COLUMN ON EACH PAGE
WHEN WORKING WITH **INDIVIDUALS**

in fact (not necessarily in title) *the most senior person responsible* for that activity or function. S/he is your Ultimate Individual Target in that organization.

b. IF THIS DOES NOT WORK (in some organizations, particularly large ones, not even the junior executives there know who is in charge of a particular function), then investigate that organization thoroughly enough so that you can at least figure out the broad general classifications of functions that that organization uses, and then analyze which one your function would have to be within; and direct your approach to (i.e., identify as your U.I.T. there) *the man at the top of that.*

c. IF YOU ARE STILL IN DOUBT always go *higher.* If you doubt whether the Executive Vice-President is the right man, then aim at the President, and label him as your Ultimate Individual Target there.

instructor

READ THE FOURTH COLUMN ON EACH PAGE
WHEN WORKING WITH **GROUPS**, WORKSHOPS, CONFERENCES, ETC.

THE PROGRAM ELEMENTS IN THIS FIRST COLUMN HELP THE STUDENT IDENTIFY HIS/HER PRIMARY **FUNCTIONAL GOAL** (WHAT)

student

THE PROGRAM ELEMENTS IN THIS SECOND COLUMN HELP THE STUDENT IDENTIFY HIS/HER PRIMARY **ORGANIZATIONAL GOAL** (WHERE)

his/her recent achievements;
some of his/her more serious organizational problems, or challenges.

This information will all be invaluable to you when you make your approach to each of your U.I.T.s, as you will see.

A summary, and example, of this systematic targeting process is to be found in Appendix N, which we recommend your reviewing at this point.

Error:
Feeling you won't really need this much detailed information.

counselor

READ THE THIRD COLUMN ON EACH PAGE
WHEN WORKING WITH **INDIVIDUALS**

WARNING. The tighter the job-market, and/or the more you are trying to go into an entirely new field (for you) the more you are going to need this information. (pp. 118–119 in *Parachute* again).

But, ultimately, the reason you are looking for this information is so that *you* can *screen out* employers who don't interest you.

instructor

READ THE FOURTH COLUMN ON EACH PAGE
WHEN WORKING WITH **GROUPS**, WORKSHOPS, CONFERENCES, ETC.

C. YOUR PERSONAL OPERATIONS PLAN. As an introduction, *before you explain about Your Personal Operations Plan,* ask each student to make an outline of how (given his/her 'druthers') s/he would *like* to spend his/her next vacation. Give time in class for this to be done, by each student individually at his/her desk (allow 15–25 minutes).

Put up on the blackboard or on a sheet of newsprint, the factors you want them to include in their vacation plan, viz.,

(1) When the vacation would start, and when they have to be back.

(2) Where they would like to go. (This can be a dream vacation; it doesn't necessarily have to be exactly what they *are* going to do next summer–though it should be close as possible to reality.)

(3) How they would get there, and how long it would take.

(4) How they would return from their vacation, and when they would have to start home.

(5) What they would like to accomplish on their vacation (sight-seeing, sports, relaxation, reading, writing? etc.)

(6) How much time they would devote to each pursuit.

(7) How they would evaluate whether the vacation lived up to their expectations, or not? and what they would do to make their next vacation better.

When they have finished writing out their vacation plan, divide the class into small groups (5–8 members) and have them read their plans to each other. Let the group say what elements of the plan they liked; what elements they contrariwise feel still need working on (and why).

Allow suitable time for discussion (25–40 minutes).

Goal:
To help you do detailed planning aimed at the successful attainment of your Specific Immediate Objective, as the first stage of your future life work.
Also:
To develop a simple device that will help you all the rest of your life to keep progressing toward whatever new aims, new interests, and new challenges you seek out, because you will discover the operational pattern that is best suited to you, and hence be able to use it essentially unchanged in structure from then on.

THE PROGRAM ELEMENTS IN THIS FIRST COLUMN HELP THE STUDENT IDENTIFY HIS/HER PRIMARY **FUNCTIONAL GOAL** (WHAT)

student

THE PROGRAM ELEMENTS IN THIS SECOND COLUMN HELP THE STUDENT IDENTIFY HIS/HER PRIMARY **ORGANIZATIONAL GOAL** (WHERE)

24. Your Personal Operations Plan

Now it is time for you to draw up a plan for the achievement of your Specific Immediate Objective. We do not intend to push you into any particular planning mold at this point. Use whatever planning technique you feel works best for you. But *do draw up a formal plan:* that states *what* you have to get done; that plans your *time* so that you are intelligently and productively busy on this whole project every waking moment you can possibly spare; and, that sets *deadlines* which you seriously intend to meet. A sample plan appears in Appendix O, page 233. Adapt it in whatever way you wish, so long as your own plan ends up with:

- a starting date;
- your own priorities;
- your own time frames for the completion of each step;
- your own progress milestones, with dates for attaining each one;
- your own measurement standards;
- and your own internal control, reporting and follow-up systems, to ensure you stick at it.

Error:
Feeling that you like to leave things open, receptive, and 'hanging loose'; and that a plan would tie you down too much.

counselor

READ THE THIRD COLUMN ON EACH PAGE
WHEN WORKING WITH **INDIVIDUALS**

MOTIVATION. A plan frees you up:

From trying to remember a multitude of details;
From having the wrong priorities begin to assert themselves.
From getting side-tracked.
From losing track of time.
From being unprepared.

You can always revise the plan at any time, as new facts and new circumstances assert themselves. But you should begin somewhere, with a statement of your plan of action—as it presently seems likely and best, to you.

instructor

READ THE FOURTH COLUMN ON EACH PAGE
WHEN WORKING WITH **GROUPS**, WORKSHOPS, CONFERENCES, ETC.

Then reconvene the whole class together and ask for any learnings or sharings.

Go on to suggest that planning is an element in all of life, and "The Personal Operations Plan" is only an attempt to bring planning over from one area of our lives to another—where it is much needed: our career and our life.

Then describe the Program Element YOUR PERSONAL OPERATIONS PLAN, to the left.

Distribute copies of Appendix O.

Looking Ahead: the instructor will want to secure (between this class session and the next) a simple inexpensive book of resumes, such as are sold by most bookstores in the large paperback section.

student

THE PROGRAM ELEMENTS IN THIS FIRST COLUMN HELP THE STUDENT IDENTIFY HIS/HER PRIMARY **FUNCTIONAL GOAL** (WHAT)

THE PROGRAM ELEMENTS IN THIS SECOND COLUMN HELP THE STUDENT IDENTIFY HIS/HER PRIMARY **ORGANIZATIONAL GOAL** (WHERE)

pro·pos·al (prə-pō′z'l), *n.* 1. a proposing. 2. a plan, scheme, etc. proposed. 3. an offer of marriage.
SYN.—**proposal** refers to a plan, offer, etc. presented for acceptance or rejection (his *proposal* for a decrease in taxes was approved); **proposition**, commonly used in place of **proposal** with reference to business dealings and the like, in a strict sense applies to a statement, theorem, etc. set forth for argument, demonstration, proof, etc. (the *proposition* that all men are created equal).

THIRTEENTH CLASS SESSION
SOME SUGGESTED PROGRAM ELEMENTS

1. **LOOKING BACK**

a. Homework to be completed by now.
YOUR IMMEDIATE JOB OBJECTIVE
YOUR PERSONAL OPERATIONS PLAN

Check to see if all the class completed this on schedule (show of hands). Any surprise learnings? Any problems? What was most satisfying about the exercise?

b. Ongoing homework assignments.

SYSTEMATIC TARGETING. Ask the class to give one or two examples of what they did in this area, as part of their homework. Ask, by a show of hands, how many did *something?* Ask for number of hours spent. If a sufficient number of students *did* spend two or more hours on this, you may want to put them into small groups to share their learnings and enthusiasm with each other. Otherwise, just keep them altogether as a class, and let what sharing takes place, happen there.

CONTACTS LIST. Check to see how many names the students have on their lists. Remind them of the urgency of adding some each week.

PERSONAL ECONOMIC SURVEY. How many have chosen a prime geographical area locally? How many have chosen a prime geographical area that is far away? You may want to divide them into small groups accordingly, to discuss methodology, present progress and any problems encountered, with each other (see Classroom Exercises below).

READING. What books have they found helpful? What books unhelpful? What new books would they like to recommend to each other? Tell briefly about each, so the rest of the class can catch some of their enthusiasm for it.

student

THE PROGRAM ELEMENTS IN THIS FIRST COLUMN HELP THE STUDENT IDENTIFY HIS/HER PRIMARY **FUNCTIONAL GOAL** (WHAT)

THE PROGRAM ELEMENTS IN THIS SECOND COLUMN HELP THE STUDENT IDENTIFY HIS/HER PRIMARY **ORGANIZATIONAL GOAL** (WHERE)

Goal:
To give you needed practice in summarizing your experiences as they are directly related to your aims and strongest assets, and within one cohesive frame-work.
And:
To look at your 'ancient history' (your past) with one last fond glance, in order to extract from it the values, insights and current abilities which you wish to represent now and in the future.
And:
To prepare you for interviews which may ask you for a 'thumb-nail sketch' of your background.

25. Your Functional Summary

Now, to supplement your Specific Immediate Objective, we ask you to write a functional (*not* chronological) summary of your back-ground, *on one page only.* By "your back-ground" we mean any and all activities and pursuits, whether or not they were part of your job. Consider yourself as a whole person.

By "functional" we mean your whole life restated on the basis of your major skill areas and your strongest life interests—rather than on chronology.

By "summary" we mean a very brief paper, stressing those personal accomplishments which most strongly support your new goals and objectives; a clear, coherent, cohesive synopsis of those past experiences which you *now* view as significant *because of* their relationship to your planned future.

The piece of paper thus produced will serve in and of itself as a thumbnail sketch of about two minutes duration; or as an outline for a thirty minute recital—whenever (as in an interview) you may need either.

Error:
Feeling this is repetitious because you have already covered this material in your Talking Papers.

Goal:
To aid you in drawing up a 'Personal Proposal' of what you can do

26. Where You are Going

In drawing up your basic working tools for this whole process, you *may* want to prepare *a one page document* (two at the most) that superficially resembles what most people call "a resume".

The defect of most "resumes" is twofold. What they are; and how they are used. Most are drab recitals of irrelevant personal trivia and dull ancient history—which the reader is left to sort out

counselor

READ THE THIRD COLUMN ON EACH PAGE
WHEN WORKING WITH **INDIVIDUALS**

UNDERLINING. Your starting point for this summary is your Specific Immediate Objective. You may indeed 'lift' material out of your Talking Papers, but they speak too generally about your talents and accomplishments. You want to lift out those achievements which specifically support the immediate objective, substantiate it, show you can do it because you have done it—*functionally*.

instructor

READ THE FOURTH COLUMN ON EACH PAGE
WHEN WORKING WITH **GROUPS**, WORKSHOPS, CONFERENCES, ETC.

2. LOOKING AHEAD

a. YOUR FUNCTIONAL SUMMARY. Present this Program Element as one of their homework assignments, to be completed by the next class session. Stress that they are only to choose experiences *related to* their planned future (i.e., their job objective).

b. WHERE YOU ARE GOING. Present this program element for homework assignment, to be completed by the next class session.

for the organization to which you are going, rather than a Resume of what you did for the organizations from which you are coming.

Goal:
To aid you in drafting something which faintly resembles a 'resume', in case you want the discipline of preparing such, and/or feel the need for such a document at any time.

student

THE PROGRAM ELEMENTS IN THIS FIRST COLUMN HELP THE STUDENT IDENTIFY HIS/HER PRIMARY **FUNCTIONAL GOAL** (WHAT)

THE PROGRAM ELEMENTS IN THIS SECOND COLUMN HELP THE STUDENT IDENTIFY HIS/HER PRIMARY **ORGANIZATIONAL GOAL** (WHERE)

for him/herself. Most resumes "short-circuit" the whole internalized self-esteem process which we have so carefully worked through, in this course thus far.

Morever, when done, it is used in a mass distribution job-seeking fashion, by people intent on *avoiding* the more difficult but infinitely more effective targeting process, described in this course.

In your case, of course, by committing yourself to the whole clustering process, and targeting, you are automatically going to keep this piece of paper from those twin defects.

We call this "A Statement of Where You Are Going" instead of a Resume, because a resume looks backward, while this Statement looks forward. As a piece of paper it is a useful exercise for your own intellectual discipline. But it cannot be your job-hunting strategy. Your strategy is *You.* This piece of paper is only useful in those rare instances where you cannot walk into a room at some particular time Yourself, and it fits *your* purposes to have some representation of Yourself present.

The mechanics of assembling this "Statement of Where You Are Going" are to be found in Appendix P, at the back of this manual.

Error:
Feeling you have got to have a resume in order to get in to see people.

Error:
Worrying too much about how this Statement sounds to (modest) You, instead of putting yourself in the shoes of a prospective employer (client, or whatever).

Goal:
To show you how all the tools you have accumulated now, can be of aid to you in the actual conducting of your active job search.

27.A The Active Job Search

Now that you have your Personal Operations Plan laid out, and all of the basic working tools you might possibly need (Contacts lists, Targeting files, your Functional Summary, and a Statement of Where You Are Going) your active job search (campaign) consists in logically following that Plan out carefully to its end.

Some of you will discover that it moves like clockwork. You will follow the Targeting procedures, according to the Time Table in your Personal Operations Plan, and will succeed in identifying the Ultimate Organizational Targets that interest you and the

counselor

READ THE THIRD COLUMN ON EACH PAGE
WHEN WORKING WITH **INDIVIDUALS**

UNDERLINING. Your problem is not that of getting past other people's 'screening out process'. Your problem is whether or not 'those other people' will get past *your* screening process.

If you understand this vital difference between our approach and the traditional approach, then you will see why you do not need to depend on resumes.

EVALUATION QUESTIONS. If you had to show this to one of your Ultimate Individual Targets:
1. Would it lead to an instant grasping on his/her part of the clear connection between you and some of his/her problems?
2. Does it spell out in detail precisely what you claim you can do for him/her?
3. Does it make him/her want to learn more about You?

instructor

READ THE FOURTH COLUMN ON EACH PAGE
WHEN WORKING WITH **GROUPS**, WORKSHOPS, CONFERENCES, ETC.

C. THE ACTIVE JOB SEARCH. Present this unit or Program Element, and assign further development of their CONTACTS LIST as the legitimate homework coming out of this.

Goal:
To learn how to deal with snags, delays, and other unforeseen problems in the job search.

THE PROGRAM ELEMENTS IN THIS FIRST COLUMN HELP THE STUDENT IDENTIFY HIS/HER PRIMARY **FUNCTIONAL GOAL** (WHAT)

student

THE PROGRAM ELEMENTS IN THIS SECOND COLUMN HELP THE STUDENT IDENTIFY HIS/HER PRIMARY **ORGANIZATIONAL GOAL** (WHERE)

people within them who are your Ultimate Individual Targets, just like clockwork.

Others of you will discover that it does not, for You, move so swiftly. *You must be prepared for this eventuality.* The process sometimes takes longer than a student at first expects. Be prepared for this; let your morale and self-confidence be unflagging.

Let us list the snags that can develop, and temporarily upset your Timetable:

1. Not being able to find enough Ultimate *Organizational* Targets that interest you.
2. Not being able to identify the Ultimate *Individual* Targets within the U.O.T.s that you have discovered.
3. Being able to identify your U.I.T.s but not able to uncover enough information about them, or the problems their organization is dealing with, to know whether or not your skills can help with those problems.
4. Being able to get enough information about your U.I.T.s and their problems, but unable to figure out how to get in to see them.
5. Being able to get in to see them, but they seem to be taking forever to decide whether they can use you or not (or whether to employ you as a consultant, or whether to become your clients, or whatever).

However thoroughly you follow this whole process, there is always an element of 'luck', 'chance', 'serendipity' or whatever you would like to call it, to Life and to the Job-Hunt—

Error:
Taking 'personally' any delay in this process that happens to you, thinking everyone else is faster.

counselor

READ THE THIRD COLUMN ON EACH PAGE
WHEN WORKING WITH **INDIVIDUALS**

instructor

READ THE FOURTH COLUMN ON EACH PAGE
WHEN WORKING WITH **GROUPS**, WORKSHOPS, CONFERENCES, ETC.

3. **CLASSROOM EXERCISES**

The agenda for this particular class session is deliberately briefer than normal, since experience has indicated there is a need—somewhere in this whole process— for a session to serve as a 'catch-up'. It is quite possible your class may—at this point—have yet to do their Specific Immediate Job Objective, etc., etc. Consequently, in this session you may actually be doing some of the exercises contained under earlier Session plans, and we are allowing for this possibility here.

a. Optional Class Exercise (if you are *really* far behind): working on any of the exercises in previous Sessions, such as YOUR IMMEDIATE JOB OBJECTIVE, etc.

b. SYSTEMATIC TARGETING. Dividing the class into small groups (5–8 members each) to discuss targeting:

(1) What have you been doing about targeting? Reading? Where? Visiting? Where?

(2) What have you learned thus far?

(3) What problems have you run into?

(4) What targets (potential) have you disqualified or dropped so far, and why? Which have you kept? And why?

c. PERSONAL ECONOMIC SURVEY. Divide the class into two 'teams': those whose prime geographical area is nearby (within commuting distance, say), and those whose prime geographical area is one that they (at this present time) have to write to, and visit later. Have each team meet as a group. If the 'teams' are too large, break each one into smaller groups (for these purposes, 'too large' would be more than 15 members). Have them discuss how they have been approaching, or will approach, their prime geographical area to get a complete picture of it and of the potential targets within it. Suggested time: 45 minutes. Have the complete class reconvene, and have each 'team' report. Summarize the *similarities*

THE PROGRAM ELEMENTS IN THIS FIRST COLUMN HELP THE STUDENT IDENTIFY HIS/HER PRIMARY **FUNCTIONAL GOAL** (WHAT)

Goal:
To tap into the invisible communications system that each of us possesses by virtue of being human and having friends, or acquaintances.

student

THE PROGRAM ELEMENTS IN THIS SECOND COLUMN HELP THE STUDENT IDENTIFY HIS/HER PRIMARY **ORGANIZATIONAL GOAL** (WHERE)

as we have repeatedly emphasized throughout this course. You may just have to lie in wait, for that 'serendipity' to swing your way—and though no-one can *guarantee* it will, it almost always does.

In the meantime, there is a tool in your work-kit that may be able to help you with each and every one of the problems listed above—the 'snags' as we called them. The tool is your list of Contacts, that you have developed all during this course. *Now* is the time to use that list.

Each of the people on that list has a circle (sometimes vast) of friends, associates and acquaintances whom you do not know—but who, together, comprise a kind of network. There is no telling what they in turn know, and who they know, that may be of interest to you. Therefore, potentially, your Contacts' Networks can overcome every one of the snags listed above; viz.,

1. They can suggest names of Ultimate Organizational Targets that you never heard of, but which might well interest you—in your chosen geographical preference area. The fact that your Contact lives in California while you are in New York and want to head for Virginia as your geographical preference is irrelevant. Your California contact may know somebody in Richmond, Virginia. Probably does. You never know.

2. If you have narrowed down your UOTs, but just can't find the name of the person in charge of your particular function, one of

Error:
Feeling that if you just organize things well enough, you can manipulate the whole scene sufficiently so that it has to work for you, just where you say, and just when you say.

Error:
Feeling that the only contacts who can help you in a particular geographical area are those who actually live there (forgetting that most of your circle of contacts have their own circles of contacts too, blanketing as much of the country as yours do.)

DEFINITION. This course is not designed to have you think of yourself as "Wo/Man the Manipulator," but rather to have you think of yourself as "Wo/Man the Taker Advantage of Situations", or whatever. It is to increase your ability to take initiative. But there are free-willed human beings out there in Radio-land; and no one can predict how or when they are going to behave.

PRACTICAL AIDS. Your contacts may not suggest an Organizational Target directly, but may give you the name of someone who would know.

You will want either to go see the name given to you (if feasible) or to write a letter to him (or her). A sample letter with suggestions of what to say to them, in order to turn up Organizational or Individual Targets, appears in Appendix Q, at the back of this manual.

and *differences* between those whose area is nearby and those who are far away, so far as their approach to surveying is concerned.

d. YOUR FUNCTIONAL SUMMARY. Assuming that the students have completed their Immediate Job Objective statements by this point, have them break into trios and practice mock interviewing. A & B 'play' interviewers to C, first of all, asking him or her to state his/her objective, and then quizzing him/her about what pertinent experience s/he has had. Then of course, after a sufficient time (10—15 minutes) B & C play interviewers to A; and thence C & A play interviewers to B. This exercise should help all members of the class to test how much their Talking Papers practice has already helped them, as well as make clearer to them what kinds of information they will need to include in their Functional Summary.

When the class reconvenes, ask them also to tell you (and list their responses on a blackboard or sheet of newsprint) what kinds of questions they asked in their 'mock interviews'. When they all are listed, ask them if they feel there are any other questions interviewers might ask.
[SAVE THESE RESPONSES: YOU WILL NEED THEM FOR THE NEXT CLASS SESSION.]

e. WHERE YOU ARE GOING. After a presentation of this Program Element, together with Appendix P, followed by questions and discussion to be sure the class comprehends completely the difference between this statement and a typical 'resume', distribute to the class copies of resumes as typically found in 'resume handbooks' sold in most bookstores. (You may want to make up your own variation on one or two of these, and mimeograph or xerox them so that each class member has a copy.) In the class, or in small groups, discuss the flaws they *now* see in these resumes. What is wrong with them? What is right about them? How could they be improved? And: would you hire somebody on the basis of *this* resume? or *any* resume?

THE PROGRAM ELEMENTS IN THIS FIRST COLUMN HELP THE STUDENT IDENTIFY HIS/HER PRIMARY **FUNCTIONAL GOAL** (WHAT)

Goal:
To give you a positive plan of something to do, when you run into delays.

student

THE PROGRAM ELEMENTS IN THIS SECOND COLUMN HELP THE STUDENT IDENTIFY HIS/HER PRIMARY **ORGANIZATIONAL GOAL** (WHERE)

your Contacts may know somebody in those UOTs who can give you *that* information.

3. If you have identified your Ultimate Individual Targets, but can't discover enough about them, again, your Contacts may turn out to actually know him/her—or know someone who does. It's a very small world, and each person is part of a mind-boggling Network of acquaintances these days.

4. Your contacts may be able to secure a personal introduction for you to one of your Ultimate Individual Targets.

5. Your contacts may be able to find out, after an interview you have with some place that fascinates you, how to accelerate the decision-making process that you are waiting on.

Consequently, since you may run into any of these snags at any time, it behooves you to get in touch with all your Contacts early in this particular phase of your Active Job Search (or Client Search if you are going the 'self-employed' route)—and then cultivate them throughout the process.

Suggestions of what to say to them (or write to them) may be found in Appendix Q, at the back of this manual.

But as your Job/Client Search goes on, *the more you run into any of the above snags, the more time you should spend getting in touch with your Contacts, for help with those snags.*

Error:
Falling into despair when you run into delays or deadends, instead of turning to your Contacts for help.

counselor

READ THE THIRD COLUMN ON EACH PAGE
WHEN WORKING WITH **INDIVIDUALS**

instructor

READ THE FOURTH COLUMN ON EACH PAGE
WHEN WORKING WITH **GROUPS**, WORKSHOPS, CONFERENCES, ETC.

f. THE ACTIVE JOB SEARCH. Give the individual students time at their desk (20–30 minutes) to draw on a blank piece of paper a diagram of their own personal contacts–drawn, of course, from their CONTACTS LIST –not by name, but by geography.

To prepare for this exercise, the instructor may want to have sheets mimeographed or xeroxed with a State map of the U.S. on it. Each student is to put a circle in each state, and approximately where each city is, where s/he has a contact.

Then have the class break into small groups (5–8 members, as usual) and let each member, in turn, ask the following questions:

(1) I have no contacts in (name a state or city). Does anyone have contacts there?

(2) My prime geographical area is ______________________________.
I think I may have approximately ____________________ contacts there.
In what fields, or organizations?

If the class is not too large (more than 30) this can be done with the whole class instead of small groups, if desired. The point of the whole exercise, obviously, is to make people aware of how large the circle of acquaintances is, that each of us possesses; and *hence* that everyone we know, in turn, possesses.

Time for the group discussion: 10–25 minutes.

[The above classroom exercises are a kind of smorgasbord, so you can choose between several of these. It is by no means necessary to use them all. You decide which areas the students need the most help in, and then choose the appropriate exercises to that need.]

Goal:
To teach you how to get in to see the people you want to, no matter how senior their position may be in a particular organization.

27.B Getting to Meet Your Individual Targets

Assuming your Personal Operations Plan is followed methodically by you, with the aid of your Contacts, the snags will be gotten over eventually. You will have identified your Ultimate Individual Targets, have learned what common interests you both share, and what problems each one faces that your skills could help solve; this will then bring you face to face with the problems that remain: how do you get in to see him/her? and: what do you say, when you *do* get in?

As to the first, there are four ways of getting in.

FOURTEENTH CLASS SESSION
SOME SUGGESTED PROGRAM ELEMENTS

1. LOOKING BACK

a. Homework to be completed by now.
YOUR FUNCTIONAL SUMMARY
WHERE YOU ARE GOING Statement

Ask how many completed these (show of hands, as usual). Any problems or difficulties encountered? If so, you may need to appoint 'a buddy system' again to aid the students who are having difficulty.

b. Ongoing homework assignments. The usual and familiar (by now):
PERSONAL ECONOMIC SURVEY
CONTACTS LIST
SYSTEMATIC TARGETING
READING

Deal with these as you did in the Thirteenth Class Session.

2. LOOKING AHEAD

a. GETTING TO MEET YOUR INDIVIDUAL TARGETS. This is not a homework assignment per se, although it is something that each student *will* need to be dealing with "on the outside" of the class. Use some imagination in presenting this subject to the class, please; i.e., keep the class interested.

Goal:
To make a personal approach to each individual target, that is recognizably so, because it lets him/her know that you know who he/she is and that you have taken the time to learn quite a bit about his/her operation, and problems.

THE PROGRAM ELEMENTS IN THIS FIRST COLUMN HELP THE STUDENT IDENTIFY HIS/HER PRIMARY **FUNCTIONAL GOAL** (WHAT)

student

THE PROGRAM ELEMENTS IN THIS SECOND COLUMN HELP THE STUDENT IDENTIFY HIS/HER PRIMARY **ORGANIZATIONAL GOAL** (WHERE)

1. *Introduction by a mutual friend.* Your targeting process, plus getting in touch with your Contacts, may result in turning up someone you know who also knows one (or more) of your Ultimate Individual Targets. S/he may be willing to introduce you in person (nothing is as valuable) or suggest you use his/her name.

2. *An appointment without an introduction.* You may not be able to turn up a person who can give you an introduction to every one of your Individual Targets. What then? *If* you have done your homework thoroughly, you will have discovered:

a. Some common ground between the two of you.

b. Some enthusiasm or deep interest that you *both* share.

c. Some problems he or she is facing which intrigue you, and which you feel your skills can help. (Or, if you are entrepreneurial in bent, then what we are talking about is some problems that you feel your product or services can help solve.)

Calling him to tell him (or his secretary) that you "have made a study of his organization, and have learned something that will be of benefit to him," may well get you in—even if there is no mutual friend to introduce you.

3. *A letter, if your Individual Target is far away* (you will not, after all, restrict all offers or leads necessarily just to your prime geographical preference areas, though you are concentrating on them). A model for such a letter is to be found in Appendix Q.

Error:
Going into an interview 'cold' without having done your thorough, competent research first.

Error:
Ignoring the secretaries.

counselor

READ THE THIRD COLUMN ON EACH PAGE
WHEN WORKING WITH **INDIVIDUALS**

EXHORTATION. Remember the name of every secretary you meet (*write it down*)—and if it isn't on a plaque on her desk, (or his) ask her to spell it, please; and thank you. If she extends any courtesy or helpfulness to you, be sure and include her in your thank you notes written *that very night.*

instructor

READ THE FOURTH COLUMN ON EACH PAGE
WHEN WORKING WITH **GROUPS**, WORKSHOPS, CONFERENCES, ETC.

Goal:
To teach you how to place yourself unobtrusively in someone's path, (your Ultimate Individual Target's) if need be.

THE PROGRAM ELEMENTS IN THIS FIRST COLUMN HELP THE STUDENT IDENTIFY HIS/HER PRIMARY **FUNCTIONAL GOAL** (WHAT)

student

THE PROGRAM ELEMENTS IN THIS SECOND COLUMN HELP THE STUDENT IDENTIFY HIS/HER PRIMARY **ORGANIZATIONAL GOAL** (WHERE)

4. *Placing yourself unobtrusively in his/her path.* Everyone is a creature of habits. Find these out for your Individual Target, and you can then place yourself unobtrusively in his/her path. The question is: how? The answer is relatively simple, if you are determined enough.

Every society has two structures or sets of communication (which can be diagrammed, simply by asking: who talks to each other?): these two structures are vocational, and avocational. If you want to meet someone important to you, you can approach that someone through either set of communications. But the subtler and more effective is the second: the avocational. Less of his/her defenses are up there, than in the office. Choose some part of his avocational scene: his/her lunching place, drinking place, hobby place, church place, or whatever. Let yourself be seen a number of times by him/her *before* making your approach. If you do it skillfully enough, s/he will think *s/he's found you.* Never disabuse him/her of that notion.

Error:
Feeling this kind of adventure just 'isn't for you'.
(If you don't get some sense of adventure and challenge out of it, don't do it.)

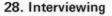

Goal:
To teach you the difference between:
Stupid Interviews,
Intelligent Interviews,
and
Quality Interviews.

28. Interviewing

INTRODUCTION: Everything we teach about interviewing makes sense only as an integral part of this whole course. It is impossible to teach Interviewing to someone, unless s/he knows what s/he wants, knows why s/he is at *this* particular place, knows exactly what s/he has to offer, knows exactly what s/he wants to do, and has found out not only a great deal about this particular organization, but also about that special part of it where the individual is whom s/he's about to talk with.

Try to put yourself first and foremost in the interviewer's viewpoint. Something about you interests him (or her), or s/he wouldn't have let you get in there, in the first place: a mutual friend, or something intriguing he (or she) has learned about you, or the fact s/he already knows

Error:
Trying to master this 'art of interviewing' as though it were some kind of trick, without yourself doing the preliminary hard work that this course is all about.

counselor

READ THE THIRD COLUMN ON EACH PAGE
WHEN WORKING WITH **INDIVIDUALS**

PRACTICAL SUGGESTIONS. If he stops off at a bar after work, and you learn which one, and you can stop off there after work yourself—do so, Two, three times at a row; then skip one or two days, before resuming. If you meet him, try thereafter to stand near where he stands (or sits).

If he lunches out regularly try to discover where and at what hour. (If in doubt, ask in the neighborhood where the big-shots eat lunch.) Come in quietly, regularly, for a while, until he gets to know your face as part of the normal scene. Fit in. The rest is relatively easy. You have your common ground already discovered in your research about him—right? When you fall to talking, use it.

instructor

READ THE FOURTH COLUMN ON EACH PAGE
WHEN WORKING WITH **GROUPS**, WORKSHOPS, CONFERENCES, ETC.

b. INTERVIEWING. Another lecture. Unavoidably so. You may want to introduce the subject by referring to the class responses at the last session, as to what they think a decent interviewer should ask. Put these responses back up on the blackboard or on a sheet of newsprint, in front of the class, and ask them if they see any way of reducing the questions to three basic categories? Let them see what they can do with this. Then make your presentation, from the Program Element INTERVIEWING.

An alternative way of getting into this subject is to have the class role-play an interview in front of the whole class. IF you do this, however, be careful to 'put people into their role' when you begin, by assigning that role to them or by allowing them to tell the class just what kind of inter-

you. If you have followed this whole course logically, point by point, *you know* what that common interest is—because you know him (or her) and have already communicated the fact that you also share this same interest. *Hence, you already know the agenda for your meeting before you get in there, because it is Your agenda.* Apart from all the careful preparation suggested in this course, however, you *don't* know the agenda, and so you would be inevitably launched upon what we can only call "a stupid interview"—an impetuous blundering fishing expedition, which can roughly be compared to being interviewed with a blindfold on, in a bat cave.

Error:
Skipping over this whole course, and leaping to 'interviewing' as though one had only to master That, in order to get a job.

However, given the careful preparation of this course, you're as prepared for this interview as anyone could possibly hope to be.

Goal:
To teach you how to attract an interviewer's interest.

THE PROPOSAL: The heart of why you are there is to make some kind of a proposal to him or her. (A so-called Resume or Statement of Where You Are Going, is really a thinly-disguised Proposal.) You have been invited by a senior person (prospective employer or prospective client) for a specific purpose: to discuss a mutual enthusiasm or interest that you both share, and to hear some proposal you wish to make about it (i.e., a bright idea of yours). That proposal, based on solid information and thorough research, on your part, is:

Error:
Not knowing what you have to offer to the employer you are talking to.

something you can do for him (or her); and/or
some problem you can help solve; and/or
some need of which this guy (or gal) is aware, but which s/he doesn't consider a problem, which you nevertheless can meet: e.g., cost reduction, sales increase, growth, new applications of their services or products, bringing in an entirely new approach, increased prestige, efficiency, etc.
some opportunity you can create, that s/he never thought of.

Error:
Deciding to settle for talking to the personnel department instead of an Ultimate Individual Target of your own choosing and research.

In any event, it has to be something which *starts* with your major skill strengths, and so you are thoroughly prepared—because you've been spending most of this course on mastering what those strengths are, to the point where they are an integral part of your total consciousness now.

Goal:
To teach you what it means when an interviewer talks about everything *but* the job.

THE 'QUALITY' INTERVIEW: a pure example of this kind of interview is rather rare; but the 'quality' factor is a part of every interview, to one degree or another. It begins with the fact that the guy you're talking to—in a pure 'quality' interview—is very very smart. Consequently, the interview will work its way rather quickly to the third of three phases. These phases are:

1. Within the framework of your general enthusiasm, what is "the great idea" that you have to contribute toward solving his or her problems? (He will probably quickly decide the proposal is so sound, it doesn't need much further discussing.)

counselor

READ THE THIRD COLUMN ON EACH PAGE
WHEN WORKING WITH **INDIVIDUALS**

SIGNPOSTS. You are in a stupid interview if you have the feeling 'I don't know what this guy has to offer me, but maybe s/he can suggest something.' The employer knows it is a stupid interview without *any* signposts.

EXHORTATION & WARNING. Explaining all of this to the personnel department of an organization is (in 999 cases out of 1000) a total waste of time. Any place accustomed to thinking in terms of how many people they can screen out and thus save the 'big bosses' from being bothered with, is simply not prepared to handle You—if you've worked your way through this whole process.

You are unique. You won't fit into any of the typical personnel experts' pigeon-holes. He (or she) won't know what to make of you, or what to do with you.

The chances are 10 to 1 that faced with this kind of unpredictability, the personnel department will take the route that is safest (for them!): screen you out.

instructor

READ THE FOURTH COLUMN ON EACH PAGE
WHEN WORKING WITH **GROUPS**, WORKSHOPS, CONFERENCES, ETC.

viewer and what kind of job-seeker they are portraying. Allow it to go on no more than five minutes, and then stop it. At that point, BE SURE to take people 'out of their role', by asking them to tell the class *how it felt* to be the person that they were portraying. *Then* ask the class what they learned about interviewing, from the role play.

Following this discussion, launch into your presentation on INTERVIEWING. Allow plenty of time for discussion, questions, and so forth, after your presentation.

However, make a herculean effort to stimulate answers from the class, *rather than playing answer man yourself.*

You may, then, want to have two other class members role-play an *intelligent* interview, as you have described it, just now. Be sure however that they are volunteers for this task. Be sure also that you 'put them into their role' and 'take them out again' when the role-play is interrupted (by you) after 5–8 minutes.

Ask the class, then, what differences they saw between this role-play and the first one? (The answer *may* be: very little. You are then in a position to point out that the last role-play was not completely realistic, because the person who played the job-seeker was probably not fully using his/her *own* job objective and supporting skills.)

student

THE PROGRAM ELEMENTS IN THIS FIRST COLUMN HELP THE STUDENT IDENTIFY HIS/HER PRIMARY **FUNCTIONAL GOAL** (WHAT)

THE PROGRAM ELEMENTS IN THIS SECOND COLUMN HELP THE STUDENT IDENTIFY HIS/HER PRIMARY **ORGANIZATIONAL GOAL** (WHERE)

2. Who can carry it out? Who better of course than the man who (or woman who) thought it up? (He will so quickly satisfy himself that you have the necessary functional skills, to carry it out, that this too doesn't need much further discussing.)
3. But what kind of a human being are you? Are you 'broad-gauged' enough to work with other human beings using imagination and creativity, or are you merely a technician–unimaginative and so forth? Do you have a broad view of the world? Do you know changing social trends? Etc. (We *assume* you know which fork is which, that your fingernails are clean, and that you aren't a falling-down drunk.)

In a *pure* quality interview, your man will devote virtually all of his (or her) time to exploring this third point; *and hence will conduct an interview which apparently beats all around the bush without coming to the point.* It will leave the normal guy (or gal) screaming. But YOU will be prepared, and will understand. You will know that the smarter your Ultimate Individual Target is, the more likely the interview will follow this sort of pattern.

Goal: To teach you why it is important never to underestimate the intelligence of your interviewer.

So, the moral of this tale is simply told: *Never* underestimate the intelligence of the guy across from you in the interview. Which means: don't start with mere ABCs. Don't waste his time on your background (unless he asks for it). Don't "try to teach your grandmother how to suck eggs". (Ancient Proverb) He'll think you're talking *down* to him, and that will be the end of Your day!

Error: Underestimating the intelligence of your interviewer. Talking down to your interviewer.

THE INTELLIGENT INTERVIEW: The first mark of an intelligent interview is that you're talking with the right person. No Ultimate Individual Target is of any value to you at this point, if he or she is either not bothered by the problems you know you can help solve, or is not possessed of the actual authority to decide whether or not to hire you for the job you want.

Goal: To teach you how to conduct an intelligent interview, where you know what the basic script is going to be before you go in.

Error: Talking to someone who isn't bothered by the problems you know you can (and want to) help solve. And/or: Talking to someone who hasn't the authority to hire you.

But, assuming you *are* conducting an intelligent interview, i.e., talking to the right person, what does he (or she) want to know? Well, ultimately *all* he wants to know is: whether or not you are an individual (or *the* individual) who can help solve his (or her) problems for him, or with him. So, how will s/he get at that? Unfortunately, nobody can predict exactly what an interviewer is going to ask. But, if we put ourselves in his/her shoes, and ask: WHAT DOES S/HE NEED TO KNOW, IN ORDER TO MAKE AN INTELLIGENT DECISION ABOUT ME? or: If *I* were doing the interviewing, what would I need to know about me in order to make an intelligent decision?–then it becomes apparent that we can predict the three *thoughts* which are inevitable, *in one form or another:*

1. *Why are you here?* The obvious answer ("Because you invited me in") is the wrong one. He already knows that. The next most obvious answer ("Because I want a job") is one he doesn't want to hear; and you're cutting your own throat if you give it. He isn't thinking about you at

counselor

READ THE THIRD COLUMN ON EACH PAGE
WHEN WORKING WITH **INDIVIDUALS**

instructor

READ THE FOURTH COLUMN ON EACH PAGE
WHEN WORKING WITH **GROUPS**, WORKSHOPS, CONFERENCES, ETC.

INTERPRETATION & WARNING. The chief office within an organization that does *not* have the authority to hire you (except for *very* low-level jobs) is, as we hope you do not need to be told by now, the personnel office. It is not, however, the only one.

Everything depends upon what particular position you want, within that organization. There may be 66 executives in an organization who do the hiring. 65 of them are irrelevant for your purposes.

Goal:
To teach you how to answer the interviewer's most obvious questions.

this moment; he's beginning the interview, naturally enough, with his sights set upon his own intelligent self-interest. So, what he really wants to know is: "Why, out of this whole world, did you choose me (or "us")?"

The answer is so simple that most people never think of it:

a. As you have learned from our earlier communication with each other, I am fascinated by what you do (if this isn't the truth, you shouldn't be there). *As is true for you, such and such a field has been one of my passions all of my life.*

b. During the last few years, I have become increasingly interested in (whatever aspect of that field you want to talk to him about). (Tell why.) I have, of course, kept a pretty close eye on developments in this, and the more I studied it the more convinced I became that the key to the solution lies in (here you introduce your proposal).

c. As this conviction grew in my mind, I began conducting an exhaustive investigation of every single leading organization that was active in our field (name others, name his/hers). Because while the key to this problem is, as I have indicated, relatively simple, it's going to take some extremely intelligent, open-minded, forward-thinking people to get it through. The outcome of my survey was the discovery that in my estimation you and your people stand head and shoulders above everyone else in this field. I believe you are the group best qualified to do it; and that is why I am here.

Error:
Being somewhere on interview where you are not actually fascinated by what that organization is up to, but claiming you are.

2. *Precisely what can you do for me?* Assuming his/her reaction to the first question was, "Great", this is the next logical question. Needless to say, having done this course, you're 'loaded for bear' on this one. Because, this is precisely why you are there.

a. Specifically, your ____x____ needs tightening up, as we both know.

b. The type of thing that I think would be invaluable in (reducing costs, or whatever problem you are zeroing in on) is ____y____. It would, I think, result in ______z______ (be totally specific here).

If you are self-employed and therefore offering a product or service, you will of course adapt the above to fit your particular situation. But the approach is basically the same. If you have done your work thoroughly, s/he will be fascinated with this 'brilliant' idea of yours. Conversation will change its focus from you, to it. There will, of course, be factors that you could not possibly

counselor

READ THE THIRD COLUMN ON EACH PAGE
WHEN WORKING WITH **INDIVIDUALS**

WARNING. If you have carefully done each exercise in this course, when you come to the interview you will be describing no more than what you have in fact done.

If you have not done it, however, most interviewers will quite quickly hear the hollow ring; and quietly throw you out.

instructor

READ THE FOURTH COLUMN ON EACH PAGE
WHEN WORKING WITH **GROUPS**, WORKSHOPS, CONFERENCES, ETC.

have known about from the outside, and hence possibly flaws in your brilliant idea. But he will be thinking: with a mind like that, based on the information s/he's gotten on the outside, what could s/he do if s/he were on the inside? So, he (or she) your interviewer will naturally want now to see your mind in actual operation. This is where you can't clam up. *Act as though you were already on his/her team.* Discuss your own idea. Ask where *s/he* thinks the problem lies. You will learn more about the company as the conversation continues; look for what factors there were that you didn't anticipate. Field them. What new light do they shed on your idea? Your expertise does not consist, at this point, in producing brilliant solutions, but in asking perceptive questions. *The more intelligent questions you can ask, the better.* The longer the interview lasts the happier you should be. S/he had the power to terminate it at any time. Hence the longer it lasts, the more s/he is moving over into trying to sell you on joining his/her organization.

Error:
Feeling there is no way you can really find out the problems of an organization from the outside, and that therefore the interviewer will quickly dismiss your amateurish diagnosis.

Goal:
To teach you how to conduct salary negotiations during an interview.

3. *How much is it going to cost me?* Obviously, this is the next logical question. Equally obviously, s/he really has no right to ask it. S/he wants to buy; therefore s/he should bid first. So much, in theory. In actual fact, of course s/he successfully gets away with reversing the roles because the whole personnel system in this country has everyone so terrorized. So, you are going to have to give an answer.

Before answering, however, you must have several things firmly in mind:

Goal:
To get him/her to *begin* near the top of his/her range, and even to think of going above it.
Also:
To confirm the view he/she has already developed of you: self-confidence, based on facts and performance.
And:
To leave him/her an out, and room to negotiate, on the basis of your future performance.

Error:
Not having done your research *before you get to the interview,* to find out what a just salary would be for the new position you are trying to get them to establish for you, with your unique talents.

a. You must know *what the general salary level is* for the kind of position you're shooting at (or asking him/her to create); or—if you're aiming to be hired as consultant—what is the appropriate level for such services; or, if you're viewing him/her as a potential client for some entrepreneurial product or service, what this should cost him/her.

b. You must understand that *s/he doesn't have a flat figure in mind* (at least at any management level, in practically any organization, including Civil Service). S/he has *a range.*

(1) It is important for you to bargain therefore. $2-3000 (the usual range) is worth bargaining for. Moreover, not to bargain reveals you are naive at best, stupid at worst.

(2) You bargain by playing 'the range game' right back at him/her. It consists in two parts, of equal and overwhelming importance; and you cannot even draw breath between these two.

(a) Well, Mr. X, (be wary about using first names without permission) I have been making my survey and I've been looking at some other situations, almost as interesting as yours, and I would be amenable to something between $x and $y (here you mention a range that overlaps

counselor

READ THE THIRD COLUMN ON EACH PAGE
WHEN WORKING WITH **INDIVIDUALS**

instructor

READ THE FOURTH COLUMN ON EACH PAGE
WHEN WORKING WITH **GROUPS**, WORKSHOPS, CONFERENCES, ETC.

PRACTICAL AIDS. Salaries are the most closely guarded secret in business life; but you can get clues:

1. If you know someone on the inside of that organization, see if they can find out the information, for you.
2. Contact State and Federal tax agencies, to find out if salaries of this organization are a part of the public record. Also if they have a Federal contract, the contract may reveal it.
3. You want to know what the guy above and the guy below your projected position, make: that is The Range. If all else fails, guess: by where they live, the car they drive, etc.

his/hers in the following manner: your minimum is just below his/her maximum. e.g., if you think his range is $15,000–$18,000, you make yours $17,000–$20,000).

AND THEN, WITHOUT PAUSING FOR ONE SINGLE INSTANT:

(b) However, I want you to know one thing. I am not half as interested in the starting amount, as I am in the intellectual challenge and the long range opportunity.

Error: Naming a flat figure.

He (or she) will almost inevitably want you even more as a result of what you have just said. And will be thinking in terms of the top salary s/he can afford. But will realize this is still not totally adequate, and so will cast about for what else s/he can throw in to the pot. You have already of course given him/her the clue: long-range opportunity. (Translated, this means you have guaranteed you will 'come through' for him (or her) and that you want more pay as time goes on, if you do come through as promised.) There are usually no budget limitations on productivity. The more you produce, the more s/he can reward you with bonuses, promotion, etc. Indeed, on the basis of that promise s/he may already be casting about for how to 'sweeten the kitty' right *now.* "What else do you want?" "Let's take a tour of the building," you reply. Here is where all your Ideal Job Specifications have a chance to make their bid. "Well, I work best with a view. . . ." Etc. Etc.

Error: Looking only at the immediate salary, and not at other considerations.

Goal: To teach you why a job offer may not come out of an interview immediately.

The above three thoughts (Why are you here? Precisely what can you do for me? How much will it cost me?) are the basic categories you must deal with in any interview; they *have* to be the thoughts that are going on in the mind of your interviewer.

Now, to the degree (precisely to the degree) that you have fielded them successfully, s/he will be unable to make you an offer right then. Because the interview went so much better than s/he had thought it would, you have succeeded in discombobulating him/her. S/he needs time to rethink the whole matter. So s/he will simply say, "Goodbye".

AND (if s/he's interested): "I'm glad you came; I'll be getting in touch with you again, within x days."

This is a very favorable end to the interview, if you are dealing with management level people. Gentlemanly. (Or womanly.) Openended. And, all in all, one for which you may be very grateful. *You must show* that gratitude with a *handwritten* thank-you note, that very night.

Error: Failing to send a thank-you letter.

REFERENCES, JUST IN CASE: You should go into the interview having already chosen, and contacted, five friends (not related to you) who could give a composite picture of you altogether: your expertise, your values, your private life as a human being. They should be substantial citizens, well-known in their own community. e.g., senior business executives, former employers (if they would be helpful), the minister at your Church, the officer at your bank, etc.

counselor

READ THE THIRD COLUMN ON EACH PAGE
WHEN WORKING WITH **INDIVIDUALS**

EXPLANATION. A flat figure will kill you. If you know his/her range, and put your figure at the bottom of that range, you will immediately convince him/her that you underestimate your own worth (and probably everything else); if you put a flat figure in the middle of his/her range, s/he says "Sold" and your bargaining power is finished. If you put your flat figure at the top of his/her range, without any escape hatch, s/he may feel you've just priced yourself right out of the market. Even if s/he says, "I'll go ask", you are probably finished; s/he can't take you.

PRACTICAL MODELS. Your letter might include the following:
(1) Cheerful bread and butter: thanks for time spent with me today. Etc.
(2) I was particularly interested in/impressed by (pick out the thing most interesting to you that he said).
(3) I look forward with pleasure to hearing from you again with (here, repeat the time limit that the guy/gal specified). Sincerely, your name.

Use it to reiterate anything you want to, as well.

instructor

READ THE FOURTH COLUMN ON EACH PAGE
WHEN WORKING WITH **GROUPS**, WORKSHOPS, CONFERENCES, ETC.

student

THE PROGRAM ELEMENTS IN THIS FIRST COLUMN HELP THE STUDENT IDENTIFY HIS/HER PRIMARY **FUNCTIONAL GOAL** (WHAT)

THE PROGRAM ELEMENTS IN THIS SECOND COLUMN HELP THE STUDENT IDENTIFY HIS/HER PRIMARY **ORGANIZATIONAL GOAL** (WHERE)

Goal:
To have the names of references, which you will give out *only* to prospective employers who have expressed a genuine interest in you.

Ask them ahead of time if they would be willing to serve as references, should they be needed (they may not be). Further, ask them if they would (now) give you a general purpose letter of recommendation. (This will help insure against later lapses of memory on their part, or inadvertent contradictions.) If you know the people well enough, you might ask them if an outline of the *kind* of things that should be included would help them. If so, give it. You will not, of course, use the names of these references unless the interview seems hopeful, from your point of view.

Error:
Giving out the names of your references to everyone.

Error:
Making all the letters alike.

Goal:
To teach you what to do after the interview, particularly if you don't hear from them for a long time—comparatively.

POSTSCRIPT TO THE INTERVIEW: The period after the interview often drags on for an agonizingly long time, even when they want you badly. BE PREPARED FOR THIS. It is not at all unusual for a month or more to elapse (the President of the organization may be out of the country, and they can't make a decision until he returns). *However,* if the time period specified by your interviewer has elapsed, *plus an extra week,* without anything happening, then *work out a reason for getting in touch with him/her again.*

e.g. "I have of course been thinking further about our conversation, and it occurs to me you may be interested in the attached article on this subject" (enclose a relevant article from a magazine or newspaper).

e.g. "An additional detail on the proposal seems to me important enough to call to your attention" Etc. Etc.

e.g. "I have had a change of address, and I assume that may be why I have not heard from you; so, here is the new address."

Most management people are under a heavy load, so *always assume the best* about why you haven't heard from him (or her). Maybe there's been a crisis at the plant. Or, whatever. You eventually *will* get a response, because s/he would be embarrassed not to give one.

Error:
Crowding them, prematurely.

Error:
Writing (or saying) "I don't know why I haven't heard from you."

Goal:
To teach you how to approach more than one Ultimate Individual Target.

29. Active Campaigning

You should have completed your Personal Operations Plan, and have all of your Ultimate Individual Targets lined up (if you can) before you approach any one of them.

Then make your approach to each of these Targets all at the same time (basically). You cannot space them out. Otherwise, offers may begin to come in (with deadlines) before

Error:
Approaching any Ultimate Individual Target before you have done your homework or research upon the rest.

counselor

READ THE THIRD COLUMN ON EACH PAGE WHEN WORKING WITH **INDIVIDUALS**

UNDERLINING. Give them only *after* a job offer has appeared, or seems likely to.

INSURANCE. Be sure, *if* you give an outline to your references, that each one is different.

WARNING. Don't do it. You mustn't let your anxiety show in any way.

WARNING. This shows PANIC on your part, and puts the other guy/gal on the defensive. You *must* use subtlety. Always treat the other guy/gal as you would want to be treated yourself.

instructor

READ THE FOURTH COLUMN ON EACH PAGE WHEN WORKING WITH **GROUPS**, WORKSHOPS, CONFERENCES, ETC.

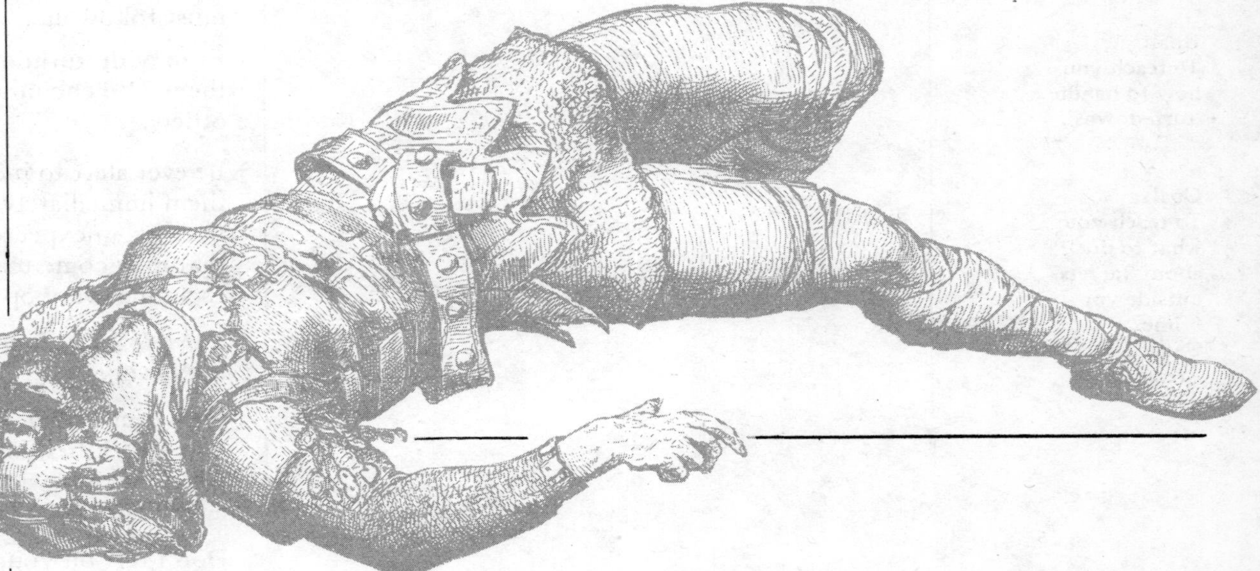

c. **CAMPAIGNING.** Again not a homework assignment per se, but a presentation by the instructor.

THE PROGRAM ELEMENTS IN THIS FIRST COLUMN HELP THE STUDENT IDENTIFY HIS/HER PRIMARY **FUNCTIONAL GOAL** (WHAT)

Goal:
To teach you how to handle 'turn-downs'.

Goal:
To teach you what to do about Targets outside your Prime Geographical Area.

student

THE PROGRAM ELEMENTS IN THIS SECOND COLUMN HELP THE STUDENT IDENTIFY HIS/HER PRIMARY **ORGANIZATIONAL GOAL** (WHERE)

you've looked at the rest of the possibilities. In which case, you would have to leap, before you've had a chance fully to look. So, in order to avoid that kind of situation, take each Target rapidly in turn. Approach it with everything you've got. Then, without pausing for one second, make your full approach to your next Target.

Keep perfect up-to-the-minute records, that show where you are with each Target. And what *you* must do next, with timelines. *You* must follow up.

Even with 'turndowns', write and thank them, and encourage them to refer you to others.

Be ever alert to incipient problems (deal with them immediately), changing situations, *and* fleeting, unexpected Targets of Opportunity that may come to your attention suddenly. Examine every opportunity.

Turn down nobody. Keep the door open with everyone.

With each target, be sure you have done your homework first; and make your approach at the right time with each, and at the highest level that is advantageous to you.

Don't rest on your oars, ever.

Error:
Leaping before you've had a chance to look.

Error:
Not keeping records.

Error:
Not following up on 'turndowns'.

Error:
Failing to examine every opportunity.

Failing to keep the door open with everyone you talk to.

d. Other Homework: Catching Up. Any part of the previous process which was supposed to be completed by the student, but has not been to date—for whatever reason.

e. Other Homework: Ongoing. PERSONAL ECONOMIC SURVEY. CONTACTS (meet three new people this week, and enter their name on your list). SYSTEMATIC TARGETING (everything you read & admire *must* go into your file and be followed-up).

3. **CLASSROOM EXERCISES**

As time allows:

a. Any of the above in connection with INTERVIEWING.

b. Any of those left over from the Thirteenth Session.

FIFTEENTH CLASS SESSION
SOME SUGGESTED PROGRAM ELEMENTS

1. **LOOKING BACK**

a. Homework to be completed by now.

None was assigned. However, you might check to see that they are all caught up, on all the previously assigned homework, viz.,

WHERE YOU ARE GOING Statement
YOUR FUNCTIONAL SUMMARY
PERSONAL OPERATIONS PLAN
YOUR IMMEDIATE JOB OBJECTIVE
YOUR ULTIMATE LIFE GOAL

etc. If someone hasn't done all of this, now is the time to find out (show of hands, of course). You may need to assign someone (or two someones) who is/are finished with it all, to work with someone who is slow—between now and the next session. IT IS CRUCIAL THAT THE COURSE END WITH EVERYONE HAVING DONE ALL THEIR ASSIGNED HOMEWORK TO COMPLETION. There is enough ongoing work when the course is done, and no student needs the added burden of extra incomplete back assignments.

student

THE PROGRAM ELEMENTS IN THIS FIRST COLUMN HELP THE STUDENT IDENTIFY HIS/HER PRIMARY **FUNCTIONAL GOAL** (WHAT)

THE PROGRAM ELEMENTS IN THIS SECOND COLUMN HELP THE STUDENT IDENTIFY HIS/HER PRIMARY **ORGANIZATIONAL GOAL** (WHERE)

sur·viv·al (sẽr-vī′v'l), *n.* 1. the act, state, or fact of surviving. 2. something that survives, as an ancient belief, custom, usage, etc.

sur·vive (sẽr-vīv′), *v.t.* [SURVIVED (-vīvd′), SURVIVING], [ME. *surviven;* OFr. *survivre;* L. *supervivere; super-*, above + *vivere*, to live], 1. to live or exist longer than or beyond the life or existence of; outlive. 2. to continue to live after or in spite of: as, we *survived* the wreck. *v.i.* to continue living or existing, as after an event or after another's death. —*SYN.* see **outlive**.

counselor

READ THE THIRD COLUMN ON EACH PAGE
WHEN WORKING WITH **INDIVIDUALS**

instructor

READ THE FOURTH COLUMN ON EACH PAGE
WHEN WORKING WITH **GROUPS**, WORKSHOPS, CONFERENCES, ETC.

b. Ongoing assignments. The usual, as you might expect:
PERSONAL ECONOMIC SURVEY
CONTACTS LIST
SYSTEMATIC TARGETING
READING

Deal with them as you did in Lesson plan for the Thirteenth Class Session.

2. LOOKING AHEAD

a. Catch-up on any Homework Assignments from the previous Class Sessions, that have not been completed to date by every student.

b. The on-going assignments:
SURVEYING
DEVELOPING CONTACTS
SYSTEMATIC TARGETING
READING
CAMPAIGNING

c. HOW TO SURVIVE AFTER YOU GET THAT JOB is presented in lecture form by the instructor, even though it is not technically a part of the homework. There is a particular way to present it, however, described below under exercises:

3. CLASSROOM EXERCISES

a. Divide the class into small groups (5–8 members in each group, naturally) to consider the question: WHAT IS WRONG WITH THE WHOLE WORLD OF WORK, AS YOU SEE IT? WHAT EXPERIENCES HAVE YOU HAD WITH THE WORLD OF WORK THAT HAVE TURNED YOU OFF?

Let each group have a convener and also another person who acts as scribe, to write the answers on a piece of newsprint. The discussion should last 15–60 minutes, depending on how the instructor thinks the discussions are going in the various groups as s/he floats around them.

Call the groups back together, and have the scribe from each small group describe the answers, to the whole class.

b. Divide the class into small groups a second time (they can be the same as before, or varied—as you decide is best) to discuss this question: IF YOU WERE RUNNING YOUR OWN ORGANIZATION, WHAT WOULD YOU

student

THE PROGRAM ELEMENTS IN THIS FIRST COLUMN HELP THE STUDENT IDENTIFY HIS/HER PRIMARY **FUNCTIONAL GOAL** (WHAT)

THE PROGRAM ELEMENTS IN THIS SECOND COLUMN HELP THE STUDENT IDENTIFY HIS/HER PRIMARY **ORGANIZATIONAL GOAL** (WHERE)

Goal:
To teach you how to hold on to a job once you get it (assuming it is a job where you are doing what you most enjoy doing, and do well).

30. How to Survive After You Get That Job

Since this process is so intelligent, you *will* get that job—in almost all cases. But just because you have successfully obtained the post you have been so carefully preparing for, does not mean that your work is done, by any means. Holding on to a job is, in many organizations, even more difficult than acquiring the job. Some organizations have a spectacular mortality rate, particularly on management levels. Consequently, you must pay as much attention to how to survive after you get the job, as you did to finding the job in the first place.

Survival, for you, consists in seven phases:

1. *Understanding the nature of the world of work.* To aid you in this, we have prepared an introductory essay in Appendix R at the back of this manual. We recommend that you read it as though your very life depended upon comprehending it.

Do it now, please.

2. *Analyzing your communications networks in that organization.* Nothing is as it would seem to be. Most organizations, of any substantial size, for which you will ever work will turn out, upon inspection, to be comprised of two groups:

counselor

READ THE THIRD COLUMN ON EACH PAGE
WHEN WORKING WITH **INDIVIDUALS**

instructor

READ THE FOURTH COLUMN ON EACH PAGE
WHEN WORKING WITH **GROUPS**, WORKSHOPS, CONFERENCES, ETC.

DO TO AVOID THE KINDS OF THINGS YOU DESCRIBED IN ANSWER TO THE FIRST QUESTION ABOVE?

Each group with a convener or moderator as above, and also a scribe & newsprint. Allow the discussion to last as long as seems profitable, and animated. (15–60 minutes)

Reconvene the whole class, and have each scribe share what his/her group concluded.

c. Keep the entire class together for the third question:
GIVEN THE WORLD OF WORK AS IT PRESENTLY IS, WHAT DO YOU THINK IS THE SECRET OF SURVIVING AND HOLDING ONTO YOUR JOB?

Let the class offer their suggestions, and do write them down on a blackboard or sheet of newsprint up front, so everyone can see. Time: 10–25 minutes.

d. *Then* make the presentation HOW TO SURVIVE AFTER YOU GET THAT JOB (the Program Element columns, to the left), including Appendix R – if it was not used at the beginning of this course.

e. Have any questions or discussion that the class wishes afterward. Do these principles seem realistic to you? If so, why? If not, why not? What alternatives can you offer from your own experience, on how to survive?

student

THE PROGRAM ELEMENTS IN THIS FIRST COLUMN HELP THE STUDENT IDENTIFY HIS/HER PRIMARY **FUNCTIONAL GOAL** (WHAT)

THE PROGRAM ELEMENTS IN THIS SECOND COLUMN HELP THE STUDENT IDENTIFY HIS/HER PRIMARY **ORGANIZATIONAL GOAL** (WHERE)

Goal:
To write up for your own use, within three months of your arrival at your new job, two reports:

[1] A very Superficial Analysis of the Organization as Officially Disseminated in Organizational Charts, Policy Statements, etc.

[2] Your Own Penetrating Analysis of the Organization, in Terms of Its Invisible Power Structure and Communications Network.

a. The drones, who are able to keep their jobs, but contribute a relatively small amount to the actual running of the organization.

b. A small minority who not only do most of the effective work there, but also most of the thinking.

The organizational chart, where you are going to work, will blend both together, without any discrimination or distinction. Memorize that chart when you are first on the job; then stick it in the back of your mind.

A chart of only the minority who actually run the place, or what we might call "The Invisible Power Structure", is much more difficult to come by. In fact, you will have to put your own such chart together for yourself, as a result of your own quiet investigation and penetrating observations. But you *can* do it, and you will greatly benefit from this kind of analysis.

By the end of three months, you should be able to diagram both the official structure and the invisible power structure as well. Therefore, draw this up as two separate reports, for your own eyes alone:

(1) A Superficial Analysis of the Organization as Officially Disseminated in Organizational Charts, Policy Statements, etc.

(2) Your Own Penetrating Analysis of the Organization, in Terms of Its Invisible Power Structure and Communications Network.

Thereafter, never confuse the two in your own mind; and never never never betray the second to the first.

Error:
Believing the organizational manuals, instead of doing your own investigation and analysis of what's going on.

Goal:
To help you understand how to become a member of the invisible communications network where you work.

3. *Becoming part of the invisible communications network yourself.* There is no way you can apply for membership in the invisible power structure, within the organization that you are going to work for. But there are two things that you can do, to put yourself in a position to be invited in—eventually.

a. Be nice to the secretaries (or "human beings, with secretarial skills") at all times. It is important for you to understand clearly that one of the most important links in the invisible communications network exists among the secretaries. They can help you at all times, aiding you in your desire to accomplish much, warning you of problems, saving you from blunders. And—if they really like you—alerting you when (and if) some trap is ever being set. If they don't like you, you will probably be the proverbial lamb led to the slaughter, when trouble develops.

b. Be a Producer, at all times. Be the one within your own sub-organization who has all the marks of a member of the invisible power structure. The one who gets things done, who goes

Error:
Catering only to 'big-wigs' and ignoring the secretaries and others who really make an organization run.

counselor

READ THE THIRD COLUMN ON EACH PAGE
WHEN WORKING WITH **INDIVIDUALS**

PRACTICAL AIDS FOR ANALYZING THE INVISIBLE POWER STRUCTURE.

(1) Ignore titles.

(2) Ask yourself (and observe): if you want to get something done in your sub-organization (dept. or whatever), who would you turn to? Who can go outside policy regulations, and get things done? Who does this regularly?

(3) Give particularly strong scrutiny to the secretaries. In many organizations, it is the boss's secretary who really runs the whole place.

(4) Once you have uncovered one member of this invisible power structure, who keeps the whole sub-organization going and makes the decisions, then notice who they turn to in other sections of your organization, when rushing to get things done. They always know their 'opposite numbers', and they maintain an invisible communications network with them.

These are "The Producers" where you work. They go into your second report (to the left).

instructor

READ THE FOURTH COLUMN ON EACH PAGE
WHEN WORKING WITH **GROUPS**, WORKSHOPS, CONFERENCES, ETC.

student

THE PROGRAM ELEMENTS IN THIS FIRST COLUMN HELP THE STUDENT IDENTIFY HIS/HER PRIMARY **FUNCTIONAL GOAL** (WHAT)

THE PROGRAM ELEMENTS IN THIS SECOND COLUMN HELP THE STUDENT IDENTIFY HIS/HER PRIMARY **ORGANIZATIONAL GOAL** (WHERE)

outside petty regulations and gets things done *regularly.* The other members of the i.p.s. will note this, and mark you as one of them.

You will know you have arrived when they invite you to lunch, or in some other way draw you into their inner circle—and communications network.

Error:
Leaning on your laurels, or oars, and ceasing to be a Producer in the present.

Goal:
To teach you how to avoid contributing to your own replacement.

4. *Taking care not to hand anyone else the tools for replacing you.* In any organization where you may work, that is of any substantial size, you may discover there is quite a bit of ambition harbored within the breast of those around you. Laudable ambition, of course. But it causes those around you to see the organization in terms of "juniors" and "seniors". Promotions occur, of course, when a 'senior' resigns, dies, or gets pirated away by another organization. That creates a vacancy, for which an ambitious 'junior' may be seriously considered. But you never know when someone below you in that organization may grow impatient of waiting for such an eventuality, and decide that the only thing keeping him (or her) from promotion is your body, which can of course be removed if s/he can convince the big boss that s/he can do just as good a job as you can, but for less money. Or, if a budget crunch is developing, that his/her job is more worth preserving than yours.

Error:
In any hierarchical organization, telling *anyone* else *everything* you know, so that he could (or she could) do your job as well as you.

Goal:
To teach you how to stay on your toes at all times.

You must take this unpleasant possibility into account, whenever you are delegating authority or training someone new in the organization. If you are in a position to delegate authority, do it with extremely tight reins—or a key part of your function may end up permanently in somebody else's hands, thus crippling you from accomplishing what you set out to do. If you are asked to train someone up to the point where s/he could effectively replace you if you were incapacitated, or otherwise out of the picture, you can be practically certain that if you tell That Person *everything* you know, s/he may not wait for that remote eventuality. Therefore, be sure some essential facts or know-how remain yours, and *Yours alone.*

All of the above caution will not of course be necessary for you to pay any attention to, if a) you are an entrepreneur, or have a position where *no-one* is junior to you, OR b) you end up in an organization that is an absolute model of what an organization ought to be, in terms of brotherly love, etc. On the other hand, we could regale you, by the hour, with stories of men and women who *thought* they were in such an organization, where none of this caution was needed, until they woke up one morning to discover their throats had been quietly cut—vocationally speaking, of course. So: be extremely cautious.

5. *Continuing to grow in your mastery of your function.* Never rest upon your laurels. Always give more than one good day's work for a day's pay. You are, hopefully, doing what you most enjoy doing, anyway; so you will probably not be thinking of this as Work, in the first place.

counselor

READ THE THIRD COLUMN ON EACH PAGE
WHEN WORKING WITH **INDIVIDUALS**

instructor

READ THE FOURTH COLUMN ON EACH PAGE
WHEN WORKING WITH **GROUPS**, WORKSHOPS, CONFERENCES, ETC.

APPLICATION. If you are going into crafts or the rendering of services, where you are pretty much in business for yourself, you still must stay on your toes about your competition.

student

THE PROGRAM ELEMENTS IN THIS FIRST COLUMN HELP THE STUDENT IDENTIFY HIS/HER PRIMARY **FUNCTIONAL GOAL** (WHAT)

THE PROGRAM ELEMENTS IN THIS SECOND COLUMN HELP THE STUDENT IDENTIFY HIS/HER PRIMARY **ORGANIZATIONAL GOAL** (WHERE)

Try to keep up to date with advances in your own field, new developments, what your competition is doing, etc. You can, of course, use at least two avenues toward this end. One is obviously reading: journals, books, periodicals, and everything you can lay your hands on. The other is conversation. Lunches (even if they must be Dutch) are an excellent opportunity to get with people who will help sharpen your mind and your wits, give you new information about your field, bring you up to date on competitive developments, etc.—especially if they are part of the Invisible Power Structure in your own outfit, or in some other organization.

Goal: To teach you how to guarantee an accurate evaluation is made of your work.

Goal: To teach you what to put in your evaluation report.

6. *Keeping your own efficiency/evaluation report.* If you are young, or naive, or both, you may suppose that the organization you are going to work for has some kind of efficiency/evaluation system; *and* that this system will meticulously notice your every achievement or good work; *and* that promotions will be legitimately based upon your boss's careful study of those efficiency/evaluation reports—most notably yours.

Error: Depending on your company's evaluation system, and waiting for promotion to come automatically.

Should it indeed work out this way for you, you may count yourself as one of the most fortunate workers in the whole country. However, in most organizations, you would be wise beyond your years not to lean on this possibility any more than you would lean on a mirage in the Sahara. Most evaluation systems are notoriously inaccurate. Some are pure charades. They will overlook many if not most of your genuine achievements. And when time for promotion comes, especially for anyone at a managerial level, promotion will be largely independent of any evaluation reports, and made rather on the basis of such factors as "I like him (or her)" or "I will promote those who can do me the most good, and make me look good (by contrast?)". The high competitiveness that exists in the world of work helps to create this unfortunate train of events. Fortunately, however, there is a way around all of this. You can ignore the whole review system that your organization may (or may not) have, and maintain your own *weekly* efficiency report. In a notebook, record weekly (or even *daily*) every achievement or accomplishment that you can legitimately claim *any* responsibility for having made happen (e.g., you diagnosed the problem, or suggested the solution, or helped supervise those who were working on the solution, or by your own efforts contributed to increased profits, social responsibility, etc.). Nothing else needs to go into that notebook. *Achievements are the only thing that count.* Keep your mind twenty-four hours a day on achievements. Then record Every One, meticulously, with figures and any other supporting data. Every six months, then, work this up into a brief one or two page efficiency report. Begin it with your stated work Objective, and then support it with the same kind of evidence as you did on your Statement of Where I'm Going, earlier in this course.

Error: Feeling you can *only* claim credit for something that you did from start to finish all by yourself.

This efficiency report is one which you now know is complete down to the last detail, and you don't have to worry whether *someone else* omitted crucial passages, or not. It is very compelling

counselor

READ THE THIRD COLUMN ON EACH PAGE
WHEN WORKING WITH **INDIVIDUALS**

PARACHUTES. As you master your own craft or field—you must always stay alert to the fact that you may be out of business at any time. Think of how many occupations or businesses thought they were very secure, until the energy crisis suddenly came along, and they were out of work.

No one can predict what factors may suddenly make an occupation obsolete tomorrow. More about this in the next Program Element: FULL CAREER/LIFE PLANNING & PROFESSIONAL DEVELOPMENT.

instructor

READ THE FOURTH COLUMN ON EACH PAGE
WHEN WORKING WITH **GROUPS**, WORKSHOPS, CONFERENCES, ETC.

student

THE PROGRAM ELEMENTS IN THIS FIRST COLUMN HELP THE STUDENT IDENTIFY HIS/HER PRIMARY **FUNCTIONAL GOAL** (WHAT)

THE PROGRAM ELEMENTS IN THIS SECOND COLUMN HELP THE STUDENT IDENTIFY HIS/HER PRIMARY **ORGANIZATIONAL GOAL** (WHERE)

to anyone who reads it. And, *it is in your hands*—to be put to whatever use *you* care to put it to. For example, when *you* feel it is time to discuss your advancement within that organization, and you are talking to the one person who has the authority to make that decision, you have the instrument for convincing him (or her) that you have, indeed, been making a profound contribution to that organization—as well as realizing your own life goals and objectives.

Error: Showing this report to anyone except the man or woman who has the authority to make the decision about your advancement.

Goal: To teach you the importance of always maintaining alternatives.

7. *Building your own future alternatives and long-term goals.* It is important for you to be proceeding with your whole-life/full career planning and professional development as a continuous on-going project. Details on how to do this systematically are provided in the next section of this course.

You must know what the next logical step is in your progression toward realizing your life-goals. And you must know this, at all times. You must also never be without a parachute—which is to say, some alternative(s) which you are ready to activate whenever the time is ripe.

It is important also to know when it fits your Objective to advance within your present organization, and when it fits your Objective to be pirated away by another organization. This is always a real possibility, of course, if you are known as a Producer of achievements, and you circulate enough with people outside your own organization so that you come to be seen and known. You will know that potential pirating is in progress when some such events as the following, begin to happen to you: you are taken out to lunch several times by a senior official from another organization, who elaborately refrains—throughout—from asking you any information about your present organization. In due course, however, he or she will ask you for a resume—strictly as a matter of information and curiosity, of course—to which you will reply that since you are not looking for a job, you don't have a resume. Far from turning him off, this will usually only whet his appetite. If he continues to press, and if you like his organization, you can at last with the greatest reluctance and diffidence confess that while you don't have a resume, you *do* have your latest personal progress report—the efficiency report we were talking about, above. You will point out it is not an official document, but just the way that you privately keep score; and it is absolutely confidential, to be burned before reading. Therefore you cannot give him a copy, but you can allow him to read it over dessert there. Because of your extreme diffidence about all this, he will clearly understand that whatever he might have had in mind for you at first—by way of position level, and remuneration,—will have to go way up, because you are

Error: Giving away any copies of your own personal efficiency report.

counselor

READ THE THIRD COLUMN ON EACH PAGE
WHEN WORKING WITH **INDIVIDUALS**

instructor

READ THE FOURTH COLUMN ON EACH PAGE
WHEN WORKING WITH **GROUPS**, WORKSHOPS, CONFERENCES, ETC.

er (kə-rêr′), n. [Early Mod. Eng. *careere, carreer;* arrière, road, racecourse; It. *carriera* < *carro;* see . 1. originally, a racing course; hence, 2. a swift se, as of the sun through the sky; hence, 3. full l. 4. one's progress through life. 5. one's advance-; or achievement in a particular vocation; hence, lifework; profession; occupation.

NOT, TO BE TAUGHT TO OTHERS UNTIL THE INSTRUCTOR HAS FIRST TAKEN THE COURSE HIM (HER) SELF.

much more valuable than he had even realized. Therefore, let the next move be his—which, if it comes, will likely be an invitation to you and your mate for "just a friendly family dinner". Act astonished, of course, when his offer comes at that dinner, and then promise to give it full consideration.

This particular little drama is even more effective when you have chosen the other party without his knowledge, and then used the methods we discussed under "Getting To Meet Your Individual Targets", part 4. Which is to say, you have unobtrusively gotten to meet the top man in the division of an organization that interests you. You have chosen him, but permitted him to believe that he has discovered you.

SIXTEENTH CLASS SESSION
SOME SUGGESTED PROGRAM ELEMENTS

1. LOOKING BACK

a. Here is the opportunity to collect feedback about the entire course, as you have led it, and as the students have experienced it. A questionnaire can be handed out and filled in *during class time.* It is outlined under Classroom Exercises, below.

b. Check to see if they have any questions about the process from here on out.

2. LOOKING AHEAD

a. Sometimes a class wants to meet with each other, to find out how they are progressing: one month hence, three months hence, six months hence. This is feasible if they will be remaining basically in the same area. However, if the class is not remaining in the same geographical area, sometimes one member of the class will volunteer to serve as 'class secretary' and put out a bulletin every two or three months, if class members will send him/her the news as to how they are progressing with their job-search.

b. More immediately, does the class feel it needs any additional sessions right now—or was all the material covered to their satisfaction?

3. CLASS EXERCISES

a. Suggested form to be distributed to class members during this session:

STUDENT FEEDBACK

It will be a great help to improving this course for others, if you will tell us your opinion about the following questions:

1. What did you find the most helpful, in this course?
2. What did you find that could be improved about this course?

Goal:
To show you what you can do in the way of ongoing planning for your career and your life, so as to be ready to take advantage of every opportunity, lucky break, and accident that comes your way, for the rest of your life.

Postscript: Full Career/ Life Planning & Professional Development

You can do planning for your whole life just as accurately, carefully, easily and logically as you plan your vacation or any other worthwhile endeavor. The problem is the same. Planning for your whole-life (or: organizing your luck) follows along the same steps as you have just traced in this course. This is the only intelligent approach, i.e., an analytic planning and implementation process that is orderly, realistic, logical and comprehensive.

The key to whole life planning, as has been the case throughout this course, is correct *identification* of the factors which are crucial to your planning/implementing process, accurate and realistic *analysis* of them for your own personal point-of-view, followed by your own happiest and most promising *decisions* on each of them.

What tools you use, and what format you use them in, is entirely up to you. It can all be as simple or as elaborate as you wish. You are the only judge as to how complex or sophisticated it should be—depending upon your own preferred way of thinking and working.

However, over the years students have reached some agreement, from experience, as to what components are essential for their overall tool-kit in life-planning, and—not surprisingly—they are the very components which you have already used in this course. For, after all, the factors you have identified, analyzed and made decisions about here are the very same factors you must always keep in mind—for intelligent planning throughout your life.

So here is a chance to organize a life-planning system, that will stand you in good stead, for years to come—if you wish.

Error:
Failing to do any more planning. Letting this course be the end of your planning, for your career and for life.

Goal:
To enable you to assemble all pertinent factors in a logically organized, summarized order, for ready use whenever you wish.

A Solution-Finding Tool: Your Estimate of the Situation

As we emphasized earlier, chance, accident, and serendipity are at the very heart of life. Using this tool will not automatically eliminate these factors from your life, by any means. It cannot deliver you from the necessity of guesswork, preclude any possibility of accidental setbacks, nor guarantee you ultimate success. It will, however, at least insure that you are giving due consideration to all pertinent factors, thereby *reducing the sheer-luck factor to as acceptable a level as is ever humanly possible in any planning process.*

counselor

READ THE THIRD COLUMN ON EACH PAGE
WHEN WORKING WITH **INDIVIDUALS**

instructor

READ THE FOURTH COLUMN ON EACH PAGE
WHEN WORKING WITH **GROUPS**, WORKSHOPS, CONFERENCES, ETC.

3. Is anything still unclear to you? If so, what?
4. Would you recommend this course to others? Why? Would you be willing to teach it to others?

(optional) ______________________________
(Signature)

b. Ask to have these turned in to you, when the students are finished answering the forms. Ask the students then to tell what they wrote in answer to question 3. See if other students can help them with the answers, at this point.

c. Tell them the problem now is how to take this process and make use of it for the rest of their lives. The problem is also what to do with all the files they have accumulated.

Tell them this inevitably leads into your subject, HOW TO DO YOUR OWN FULL CAREER/LIFE PLANNING AND DEVELOPMENT FOR THE REST OF YOUR LIFE. Present the program element to them, in as imaginative form as you can.

d. Ask for reactions, questions, discussion.

e. Dismiss the class early.

A suggested outline will be found in Appendix S, at the back of this manual. It offers, needless to say, a beautiful way to organize and file all of the material which you have gathered in this course; so that this material becomes the nucleus of your on-going full life planning.

We suggest you then take a calendar (if you have one) and 'flag' on it the times when you will particularly deal with this Solution-Finding Tool (entitled Your Estimate of the Situation; or: Your Personal Lifework Planning System; or, whatever).

E.g. *Six months from now:* a note on your calendar to review the whole system.

One month from now and every month thereafter: a note to update your autobiography, and the analysis thereof to extract skills & qualities. Also, to update your Contact List, if you have let is slide.

Needless to say, you will continue to file all the things you read, that interest you, in the appropriate file.

A Short-Term Planning Tool: Your New Personal Operations Plan No. 2

(The Personal Operations Plan drawn up earlier in this course was your no. 1, of course.) The title here, as earlier, is not important—so long as you draw up your own comprehensive, logical, realistic plan for the achievement of the next Specific Immediate Objective, that you listed in section II, of your Personal Lifework Planning System (Appendix S, page 246 of this manual).

This is to prepare you for the next step in your life, so that you will always be prepared to capitalize on whatever luck or accident may come your way.

A suggested outline for this Operations Plan is:

I. *Your Next Objective* (simply copy the next Objective you have for your life, now that you've gotten this job, from Section II of Appendix S.)

II. *Where* (list your top three geographical preferences, in descending order).

III. *With Whom* (list your potential targets for this next Objective, any Live targets you are already aware of, and—if you know them—any Ultimate Organizational targets *for this Objective.*

IV. *Organizational Targets Information.* Footnote here where you are keeping information about Targets which you have identified (the folders for Sections VII, OR VIII below, for example).

V. *Ultimate Individual Targets* (list any whom you have identified as people who have authority to hire for the function you are interested in, in whatever organization you might be interested in 'doing your thing' next).

VI. *General Plan of Approach to These Kinds of Targets.*

VII. *What Additional Information Is Needed* (list it and how you plan to acquire it; also give yourself deadlines on getting it).

VIII. *Your Plan of Approach to Ultimate Individual Target No. 1* (if you don't know who this might be, as yet, you will obviously have to fill this section in at some later time; but leave the heading here, anyway. It is to remind you to spell out *in detail* the contacts who might be able to help, others you should and can meet, your further plan for obtaining every bit of information you will need to know about this individual and his particular organization before you approach him (or her). Establish time tables. Decide when you will want to begin to think of taking this next step beyond your present job).

IX. *Your Plan of Approach to Ultimate Individual Target No. 2* (fill it in when you can).

X, XI, XII, etc. Same for other targets____.

XIII. *Campaign Coordination* (filled in at the appropriate time, this is how you plan to integrate your approach to all the Individual Targets at the same time).

XIV. *Milestones and Timetables* (how you'll know whether you're ahead of schedule, behind, etc.; whether you ought to reassess your priorities in order to get at this).

XV. *Control, Measurement, Reporting & Follow-Up Systems* (checks on yourself).

XVI. *Special Procedures and Techniques.*

If the above planning tool does not please you, draw up your own. Just be clear that what happens with your life depends on what *you* do. If loose threads are to be picked up, of problems are to be unraveled, if luck is to be capitalized upon, in your life, it will be largely if not entirely up to *You.* So plan it at least as carefully as you plan *anything* else in your life; and if you have caught our vision, plan it *more carefully* than anything else you will ever do.

If you will only realize that who you are is already written upon your members in the unique blend of skills, interests, talents, values and directions that make up You, and if you will only consciously direct each day's effort from now on to the deliberate exercise of your own greatest strengths that you are conscious of, AND to the deliberate expansion of your own knowledge and skills, AND to the deliberate attainment of significant personal accomplishments,

you can hardly fail to *enjoy* yourself more, earn continuously growing respect from the people who matter to you, and continue building your own self-confidence, with the rewards to which you are legitimately entitled as a consequence.

AMEN

Appendix A

An Overview of This Course

Who is this course for?

This course is for you if you are between the ages of 16 and 86, and would like to find more fulfillment and happiness in your life, through commitment to a concentrated developmental program of personalized, individual exploration of what makes you unique.

It is for you if you work, or would like to begin working, or would like to find more fulfillment in both your work and your life.

It is for you if you want help in choosing a career, or in changing careers without traditional retraining, or in finding alternative kinds of employment.

It is for you if you are unemployed or if you are having difficulty in finding employment, and you want an alternative to the traditional job-hunting 'system'—as it is laughingly called.

It is for you if you seek improvement in your self-confidence and in your decision-making ability and in your knowledge of how to accomplish what you want to accomplish.

It is for you if you would like help in planning where your life is going next, and if you would like help in developing alternatives.

This is more than a job-hunting workshop. It is more, even, than a life-planning course. It is, in some sense, a whole different way of educating you.

What is expected of the student?

First of all, motivation. It is crucial that you must want something of what this course has to give. You must believe in your life, and must be willing to do some hard thinking about that life of yours, so that you may find as much fulfillment and happiness as any human being can reasonably expect. This motivation must be your own. No one should take this course simply because someone else thought you should.

Secondly, commitment is expected of you. It is a most concentrated course. The fifty hours of class time, spent in group process experiences of personal exploration of what makes you unique, is only the beginning. There is extensive homework, which can run the equivalent of two to four hours a day, at times. But while there is a minimum amount of time which you must commit to this course, there is no maximum. The value of the course will be directly proportional to how much time you can lavish on it outside the classroom. The harder and longer you work on it, the more you will change your future.

The test, so to speak, of your motivation and commitment will be found in the very first exercise, for it is the hardest part of the whole course: the writing of your very detailed work-autobiography, the equivalent of a small book. Anyone who gives evidence of lack of commitment and motivation, by failing to fulfill this assignment within the allotted time of three weeks, will automatically be dropped from this course. There is no point to wasting your time further.

Third, what is expected of you is a willingness to re-examine some of our country's most cherished presuppositions about how you choose work, how you find work, and how you find fulfillment in your work. Not only will these presuppositions be searchingly critiqued, but new methods and ideas will be proposed which will at first sight cause some incredulity. We ask you for a temporary suspension of disbelief until you have had a chance to test them for yourself; and to that end, early on in this course there is a practice field survey in which—after careful instruction—you are asked to go out into the community and test some of these principles, so that you may validate them in your own experience. The most radical principle—be forewarned!—is that you *can* overcome most if not all of the obstacles that other people will tell you you cannot overcome.

Finally, each student is expected to share with others what you will learn in this course. In both its method and its subject matter, this course is committed to our mutual interdependence upon one another. If we are not precisely our brother's keeper, we are at least our brother's helper. (And sister's.) If you pick up the principles of this course faster than others, we expect you to be willing to give some of your time to helping those who are slower. On the other hand, if you are slower, we expect you to be open to receiving help from others (it is sometimes harder to receive than to give). We ask you also to share these insights and learnings outside of the classroom. With your loved ones. Your family. Your friends. Whatever this course may be, the one thing it is *not* is a set of principles and secrets meant to be hoarded by those privileged few who have had access to them. It is a course for all mankind, and part of the price of taking it is that you must be willing to take the time throughout the rest of your life to share its insights with others, wherever you go.

What is the course all about?

It is about how you can take fuller charge of your own life, to do with it what you most want to do, and accomplish that which you most want to accomplish with it. It is about your uniqueness and how you do not need to allow the world to frustrate that uniqueness. It is about the false dichotomy between jobs with meaning and jobs with money, and how it is that you can find work which really is enjoyable and fulfilling, and at the same time enjoy those legitimate rewards and benefits to which you are, as a human being, entitled.

The purpose of the course is to give you a process through which you can determine exactly who you are, and what you have that is of value to yourself and to others; to give you an accurate and honest picture of the world with which you have to cope in order to manage your life fully and without fear; and to help you identify what you want to accomplish with your life; and, how to go about doing this successfully.

To this end, the course gives you a whole series of questions to answer and decisions to make, which may be briefly summarized under four headings:

• *Who am I?*

The course opens with a careful self-examination of your entire past, in order to identify down to the last detail your specific skills and strongest personal qualities, so that each can then be scrupulously examined individually. The purpose of this examination is to permit you for perhaps the first time to render your own value judgment on *each* skill in terms of your interest in it, the pleasure which you do or do not derive from exercising it, and the degree of expertise you enjoy in it. You will also, in the process, see how completely transferable to other fields are your skills, assets, traits, and qualities. This opening stage of the course culminates in your preparation of a complete list of all your strongest skills, which are then grouped by you into new logically related, creative clusters—which bring sense out of the random work-experiences and seemingly varied but unrelated accomplishments that have characterized your life to date. This is done according to your own creative insights and language, rather than according to the artificial categories of so-called 'personnel experts'. And your uniqueness as an individual becomes apparent, in the uncommon way that your skills are blended together, in the service of your own values, interests, and concerns.

• *What is the truth about the realities of the world of work, as seen from the only point of view that carries weight, namely my own?*

At this stage, you are taught the simple truth about the work environment in this country as it affects the individual. Further, you are taught how to cope with it successfully, a la David and Goliath. The method by which this is done is:

a. The imparting of simple truths by the instructor, and his (or her) answering any question you wish to ask—but never dared to.

b. Your sudden realization that his/her explanations of everyday situations jibe with your own past experiences.

c. His/her proposal of new methodologies—surveying, contacts, and targeting—and your testing each of these new concepts in practice, out in the field.

The truths that are dealt with are: how does the job market, so called, actually work? Or doesn't it exist, at all? How do people get jobs that have meaning? Or how do people find meaningful self-employment? What is the truth about the whole employment process and 'system' in this country? And: how do some lucky people manage to enjoy life in meaningful and fulfilling work, and at the same time enjoy the standard of living they want?

• *What do I really want to accomplish with my life?*

Having gotten to know yourself better than ever before, and having seen the realities of the world of work as they really are, you are then ready to decide exactly what you most want to accomplish in that world. This requires a series of carefully sequenced decisions (the rationale being carefully explained for each) on the various matters which will be of greatest significance to you for your future. And then the melding of these decisions with your strongest skills and assets in order to fashion a clear-cut statement of precisely what you most want to do, and where you most want to do it, summarized as a short-range immediate objective that is formulated in the light of your ultimate personal goals.

Specifically, what this involves is:

a. You are given the tools and guidance necessary to reach your own thoughtful decisions on these keys to your future fulfillment and happiness:

(1) Where you want to live.
(2) The kinds of people you want to work with.
(3) The kinds of activities you would like to do.
(4) The working and living conditions you really like.
(5) Your ideal job specifications.
(6) The business ethics you want to be working with.
(7) The values you hold important and beyond compromise.
(8) Your major interests.
(9) The kinds of issues you want to help solve, or the other ends to which you want your creativity to be set.
(10) The care of your family and what that requires.
(11) Your future lifestyle, and your loved ones' involvement in it.
(12) Your immediate and long-range financial needs and desires.
(13) How you want further to develop your own skills and knowledge.
(14) What alternatives you want always to have ready at hand.

b. You are taught the key to personal fulfillment, viz., the knowledge that you can contribute to the accomplishment of a human or societal function in which you truly believe. That may be feeding or clothing people, or helping solve energy problems, or working on behalf of ecology, or helping to build something, or whatever. But every job is in some measure the answer to a societal need. Specifically, this step involves:

(1) Learning to ignore the lifelong brainwashing our culture has given each of us, that we should not visualize what we would most like to do because it will be impossible to achieve it anyway. You are required to spell out your impossible dreams, to translate them into alternative ways and means, and to pursue vigorously your whole dream with your whole heart. What is the societal need or situation which you would be most pleased to meet, solve, or improve, if you had the power to do so?

(2) Each of your choices is examined by you in terms of how you can make constructive entry into it on your own terms, and in accordance with a plan that successfully eliminates most or all of the things formerly alleged by 'personnel experts' to be roadblocks, handicaps, or even insurmountable obstacles on your path.

(3) You then choose which of your formerly impossible dreams shall become the target of your pending entry or re-entry into the world of work on an entirely new, stronger, and far freer basis.

c. You then blend all these working materials—the prioritized skill-clusters, your decisions about your goals, values, interests, and preferred working conditions—into some clear statements of where you want to go with your life. First, in terms of ultimate life-goal (as you presently perceive it), and then working backward from that, your immediate and intermediate accomplishment objectives. These are developed so that your next stage and feasible alternatives are always readily identifiable.

• *Lastly, how do I go about accomplishing it?*

Knowing exactly what all your assets are, and precisely what you want to do, and where, with whom, at what level, and under what circumstances; and, above all, precisely what it is you most wish to do or accomplish, the actual mechanics of getting where you want to go become relatively simple, contrary to what everyone supposes. The mechanics you are taught are:

a. How to identify those individuals and/or organizations which share your major interests and meet all your requirements, either as prospective employer, or as client, or in whatever role you need them.

b. How to learn everything you will need to know about them in advance, and how to identify that one individual in each case whom you must convince of your overwhelming value to his or her effort.

c. How to meet him or her under non-stress conditions, and how to give him or her the best possible opportunity to conclude for him/herself that s/he would be a fool not to avail him/herself of your abilities and shining enthusiasm.

d. How to survive, afterward, by the simple expedient of remaining outstandingly productive and creative, for the rest of your active life.

e. How to continue planning and managing your own life, through your choice of successive objectives, and even changes of interests, over the succeeding years.

In the case of individuals who want an independent lifework or alternative form of employment (jobs without bosses, profits or competition, because you want to avoid buying things you don't want, with money you don't have, to impress people you don't like), you will be taught how these same principles apply in your particular case equally helpfully.

What is the exact process of this course, step by step?

On the facing page we have diagrammed how this course is constructed, lesson by lesson.

Does it work?

Each of you is unique, thank God, and the moment you know enough about your uniqueness, you will lose your fear of 'the system', because you will know it cannot stop you. Our so-called employment system in this country is, to be sure, a horror. But it is 'a paper tiger' once you or any intelligent, disciplined and highly motivated individual can forget the bonds we foist upon ourselves, and drive singlemindedly and unswervingly toward your own self-fulfillment and life-goals. The world, as someone has well said, stands in awe of someone with purpose who knows where he or she is going with his or her life. That is because it is, unhappily, not a very common sight. Very, very few people have ever dared to set their own personal, optimum goals. Fewer have ever bothered to examine "the system" to discover that it is indeed a paper tiger. Most workers appear to have no real idea of where they are, how they got there, or where they might be going. The individual who does, is not, to be sure, *guaranteed* success. But his or her chances of realizing his or her life goal are increased a thousandfold. Statistics and records of those who have taken this course over a period of more than fourteen years indicate that at least 86% do realize their goals. That, compared to the usual 'success' rate of 5% for the traditional avenues of our so-called 'employment system' in this country, is worth your fighting for. This course is the doorway.

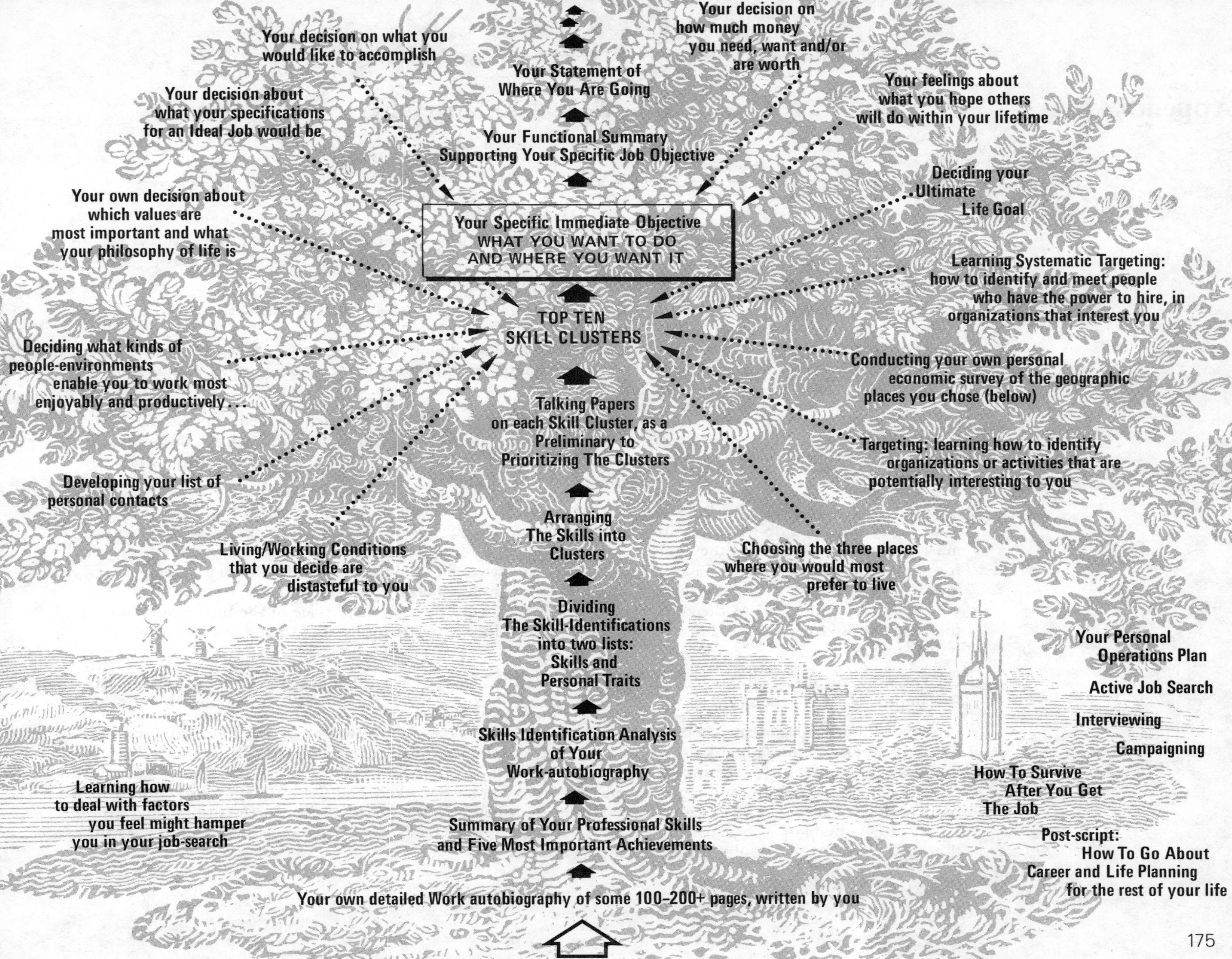
Your decision on what you would like to accomplish
Your decision on how much money you need, want and/or are worth
Your Statement of Where You Are Going
Your decision about what your specifications for an Ideal Job would be
Your feelings about what you hope others will do within your lifetime
Your Functional Summary Supporting Your Specific Job Objective
Deciding your Ultimate Life Goal
Your own decision about which values are most important and what your philosophy of life is
Your Specific Immediate Objective
WHAT YOU WANT TO DO
AND WHERE YOU WANT IT
Learning Systematic Targeting: how to identify and meet people who have the power to hire, in organizations that interest you
TOP TEN
SKILL CLUSTERS
Deciding what kinds of people-environments enable you to work most enjoyably and productively . . .
Conducting your own personal economic survey of the geographic places you chose (below)
Talking Papers on each Skill Cluster, as a Preliminary to Prioritizing The Clusters
Targeting: learning how to identify organizations or activities that are potentially interesting to you
Developing your list of personal contacts
Arranging The Skills into Clusters
Living/Working Conditions that you decide are distasteful to you
Choosing the three places where you would most prefer to live
Dividing The Skill-Identifications into two lists: Skills and Personal Traits
Your Personal Operations Plan
Active Job Search
Interviewing
Campaigning
Skills Identification Analysis of Your Work-autobiography
How To Survive After You Get The Job
Learning how to deal with factors you feel might hamper you in your job-search
Summary of Your Professional Skills and Five Most Important Achievements
Post-script: How To Go About Career and Life Planning for the rest of your life
Your own detailed Work autobiography of some 100–200+ pages, written by you

Appendix B

Your Work Autobiography

RATIONALE

Reasons for each program element have been carefully thought out, by John Crystal over many years. Reasons primarily for the instructor/counselor's own awareness, have been placed in brackets [ ]. Reasons that *should be shared with the student,* have been left unbracketed.

There are several reasons why this course begins with a detailed work-autobiography, and these reasons are important for both student and instructor to understand—lest, in the interests of saving time, you be tempted to try to "leap over" this element—a fatal error.

(1) Self-esteem and good feelings about oneself come from remembering past achievements and strengths. Beginning this program by going back over the past, helps your self-esteem immeasurably—and thus makes it all the easier to do the remainder of the program. You begin to see that you have a veritable army of talents and skills at your command. As you have already demonstrated.

(2) You begin to realize that whole life-planning is a matter of taking charge of your own life, from now on. You realize what you do with your life from here on out is your business. What decisions you make about it must be your decisions. And they must be as rational and informed as you can possibly make them. In order for them to be that, you must have all the possible data at your command. *Part* of that data is a complete inventory of the past. The work-autobiography is a means of gathering together all of the relevant data that you need out of the past. As the course goes on, this data will be put to the service of the future directions that you choose for your life. For it is only as the past is linked to the future that the present becomes transformed.

(3) The work-autobiography is the 'goldmine' out of which will be carted the 'nuggets' of your skills and talents. It is impossible to do the skill-identification exercises, unless this autobiography is first completed.

(4) We could probably identify a number of your skills just from a description of a typical week in your life. But beyond just enumerating skills, we are looking for *patterns.* This is the reason why, after completing your summary of your adult (or significant) working experience, we ask you to review the past, segment by segment. These segments correspond to the various places where you have worked, and the different jobs you have held. By devoting equal care to each segment, you begin to discover the existence of the aforementioned patterns. That is, the same families or clusters of skills tend to keep resurfacing, in each time-segment. Only a careful, thorough work-autobiography will reveal these patterns.

THE RATIONALE OF "SKILLS"

In the entire field of life planning, career development, or whatever, there is probably no subject more misunderstood than the subject of Skills.

The average person, when asked to enumerate her/his skills, will probably give you an answer that has the following two characteristics:

(A) S/he will name about six *broad* areas, like "I am good with people", or "I'm good at analyzing situations", and let it go at that.

(B) S/he will, generally speaking, refer to skills as something taught in high school or college.

A more thoughtful approach to the subject of skills, will reveal that they fall into at least three different categories, corresponding to the three stages by which skills develop. (Or three levels.)

(1) Skills which you do only with great difficulty, *and* it looks difficult to the onlooker, as well.

(2) Skills which you do only with great difficulty, *but* it looks effortless to the onlooker.

(3) Skills which you do effortlessly, *and* it looks effortless to the onlooker as well.

The crucial point is, that if you are trying to recall what your skills are, you will find no. 1 the easiest to identify, no. 2 the next easiest, and no. 3 the least easy to put your finger on. To illustrate, let us suppose you are at level no. 1 with typewriting, at level no. 2 with skiing, and at level no. 3 with handwriting. When asked what your skills are, you will find it easiest to recall the typing, harder to think of the skiing, and hardest to name the handwriting. Which is to say, the longer you have effortlessly been doing something, the harder it is to recall the time when you were first mastering it.

All this is but a prelude to our major contention, however, which is that there is a fourth category of Skills; namely:

(4) *The talents that you were born with, which you have always been able to do effortlessly.*

The difference between this category, and the earlier ones, may be illustrated with, let us say, typewriting. Typing may be on any one of the first three levels, and hence in any one of the first three categories, depending on the person we are talking about. But it cannot be on the fourth level. That would be, rather, such a talent as finger-dexterity.

Just because you have always had such natural-born talents, and can never recall a time when you did not have them, *you will have the hardest time naming this fourth category.*

All of this is by way of further explaining why the work-autobiography is needed. *The more you can talk* intelligently and meaningfully about your past, the more you are likely to begin to sense not only levels no. 2 and no. 3, but—most importantly—category no. 4, which is what we are urgently looking for. For there lie your greatest strengths.

APPENDIX B.
YOUR
WORK-AUTOBIOGRAPHY

OUTLINE FOR EXPERIENCE ANALYSIS AND CAPABILITY INVENTORY

Name ______________________________ Birthdate ______________

Height ____________ Weight ____________ Marital status ____________ No. children ________

General state of health (any physical limitations?) ______________________________

____

EDUCATION—UNDERGRADUATE

College(s) ______________________________ Degree(s) ____________

Year(s) ____

EDUCATION—GRADUATE, POSTGRADUATE

University(ies) ______________________________ Degree(s) ____________

Year(s) ____

Title of theses, significant term papers, etc. ______________________________

____

Articles published, significant speeches, papers, etc. ______________________________

____

Special schools, armed forces schools (name, course title, duration, date completed) ____________

____

____

____

Business/professional seminars, extension courses, etc. ______________________

____

____

Any other courses completed, including correspondence courses, etc. ______________

____

____

SPECIALIST QUALIFICATIONS

Any military specialist qualifications, by title; or non-military, professional specialties ________

____

____

____

FOREIGN LANGUAGE PROFICIENCIES

Give name of the language, and your quality estimate (G=Good, F=Fair, P=Poor) of your ability under three headings: Speak, Read, Write. (If even better than Good, please say so.)

____

____

____

PROFESSIONAL SOCIETIES

List memberships held at any time, including offices ______________________

____

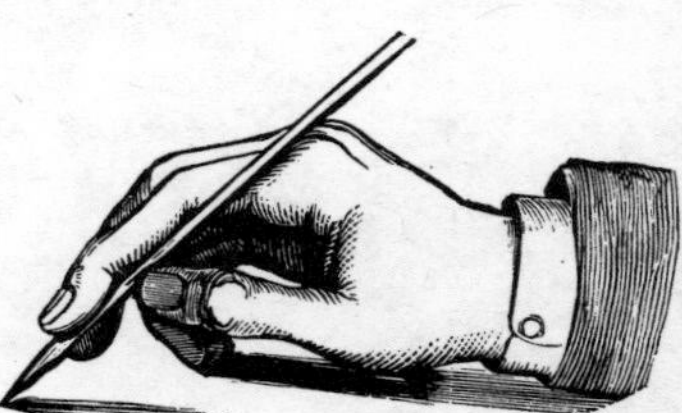

SPORTS AND HOBBIES

What you do in your spare time ____

____

____

PROFESSIONAL LICENSES OR RATINGS HELD

List civilian and military, if any ____

____

REMARKS

Any other information you wish to have included in this outline, to which you may later wish to refer, in writing up your work-autobiography ____________________________

____

____

If government worker, your security clearance status ____________________________

SUMMARY OF YOUR ADULT WORKING EXPERIENCE (BY TIME SEGMENTS)

Please commence with your *earliest* adult work experience or significant work experience (whenever it occurred). Do not leave gaps in your chronology, since this summary serves as the "pegs" on which your work-autobiography is to be hung. If you had periods of unemployment (or of hunting around to see what you wanted to do next), please list the time period, and simply write "Not Employed" during that period. There is no need to list leave, vacation times, times between jobs, or assignments of short duration; simply give as the first date of a new assignment/job, the calendar date immediately following the last day at your preceding assignment/job. An example of how to fill out the outline is given under *a* and *b*, below.

a.	6/60	1/62	Mechanic	Asst. Parts Mgr.	Cory Motors	Richmond, Va.
b.	1/62	7/65	Sales Mgr.	Southeast Region	Renway Inc.	Washington, D.C.

APPENDIX B.
YOUR
WORK-AUTOBIOGRAPHY

	FROM	*TO*	*TITLE/RANK*	*ASSIGNMENT/DUTIES*	*ORGANIZATION/COMPANY/GROUP*	*LOCATION*
1.						
2.						
3.						
4.						
5.						
6.						
7.						
8.						
9.						
10.						
11.						
12.						
13.						
14.						
15.						
16.						
17.						
18.						

Appendix C A Summary of Professional Skills

RATIONALE

Reasons for each program element have been carefully thought out, by John Crystal over many years. Reasons primarily for the instructor/counselor's own awareness, have been placed in brackets [ ]. Reasons that *should be shared with the student,* have been left unbracketed.

Why start on a (preliminary) list of your skills, at this point in the process? There are a number of reasons:

1. **A NEW METHODOLOGY.** To look for skills is to begin to learn a new way (or to reinforce that learning) of understanding and communicating anything: taking the factual, and analyzing it in order to:

   a. SEPARATE IT FROM ITS ENVIRONMENT. "I did it sitting at a desk." Who cares whether you were sitting at a desk, or at the end of a log? What you did, and what you used to do it, is important; not the environment in which it was done, necessarily.

   b. GET BENEATH ITS SURFACE. The important question is not what you achieved, but What You Used in accomplishing those achievements. This exercise begins to get at that. Skills are ageless, colorless, and sexless. They are universal.

   c. DISTINGUISH BETWEEN OUTER AND INNER. You must learn (if you do not already know) how to remove the outer shell of the Hard Facts, in order to get at the inner kernel of Your Strengths—and concentrate on these. This is a learned technique, and therefore has to be practiced (as in this exercise)—because it is not taught in most schools, at all.

   d. SORT OUT 'THE IMPORTANT' VS. TRIVIA. The skills you used are the important things, not the experiences per se, or the trivia—the latter being most of the things that other people put in their resumes.

2. **CONCENTRATION ON FEELINGS.** Everybody has a screening device, and everybody's afraid of boring others to death—so we have all learned to screen out things—even from ourselves. You were taught, early on—as in almost all cultures—that emphasis should be placed on hard facts, while the truly important material—your feelings—is to be dismissed. This exercise is designed to begin to reverse that process, and thus to turn off some of your screening devices—through emphasis upon the validity of your own personal feelings and estimations.

3. **REINFORCING YOUR SELF-ESTEEM.** As you work through this exercise, you begin to spot the fact that you have skills, abilities and talents which are universally recognized as important. For this reason, the list of skills that is attached to this exercise by way of illustration or example is deliberately *high executive* skills. You may protest that these do not apply to you because you have not been (nor do you, perhaps, desire to be) an executive. But no matter how simple or even demeaning you may imagine some of your previous jobs to have been, you *have* used 'high' executive skills. The purpose of this illustrative list, without explicitly saying so, is

to lead you to see—midst a culture which defines 'executive' as 'high level'—that *everyone* has such executive skills. Increased self-esteem inevitably flows out of this realization, for women as well as for men. [THIS, INCIDENTALLY, IS WHY SO MUCH OF THIS WHOLE COURSE SEEMS TO HAVE SUCH A 'MANAGEMENT CAST' TO IT; IT IS NOT IN ANY SENSE DESIGNED TO STEER PEOPLE INTO MANAGEMENT OR EXECUTIVE POSITIONS. BUT IT *IS* DESIGNED TO HEIGHTEN PEOPLE'S SELF-ESTEEM BY USING THE LANGUAGE AND SYMBOLS OF OUR CULTURE (EXECUTIVE=HIGH LEVEL). WHATEVER YOU CHOOSE AS YOUR FUTURE, WE WANT YOU TO CHOOSE OUT OF A HEIGHTENED SENSE OF SELF-ESTEEM, AND THE REALIZATION THAT YOU *HAVE* THE SKILLS TO CHOOSE ANY PATH YOU WANT TO.]

4. **PREPARING FOR INTERVIEWS.** By learning to concentrate on your skills, and to separate them out from their environment, their outer shell, and so forth, you are beginning to learn how to handle yourself at an interview, what to talk about at an interview, and how to avoid boring people. Priceless preparation for any kind of interview, whether it be for information, or for a job.

5. [**SAFETY-NET.** If we did not, all of us, have our built-in cultural screening devices as mentioned earlier, much of the material that is uncovered by this particular exercise would have already surfaced as you were writing your work-autobiography. So this exercise is a way of taking our screening devices seriously, and therefore going back deliberately to pick up what they kept us from seeing. Of course, it goes without saying that some of the screening still operates; this is one of the reasons that a counselor is usually so crucial, in one-to-one counseling at this point in the process—and why a buddy-system is crucial in group-counseling situations. We all need *another person's eyes* to look at our material, to see what we missed.]

SAMPLE LIST OF MANAGERIAL, EXECUTIVE, AND PROFESSIONAL SKILLS

PLANNING

- Determining/establishing objectives
- Forecasting
- Scheduling
- Programing
- Plan/program evaluation and revision
- Formulating/determining
  - Progress milestones
  - Policies
  - Procedures
  - Budgets
  - Requirements

ORGANIZING

- Designing organizational structure
- Assessing reorganization proposals
- Establishing/adjusting relationships
  - Coordination
  - Procedural
  - Team work
  - Liaison
  - Inspection
  - Technical
  - Administrative
  - Production
  - Representation
  - Delegation
  - Disciplinary
  - Supervisory

CONTROLLING

- Establishing standards
- Revising standards
- Performance assessment
- Analysis and review
- Adjustment
- Correction

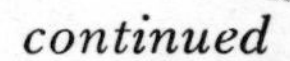

continued

APPENDIX C.
PROFESSIONAL SKILLS

LEADERSHIP

Conceptual acuity
Initiative
Formulating objectives
Defining objectives
Selecting people
Developing people
- Executive
- Technical
- Administrative
- Other

Communicating
- Addressing groups
- Speech writing
- Conferences
- Negotiations
- Conversation
- Supervisory
- Oral presentations
- Analysis, review, assessment
- Technical writing
- Promotional writing
- Historical writing
- Letter writing
- Reports
- Summations
- Position papers
- Industrial relations

Problem identification
Problem definition
Problem solving
Motivating
Decision making
Other

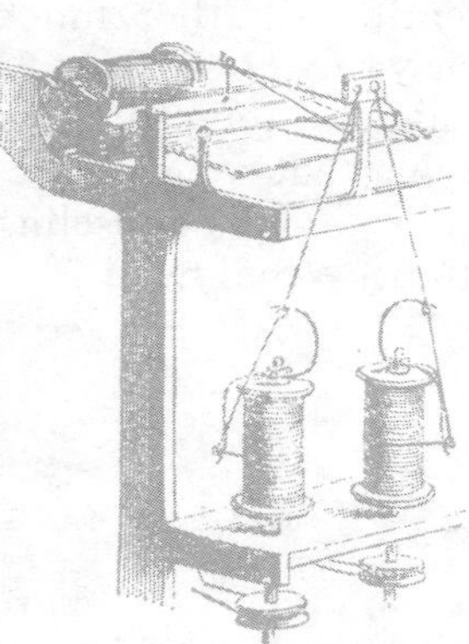

Distasteful Living/Working Conditions

Appendix D

RATIONALE

Reasons for each program element have been carefully thought out, by CMS over many years. Reasons primarily for the instructor/counselor's own awareness, have been placed in brackets [ ]. Reasons that *should be shared with the student,* have been left unbracketed.

TIMING OF THIS PROGRAM ELEMENT ON DISTASTEFUL LIVING/WORKING CONDITIONS:

The work-autobiography and almost all of the preceding elements in this course have been dealing with the question, "Who am I?" But a heavy dose of this theme can tire one, so we turn here to another theme: The Ideal Job Environment. Thus your imagination and interest is kept alive. Moreover, this theme is uplifting and optimistic, which is a helpful counter-mood to the preceding program element which—since it dealt with fears—can get pretty depressing. Thus this element comes as a corrective. Or—to use a musical illustration—these two elements together comprise point and counterpoint.

THE METHODOLOGY OF THIS PROGRAM ELEMENT:

We want to deal in terms of the question: "What do you want?" But, at this point in the course, if we started there we would get only vague answers. So, we start at the other end. Complaining (or 'bitching' or whatever you want to call it) is accepted in our culture. If one listens to The Dislikes, problems almost automatically answer themselves with solutions. Thus this program element encourages the student to talk about his distastes, dislikes, complaints, bitches or whatever—from his past experience; things he wants to be sure he never runs into again (likewise, for women). Or things s/he has always disliked. This is then analyzed in reverse. Because if you know what's wrong, then you know what's right. (See: ANALYZING DISLIKES, on the next page.)

HOPED-FOR RESULTS OF THIS PROGRAM ELEMENT:

This element serves up an opportunity for the instructor to emphasize (as s/he will, many times throughout this course): You can build anything you want, but before that, you have to know *what* you want to build. You won't get it until you ask for it. There is of course no guarantee you will necessarily get it, even then; but we can practically guarantee you will not get it, if you don't even know what you're looking for.

This element will, hopefully, begin to enable the student to see that it's the total environment that counts, in thinking about one's life and one's lifework. And this total environment can be controlled for *your* life, at least.

APPENDIX D.
DISTASTEFUL CONDITIONS

This element is designed also to begin the student thinking about her/his environment in terms of geographical preference. And it is designed to begin the student in writing her/his ideal job specifications. In other words, as in a symphony, this is the first sounding of a few bars of two or three themes, which will become more pronounced and developed, later in the course.

[ANALYZING THE STUDENT'S DISLIKES: A GUIDE

1. The Instructor should be aware that his/her nervousness about how 'to field' or respond to students' remarks in this program element, must not betray him/her into making a cheap remark for an easy laugh, at someone else's (i.e., the student's) expense. Don't laugh (or lead others to laugh) *at anybody.* This is deadly serious business. It's not your life; it's the other guy's (or gal's). Therefore, treat it with the utmost gravity and respect. S/he is beginning timidly to expose her/himself; if you laugh at it in any way, you downgrade it—and therefore him (or her). S/he will consequently clam up, and thus destroy the candor and openness upon which job-hunting in general, and this course in particular, absolutely depend.

2. Generally speaking, the student's description of living or working conditions that s/he finds, or would find, distasteful, will be drawn from his/her own past experience. In general, the way to deal with his/her accounts of disagreeable past experiences, might well be as follows:

a. First of all, sympathize.

b. Validate how distasteful such an experience is, from the instructor's own experience—or the experience of those he knows. "By George, you're right."

c. Always, then, add: "The whole purpose of our work together is to see that you never have to put up with this kind of situation again. So, let us go on to build the picture of what an ideal job situation would look like, for you."

3. If the distasteful living or working conditions are drawn from the experiences of others, because—say—the student has not yet had enough working experiences of his/her own, the same general steps above (a., b. and c.) can still be followed, with slight modifications, in your response.

4. To complete the analyzing of the student's dislikes, you must then go on to change negative statements into positive ones. Which is to say, gripes about the past, when restated, become positive goals for the future. Here are two examples:

Student's statement: "I don't want to be oversupervised, as I have been in the past."

Revision of this into positive goal for the future: "I insist upon being my own boss within nothing less than very clear policy guidelines which I can question at any time, and with no more than one review of my work annually, with me present to defend my position."

Again, *Student's statement:* "Maybe I'm lazy, but I don't know that I really want to work at all."

Revision of this into positive goal for the future: "Considering what work is commonly regarded to be in our culture today, namely drudgery and tedium, I want to discover my own enthusiasms and values so that when I set about doing what most people would call my life's work, it will actually be so enjoyable to me that I will not even think of it as work."]

Practice Field Survey

Appendix E

> RATIONALE
>
> Reasons for each program element have been carefully thought out, by CMS over many years.
> Reasons primarily for the instructor/counselor's own awareness, have been placed in brackets [ ].
> Reasons that *should be shared with the student,* have been left unbracketed.

RATIONALE FOR THE TIMING OF THE PRACTICE FIELD SURVEY

1. Change of Pace. There has been enough time spent within the classroom by this point in the course. It is necessary for you to go out and look hard at the real world, through some new eyes and with a new viewpoint. This exercise gets you out, *but only after you have had enough of the course thus far to ensure that it will be with new eyes and a new viewpoint.*

2. Compelling Personal Evidence. As the course proceeds from this point, some of the ideas in it will seem more and more surprising. We are at the point where you are examining the first surprising concept: that you may indeed be able to choose exactly where you want to live and work, rather than being at the mercy of 'what's available'. It is important for you to gather compelling personal evidence *that will be convincing to you* precisely at this point. For if you remain unconvinced on this point, your ambivalence will erode much of the usefulness of the rest of the process to you. We could, of course, show or tell you stories of literally hundreds of people who have successfully done their own personal field survey. But such success stories have not, in the past with others like you, proved sufficient. You may therefore dismiss the success stories of others, and understandably so, with the rationalization that each of them had something going for him or her that you do not have. Only evidence gathered by you, for yourself, will ultimately convince.

3. Increasing Self-Confidence. The very thought of barging in on a lot of strangers, shakes most beginners. You will never know how easy it is, until and unless you try it for yourself. So, that is just what you are about to do with the Practice Field Survey Exercise. Practice may make you (eventually) perfect; but more immediately, it will remove the natural fear of the unknown. And thereby add to your self-confidence–which, ultimately, is THE secret of this whole process.

RATIONALE FOR THE METHOD OF THE PRACTICE FIELD SURVEY, AND THE GEOGRAPHICAL PREFERENCES EXERCISES

1. Narrowing Down the Area to be Researched. This country is just too big and our economy too complex for any one individual to make anything even approaching a thorough Survey of all the places and organizations relevant to his or her particular field of major interest. The numbers of possibilities are so incredibly vast that

you have no choice but to reduce them to manageable proportions, as soon as you can. And then to set up a systematic research process, that works through the three logical stages of identifying a) potential 'targets', b) 'live' targets, and c) ultimate targets. There might be many ways of narrowing down the area to be researched, but experience has proved that selecting your top three geographical choices is the best way of thus narrowing the research area. This does not mean that if attractive offers appear outside those areas, you will automatically dismiss them. You will want to consider and weigh them very carefully. But the purpose of this exercise is to enable you to concentrate the bulk of *your research efforts* in a manageable area.

2. Increasing Your Chances of Success. Contrary to a popular misconception, selecting the place in which you wish to live *vastly* increases your chances of getting a job or other economic position *that you really want,* rather than diminishing those chances. The misguided soul who bases his career search on "want job, will travel anywhere to get it" thinks that by staying 'loose', s/he is improving her/his chances of ultimate success. S/he is kidding her/himself. Success is dependent upon *the depth of your effort,* which is only possible under manageable circumstances. It is clearly impossible if you commit yourself to indiscriminate and superficial chasing of leads all over thousands or even millions of miles, so to speak.

3. Organizing Your Luck. No one can guarantee that you are going to get what you want wherever you choose to go. Nor can anyone guarantee that you are going to get exactly what you want, anywhere. There is always an element of 'luck', 'the fortuitous crossing of paths', 'serendipity'—or whatever you choose to call it, that is beyond your control. But the question is: 'how can you best organize your luck, so that the factors which *are* within your control are working for you, instead of against you?' The answer is: by choosing a manageable target area, and mining it to death.

4. Choosing Your Happiest Environment. The purpose of all your efforts in this course is to find the greatest amount of day-by-day happiness that can reasonably be expected by any mortal. And to find this by working very hard at the activities which you are most fitted to do because you most enjoy doing them. But environment deeply affects happiness also. And if it is possible to help choose your environment, then it is important you choose an environment where you would be happiest. Indeed, the experience of those who have followed this process religiously, so to speak, before you, is that it *is* possible to choose. While a few were unable to find jobs to their liking in any of their three top geographical choices, and true, some had to accept their second or third choice at the end, the vast majority have actually been able to get the jobs they wanted right where they most wanted to settle down permanently. So, we are asking you to work on the premise that—with luck and serendipity—you should not have to live in an environment you do not like. You are going to have to work hard at this process, anyway. You might as well devote that effort to developing your own dream activity in the place you find most enjoyable, rather than expending the same energy over a place that is only so-so in your opinion, or perhaps even disagreeable.

YOUR PERSONAL PRACTICE FIELD SURVEY EXERCISE

Outline

I. Before you go out
   A. Preparation for obtaining general info about the community
      1. Identify factors
         a. On basis of your past experience
         b. On basis of a checklist
      2. Prioritize the factors
         a. Any way you wish
         b. Or by means of a systematic exercise
      3. Use this prioritized factors list to guide your survey
      4. Do some information gathering before you go out
      5. Think out who you want to see and talk to
   B. Preparation for obtaining particular info on your hobby or interest
      1. Choose one—preferably a genuine enthusiasm of yours
      2. Think out how to dissect the community in this field of interest
         a. Disregard textbook analyses
         b. Do it functionally. An illustration, using "education."
      3. Then draw up a plan of action

II. When you go out
   A. Go "on site."
   B. Go with your eyes and ears open.
   C. Go talk to everyone.
      1. Calling cards
      2. Names
      3. Informational material

III. After you go out
   A. Records.
   B. Thank you notes. Contacts.
   C. Begin applying this to your actual geographical preference areas.

Now, to 'flesh out' this outline ...

APPENDIX E.
PRACTICE
FIELD SURVEY

I. BEFORE YOU GO OUT

A. PREPARATION FOR OBTAINING GENERAL INFORMATION ABOUT THAT TOWN OR CITY

1. Identify the *factors* about a place to live that are most important to you.
   a. List, discuss with your mate or with a group, the things you liked or disliked about the various places you have thus far lived, since birth. Make two lists: one of your likes; one of your dislikes.
   b. Among the factors you may wish to consider in the preceding lists are:
      weather, temperature, rainfall, winds, dust, seasons, humidity, pollution, topography or terrain, open spaces
      ethnic groupings or communities, the pace of life, congeniality of people, food, housing, clothing
      political or legal climate, corruption or its absence, crime rate
      the arts and educational facilities available, entertainment available
      closedness or openness of the community, accessibility, remoteness
      urban vs. rural, access to country or to city, to mountains or to beaches
      architecture, degree of sophistication, cosmopolitan, hi or lo-rises
      safety of streets, heaviness of traffic
      school system, libraries, churches, medical system, and other services
      public transportation, freeways, rapid transit, family health services
      parks, camping, sports, skiing facilities nearby, water nearby
      kind of help available, expensive or inexpensive
      costs, free things to do, taxes
      population density, turnover, degree to which people know each other
      restaurants
      friendliness of the people, proximity to friends
      variety of things to do
      town identity, unity, cohesion, attitude of people toward civic responsibility
      department stores
      color, excitement
      neighborhood or community where your lifestyle didn't matter; or did
      miles between home and work
      t.v., radio, and f.m. stations
      newspapers, magazines, and technical journals
      place with a sense of history, or not
      growth; controlled or uncontrolled? tax rates, property values
      liberal or conservative community
      mail service
      cleanliness of the streets; garbage disposal system, pest control
      types of housing
      other

Disregard any factor not of interest to *you.* The point of this exercise is to discover what makes a place good *for you,* or bad for you (and your loved one/s). Use "b." as checklist *only after* you have *completed* "a."

2. Once you have your two lists: likes, and dislikes—based on your past experiences, put each list in some sort of priority. Most important likes (or dislikes) at the top; least important at the bottom.
   a. You can prioritize each list simply by intuition, discussion, or some other way you may prefer for doing it.
   b. Or you may do it according to some kind of systematic evaluation, such as the following:
      (1) Assign a number (1, 2, 3, etc.) to each of the factors (previous page) that you are going to put in some order of priority.
      (2) Then draw a chart with each of those numbers compared, in turn, to just one other number at a time. The two numbers to be compared should be immediately above and below each other. E.g., a chart comparing ten factors (hence, ten numbers) would look like this:

```
1 1 1 1 1 1 1 1 1
2 3 4 5 6 7 8 9 10

  2 2 2 2 2 2 2 2
  3 4 5 6 7 8 9 10

    3 3 3 3 3 3 3
    4 5 6 7 8 9 10

      4 4 4 4 4 4
      5 6 7 8 9 10

        5 5 5 5 5
        6 7 8 9 10

          6 6 6 6
          7 8 9 10

            7 7 7
            8 9 10

              8 8
              9 10

                9
                10
```

You can add as many more numbers (i.e., pairs) as you need to, for the total number of factors you want to prioritize. Just be sure that, on the first line, no. 1 is compared to all the other numbers you are using; the rest of the chart will then take care of itself.

(3) Once you have completed the chart, use it as a device for comparing two of the factors to each other, and only to each other. Beginning with the first line, for example, the first pair is: 1
2

This means: if you only had time, energy, opportunity or whatever to achieve your preference for the factor you have numbered "1", OR the factor you have numbered "2", which of the two would you prefer?–as more important? Circle that number in the pair. E.g., if you preferred no. 2 over no. 1, your pair would look like: 1
(2)

(4) Go on to each of the other pairs, in turn, and deal with the same kind of question. Circle the preferred number in each pair. The only question: which one do *I* (and my loved ones) prefer? What you think you *should* choose, or what *others* would choose, is not the issue.

(5) When you have compared every pair, go back and count how many times you circled "1" anywhere on the chart; then how many times you circled "2" anywhere on the chart; etc. When you have counted all the circles, the number with the most circles is your first priority; the number with the next most circles is your second priority; etc. E.g., let us say your chart came out like this in the end:

I circled no. 1 5 times
I circled no. 2 6 times
I circled no. 3 2 times
I circled no. 4 2 times
I circled no. 5 5 times
I circled no. 6 7 times
I circled no. 7 3 times
I circled no. 8 4 times
I circled no. 9 5 times
I circled no. 10 6 times

Then my priority list would consequently read as follows:

No. 6 is my top priority
Nos. 2 and 10 are tied as my second priority
Nos. 1, 5, 9 are my third priority (again, a tie)
No. 8 is my fourth priority
No. 7 is my fifth priority
No. 3 is my bottom priority

(6) Take your factors, and make up a new list of your "Likes" and "Dislikes" according to where their numbers occurred in step (5): e.g., in the example above, write out in full the factor that was no. 6, at the head of your new priority list. Then write out the factor that was no. 2 and the factor that was no. 10, together, on the next line, with a bracket lumping them together. Etc.

(7) You will have to repeat steps (1) through (6) all over again for each list you have. Since you have two lists: "Likes" and "Dislikes" you will have to go through those steps twice, once for each list.

3. Now that you have your two lists prioritized, you will know which factors are most important to you, and *therefore which factors you most need to gather information about,* when you do your on-site, eyes and ears wide open, practice personal field survey. And while the town or city you have chosen to practice on, may not in any sense be like your Shangri-La, you can still practice gathering information about the factors that are on your list, anyway; and in their order of priority. So that, if you run out of time, you will at least have gotten information concerning the things most important *to you,* in that community.
4. Before you go out to do the survey, *gather some basic information.* Get a good map of the community (from the Chamber of Commerce, the library, or wherever else they suggest). Get other printed materials about the town from the Chamber, etc.
5. Before you go out, *think out who you want to see* and talk to. Decide if you want to visit the mayor? the local college president? the superintendent of schools? the local congressman? Senator? Chief of Police? County supervisor? local delegate to the state assembly? planning board director? leading real estate office manager? local newspaper editor? bank president? etc., etc. Make appointments where necessary, for the day of your survey.

B. PREPARATION FOR OBTAINING INFORMATION ABOUT THAT PART OF THE COMMUNITY WHICH SHARES THE HOBBY OR INTEREST YOU HAVE CHOSEN TO EXPLORE IN THIS PRACTICE EXERCISE

1. List what the hobby or spare-time interest of yours is, that you are going to explore. If possible, it should be something you are *genuinely enthusiastic* about—since in this practice survey, as well as later when it is "for real", you ought to be going out to discover *who shares your enthusiasms.* The symphony? Art? Learning? Books? You choose.
2. Learn to dissect the community, that you are going to practice on, in the interest area that you have chosen. Your goal, remember, is to know all there is to know about the people and organizations doing, involved in, or making their living at, whatever it is that you have chosen in 1., above.
   a. Textbook distinctions among societal work groups are much too crude for your purposes. No human society is quite as simple as it may appear at first. And you want to insure that you do not carelessly overlook any individuals or groups who could be of great interest to you, in your area of interest.
   b. Many people are in fact doing unexpected and fascinating things in places where they are hardly supposed to be (according to the traditionalists and occupational guidebooks). The task of your practice field survey is to discover where they are, and who they are. The method for analyzing where they are is to think in terms of *real skill requirements* and *actual functional responsibilities.*

   E.g., suppose your interest were *education.* How would you dissect a community, to find all the places where people are engaged in education? You would begin with the obvious. Education breaks down into public, and also private. Then they are subdivided into: pre-school; kindergarten; elementary; high school; college; and grad school. Now, beyond the obvious, you have to begin to put your thinking cap on. If you do, you will realize (or uncover) the fact that education is done in the following places where traditionalists and occupational guidebooks do not often go:

continuing adult education, in places like the "Y", churches, union halls, lodges, professional and trade societies, music clubs, military bases, investment clubs, seminars—held for all kinds of for-profit and not-for-profit groups, etc.
adjuncts to youth education: in Scout Troops, churches, etc.
educational support activities
teachers associations
foundations
private research firms
designers and manufacturers of educational equipment
consultants on every aspect of the field
state and local councils on higher education
elementary education
experts on educational budgeting and cost controls
national and regional associations of universities, land grant colleges, and junior colleges
congressional and state legislature committees on education
fire and police training academies
authors of good and bad books
specialized educational publishing houses
corporate training and sponsored educational departments
etc., etc.

Any one of these activities, and every one of them, is contributing in one way or another and to one extent or other to "education". There is much more to "education" in any given geographical area, than the casual observer might think. The purpose of your practice survey is to uncover this, for the field of interest that *you* have chosen. So, think out as much of this ahead of time as you can; the rest of it you will discover during your survey.

3. After thinking through how you might dissect the community in your field of interest, draw up some plan of action for investigating this when you go out to make your own survey. Where will you start? Who might give you the best clues about where else and who else might give you the information you are looking for.

   [If a whole class is going to do this Practice Field Survey, check to see if two or more people share the same field of interest. If so, let them divide the appointments so that two or more from the class do not visit the same information source during the survey. Who will visit the mayor on behalf of the whole class? Who will visit the newspaper editor? etc.]

II. WHEN YOU GO OUT TO GATHER INFORMATION ABOUT THE COMMUNITY IN GENERAL, AND YOUR OWN FIELD OF INTEREST IN PARTICULAR

A. **YOUR PRACTICE FIELD SURVEY IS TO BE ON-SITE,** and to use whatever spare time you have within one week (seven days). Pretend that this community really is your Shangri-La. Spend as much time, with as much curiosity as you can muster, trying to see how you would go about learning all you wanted to know about your Shangri-La. Your job is not to find a job, but to uncover *information* that will aid *you as decision-maker* in deciding where you want to go in the time to come. Assume (or pretend) at this point that you could find a job doing what you most want to do *anywhere;* so the question is, would you like it to be here? And why? Or why not? And how do you go about uncovering that information? Use the prioritized *factors* list that you prepared.

B. **YOUR PRACTICE FIELD SURVEY IS TO BE WITH YOUR EYES AND EARS OPEN.** Walk the streets. Be alert. Look at everything with the eyes and ears of a young child who is a brand newcomer to this community. What do you notice about it? Sense the attitudes and moods around you. Take the time to stop, look at, and ask about anything which interests you for any reason. You particularly, of course, want to gather information about the *factors* on your list which are important to you for any community you might live in. You also want to gather information about your special field of interest. Read nameplates on office doors, look at directories in buildings that intrigue you. Go in and ask whoever is in charge just what he/she is doing. Tell him you are intrigued by his/her operation, as you are going about making a survey of this particular community.

C. **YOUR PRACTICE FIELD SURVEY IS TO TALK WITH ANYBODY AND EVERYBODY.** Taxi drivers. Interesting or friendly people on the street. If you walk in on an organization that looks interesting, talk to both clerks *and* head honchos. Aim high. He may throw you out or refuse to see you, but chances are he/she won't. S/he enjoys meeting interesting people just as much as you do. Wherever you go, talk to every social strata and kind of profession: social workers, editors, doctors, bankers, lawyers, clergy, etc. And always

1. Carry plenty of personal calling cards (if you don't have them, they can be inexpensively printed up by a local printer), and *exchange* them (get his/hers, in return).
2. *Always* get the name of *anybody* you talk to. (Unless it's someone on the street, and they're obviously reluctant to give it.)
3. Get any and all informational material that any place you visit may have. Ask for it.

III. AFTER YOU GO OUT

A. Keep careful records at the end of *each day* during your practice survey week. Names of people you saw. Addresses and phone numbers. Brief notes on the information they gave you. *Write it all down.*

B. Send the briefest of thank you notes to each person you talked with at any length. (One or two-sentence notes are quite sufficient.) Write a brief, graceful bread and butter note. Such old-fashioned courtesy is so rare these days you cannot fail to be remembered; and that, dear brethren and sistern, is the name of the game. You are practicing building-up what is called a List of Contacts—about which, more later on in this course. Be as faithful about this during your practice, as you will have to be later on, for real.

C. Then identify your three preferred geographical areas For Real (see the exercise in the early part of this manual) and begin applying all the principles you learned in your Practice Field Survey in earnest. Begin your survey, even if your chosen community(ies) are at some distance. Here is a sample letter to the President of the Chamber of Commerce, or anyone who can give you similar information, in outline:

1. Start by telling him the truth, that you have selected his city above all others as *the* place where you want to locate—or stay permanently.
2. Be diplomatic. Mention a few of the pleasanter cultural or economic aspects of his town or city which actually led you (and your mate) to choose it.
3. Tell him that since you plan to settle (or, if you are already there, remain) there you would appreciate his providing detailed information on specific conditions, schools, recreation facilities, etc. You will almost invariably receive a courteous reply and a considerable amount of useful information.
4. Add another paragraph to the effect that you are much too young and vigorous to ever rest solely on your previous accomplishments, and you therefore intend to contribute your skills to some dynamic local concern needing the unusual qualifications which you have to offer. (With luck, you may succeed in stimulating invitations to interviews by local firms, through this initial contact.)
5. Having announced your intentions, ask him to give you all available data on business firms in his area. (If you know at this point in the course what kinds of firms particularly interest you, say so.)
6. Add any pertinent summary of your abilities or experience that you wish.
7. Close by thanking him for his courtesy and expressing the hope that you may be able to call on him in person in the fairly near future.

Starting Your Contacts List

Appendix F

RATIONALE

Reasons for each program element have been carefully thought out, by CMS over many years.
Reasons primarily for the instructor/counselor's own awareness, have been placed in brackets [ ].
Reasons that *should be shared with the student,* have been left unbracketed.

THE RATIONALE FOR THE TIMING OF THE CONTACTS-LIST EXERCISE

1. Momentum. With the Practice Field Survey fresh in your mind, you begin to see how much information can be quickly gathered by an on-site survey of a community. It is natural to want to know how to organize this information, so that none of it gets lost. Hence, now is the logical time to talk about organizing people-contacts that you have made—and will make.

2. Practicality. Having gotten out into a community to do the Practice Field Survey, many if not most students want to get immensely practical at this point. Impatience with classroom philosophizing grows apace. Interest begins to be "out there". And pressure increases at this point in the course to "get out". "How do we do it, chief?" This exercise deals with *who's out there,* thus fitting in with the student's natural questions at this point.

3. Length of time. It takes time to compile this list. By starting now, it will be ready when you need it. If you wait, the process will be delayed at one point while you have to stop to compile the list.

THE RATIONALE FOR BUILDING A CONTACTS LIST

1. Since experience shows that the single best source of vital information and direct job leads is your circle of friends and acquaintances, this is a systematic survey of that complete circle, on your part.

2. Every person you know has his own complete circle of friends and acquaintances, too. If you can compile a list with 200-500 names, each one of those names, in turn, has his/her own circle of 200-500 names. Thus, to compile a list of 200 contacts on your part, is to tap into a potential network of 40,000+ information sources or job-leads. It all ends up looking something like this:

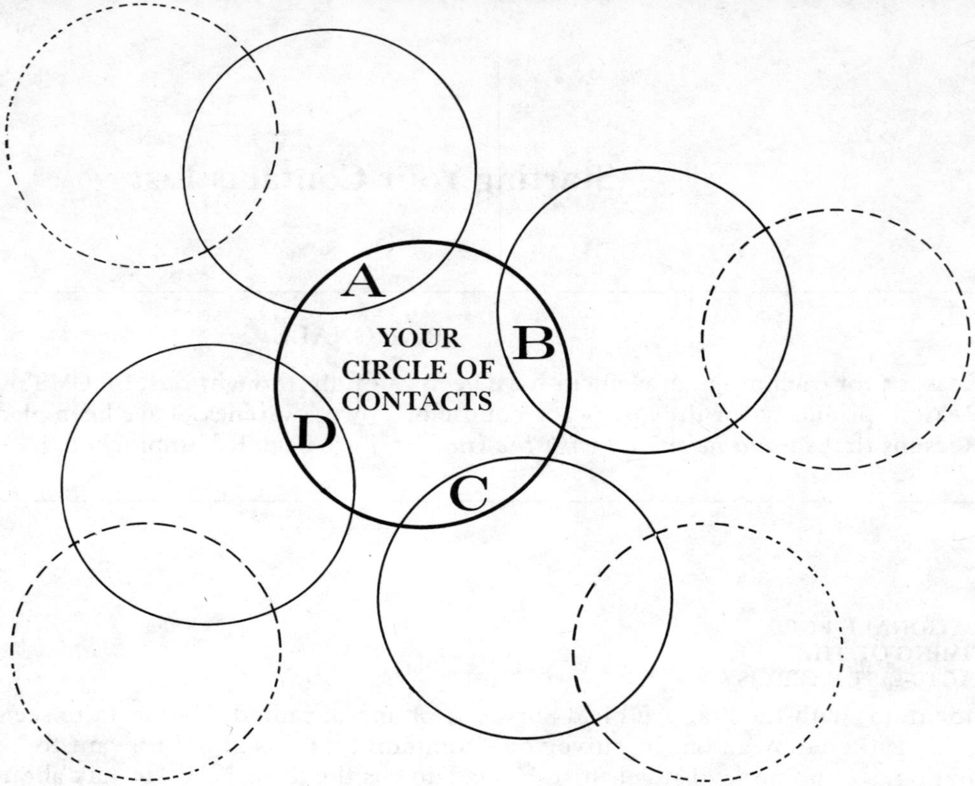

This diagrams the circles available from just four potential contacts: A, B, C, and D.

A
YOUR CIRCLE OF CONTACTS
B
C
D

It is not unusual for students to end up with 1000 on their list.

3. Going back to think of your potential Contacts stimulates your memory banks about many other things as well. We suggest the following memory starters, in compiling your list:

CONTACTS FROM THE PAST AND PRESENT

1. Your Christmas card list—names of *everyone* on it.
2. Classmates and the alumni list from high-school (and college if you attended or are attending).
3. Relatives, in-laws.
4. Fellow Church/committee members
5. Colleagues in civic associations, political groups, volunteer groups.
6. Sports partners.
7. People you know professionally (your banker, etc.).
8. Ex-teachers.
9. Every responsible adult you know: "Your Uncle Charlie, and your Aunt Minnie, that Reserve co-pilot who flew with you in Korea, that old pastor of the Little Church in the Boondocks where you served your first apprenticeship in the front line of the Lord's service, the kid who helped you set up your first advertising account, the reporter who interviewed you the day you won the Big Game, the pleasant-mannered and voiced lady who ran your switchboard back in Kalamazoo, etc."

4. It is essential to keep building your Contacts list, by adding to it ongoing names of people as you meet them, day by day. This succeeds in deliberately expanding your circle of contacts, and also serves *to get you out.* You have to get moving, out talking to people; and hopefully this habit will stay with you for the rest of your life. This is helpful not only to your Job Search campaign, but to everything you want to accomplish throughout the rest of your active life.

CONTACTS FROM THE PRESENT AND THE FUTURE

1. Every new person you meet gets added to the list.
2. Resource people you go out of your way to meet, because they share your interest in your chosen area of interest.
3. People particularly in your target area, uncovered through your Personal Economic Survey and subsequent research of your prime geographical preference area.
4. Leads your friends turn up for you (people "you ought to look up").
5. Executives you meet anywhere (they often have large networks of friends and hence potential contacts for you).

Appendix G

Targeting

RATIONALE

Reasons for each program element have been carefully thought out, by CMS over many years.
Reasons primarily for the instructor/counselor's own awareness, have been placed in brackets [ ].
Reasons that *should be shared with the student,* have been left unbracketed.

THE RATIONALE FOR TARGETING

1. *It puts the information-gathering about good places to work, in the hands of the one who will do the best job of gathering that information: You.* In the past, we were all brainwashed into thinking there is some kind of 'personnel system' in this country that is knowledgeable about jobs, and anxious to share that information with hungry job-hunters. Unfortunately, the truth is that 'personnel experts' who write job descriptions, and who establish 'qualifications' for those jobs, rarely have the faintest idea of what they are doing. And, for a very good reason: they have never performed the job in question. It is up to you, and you alone, to gather whatever information you need, about good places to work. Only you will take the time necessary, only you will do it with the thoroughness that is necessary, and only you can know which information is important to your ultimate goals, and which is not.

2. *It systematizes the research, and makes certain that all options are looked at.* Most personnel departments—and their handmaidens, the public and private employment agencies—do not know the rich variety of options that are available to someone with particular talents; or do not have the time to share what they know. The consequent result: if you depend upon them, or any other, you will end up with only a sampling (at best) of all the options that might be available to you. And, whatever job you would then end up with, would be only one of countless options open to you—most of which you did not know about, and so, could not choose.
As a free wo/man, it is crucial for you to choose from among *all* your options. And essential that, before you choose, you *know* what all your options are. Obviously the best way to do this is to choose a manageable geographical area (as we have already asked you to do), then learn about *all* the economic entities within that area (as we will ask you to do, shortly, in your Personal Economic Survey), and then begin to narrow all these options down to the ones which please you the most. Targeting is a process designed to do exactly that. It asks you to set up—first of all—a general file, called Potential Organizational Targets, into which you can throw every name and every bit of information about anything that looks even mildly interesting to you as a possible place to work or thing to do. This first phase of Targeting is designed to let no bit of information get away, however peripheral or extraneous it may seem to your major interests. Then, in successive phases of Targeting, you will be asked to sift and refine this information—first into Live Organizational Targets, then Ultimate Organizational Targets, and finally, Ultimate Individual Targets (about which, more later on in this course, at the appropriate time).

3. *It puts the ultimate success of your job-search in the hands of the person who cares the most about it: You.* Dreamers like to dream that somewhere Out There there is Something or Someone who holds the key to their job-search, and who cares. Dreamers like to dream that there is, in this country, 'an employment system' which provides for a rational matching of people with jobs—once people know what they want to do. On the lowest levels of jobs, such as dishwasher, perhaps this is true. On any other levels, this is purely a dream. And any individual foolish enough to rely on this dream or on any portion of the so-called 'employment system' to match her/him up with appropriate employment, is at best betting on a 1000 to 1 shot, and at worst committing vocational suicide. Eliminating from your consciousness all the falsehoods taught to you throughout your life about how to get a job, is the first beginning of wisdom. For the very practical purposes of your vocational survival, you must understand that the so-called 'employment system' does not exist. Finding a rational matching of you with appropriate employment is *solely up to you*—aided by whatever persons *you* choose. You must determine exactly what it is you want to do. You must select precisely that organization which you find most attractive. You must identify the one official there who shares your major interest, and who does have the authority to create for you the position you wish. And then you must go about convincing him or her of the overwhelming logic of your thesis in order to get what you want. There is no other way.

This applies equally to those of you who do not care to work for anyone else, but would rather establish your own independent professional economic position, or other entrepreneurial pursuit. You must still go through this Targeting process, because you will have to determine precisely where you fit in our economy, and which individuals and organizations will be your allies, which will be your opposition or enemies, and which will be your clients. It is only by researching the area sufficiently so that you can define your own most advantageous position within the economy that affects your interests, that you will be able to intelligently plan, organize and establish your own economic entity and independence.

4. *It starts you off in the very place you would end up, anyway.* Let us suppose you went through the normal 'personnel system' in this country. You would, sooner or later, hear of a job-opening. You would go over, and find yourself in an interview with a personnel official, who is equally ignorant (with you) of the real requirements of the job, and who had no authority to hire anybody, anyway. The most this 'low man on the corporate totem pole' could do would be to permit you to be one of the few lucky ones who survive this irrelevant 'screening', in which case you would move on to the next echelon for further irrelevant 'screening' and so on. If you survived it all, you would ultimately find yourself talking to the person you should have started with in the first place—what we call your Ultimate Individual Target. And one of his/her questions would be: why are you here? What made you choose this place? Targeting begins with that question, from the start, and short-circuits all the irrelevant 'screening'—since we will teach you how you get in to see the wo/man you need to see, without working your way up through the personnel system, that knows nothing about you, and cares less.

Appendix H

Ideal Job Specifications

RATIONALE

Reasons for each program element have been carefully thought out, by CMS over many years.
Reasons primarily for the instructor/counselor's own awareness, have been placed in brackets [ ].
Reasons that *should be shared with the student,* have been left unbracketed.

RATIONALE FOR THE TIMING OF THE 'IDEAL JOB SPECIFICATIONS' EXERCISE

1. It shouldn't be earlier in this course because you need to have done the Practice Field Survey, and have had the introduction to Contacts and Targeting–with its attendant explanation of how the whole 'personnel system' works–before you begin *to believe* that you really might, just possibly, be actually able to create whatever you want–in the way of your life's work. To attempt this exercise any earlier, is to run into an absolute wall of incredulity. You also need to have dealt with your preferred people-environments and your values (philosophy of life) before attempting to define the ideal job specifications.

2. It shouldn't be any later in this course, because you need to be aware of your specifications before you go out on your Personal Economic Survey. That Survey will help to refine the specifications, because you will be looking at the community with new eyes; and, on the other hand, having the specifications firmly in your mind before you begin the Survey will save you a lot of time, since you will more instantly recognize when a particular economic entity just isn't of any great interest to you; and so you will not waste your time on it. Moreover, by beginning your list of ideal job specifications at this point in the course, you give the list time to percolate in your mind, for reflection, refinement and redefinition.

RATIONALE FOR SETTING DOWN YOUR IDEAL JOB SPECIFICATIONS

1. *To further sharpen and hone your personal direction.* By the time you go out job-hunting, you will really know exactly what you are looking for. This is part of the preparation for that. You can't answer this question in any final way, at the moment, because you haven't got your *job objective* defined yet; but you can begin circling toward a landing. And, strangely enough, many times this circling for a landing actually helps a student define part of his ultimate Objective.

2. *To describe the milieu in which you would do your best and be most productive; and, by describing that milieu, to also surface more things about your Self.* It is important for you to be as specific as possible about the conditions under which you would work the happiest and best. Suppose, for example, you have always dreamed of being able to work "in a relatively large office with a fireplace, a well-stocked wall of books,

nicely-furnished, with a nice picture window, where the sun streams in during the afternoon hours particularly." Then say so. Your ideal job specifications should be precisely that specific, and detailed. It will help you better to recognize it, if it is in the cards for you to find it; and it will also help you to define your Self better. For example, the previous picture obviously says a lot about that particular person. S/he is clearly a thinker type, who needs that kind of office, because s/he's going to be there most of every day. A person who intends always to be on the go, usually only wants a cubby-hole, because s/he'll never be there; and consequently, would not lay down these requirements or specifications in her/his list; but would specify other kinds of things.

3. *To focus down further the number of possibilities that you will later have to examine.* The more thoroughly you do this ideal job specifications exercise, the less time you'll have to waste looking at possibilities that don't really interest you. But first, you have to know *what* doesn't really interest you; and this exercise helps to nail that down, very firmly.

4. *To increase the chances of your finding what you really want.* With all the variety of possibilities in the world today, the chances that anything you want is really 'out there' are staggeringly in your favor. But most people brush right past what they really want, because they haven't thought it out carefully enough. The more clearly visualized your ideal job specifications are, before you go out, the easier it will be for you to recognize what you are looking for *whenever you see any part of it.* No one can guarantee positively that you *will* find exactly what you want; but, *if* you don't at least know what you are looking for, we can practically guarantee that you won't find it.

5. *To begin preparing you for job-interviews later in this process.* When the time comes for you to go choose whom *you* want to interview for a job, you will be coming in completely informed as to what you want, thus avoiding 'fishing expeditions' (I don't really know why I'm here; uh, what do you have that I might be interested in?). Interviewers have had their fill of such dumb interviews. You, on the other hand, will stand out. The interviewer cannot help but think, "This is a very impressive gal/guy. S/he really knows where s/he's going."

6. *To raise the level of job that you are considered for, and can handle.* People with responsibility, such as those you will likely be approaching for job-interviews later, have certain similar characteristics: they see themselves as initiators, they are concerned about productivity and doing their best, they are anxious to change things if necessary in order to increase personal productivity, etc. (unless, of course, they are outstanding illustrations of the Peter Principle). When you walk in, the best of them at least will instinctively recognize you an 'another member of the club'. Consequently, they are not going to end up offering you 'just a crumb job'.

7. *To identify your best working conditions is to set this goal for not only now but for the rest of your life, and not only for yourself but for other people as well.* Half the problem with the world today is that people do not make clear what they believe they need in order to do their work properly and creatively, nor do they make clear those aspects of their job or job environment that bug them so much that they cannot be creative and productive. You refuse to be a part of that problem, by visualizing your own ideal job specifications. And this will inevitably raise your consciousness about this for the rest of your life; as well as making you more sensitive to how you can help those around you increase their creativity and productivity as well, through improving the circumstances under which *they* work.

Appendix I To Help You in Understanding Skills-Identification

I. SAMPLES AND EXAMPLES

The most useful way to get into this subject, is to begin by simply studying some samples and examples, as they have appeared in previous students' analysis of their work-autobiographies:

Artistic Talent
Unusual Perception in Human Relations
Handling Prima Donnas Tactfully and Effectively
Accurately Assessing Public Moods
Selling Intangibles to Senior Executives and Other Opinion-Molders
Musical Knowledge and Taste
Organization and Administration of In-House Training Programs
Effective in Dealing with Many Kinds of People
Deft in Directing Creative Talent
Conducting and Directing Public Events and Ceremonies
Fiscal Analysis and Programming
R&D Program and Project Management
Supervising and Administering Highly Skilled Engineers and Other Professionals
Design Engineering
Lecturing with Poise Before the Public
Planning, Organizing, Coordinating and Directing Production of New Scientific and Engineering Procedures, Guidebooks, and Manuals
Reliability
Outstanding Writing Skills
Cost Analyses, Estimates, Projections and Comparisons
Policy Interpretation
Redesigning Structures
Creative, Perceptive, Effective Innovator
Special Study Projects Planning, Organization and Management
Planning for Change
Training Discussion Leaders
Readily Establishes Warm Mutual Rapport with Students and Other Youths
Schooled in Instructional Principles and Techniques
Bringing New Life to Traditional Art Forms
Interviewing
Organizing and Coordinating Effective Press, Radio and TV Coverage of Major Events
Aware of the Value of Symbolism and Deft in Its Use
A Good, Trained, Effective Listener

Highly Observant
Discussion Group and Forum Leadership
Repeatedly Elected to Senior Posts
Imagination and the Courage to Use It
Humanly Oriented Technical Management
Manpower Requirements Analysis and Planning
Analyzing Performance Specifications
Significant Theoretical Modeling
Very Sophisticated Mathematical Abilities
Conceptual Acuity of the Highest Order
Engineering Planning, Program Organization and Supervision
Establishing Priorities Among Many Urgently Repeating Requirements
Courage of Convictions

II. REFLECTIONS UPON THESE EXAMPLES IN ORDER TO DISCOVER PRINCIPLES

Out of your study of the foregoing examples, you doubtless have made several observations. So have we. Putting yours and ours together, we arrive at the following principles or guidelines for Skills Identification:

1. *The word "Skills" is being used in the most general sense possible.* You are not looking for skills which you, and you alone, possess, in all the world. It is sufficient that you should have it, to any degree, and that not everyone else in the world does. (E.g., cf. the previous page: "Highly Observant"—lots of other people are; but not everyone is. So it gets listed.) You are looking for any of the following, that you may have exhibited, when you were *doing something:* a capacity, or a natural gift, or an instinct, or an ability, or an aptness, or an eye for, or an ear for, or a knack, or something you have a good head for, or a proficiency, or a handiness, or a facility, or a know-how, or some savvy about something, or some forte, or strong point, or some quality, etc. If you simply demonstrated you could do it, then list it (e.g., Fiscal Analysis and Programming). If you feel you did it better than others would have, say so (e.g., Very Sophisticated Mathematical Abilities; or: Unusual Perception in Human Relations).
2. *Do not stick simply to traditional job titles, job descriptions, or historical statements.* There is no vocabulary to memorize, no list from which you must choose, no categories into which you must fit. You are to capture your own uniqueness, which means you are encouraged to be as creative as possible in the very naming or identification of your skills. Describe even common skills in any uncommon way that occurs to you.

   Examples: "Innovative Engineer"—not very useful. Mainly a job title.
   Try, instead, "Innovative, Creative Technical Ideas".
   Again,
   "Managed R&D Project"—not very useful in this form, as an historical statement.
   But it can be turned into a functional identification. Try, instead, "R&D Program and Project Management", or—better yet—"Managing R&D Projects".

3. *Describe what you did, purely in functional terms.* Action verbs have a stronger force than nouns, which seem more static.

   Examples: good: Conductor and Director of Public Events and Ceremonies
   better: Conducting and Directing Public Events and Ceremonies
   Again,
   good: Lecturer
   better: Lecturing
   best: Lecturing with Poise Before the Public

4. *Overall, you are aiming for as general a description as possible of the skill, so that the transferability of the skill to other fields is readily obvious.*

   Examples: not very useful: "Works Wells with Boy Scouts, Church Groups, etc."
   much better: "Readily Establishes Warm Mutual Rapport with Students and Other Youths"
   Again,
   not very useful: "I preached persuasively to upper-class congregation"
   much better: "Selling Intangibles to Senior Executives and Other Opinion-Molders"

   This "transferability" of your skills is the key to the whole exercise; and is another reason why ongoing, action verbs are preferred.

   Examples: "Established" puts your skill in the past only.
   "Readily Establishes" puts it in past, present and future.
   Or, again,
   "I was effective in dealing" puts it in the past; but simply dropping the "I was", puts it in an ongoing mode.

5. *You are also aiming for the sub-components of big, general skills.* Because "big" skills often conceal lots more sub-skills, each of which is important in its own right. So don't leave them concealed under some "blanket" designation.

   Examples: too general: "Management"
   broken down into components: "Planning, Organizing, Programming, Directing, Administering, Supervising, Analyzing, Evaluating, etc."
   Or, again:
   too general: "Money Management"
   broken down into components, in terms of decreasing level of complexity and responsibility, it goes like this:

   1. Financial Planning and Management;
   2. Fiscal Analysis and Programming;
   3. Budget Planning, Preparation, Justification, Administration, Analysis and Review;
   4. Cost Analyses, Estimates, Projections, and Comparisons;
   5. Fiscal Controls and Audits.

6. *Avoid identifications that are too brief: add the details about the public (or object) that was being dealt with, and some adjectives if possible.* We have discovered, with students in the past, the greatest error is that they try to be too brief in their description or identification of their skills.

Examples: barely decent: "Management"
better: "Technical Management"
best: "Humanly Oriented Technical Management"
Or, again,
barely decent: "Analyzing"
better: "Analyzing Performance Specifications"
best: "Perceptively Analyzing Performance Specifications"
Or, again,
barely decent: "Administering"
better: "Supervising and Administering Engineers"
best: "Supervising and Administering Highly Skilled Engineers"

(The more complex the public (or object) that the skill is being exercised with, the more complex the skill; and the more worthy it is of mentioning.)

7. *Finally, it is helpful to capitalize all the words in each identification.* Or: Finally, It Is Helpful To Capitalize All The Words In Each Identification. Capitalizing makes things more important (just naturally), and more like titles without being titles in the traditional sense of personnel "experts". You will notice this was done with all the samples and examples, at the beginning of this Appendix.

III. EXERCISE TO PRACTICE SKILL-IDENTIFICATION

We ask you to read this excerpt from another student's work-autobiography, and in the right-hand margin jot down *your* first, tentative, exploratory identifications of the skills you see there.

WORK-AUTOBIOGRAPHY	YOUR IDENTIFICATION OF HIS SKILLS
I want to describe my period as a graduate student, Department of Nuclear Engineering, at the University of Washington. I was one of only twelve students selected for the class entering in September 1965. The department of Nuclear Engineering had a total of about 30 to 35 students enrolled, most of them full-time. A couple of these students had been there longer than five years. I decided right then and there that it would be wise to finish the master's degree ASAP, and get going. I was the recipient of an Atomic Energy Commission Traineeship, which is a fancier word for Fellowship. Before I forget to mention it, there was one rather special situation	

WORK-AUTOBIOGRAPHY	YOUR IDENTIFICATION OF HIS SKILLS
that I lucked into: this was living in a graduate student house made up of about 90 of some of the most talented people I have ever known. They helped make education a varied and stimulating experience partly by way of a cultural hour we had every Sunday evening, partly by way of turning a rather banal dormitory existence into a lively one. Now, I am not sure how much of this info is going to be relevant but I'll go ahead anyway. I was instrumental in helping to plan a group of dorm evenings. But we really hit our stride when we decided to communicate with the freshmen and sophomore men and women who populated the rest of this particular dormitory. That is, apathy was rampant, and there was a significant communications gap existing between us grad students and the underclass types that we did not feel was either justified or necessary. So, what we did was to involve these people by way of staging a series of plays: the first was a version of the "Christmas Carol" by Dickens, later followed by our own productions which I had a hand in writing, staging, and publicizing; these last were respectively a satire on dorm life (based on "Alice in Wonderland") and a horse opera based on the old clash between the cattlemen and the sheepmen in the wild wild west ... I should add that all three productions were overwhelming successes, even in spite of free admission. Even the dean of the graduate school, who attended one performance, sent a congratulatory letter.	

IV. AFTER YOU HAVE IDENTIFIED SKILLS IN YOUR OWN WORDS, HERE IS A SAMPLE VOCABULARY WORTH LOOKING AT TO BROADEN YOUR IDENTIFICATION OF SKILL COMPONENTS, SO THAT THEIR TRANSFERABILITY IS MOST EVIDENT:
(These are universal words, applying across all fields.)

Name of a Person with a Particular Skill/Function	*The Skill/Function As a Noun*	*The Skill/Function As an Ongoing Action Verb*	*The Product Resulting from the Function or Skill's Use*	*When Speaking of the History of a Function's Use*
Communicator	Communication	Communicating	Communications	Communicated
Manager	Management	Managing		Managed
Reporter	Report	Reporting	Reports	Reported
Writer		Writing		Wrote
Interpreter	Interpretation	Interpreting	Interpretations	Interpreted
Researcher	Research	Researching	Research Reports	Researched
Artist	Artistic Talent			
Planner		Planning	Plans	Planned
Designer	Design	Designing	Designs	Designed
	Conception	Conceiving	Conceptions	Conceived
Analyst	Analysis	Analyzing	Analyses	Analyzed
Definer	Definition	Defining	Definitions	Defined
Evaluator	Evaluation	Evaluating	Evaluations	Evaluated
	Perception	Perceiving	Perceptions	Perceived
Forecaster	Forecast	Forecasting	Forecasts	Forecast
Estimator	Estimation	Estimating	Estimates	Estimated
Programmer	Program	Programming	Programs	Programmed
Organizer	Organization	Organizing		Organized
	Selection	Selecting	Selections	Selected
		Bringing		Brought
	Enlistment	Enlisting	Enlistments	Enlisted
Developer	Development	Developing	Developments	Developed
Administrator	Administration	Administering		Administered
	Application	Applying	Applications	Applied
Coordinator	Coordination	Coordinating	Coordinations	Coordinated
Director	Direction	Directing	Directions	Directed
Dealer	Deal	Dealing	Deals	Dealt
	Implementation	Implementing	Implementations	Implemented
Chairman		Chairing		Chaired
	Guidance	Guiding		Guided
Leader	Leadership	Leading		Led
	Delegation	Delegating		Delegated

APPENDIX I.
SKILLS-IDENTIFICATION

DON'T USE

Name of a Person with a Particular Skill/Function	*The Skill/Function As a Noun*	*The Skill/Function As an Ongoing Action Verb*	*The Product Resulting from the Function or Skill's Use*	*When Speaking of the History of a Function's Use*
		Molding	Molds	Molded
Producer	Production	Producing	Productions	Produced
Expediter		Expediting		Expedited
Promoter	Promotion	Promoting	Promotions	Promoted
Performer	Performance	Performing	Performances	Performed
Counselor		Counseling		Counseled
	Encouragement	Encouraging		Encouraged
Achiever	Achievement	Achieving	Achievements	Achieved
Instructor	Instruction	Instructing	Instructions	Instructed
Persuader	Persuasion	Persuading	Persuasions	Persuaded
Motivator	Motivation	Motivating	Motivations	Motivated
Trainer	Train	Training		Trained
	Stimulation	Stimulating		Stimulated
	Attainment	Attaining		Attained
	Summarization	Summarizing	Summarizations	Summarized
Inspector	Inspection	Inspecting	Inspections	Inspected
Comparer	Comparison	Comparing	Comparisons	Compared
Reviewer	Review	Reviewing	Reviews	Reviewed
	Maintenance	Maintaining		Maintained
Negotiator	Negotiation	Negotiating	Negotiations	Negotiated
	Renegotiation	Renegotiating	Renegotiations	Renegotiated
Adjuster	Adjustment	Adjusting	Adjustments	Adjusted
Reconciler	Reconciliation	Reconciling	Reconciliations	Reconciled
	Recommendation	Recommending	Recommendations	Recommended
		Updating		Updated
	Improvement	Improving	Improvements	Improved
	Reevaluation	Reevaluating	Reevaluations	Reevaluated

For reasons made clear earlier in this Appendix, the first column above—and on the previous page—should be used as little as possible, since it locks you into job titles prematurely, and prevents you from thinking of yourself in a much wider perspective.

SAMPLE PERSONAL TRAITS OR ADJECTIVES DESCRIBING THE WAY YOU DID (AND DO) VARIOUS SKILL/FUNCTIONS

exceptional
unique
challenging
mastery
strong
dynamic
versatile
responsive
attractive
sophisticated
earning respect
artful
responsible
innovative
diplomatically
perceptive
highly
readily
repeatedly
very sophisticated
deeply concerned
discretion
contagious

unusually good grasp
new and improved
outstanding
broad
instrumental
successful
unusual
natural
creative
tactful
significantly
with candor
enjoying challenge
exceptional
increasingly responsible
greatly contributed toward
effectively
deft
reliability
bringing new life
humanly oriented
acuity
lifelong

quickly
driving
adept
vigorous
uncommon
pioneering
leading
competent
penetrating
driving
sensitive
objectivity
dependable
honesty
courage of convictions
repeatedly
initiative
highest
extensively
accurately
warm
aware
significant

urgently
exceptionally broad
thinks on her/his feet
trained
strongly
outgoing
humanizing
open-minded
firm
deep insight
expert
experienced
talented
astute
high-level
empathy
participative
diverse
calm
sensitive
easily
foresight
imaginative

As we indicated earlier, students as a rule are too brief in their description of their skills. Qualities, traits, and adjectives such as the above should be used wherever appropriate, to make clear the unusual degree to which certain skills or functions are possessed by you. And since students tend to be too modest, and end up *under-rating* themselves, we urge you to use such adjectives as the above wherever you even *dare to hope* they might be appropriate. You can always edit, modify, or tone down later—if, upon reflection, that seems necessary in any particular.

SAMPLE OBJECTS OR PUBLICS THAT SKILL/FUNCTIONS ARE EXERCISED WITH

As we said earlier, there are typically three kinds of words that appear in skill identifications. One is the noun or verb indicating the function itself; we have given samples of these. The second is the trait or adjective indicating how the skill/function is used; we have just given examples of these. The third is the object or public that the skill is demonstrated upon. That is the purpose of this section: to give samples of these. Typically, as Sidney Fine, the "father" of the Dictionary of Occupational Titles has pointed out, all of us work (in varying degree and admixture) with People, Data, and Things. However, we have simply listed the objects or publics without categorizing them in any way. We leave this to the reader (and student):

data
work aids
reports
schematic analyses
standards
discipline
designs
recommendations
unusual conditions
principles
systems analysis
capabilities
inefficiencies
high proficiency level
statistical analysis
communications systems
interpretation systems
R&D project management
research projects
programs
conclusions
facts
groups
performance reviews
boundary conditions
feelings
new approaches
schema

standards
prescribed action
system
art
technique
procedures
methods
frameworks
organizational contexts
proficiency
deficiencies
responsibilities
records management
presentations
reporting systems
policy formulation
project planning
objectives
reports, summary
problems
relations
individuals
goals
events
ideas
solutions
plan
operations

information
criteria
materials
craft
methods
specifications
theories
process
controls
peak performance
records
statistics
journals
control systems
policy recommendation
project goals
plans
findings
fiscal accounting
resources
human resources
policies
intuitions
parameters
resolutions
handbooks
professional literature
needs

performance characteristics
data analysis studies
strategic needs
expressed wishes
one to one
product
competing needs
treatment
performance
privileges
life adjustment
objects
equipment
controls
solids
blueprints
inputs
sources
public moods
opinion-makers
cost
principles application
repeating requirements
living things
catalogs
trade literature
variables
investigations

tactical needs
financial needs
response
small group
service
demonstrations
duties
efficiency
contractual obligations
courses of action
tools
precision requirements
power tools

gauges
fixtures
outputs
sequences
intangibles
in-house training programs
structures
symbolism
plants
environment
wall charts
staff reports
priorities

surveys
organizational needs
work assignments
assignment
institutional services
points of view
specialized procedures
harmonious relations
rights
giving and taking
strategy
machines
specifications

liquids
gases
attachments
timing
prima donnas
senior executives
creative talent
change
manpower
trees
energy
grass-roots projects
controlled growth

With these sample lists all in hand (and they are samples, only; you can expand them as much as you wish, or ignore them completely), you can return to the first part of this Appendix and look at the samples of skills-identification all over again. But, hopefully, now with new eyes and new understanding.

Look also, when you have completed analyzing your own work-autobiography, at your own skill-identifications, to see where you have overlooked some altogether: or where you can be *more expansive* in your description of particular skill/functions.

Appendix J

Clustering of Your Skills

I. SAMPLES AND EXAMPLES

As with skills, so with clustering: the most useful way to get into this subject is simply to begin by studying some samples and examples, as they have appeared in previous students' analysis of their skills, and their subsequent organizing them into families:

PUBLIC SPEAKING: Making Radio and TV Presentations; Speech Writing; Teaching Public Speaking; Using Audio-Visual Aids; Lecturing; University Guest Lecturer; Expert in Reasoning Persuasively, Developing a Thought, Making a Point and Cogently Expressing a Position; Poise in Public Appearances; Showmanship; Debating.

DYNAMIC LEADERSHIP OF ALL AGE GROUPS, ESPECIALLY YOUTH: Motivation; Exceptionally Perceptive Human Relations; Driving Initiative; Readily Establishes Warm Mutual Rapport with Students and Other Youths; Creating Atmospheres Conducive to Enthusiasm, Personal Growth and Creativity; In Tune with Youth; Church and Community Activities Leadership; No Fear of Risks; Good Judgment.

PERSONNEL ADMINISTRATION: Recruiting, Interviewing, Evaluation, Selection, Classification and Assignment; Staff Counseling and Guidance; Evaluating Individual Performance; Progress and Potential; Employee Morale, Character-Building and Internal Communications Programs Management; Employee Information and Educational Programs Planning, Organization and Management.

SHOW PLANNING, ORGANIZATION AND MANAGEMENT: A Strong Theatrical Sense; Aware of the Value of Symbolism and Deft in Its Use; Artistic Talent; Unusually Good Grasp of Time and Spatial Relationships in Creating a Group Impact; Planning, Organizing and Orchestrating Dramatic and Supporting Elements; Writing Scripts and Scenarios; Screening and Selecting Many Kinds of Talents; Handling Prima Donnas Tactfully and Effectively; Teaching Dramatic Concepts and Techniques; Assessing Audience Attitudes and Reactions; Stage Direction; Musical Knowledge and Taste; Planning, Organizing, Staging, Producing and Directing Student Events; Mastery of All Forms of Communication; Deep Insight into Linguistic and Symbolic Meanings; Musical Groups and Programs Planning, Organization and Management; Bringing New Life to Traditional Art Forms; No Fear of Change or Progress; Artistic Management; Deft in Directing Creative Talent.

GROUP DYNAMICS: Discussion Group and Forum Leadership; Training Discussion Leaders; Selected As Coordinator for Major Subject at National Political Experts Conference.

MANAGEMENT SYSTEMS ANALYSIS AND ENGINEERING: Directing Formal Management Improvement Programs; Devising New or Improved Management Systems and Procedures; Efficiency Engineering; Management Inspections and Audits; Cost Effectiveness Analysis Techniques; Supervising Educational Programs Designed to Upgrade Skill Level of Professional Controller Personnel; Work Simplifications Training Methods.

II. SOME GENERAL OBSERVATIONS ABOUT THESE EXAMPLES

As you will have noticed from reading these over carefully:

A. *Clusters can be of any length.* The clusters above vary from one which includes only four skill-identifications, to one which includes twenty-one skill-identifications. Had the student wished, the longest one could have been broken into two shorter clusters.

B. *Clusters begin with some general, or generic, skill-identification—and then every skill that is related to it (in the eyes of the student) is put with it, in that same cluster.* The first skill-identification is underlined, and serves as the title for the cluster. Which skills the student chooses as the generic ones, to head-up clusters, is entirely up to that student.

C. *Once the generic skill that heads-up a cluster is chosen, it is entirely up to the student as to which skills s/he then includes in that cluster.* In the above clusters, "A Strong Theatrical Sense" might with equal justification have gone in the first cluster (Public Speaking) as in the fourth cluster (Show Planning, Organization and Management). There is no "right" or "wrong" place for a skill-identification—within certain broad limits, at least.

D. *The skills are copied into the clusters in exactly the same language as they appeared in their original identification.* There is no particular attempt to "tidy up" the identifications as they go into clusters.

E. *Almost any cluster could stand by itself as a full-time job.* If you look over the clusters again, you will be very struck by the way in which there are—in fact—people who make a full-time living doing solely what is in one cluster. In other words, each cluster is (generally speaking) strong enough to stand by itself.

With these observations (plus any other you care to make) under your belt, you are ready to move on to the actual principles as to how you go about clustering.

III. DIRECTIONS FOR DOING CLUSTERING OF YOUR SKILLS

A. *Take your whole list of skill-identifications, and read it over, without preconceptions. As you read, look for which general strength areas seem to stand out.* It is entirely up to you, though you may be helped if you know which general strength areas have stood out, in previous students' lists:

1. Training someone in something, or other educational activity
2. Money management, of one kind or another
3. The administrative side of handling people (personnel, etc.)
4. Organization-building activities with respect to manpower, resources, etc.
5. Addressing people (public speaking)
6. Selling (tangibles or intangibles)
7. Group dynamics or work with groups in general
8. Problem-solving or other types of trouble-shooting with *operations* (planning-decisions) or with *management systems* (devising the means whereby other things can be done)

9. Values or interests of the student (environment, the international scene, etc.)
10. Any "executive activities": planning, organizing, scheduling, coordinating, interpreting, communicating, etc.
11. Any management-administration activities, not already covered: design projects, R&D, resources, technical, financial, human resources, administrative
12. Voluntary activities not already clustered
13. Public relations (relations with the public, not just publicity)
14. Writing, general or specialized variety
15. Leadership traits (charisma, personality factors, etc.)

Your own strength-areas may, of course, be quite different from the above; but, for most students, the preceding list is a useful framework to keep in mind, as you read your skill-identifications list over to find your own general strength-areas.

B. *Choose what cluster is, for you, the most obvious and easiest to sort out, and begin with that.*

1. Take a piece of paper, and use it to write your new clusters on.
2. Begin this cluster by writing down that skill which you feel is the most general one, and could therefore serve as the title or heading for the cluster, copied from your very own skill-identifications list.
3. Identify the other members of the cluster, on your skill-identifications list. Some students prefer to run all the way through the list, putting a dot in front of the ones they intend to use, and then copying; others prefer to just go down the list, copying as they go. Copying, of course, only those skills which you feel belong to this particular cluster.
4. Your object is, one by one, to eliminate each skill, that you copy, from the skill-identifications list. We suggest you draw a fine-line through each skill-identification that you copy, after you copy it. A line, so you'll know you have already used it. A fine line, so you can still read the identification *in case* you want to use it again in a later cluster (this *sometimes* may seem wise, to you).
5. It is quite permissible to break up a skill-identification into its sub-components, if you decide you want to use one part in one cluster and another part in another cluster later on.

C. *Go on, and do your next cluster—next easiest and most obvious one.*

1. Your strongest clusters are usually the easiest and most obvious ones to pick off your skill-identifications list. Strength of a skill-area is measured by one or more of the following:
   a. Its priority, in your mind; and/or
   b. The amount of your time that you have devoted to it, over the years; and/or
   c. The intensity the skill required of you, or that you willingly gave to it; and/or
   d. The depth of the skill-area, or the public served; and/or
   e. The scope of the skill, the amount of territory, etc., that it embraced.
2. Follow the same directions as in B. above for your first cluster. You are eliminating part of your skill-identifications list, however, each time you do another cluster, so you need only look at the skills that are not crossed out (as a rule). As you copy the skills you want to include in this second cluster, draw a fine-line through them, one by one.

D. *Look at the skill-identifications list, at the skills not yet crossed out, and proceed in turn to the remaining clusters that occur to you, one cluster at a time.*

1. The whole process of clustering is (obviously) a process of elimination. Therefore, as you go on, crossing out each skill as you copy it into a new cluster, there are fewer and fewer skills remaining for you to look at, and figure out how to cluster.
2. Separate clusters according to where you use it. If you do *writing* "in-house" and also "externally, with the outside public", that is two different clusters.
3. Separate your clusters according to whether you do it, or you manage others doing it. Those are two different clusters, ordinarily.
4. As you study the skills that still remain on your skill-identifications list, eliminate any that—upon reflection—now seem to you to be overstating the case. Don't claim anything that isn't true. But guard equally against false modesty. Also eliminate any skill-identifications that seem to you to be very very low-level skills *(for you),* way beneath the general level of the remainder of your skills in general.
5. If you come to a skill-identification that puzzles you—you just cannot figure out where it belongs, or even, perhaps, what the skill involves—there are two devices that may help you:
   a. Visualize yourself moving around and doing this thing, as much as you can. What's going on here, as you go about it? This may open up for you the solution as to what kind of a cluster it belongs in.
   b. And/or, go back and ask yourself how the skill is done if it is done very badly. Then reverse this picture and the adjectives, add the positive description and see if this helps.
6. Take care that in putting the clusters together, you don't do it in such a way that it commits you to only work in one industry. You are looking for clusters that are *transferable.*
7. Do not be dismayed if, toward the end, you find yourself having to put together clusters that have only one, two, or three skills in them. This *may* happen, in one or two instances—for each student. Then again, it may not.
8. When you are all done, every skill on your original skill-identifications list should now have a line drawn through it. You have completed the clustering.

E. *Check over your clustering when it is done.*

1. Any skills, as you now see it, that you would like to transfer from one cluster to another? Or use in more than one cluster? If so, take care of this, at this point.
2. Then copy all your clusters, underlining the heading (as we did on the first page of this Appendix), and then—*as much as possible*—organizing the sub-components *in each cluster* in order of descending usefulness, within that cluster. (Or descending importance, or descending strength, or descending priority to you, or whatever.)
3. You probably will end up with twenty to thirty clusters; but there is no "right" or "wrong" total number, so don't fret about it, one way or the other.

IV. SUMMARY: TITLES OR HEADINGS OF CLUSTERS THAT OTHER STUDENTS HAVE CHOSEN

Financial Planning and Management
Leadership in Perceptive Human Relations Techniques
Contracting, Purchasing and Procurement Management
Public Speaking—Briefing—Group Dynamics
Logistics Systems Planning, Organization, Installation and Management
Management Systems Analysis and Engineering
Selling Intangibles—Persuasion—Negotiation and Bargaining
Public and Plan/Community Relations
Strong Medical and Health Care Services Management Orientation
Community, Housing and Food Services Management
Manpower and Organizational Analysis and Planning—Human Resources Management
Foreign Affairs—International Relations and Diplomatic Representation
Construction Engineering Programs Planning and Supervision
Resources Management—Economic Research and Analysis
Large-Scale R&D Programs Planning, Organization and Management
Cost Control and Reduction Programs Management
Marketing and Public Relations Programs Management
Voluntary Group Activities Leadership
Writing
Supply Administration: Property Accountability and Control Procedures
Creative Management Systems Analysis and Engineering
Administrative Management
Organizational Analysis and Planning: Planning for Change
Mountaineering and Outdoor Skills and Enthusiasm
Applied Research: Design Analysis and Engineering
Technical and Scientific Liaison, Coordination, Investigation, Information-Gathering and Representation
Organization and Administration of Training Programs
Manpower Analysis, Planning and Management; Personnel Administration
Administrative, Administrative Support Services, Office and Branch Office Management
Property and Supplies Management
Plant, Facilities and Real Property Management
Theatrical Production Planning and Management
Ombudsman: Civic Administration: Municipal, Social Services, Legal Aid and Travelers Aid Programs Management
Linguistics
Church, Community and Recreational Activities Participation and Leadership

Customer Relations and Services Management
Research, Writing, Editing and Reporting
Group Dynamics
Senior Staff Planning, Organization, Coordination, Administration, Supervision, Writing, Policy Formulation and Recommendation
Market Research and Analysis; Regional Economic and Industrial Research
Negotiation and Bargaining
Organization and Administration of In-House Training Programs
Journalistic Interviewing, Reporting, Writing; Editing; Publishing
Professional Society Organization and Leadership
High-Level Representation, Tact, Diplomacy, Discretion
Counseling; Counseling Centers and Programs Management
Adult Education, Adult Discussion and Youth Programs Management
Humanizing Corporate Relationships

These can help give you "the feel" of the process; but, in the end, the clusters you choose should have your own inimitable headings. If any of the above are appropriate also to you, fine. If not, create those that are.

Appendix K Prioritizing Your Skill Clusters

I. THREE METHODS FOR PRIORITIZING YOUR TALKING PAPERS (SKILL CLUSTERS)

A. Sort your Talking Papers into two groups.

1. In the first group: those skill clusters which you feel represent your strongest abilities *and* which you take the greatest pleasure in performing. This will include five or more, usually.
2. In the second group: those which in your opinion represent your relatively minor skill clusters, in which you feel somewhat less confident, or which hold a lesser interest for you.

Concentrate, then, on the first group. Identify the one skill above all, in that group, in which you feel most *competent,* most *confident,* in which you find the greatest *interest,* and in which you take the greatest *pleasure.* Number it no. 1, at the top of that Talking Paper. Set it aside. Return to the first group, and continue the process: of those which remain, which is your top skill, now? And so on, until the entire group has been thus arranged, and numbered. You can largely ignore the second group, unless the first group doesn't even have five in it; in which case, draw on the second group, in the same manner as you have in the first until you have from a half dozen to ten clusters prioritized. Or as many as you wish.

OR

B. Sort your Talking Papers twice.

1. Go through all your Talking Papers, asking yourself what is the one skill in which you feel most competent and most confident; *ignore all other criteria, this time out.* Number that Talking Paper no. 1, at the top, and set it aside. Go back to the Talking Papers that remain in the pile, and ask which of those remaining is now the one in which you feel most competent. Number that Talking Paper no. 2, and set is aside. Continue with all your Talking Papers/Skill Clusters until the whole pile is prioritized.
2. Now start all over again. Take all the Talking Papers, and ask yourself how to prioritize them according to another criteria, namely, what is the one stkill in which you find the greatest pleasure; *ignore all other criteria, this time out.* As you go through this process, number them with a circle around the number.

When you are done, see how closely the two lists match. Do not be surprised if there is a great deal of agreement.

OR

C. Use the number method found in Appendix E (at I.A.2.b.) in order to prioritize your Talking Papers/ Skill Clusters according to method A., above, or with method B.

II. A CHART ON WHICH TO RECORD YOUR RANKING OF THE TALKING PAPERS/SKILL CLUSTERS

See the next page, please.

YOUR TOP TEN SKILLS

After you have arranged your Talking Papers in your preferred order, and have numbered each of them, please copy *the full names* of the top ten, in turn, on the sheet below or on one like it. Since Method B of prioritizing, on the previous page, is the more complicated, we have put enough columns below to accommodate it. If, however, you used Method A only, you will need only the column below on the extreme right.

THE CLUSTER (Copy it completely, please)	*Ranking on Basis of Your COMPETENCY Only*	*Ranking on Basis of Your PLEASURE Only*	*Your Final Decision on Basis of Everything*
1.			
2.			
3.			
4.			
5.			
6.			
7.			
8.			
9.			
10.			

Check your intuition, now. Does it agree with the final ranking, above? If not, feel free to rearrange it. Trust your intuition. You know yourself best!

Appendix L

Finances: How to Compute What You Need or Want

	Bare-Bones Budget for a Year	*Peak Salary Someday*	*Asking for Next Job*
FIXED OR COMMITTED EXPENSES MONTH BY MONTH			
1. Rent and household needs:			
2. Medical needs:			
3. Insurance:			
4. Phone and utilities:			
5. Car, gas and oil:			
6. Debts:			
7. Taxes: Federal, State and Local:			
VARIABLE EXPENSES MONTH BY MONTH			
8. Food and toiletries:			
9. Clothing:			
10. Recreation, sitter, etc.:			
11. Church, charity, gifts:			
12. Emergency fund:			
SAVINGS (Omit, for Bare-Bones Budget)			
13. Car replacement:			
14. Children's future (college):			
15. Investments or unrestricted, or undesignated:			
TOTAL BUDGET NEEDS			

Your Immediate Job Objective

Appendix M

RATIONALE

Reasons for each program element have been carefully thought out, by CMS over many years.
Reasons primarily for the instructor/counselor's own awareness, have been placed in brackets [ ].
Reasons that *should be shared with the student,* have been left unbracketed.

THE RATIONALE FOR RARELY USING JOB TITLES IN YOUR JOB OBJECTIVE

1. The meanings of job titles frequently vary wildly from one organization to another. Responsibilities required within a particular title in one company or organization are often completely different from those required for the same title in another company or organization.

2. Shooting for a job purely by title gives you little opportunity to expose the full range of skills which you can offer. "The wo/man makes the job" is true throughout the world of work today. If you let the job make the wo/man, you will be trying to compress yourself into a very small slot indeed.

3. If the post is of very limited scope, it is sometimes given a very impressive title in order to disguise this fact. This, to trap the unwary. Or to give him/her a 'fringe benefit' to compensate for the fact that the job is rather dreary. (The work may be monotonous, but with that title you'll at least impress outsiders to death). In any case, it is likely to be work which you—with your broadly based skills—will find neither interesting nor rewarding. You are far wiser to begin by concluding that titles are meaningless, and the only thing worth looking at is how interesting the job is *to You.*

4. If the post is of some importance, the chances are excellent that if it is vacant, someone is temporarily sitting in. The chances are also excellent that he might wish to hold on to it permanently. And (of course) the chances are excellent that his bosses are oblivious to this, and have therefore allowed him to become part of the decision making process as to who will take over this post permanently. By announcing—through the use of that post's title—that you are shooting for it, you have identified yourself to him as a competitor to be eliminated, no matter how excellent your qualifications. He will accordingly take good care of you—according to *his* own intelligent best interests, at least. On the other hand, if you don't announce—by using a job title—that you are shooting for his post, you save yourself a lot of this unnecessary grief.

5. He is free to suppose that his boss, if interested in you, may create an entirely new post—just in order to utilize the remarkable blend of assets which you offer. And, in fact, this is a very very common practice in organizations. And one which has happened to many many students who have taken this program. Precisely because they didn't go in, aiming at a particular job title. They let the man with the power to hire take their measure first, then create a title to fit them; rather than vice-versa.

DEVELOPING YOUR SPECIFIC IMMEDIATE OBJECTIVE
(A Final Clustering)

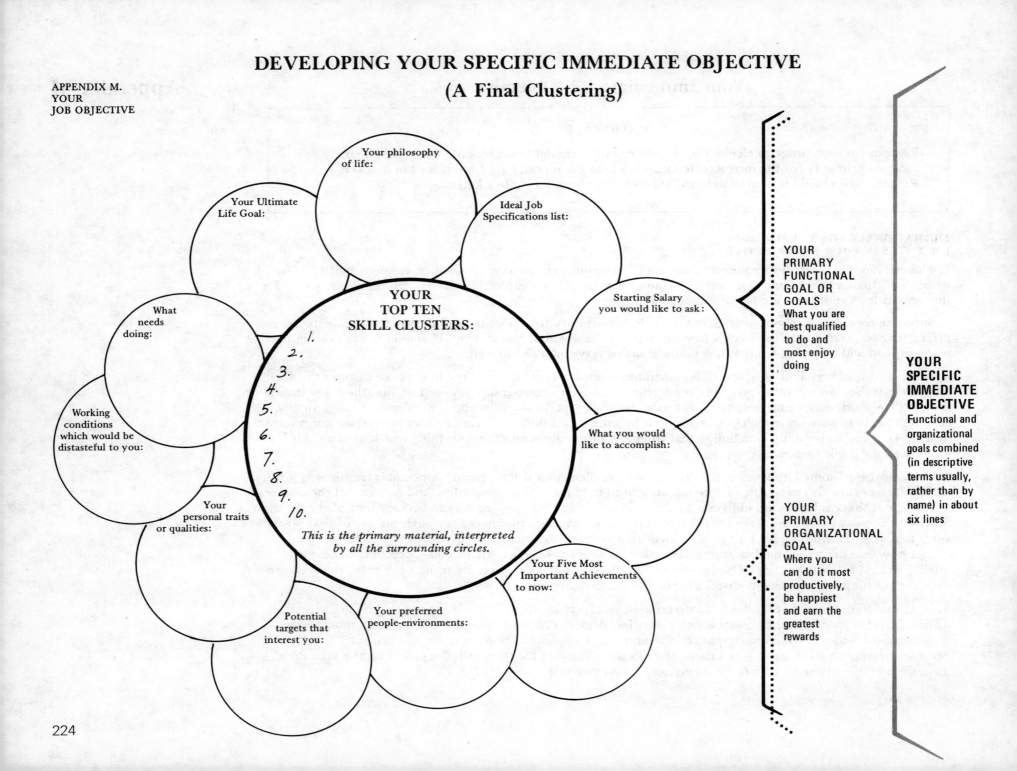

Your philosophy of life:

Your Ultimate Life Goal:

Ideal Job Specifications list:

Starting Salary you would like to ask:

What needs doing:

YOUR TOP TEN SKILL CLUSTERS:

1.
2.
3.
4.
5.
6.
7.
8.
9.
10.

This is the primary material, interpreted by all the surrounding circles.

Working conditions which would be distasteful to you:

What you would like to accomplish:

Your personal traits or qualities:

Your Five Most Important Achievements to now:

Potential targets that interest you:

Your preferred people-environments:

YOUR PRIMARY FUNCTIONAL GOAL OR GOALS
What you are best qualified to do and most enjoy doing

YOUR PRIMARY ORGANIZATIONAL GOAL
Where you can do it most productively, be happiest and earn the greatest rewards

YOUR SPECIFIC IMMEDIATE OBJECTIVE
Functional and organizational goals combined (in descriptive terms usually, rather than by name) in about six lines

DRAFTING YOUR JOB OBJECTIVE

It cannot be over-emphasized that all of the analysis referred to, below, *must* take place in the context of all that you have articulated about yourself in the other parts of this program, as summarized in the chart on the left. That is to say, those other parts of the program often serve to interpret, illuminate and develop themes within your top ten skills (clusters) which otherwise might be obscure, ambiguous, or too general.

I. HOW TO ANALYZE YOUR TOP TEN SKILLS (CLUSTERS) IN ORDER TO OBTAIN YOUR PRIMARY FUNCTIONAL GOAL

Remember, we may be looking for a title here, such as "Director of Plant Maintenance and Engineering Services"; but in most cases you would be more accurate and effective to describe your functional goal in terms of the skills required in it. Now, to some samples in order to show you how to analyze your clusters:

A. *Original name of cluster:* "Operational Analysis, Planning, Organization, Scheduling, Coordination, Supervision and Direction"
Student's ranking of it in his/her top ten: First
Analysis: We look at it to see if it is a) a clear indication as to either goal (functional or organizational); OR b) strong supporting skill; OR c) secondary supporting skill; OR d) unrelated to any other skill (cluster)? In this case we conclude it does not give clear indication as to either goal, because it is a good asset which can be used almost anywhere.
Conclusion: Strong supporting role.

B. *Original name of cluster:* "Selling; Salesmanship; Showmanship; Tremendous Representative; Customer Relations"
Student's ranking of it in his/her top ten: First
Analysis: This gives a clear indication as to a functional goal, and fortunately it is also the student's top ranking. Standing all by itself, it could have a job-title, such as "Account Executive". But, if this is clustered with other strongly supportive skills (clusters), it becomes even broader and stronger; viz., the student's no. 5 has strong representational aspects supportive of selling ("High-Level Scientific, Engineering, Technical and Inter-Agency Liaison, Coordination and Representation; Familiar with Workings of Top National R&D Agencies"); the student's no. 7 has strong presentational aspects ("Public Speaking; Speech Writing; Lecturing Before Scientists and Other R&D Professionals; Briefing top Executives and Committees; Other Formal Oral Presentations; Expert in Using and Improving Visual and Graphic Aids"); and—dipping below the top ten, as is sometimes quite appropriate—the student's no. 14 is also strongly supportive ("Exceptional Leadership and Motivational Talents; Imparting High Morale, Enthusiasm and Team Spirit").
Conclusion: The first part of the objective comes out of this "clustering" of no. 1, part of no. 5, part of no. 7, and no. 14, yielding a much broader management post than if just no. 1 were taken by itself; viz., "CHALLENGING SALES AND MARKETING MANAGEMENT RESPONSIBILITIES FOR PROFITABLY SPEEDING THE FLOW OF INFORMATION . . ."
Commentary: This is typical of the analysis process. When you have found one skill (cluster) in your top ten that yields a clear indication as to functional goal, look around to see what other clusters can then be combined with it, to make a much broader position—where you are free to use *all* your skills.

C. *Original name of cluster:* "Personnel Administration; Interviewing; Specialized Personnel Evaluation and Classification; Evaluating Individual Executive Performance, Progress and Potential; Employee Motivation Program Management"
Student's ranking of it in his/her top ten: First
Analysis: The student had indicated earlier that he was interested in *personnel administration,* in the aviation field. He had had experience—as this skill (cluster) indicated—in this field, but it was in the military and was, by civilian standards, quite limited. His exploration of civilian personnel administration showed him that this included certain activities which were simply not present in military personnel work, viz: Wage and Salary Administration; Labor Relations—including intimate knowledge of our exceedingly complex labor laws; Union Negotiation, etc. This awareness did not make him discard this interest or his ranking of this skill (cluster). It only meant he would have to be very careful in what he said, so that he did not misrepresent himself as a fully qualified personnel expert by civilian standards. Thus, by itself, this cluster is a little weak as a primary job function goal. Instinctively, therefore, the student must hunt for other skills (clusters) which would back up and be supportive of this one. These were found in his no. 2 ("Academic Administration at Formal Educational Institutions and Graduate Level Management Schools; Course and Curriculum Planning and Writing; Writing Management School Catalogs; Preparing and Presenting Field Demonstrations for Technical Schools; Student Counseling and Guidance; Teaching Management Courses to Senior Executives") and in his no. 6 ("Organization and Administration of In-House Training Programs; Training and Supervising In-House Instructors").
Conclusion: When no. 1, no. 2, and no. 6 were clustered together, they indicated the following, which became the first part of the objective: POST AS TRAINING AND EMPLOYEE SERVICES SPECIALIST with a corporation requiring BROAD EXPERIENCE IN ORGANIZING AND DIRECTING TECHNICAL TRAINING PROGRAMS, PERSONNEL AND ADMINISTRATIVE SERVICES, STAFF SUPERVISION, AND OPERATIONAL MANAGEMENT . . .
Commentary: By calling it "employee services" rather than "personnel administration" the student avoided claiming too much; by linking it with "training" from his no. 2 skill (cluster) and his no. 6, he made it a broader skill, allowing him to utilize the rest of his impressive talents. At the same time "personnel administration" got included in the supporting skills list, though it was altered to read "personnel and administrative *services*", which made clear that he was not claiming to be a fully qualified personnel administr*ator,* per se; i.e., he avoided job *titles.*

D. *Original name of cluster:* "Civil administration; Airport and Aviation Services and Training; Municipal, Real Property, Plant, Shop, and All Community and Supporting Services Management"
Student's ranking of it in his/her top ten: Ninth
Analysis: This gives not only a perfectly clear functional goal, but organizational as well, for which all the earlier skills (clusters) could serve as fine supporting assets. But this was the ninth choice out of ten —rather far down the line, all things considered; one normally hopes to find a clear functional goal within the first five or six, in the top ten. However, this could strongly support any other goal.
Conclusion: Prepare two objectives. Make this the center of the second one, and a supporting asset in the first.

II. HOW TO ANALYZE YOUR TOP TEN SKILLS (CLUSTERS) IN ORDER TO OBTAIN YOUR PRIMARY ORGANIZATIONAL GOAL

Remember, here we are looking (rarely) for an organization by name; OR for (much more commonly) some descriptive terms which could fit a reasonable number of targets, without specifying them by name. Samples (ranging from very simple description, to more complex ones):
"Major industrial manufacturer"
"Leading insurance firm"
"A corporation requiring broad experience in . . ."
"Growth-oriented consumer services / industrial complex where broad experience in . . ."
"Surface transportation systems or environmental resources control organization"
"An electronics communications systems manufacturer supplying the aerospace industry"
"Large, diversified and aggressively expanding company offering a challenge in cost reduction programming. . ."

Now, let us see how we zero in on this organizational goal, by analyzing the Top Ten skills (clusters) in the light of everything else in this program:

A. *Example:* one of the top five skill clusters says "planning, design". What does this suggest about an organizational goal?
Answer: It suggests it would have to be *growing* (whatever kind of organization other skills (clusters) may indicate).

B. *Example:* one of the top skill clusters revolves around "international interests" of the student. What does this suggest about an organizational goal?
Answer: It suggests the place he eventually goes to work must be large enough to be *international*, even if s/he is working in the home office.

C. *Example:* Her/his skills, but even more her/his other supporting material reveals great interest in reforming parts of the country. What does this suggest about an organizational goal?
Answer: It suggests some kind of occupation working from an outside base to 'the establishment', or else working within the establishment. If the latter, we look for places where reforming is possible and this in the end tends to be within educational type activities. This therefore would suggest the student should look at: Educational enterprises; the Church; governmental enterprises; big corporations; private organizations, for profit/not for profit; the press, etc.

D. *Example:* "Operational Aviation, Airport, Air Taxi & Charter Flight Services & Flying Club Management; Municipal Aviation Program Planning", was ranked second by the student in his top ten skills (clusters). What does this suggest about an organizational goal?
Answer: Aviation. But because other skills (clusters) revealed he was much interested in information flow, the organizational goal was described as "management responsibilities for profitably speeding the flow of information on modern aviation, etc. . . ." leaving him free to aim at any organization, even outside of aviation per se, that accomplished such information flow (e.g., the press, government, etc.).

E. *Example:* The student said in another part of the program that he was interested in the aviation industry. Nothing of this showed up in his skills (clusters); i.e., his past experience. What does this suggest?
Answer: Aviation. A second objective can be written up, spelling out alternative targets, if aviation proves to be too tough to break into at his high level (as indicated by his other skills clusters).

III. HOW THE TOP TEN SKILLS (CLUSTERS) AND OTHER MATERIAL IN THIS PROGRAM FINALLY COMBINE FUNCTIONAL GOAL AND ORGANIZATIONAL GOAL INTO YOUR OBJECTIVE

The top ten, as we saw earlier, have now been analyzed by you into

a) your functional goal
b) your organizational goal
c) your strong supporting functional skills
d) your secondary supporting functional skills
e) mavericks or 'odd men out': skills which don't fit with any of the above

We want now to see how they all fit together, into a formula which runs something like the following, for the sake of conciseness:

Post as ______________ OR (Challenging) ______________ post/position
in my own organization/shop OR ______________
with (leading) ______________ firm/institution/organization (seeking to
______________) where/in which requiring ______________ knowledge,
(broad) experience in ______________, (proven/demonstrated) skills
in ______________
____
plus ______________
can be (fully) used/utilized to (the fullest) advantage, preferably where strong
background/interest in ______________
can also be additional assets.

Now, let us take two examples—in full detail—to see how this all works out:

A. *Example:* analysis of the top ten and other material yielded the following:

1. FUNCTIONAL GOAL: a human development specialist (nee, professional career counseling) (This came out of the student's other exercises.)
2. ORGANIZATIONAL GOAL: an educational institution
3. STRONG SUPPORTING FUNCTIONAL SKILLS: No. 4 in the Top Ten: *Counseling*: Counseling Centers and Programs Management. No. 5: *Academic Administration, Teaching,* Educational Research and Planning. No. 1: Dynamic *Leadership* of All Age Groups, Especially Youth.

4. SECONDARY SUPPORTING FUNCTIONAL SKILLS: No. 8: *Group Dynamics.* No. 2: Public *Speaking.* No. 6: *Theatrical Productions* Planning, Organization & Management. No. 7: *Public Relations & Publicity* Programs Planning, Organization and Management. No. 3: *Selling.* No. 10: *High-Level Representation,* Tact, Diplomacy, Discretion. No. 9: *Adult Education.*

5. MAVERICKS: none, except possibly "Theatrical Productions Planning, etc."

6. PUTTING IT ALL TOGETHER in an Objective (first draft):

functional & organizational goals	Post as a human development specialist with educational institution seeking to enable students to establish their own work identities, define their own life goals, choose their preferred vocations and to secure those jobs and careers most meaningful to them,
strong support-supporting skills	in which unique *counseling* process knowledge, successful experience in *university teaching,* guidance and *administration, adult education,* the *performing arts, public relations and publicity*, plus polished
secondary supporting skills	polished *leadership, speaking, group dynamics, selling* and *high-level representational* talents can also be utilized to the fullest advantage.

(We have italicized words *or concepts* taken directly from the skills, and italicized those same words in the skills themselves.)

7. PUTTING IT ALL TOGETHER in an Objective (final draft):

functional & organizational goals	Position as human development specialist on staff of educational institution seeking to motivate and develop students to become all that they can be through *leadership*, initiative, and creativity, where
strong supporting skills	successful experience in *university administration, teaching* and *counseling, program* development, and student and *public relations,* plus
secondary supporting skills	an uncommon ability to communicate, influence, and persuade through *public speaking, group dynamics,* and *high-level representational* talents can be utilized to the fullest advantage.

(In the above Objectives, we have italicized the words which came directly from the Top Ten Skills (Clusters). We have also italicized those same words in the Skills themselves, so you can see how many of them were utilized in the objective.)

B. *One More Example:* analysis has already yielded the following:

1. FUNCTIONAL GOAL: No. 1 in student's Top Ten Skills: Operational *Management* of Major, Computerized International *C-E Systems Centers* + his No. 6: C-E Systems *Planning, Design & Installation.*
2. ORGANIZATIONAL GOAL: C-E company operating communications systems and centers.
3. STRONG SUPPORTING FUNCTIONAL SKILLS: No. 9: C-E Resources Analysis, Planning, and Management. No. 4: Large-Scale International *Logistics & Technical Support* Cooperation *Program Management.* No. 2: *Personnel & Administrative Services Management.* No. 5: *Technical Staff* Planning, Organization, Coordination, Administration and Supervision; *Policy Formulation* & Recommendation
4. SECONDARY SUPPORTING FUNCTIONAL SKILLS: No. 7: *International Relations*, High-Level Representation. No. 3: Multi-National Administrative Staff Management, Liaison & Coordination; *Bi-Lingual* Administration. No. 10: International Sponsored *Education,* Student *Exchange* & Technical Training Program Management.
5. MAVERICKS: none
6. PUTTING IT ALL TOGETHER in an Objective (first draft):

functional & organizational goals | Challenging *C-E Systems* and *Centers Management* post with growing communications firm requiring broad operational, *planning, design, and installation management* experience in which skill in large-scale *C-E Resources Analysis* and allocation. *Logistics and technical support*

strong supporting skills | *program* direction, *personnel and administrative services management, technical staff* liaison and *policy formulation,* fiscal planning and control, and business administration can be utilized to the fullest advantage—preferably where strong background in

secondary supporting skills | background in *international relations, bilingual representation,* marketing and *educational exchange program management* can also be additional assets.

(In the above Objective, we have italicized the words or concepts which came verbatim from the Top Ten Skills (Clusters), and we have underlined those same words in the Skills themselves, so that you can see how fully those Skills were utilized in the Objective itself.)

Systematic Targeting: A Brief Example

Appendix N

One recent student in this course decided that he wanted, above all, to contribute to the effective and efficient management of the investment aspects of an organization which (as he defined it) "was itself contributing to the well-planned growth" of the midwestern city which he had chosen as his geographical preference.

Working from the East coast, his initial investigations uncovered at least forty organizations which ostensibly fit his criteria. A careful study of each, based on information available to him at that distance, quickly narrowed the field down to fewer than a dozen serious contenders.

His first on-site survey, a visit of only one week's duration, allowed him to reject roughly half of these Live Organizational Targets, because even the most cursory investigation on the scene showed him that they did not meet enough of his personal requirements (Ideal Job Specifications, etc.) to warrant his further interest. But this investigation developed numerous knowledgeable sources of information and contacts, whom he was careful to add to his contacts list as he went.

It had now become clear to him that the local kind of organization which came closest to meeting his criteria and desires, was a handful of banks. His major concern in each case, because of his interest in investments, was of course their trust departments. However, it was important to him that this be put in the context of that bank's (or those banks') general outlook, and what one might call the spirit of each such organization. Although the student was no longer young in years, his attitude was still very youthful, and much attuned to the modern concern about corporate social responsibility. So he looked very hard and carefully at each bank that interested him, to determine its attitude toward the community—searching for that one which, above all others, saw itself at least as much of a good neighbor as a business enterprise.

The physical appearance of the banks, to begin with, gave some useful clues. Those which were built like medieval fortresses, with small heavy guarded doors, few or no ground-floor windows, relatively gloomy interiors, and an overall forbidding negative attitude within its staff, instantly lost points with him: they looked closed in upon themselves. On the other hand, those which were bright and cheerful buildings, with plenty of glass that people could see both in and out of, plus a happy outgoing attitude among the staff, attracted his attention.

Local contacts that he had made were able to provide further insights then into the general reputation of each bank for community participation. Moreover, they also provided a good assessment of each trust department's reputation for both efficiency and humanity.

The next step logically was for him to meet key officials of each bank under strictly no-stress circumstances, in order that he might get an even closer feel for the prevalent attitude among that bank's pace-setters and opinion-molders. Such meetings were comparatively easy to arrange, through the contacts he had made—who served as mutual friends on a social basis.

APPENDIX N.
SYSTEMATIC TARGETING

Having met with representatives of each remaining Organizational candidate, it was not difficult to narrow down his Ultimate Organizational Targets to those two banks with the people-environments that were most compatible with his own interests, criteria, views and personality. By this time, indeed, enough internal contacts had been established within those two targets, to make it easy to arrange to lunch with the Presidents and Trust Department Vice-Presidents in each case. From thereon in, it was simply a matter of giving them the opportunity to recognize that he was indeed one of them in spirit and, because of his intense interest in the same activities that they were interested in, an additional resource for implementing their corporate social responsibility that they simply could not afford to let get away.

Thus not only the targeting, but the active search campaign itself, was over almost before it had begun.

Your Personal Operations Plan: A Suggested Format

Appendix O

I. Objective

There is only one way to start and that is by defining what it is you are trying to accomplish—your objective or mission at this particular stage of your life. For your first Personal Operations Plan, simply copy down your Specific Immediate Objective, as you so carefully defined it earlier in this course.

II. Where

List your top three geographical preferences, in descending order.

III. With Whom

List your original Potential Organizational Targets, your Live (Probable) Organizational Targets, and your Ultimate (Confirmed) Organizational Targets.

IV. Targets Information

Referende how much information you have gathered thus far on the Targets that you have identified; and where this information is filed.

V. Ultimate Individual Targets

List those whom you have already identified. How much information you have gathered on each, and where this is filed. Indicate those whom you have not yet been able to identify.

VI. General Plan of Approach to These Kinds of Targets

VII. What Additional Information Is Needed

List is, and how you plan to get it. Also, give yourself deadlines on getting it.

VIII. Plan of Approach to Ultimate Individual Target No. 1

Spell it out in detail. List the contacts who might be able to help. Identify others you can, and should, meet. Work out your plan for obtaining every bit of information you will need to know about this individual and his particular activity or organization. Establish time tables. Decide when is the earliest and best time for you to begin the action. Estimate how long it will take you to complete each stage of your attack. Could you coordinate visits to that target with similar visits to other Ultimate Individual Targets in the same area, etc?

IX. Plan of Approach to Ultimate Individual Target No. 2

The same details as spelled out under VIII.

X, XI, XII, etc. Plan of Approach to Ultimate Individual Targets Nos. 3, 4, 5, etc.

The same details as spelled out under VIII.

XIII. Campaign Coordination

How all of this seems to you to mesh together.

XIV. Milestones and Timetables

Ways in which you can divide the large task up into manageable segments.

XV. Control, Measurement, Reporting & Follow-up Systems

Ways in which you can check yourself, by deadlines and such, to see that a) you did the task, and b) how well.

XVI. Special Procedures and Techniques

Anything not covered in the above. Highlighting the unusual.

How to Draft A Statement of Where You Are Going (Née, Resumé)

Appendix P

Introduction: There is no 'right way' of doing this Statement, no 'approved formula' or 'standard format'. With one exception: Make your Statement functional, in its outline, rather than chronological.

Purpose: To state where you are going, most immediately, with your life. Therefore, the heart of this Statement is your Specific Immediate Objective. Verbatim, word for word, just the way you drafted it earlier in this course. Six typed lines. Everything else on the page must flow from this Objective, justify it, and support it.

General Format: Your Statement of Where You Are Going might have the following format, as one which has come out of a number of students' successful experience:

1. Name, street, city and state, and telephone, on the four successive top lines.
2. The first section, thereafter, is entitled "OBJECTIVE:" in the left hand margin even with the first line. This is your Specific Immediate Objective.
3. The next section is entitled "QUALIFIED BY:". In your own words, explain exactly (and in as interesting a manner as possible) just what you want to do. Some clues may be obtained from your Objective. You recall that you arranged your skills there in descending order of relevance to the post or work that you want to aim toward; the most important skills first. Go now to the Talking Papers that you wrote for each of those clusters, *in the same order* as they now appear in your Objective, and quote from them the most relevant and supportive data as to your qualifying experiences, knowledge, and achievements. Thus, as it appears in this section, you will allude first of all to your most powerful qualifications that are supportive of the position you are aiming for in your Objective, so that the reader's attention is caught immediately (should there ever be any reader besides yourself); then to your less powerful but still impressive qualifications. And so on. Check over your Functional Summary (the one you just completed) then, to be sure nothing is left out, that is relevant. Look at the total section now. Is there anything written there that does not directly strengthen your case about Where You Are Going, and is not immediately relevant to the claim you make in your Objective? If so, strike it out. Now snip and prune all that is left, until you have a brief paragraph (probably no more than ten lines)

   Keep it short. Barebones. Resist the temptation to write at length here. Check over your verbs: did you use the passive, or past tense? Strike it out, and substitute action verbs (determining, supervising, etc.). On-going. Present. Be sure you included personal qualities, and not just experiences. Polish it lovingly. Enjoy writing it.
4. The next section is optional; you may or may not want to include it. It is entitled "SUMMARY OF BACK-GROUND:" If your background was clearly relavant to where it is that you are going, your field and job

titles were *obviously* clearly related, then here is your chance to tell people what jobs you held probably without dates), and what you did there by way of achievement while you held each job. And underline each title you held. However, if your background has not been obviously related to where you are going, omit this section. *Nothing should go on this Statement that is not clearly and manifestly supportive of your Objective at the top of the page.*

5. The final sections (a couple of lines apiece, at most) are for the more mundane aspects of your life. "EDUCATION": If your degree(s) strongly support your Objective, list them here in caps. If not, just list them quietly. "PERSONAL": Here is where your age, height, weight, health, marital status, and children go (except don't say "divorced"; just say "single", or—if you've remarried, "married"). Are any of your hobbies, avocations, sports, professional societies, or other memberships supportive of your Objective, in your view? If so, list. If not, forget them. Avoid the irrelevant like the plague. "LANGUAGES": List if, again, they are relevant to your Objective, in your view.

In writing this page, the only thing that should be on it—in the end—is information that *you* want others to know. Do not, ever, try to write it as though it were an answer to information that *others* are thought to want—least of all people in Personnel, whom you will steer clear of, anyway.

Rewrite: Polish this Statement, until it is *entirely* You. Be yourself. Make it fun. Unconventional. Happy. Self-assured. Confident. Neat but not gaudy. No pictures, colors, fancy ribbons, or other attempts to 'stand out.' If you wrote it as a part of this whole program, it *will* stand out anyway. If you didn't, nothing will compensate for that lack.

Alternate Versions: You may never need to use this Statement anywhere. But the discipline of writing it was good for you. And, if you do need it—with any of your Contacts, as you write to tell them Where You Are Going—or with any of your Ultimate Individual Targets, you've got it all ready. You can (as so many of the students in this course have, in the past) draft a different version of it for each Ultimate Individual Target that you decide to use it with, depending on what will be most persuasive *to him (or her).*

An example is to be found at the right.

[example]

ADAM SMITH
1950 Fairmont Road
Mark Twain, Missouri 66303
Tel.: 912-456-8938

OBJECTIVE: Position as a human development specialist with educational institution seeking to enable students to discover their unique identities, clarify their values and interests, define their life goals, choose their preferred vocations, and secure those career projects most meaningful to them in which unique counseling process knowledge and successful experience in university counseling, teaching, and administration, program planning, public relations, and adult education, plus the ability to communicate, influence, and persuade through public speaking, group dynamics, and high-level representational talents can be utilized to the fullest advantage.

QUALIFIED BY: Specialized training in career counseling and development. Five years of successfully counselling young people and students at both secondary and post-secondary educational institutions. Experience and skill in group dynamics. Leadership of student sharing experiences, student community, morale, and character building programs. Proven ability to enable human development by creating an atmosphere conducive to enthusiasm, personal growth, and creativity. Exceptionally perceptive human relations skills. Ease in establishing warm, mutual rapport with students. Ability to relate easily and well at all levels. Broad experience in all forms of communication. Extensive public speaking experience. Poise and confidence in public appearances. Communicates with honesty, sincerity and conviction. Experience in analyzing student needs and concerns, evaluating educational practices, concepts, structures and systems, determining and formulating goals and objectives, and planning, organizing and coordinating successful student programs and activities. Member of Dean of Students' staff and department head at large university with an enrollment of 20,000. Director of university student center. Schooling and experience in educational techniques, principles, and organization. University lecturer. Coordinator of free university. Coordinator of state and regional staff development converences. Director of regional continuing education program involving 600 professionals and thousands of participants. Coordinator for a major student subject area at a national convention of professional educators attended by 8,000. Effective liaison with community and educational groups and resources.

EDUCATION: University of Miami, Coral Gables, Florida, Masters program in Education, 1971–1972.
University of Louvain, Louvain, Belgium, M.A., Theology, cum laude, 1967.
University of Louvain, Louvain, Belgium, A.B. Theology, cum laude, 1965.
St. Mary's University, Baltimore, Maryland, B.A. Philosophy, cum laude, 1963.
Training program in career counseling and development, Crystal Institute, McLean, Virginia, 1972–1973. Won offer of four years of sponsored graduate studies abroad leading to doctorate.

PERSONAL: Born, March 13, 1941. Height, 6′6″. Weight, 175. Health, excellent. A concerned citizen and a highly moral person who has repeatedly won election to senior posts in community organizations and professional associations.

Appendix Q

Writing Letters To Contacts

Everyone you know, no matter what his/her position, has his/her own circle of friends and associates whom you do not know. Your goal is to tap in to each of these networks, without imposing on anyone. Your friends or acquaintances will be glad to give you a hand if they can, provided you do not ask too much, and you handle your request properly. After all, you would do the same for them were the positions reversed.

OUTLINE FOR A LETTER TO ONE OF YOUR FRIENDS OR ACQUAINTANCES FROM THE OLD DAYS

1 Open by saying whatever you would naturally say under the circumstances. Chat a little about anything at all just as you normally would with him or her. Then tell him/her that after many (or few) happy years where you have been you are thinking of offering your skills in the new field you have chosen in this course (or in a different geographical area in your old field, or whatever). Say that this experience is new and that you would like to have whatever advice and suggestions s/he might care to offer about how to go about such a transition successfully.

2 Then get down to the real purpose of your letter. Explain that after your previous experience elsewhere, your greatest need is introductions to officials of the kinds of organizations whom s/he thinks could benefit from your skills, or might already be desperately searching for just what you have to offer. Describe your Specific Immediate Objective at this point, and your preferred geographical area.

3 S/he may not know anyone like this him/herself, but have another friend who could give you just the lead you want. Suggest this possibility, and ask him/her to see what s/he can do for you.

4 Tell him/her you would be glad to bring him/her up to date on your activities, should s/he deem that would be helpful (if s/he responds affirmatively, you can write up a special edition of your Summary of Where You Are Going for him/her—at that point!).

5 Thank him/her and tell him/her that you would certainly appreciate anything s/he could do for you along these lines.

6 Close by saying whatever you would most naturally say to this particular friend or acquaintance. News about your family, asking about his/hers, etc. Whatever it may be, do what comes naturally to you.

Flesh out the above outline in any way that is natural to you. When his/her answer comes, sort out their advice about how to find a job, from their introductions or leads to other people. It is the latter that you really want, from this type of letter. Don't say so directly, however.

SAMPLE LETTER FOR WRITING A SENIOR OFFICIAL TO WHOM YOU HAVE BEEN SUBSEQUENTLY REFERRED BY ONE OF YOUR CONTACTS

1124 Maribob Circle
Savannah, Georgia 31406
July 15, 1974

Mr. Joseph F. Smith
Vice President
Bear Paw Manufacturing Inc.
5700 Fursman Avenue
San Francisco, California 98412

Dear Mr. Smith:

Our mutual friend, Mr. Charles M. Jones of ITT in New York, has suggested that I get in touch with you because of your familiarity with international activities in the San Francisco area, and your wide acquaintanceship among leading figures in that field.

Charlie knows that I am contemplating a change in my current association, in the fairly near future, and feels that you are in a good position to be aware of those executives among your friends and acquaintances who might be looking for someone with my skills and experience for their own organizations. If you do happen to know of such needs, I would certainly appreciate your arranging introductions to the appropriate people for me.

Should this not be the case, on the other hand—at least at this moment—perhaps you could refer me to someone else whom you feel might be in a better position to have such information.

I have had considerable experience in international operations as follows: [here summarize briefly relevant excerpts from your Functional Summary, or from your Statement of Where I'm Going].

Should you or any of your friends desire additional detail, I would needless to say be happy to furnish it.

I would also be grateful for an opportunity to call on you at your convenience when I am out there next month, to discuss my plans in greater detail and to benefit from your helpful advice in person, should you be able to spare a few minutes for this purpose.

Looking forward with interest to hearing from you soon, I remain,

Sincerely,

- **Again, do not just copy this letter. Adapt and rewrite it in your own natural language. Relate it to your own particular circumstances (just out of school, or whatever).**

WRITING LETTERS TO TARGETS

OUTLINE FOR A LETTER TO A SENIOR OFFICIAL AT SOME DISTANCE, TO WHOM YOU HAVE NO REFERRAL OR INTRODUCTION

You will still not approach him (or her) completely blind. Know the official by name, rather than just by title. Know what section or department s/he is in, and be sure it is the section or department you would be interested in. Inform yourself as fully as you can about his/her operation. Make sure that you know what his/her department does. See if you can dig up some of its recent achievements. Ideally, you will be able to identify some of his/her more serious problems, so that you can come right to the point and offer to help solve them. Acquire as much personal information on him/her as may be available.

Use standard business stationery, 8½ x 11", and good quality bond paper. Follow standard business correspondence practices and formats. Have each letter individually typed by a good secretary, or secretarial service (see phone book) if necessary.

1 Find something specific for your very opening sentence which will convince him (or her) that you know who you are talking to, and are informed about his firm's or department's activities. Choose some item on which you can be honestly complimentary to him (or her), and which is also logically related to your own qualifications and goals.

2 Tell him (her) why you are confident that you could contribute to the further success of his/her operation, and by way of example outline a problem area which you could help him/her solve. State that this is the reason why you are interested in joining his/her staff now that you are comtemplating a move in the near future.

3 By way of satisfying him/her that you have the skills necessary, summarize a few *relevant* sections from your Functional Summary, or your Specific Immediate Objective, or your Statement of Where You're Going.

4 Close by suggesting that a meeting to discuss the possibility of your joining his/her staff might be mutually beneficial, and that you would be happy to arrange to call on him/her for this purpose, at his/her convenience.

You may never need to write such a letter as this, because you may find all of the Ultimate Individual Targets that interest you are near at hand, and you are able to visit them first hand without the aid of any correspondence—after, of course, you have done an intensive job of researching them. But occasionally Targets of Opportunity come along, that are in an entirely different section of the country, but which nonetheless look interesting enough to pursue. At such times, a letter such as the above, firmly in your own language and thought-forms, may be the second step in exploring that Opportunity. (The first step, of course, is all the research alluded to, in the introductory paragraph above.)

Understanding The Nature of The World of Work

Appendix R

ENTERING THE UNKNOWN

As you go to your next job, you may be leaving a reasonably structured society where the rules of the game were comparatively clear, viz., school, the military, the church, or your own private enterprise. If you are to survive in your new job, you must be prepared for the fact that not only may the rules not be clear, but that things may not be at all as they seem.

Manuals, policy statements, and personnel handbooks should be viewed with appreciation, as the way in which the organization might *like* to operate? but with large skepticism, as to whether in fact these reflect the way the organization operates in actuality.

Your first rule should be to suspend judgment for a while, and seek to understand what is actually happening there in that organization; how the life of this social organism actually functions. Observe the rules and rationale of its members, but withhold any value judgments as much as you can, about their mores, until you understand why they act as they do.

COMPETITION

The one and only name of the business game—no matter what line you're in— is, let's face it, profit. Yes, money makes the world go 'round, and the *only* test of your worth in the eyes of those who employ you is your ability in one way or another, directly or indirectly, to contribute toward helping your organization make a profit. Profits are sometimes difficult to come by because no matter what it is that you are helping produce, there is someone somewhere who is trying to compete with you for the consumer dollar. And your success may mean his failure; or vice versa.

If this were only competition *between* whole organizations, or between consultants, or between entrepreneurs or craftspeople, things might not be so bad. But, unhappily, the competitive spirit has been overstimulated even within organizations, so that if someone there wants a larger paycheck s/he may only be able to secure that enviable goal by successfully competing with you. And were this internal competition out in the open so that everyone could be prepared for it, deal with it, and hopefully master it, *that* would be bad enough. But, in altogether too large a part of the world of work, this internal competition is covert, masked and underground.

The end of this tale, and its moral, is that you would do terribly well to make the assumption from the beginning that you are essentially ALONE in your job. You win or lose alone. You will need the good will and helpful cooperation, in most jobs, of your fellow workers, in order to get your job done and done well. But you will, likely as not, have to work very hard for this cooperation, and have to spend much time trying to show them why it is in their own intelligent self-interest thus to help you.

You will be wise beyond your years if you always remember that these are—sad to say—two competitors forming an uneasy alliance, which may be rent asunder in a moment, in the twinkling of an eye, as when—for example—a budget crunch suddenly appears, and a decision has to be made 'upstairs' whether to terminate your job or his (hers). It will then be 'man the lifeboats'; and: 'everyman (or woman) for himself (or herself)'.

LOYALTY

Millions of trusting souls enter the labor force every year, thinking they understand this word. It means, does it not, that if you are loyal to your superiors in that organization, they in turn will look out for your welfare? In some organizations, yes. Your boss may be the very model of concern for you, your advancement, and everything you ever hoped for. But in other organizations, no. Loyalty may be honored in rhetoric, but in actuality the law of the jungle prevails. Your boss, beneath his cool exterior, may be the most frightened person you have ever met. He may fear you, as an up and comer who may eventually displace him (or her). And, given this fear, may undermine you when you least expect it. Or, when something he has told you to do starts to turn sour, may swear on a stack of bibles that he never told you any such thing, and it was all your fault and responsibility.

Now, how are you to know which of these two types of organizations you are in? One where loyalty is a fact, or one where it is honored only in rhetoric? The difficulty is, both will look the same in appearances until (for you) the chips are down; *and then it may be too late.*

So, just as you take out life insurance against the eventuality and possibility that you may die sooner than you had intended, you would be exceedingly wise to take out insurance against the possibility that the organization you are in (and the bosses you have) are the latter type (above), rather than the former.

And your best insurance is, while maintaining a friendly and cordial relationship with everyone, to operate under the surface *as you would if you knew for a fact that you were in the second type of organization*—the one where loyalty is a gentle charade, to be discarded the minute the going gets tough for someone else.

<u>If you knew this for a fact, you would obviously:</u>

- assume that your survival within that organization is entirely your own business, and nobody else's. You cannot expect (or count on, at least) anyone else coming to your rescue if your budget is in trouble.
- assume that trouble could develop both from those above you and from those below you, in the organizational hierarchy. You would not make the bland assumption that just because someone makes less money than you do, that you can relax with him (or her) because they are no threat to you at all.
- assume that just because someone is close to you in the organization, able to see all your splendid virtues writ larger than life, does not mean that s/he is immune to the competitive virus—or will make an exception om your case while stepping over the bodies of others. The virus may attack anybody, at any time, and such considerations as how much you have helped them in the past may go right out the window, if your removal (or castration) is the logical precondition for their advancement, or for their saving their present position.
- assume that 'justice' may be sacrificed at any moment to 'expediency', and that therefore planning, strategy, and defense cannot be confidently based on such high-minded principles as 'who is actually right, and who is actually wrong'. It is infinitely more realistic to assume that whenever a conflict develops between two people, and one is junior in position to the other, the junior is going to end up being in the wrong.

- assume that just because for quite a spell things go splendidly between you and all of those around you, above you, et cetera, is no guarantee that some strange aberration may not suddenly manifest itself—with all of the past being, in effect, thrown out the window, and trust suddenly dissolved—because, unbeknownst to you, someone has suddenly become very frightened about his future (or hers). Consequently, 'eternal vigilance is the price' of your liberty, your success, and your survival.
- assume that you cannot completely 'relax' with anyone, not your own deputy (who may suddenly conclude one day that s/he can do your job better than you), not your 'friend' who is in a completely different section of the organization altogether (his or her budget next year may turn out to be in competition with yours), not the friendly personnel man downstairs who has all the manner of a good pastor (he knows his survival depends on being primarily loyal to the organization, rather than to you, so anything he knows, the organization may end up knowing), or anyone.
- assume that if you fall, by being fired or whatever, no one will stop to console or help you—pious platitudes and phrases notwithstanding. In fact you will probably be studiously avoided like the plague, because of most people's fear of becoming contaminated with the same disease: failure. ('Birds of a feather flock together'? etc.) To quote one who went through this experience and made this sad discovery only after the fact: "I don't know what I expected, but certainly not leprosy."

All these things would you do, if you knew for a fact that the organization you are working for is a typically bad example of what is to be found in the world of work today. (Cf. Robert Townsend, *Up the Organization*; Lawrence Peter, *The Peter Principle*; and some of the other reading in this course—all of which imply this sort of thing goes on only in executive position. Unhappily, the disease has not been so isolated.)

If you operate on these principles, as outlined above, and then discover that the organization you are in is a happy exception to the rule, you may celebrate this pleasant discovery as you would celebrate your 110th birthday and the discovery you didn't need your life insurance after all. No, but you were sure glad to have it—just in case.

That's the way it always is. So, you would be wise beyond belief to take out the insurance we have suggested above—against the possibility that you may need it. Or, as the Boy Scouts say, "Be prepared".

PRINCIPLES

While, at its worst, the world of work seems to be the worst expression of human unprincipledness, there are plenty of good and noble souls who have not compromised themselves one inch, while still earning their living in this profit-oriented, highly-competitive world.

Which is to say, understanding that you may have to operate in that world does not mean you need to lower your own high ethical standards one bit. You can, and *must*, devise your own soundly conceived strategy for not only surviving, but flourishing in it—while remaining yourself, and holding on firmly to your own prized integrity.

You may be helped by realizing that in our description, above, of the way in which you must view your fellow-workers, the key word is "frightened". All the unfortunate behaviour which we described as all too common in the world of work, is rooted in that word.

Hard on the heels of 'fright' is 'avarice'. Millions of our fellow citizens have fallen prey to unprincipled avarice, in their single-minded striving for 'the filthy lucre' (as they say).

In setting yor own principles clearly before you, it is important therefore that—insofar as possible—you flee from fright and avarice. You have, after all, selected (hopefully) as a result of this course that one position in which you can really and honestly be happiest. Very few of your competitors will ever be able to outproduce you. Therefore whatever monetary rewards in this life are justly yours, will almost surely come. And because you know how to find another rewarding position whenever you need to, you can afford not to be frightened of your fellow-workers.

Out of this awareness, and self-confidence, you can reach out and relate to your fellow-workers with genuine compassion, knowing they are indeed frightened about their future, and that you can be missionary to them—in gentle ways—to tell them some of the things you have learned in this course.

Now, to some subsidiary principles that may guide you in your work:

- Never frighten your boss or threaten his self-esteem in any way, if you can possibly avoid it. He is no less frightened about his future than anyone else.
- Delegate wisely and cautiously, and never tell anybody anything that you would not want stolen—or used against you. To paraphrase Mark Twain, "So conduct your work, that you would not be afraid to sell your office parrot to the organization's worst gossip."
- Use tact and diplomacy at all times with your fellow-workers, remembering how hungry everyone is for boosts to their self-esteem. Praise others as you would yourself be praised—not with blarney, but with truth.
- Remember always that those who practice jobs which have, on their face, a simpler (or lower) level than your own, probably have skills as rich as yours but are the victims of a world that has never told them how to harness them and find appropriate work for them. So treat everyone as your peer in terms of talent, if not recognition.

- If you are given the privilege of selecting people, who will be aiding you in your function, give equal weight to their brightness, intelligence, and sense of direction in their life (and how much this is really what they want to do) *and* to the degree to which you feel you can count on them, because of their own intelligent self-interest (your achievements and theirs will be mutually supportive and 'synergistic').
- Always be willing to reevaluate your perceptions—of how the organization really runs, of who are the movers within that organization, etc. The beginning of wisdom is humility. The longer you work in a place the more you may be tempted to say that you don't really understand what's going on, at all. But careful observation on your part, particularly of the invisible communications network, will ultimately unravel much of this mystery.
- No matter how you may perceive others compromising their principles, do not compromise yours. You *can* get another job, and therefore you cannot (and need not) allow this present position to hold your principles hostage to fear. Since you will always be pursuing a position which will use your talents to the fullest, you will inevitably be a Producer and Achiever—and therefore prized by one organization if not another—sometimes reluctantly, and sometimes in spite of themselves. But prized, nonetheless. At the same time, you must always be prepared for this state of of affairs to come to an end *in that particular organization*—as you threaten a non-achieving boss, by your achievements—or whatever. Hence the final principle is this:

Always have your parachute prepared, for you never know when you will need it. Your own personal future planning, continuously, should be your firmest principle.

Note: John C. Crystal is preparing a videotape expanding on this subject of "Understanding the World of Work." Those desiring such a tool should contact him at 6825 Redmond Drive
McLean, Virginia 22101

Appendix S

Your Personal Lifework Planning System

All your future planning is inter-dependent, and should therefore be integrated into one Personal Master Plan and Filing System. The name you give it should be your very own: e.g., My Future; Personal Planning; Lifework Planning System; Life Management by Objectives; My Comprehensive Personal Information System; Career Planning File; or whatever.

The key to this is a five–six page paper (or less) which is: a summary of your thinking on each of a variety of factors + cross-reference to your filing system, where more information may be found. The factors we suggest you include (in the SUMMARY PAPER and in your filing system) are as follows:

I.
My Ultimate Life Goal

1. For the first section of your 5–6 page Summary Paper, simply sit down and write out your ideal Ultimate Life Goal *as you see it today*. Say anything you want, without worrying about the possible reaction of others to it. This is *your* plan. You will never have to show it to anybody else unless you want to. In this Paper, you are only talking to yourself. So do not hesitate to speak freely and frankly. (You can, of course, change your mind at any time in the future. When you do, revise this, refine it, or otherwise change it, as you grow.)

2. Then reference where additional material on this subject can be found. Indicate that it is in your first file file folder for this System, which should be called "Appendix I" (coded to the same letter as this section of your Summary Paper). In that file, place all the pertinent material which you completed earlier in this course. Everything you wrote, for example, on "What I Think Needs Doing", "What I Would Like to Accomplish Before I Die", etc. Do not hesitate to include anything else which strongly influences your thinking on this vital subject. And continue to be alert in the days to come, as you read or think, to put any relevant articles or notes into this file, for future reference–particularly when it comes time (every six months) to review this section of your Paper.

II.
My Specific Objectives

1. The chances are that you will have developed several interesting objectives, specific ones, as a result of your most recent work in this course. Sort them out, now, in descending order according to your own preferred time priorities–using the various decision-making devices found in Appendices E and K of this manual. Number One, therefore, will turn out to be the next most immediate objective in terms of a timeline, Number Two, the the next nearest dateline, etc. Then, for this section of your Summary Paper, simply list each of your cherished Objectives, in that order. Your time milestones may be very tentative, but place tentative ones behind whatever Objectives you can, even at this early stage.
These can, of course, be revised at any time; and should be carefully reviewed every six months, when you review this entire Summary Paper.

2. Reference where additional material can be found on this subject. Put it in Appendix II, in your files (and place that title on your second file folder there, of course). Also, we are going to suggest you prepare a Personal Operations Plan for the Number One Objective on your list, above; so indicate where you are going to place that, also; so you'll know where to find it, whenever you need it.

III.
Resources Available

A. My Experience

1. You may wish to put a brief paragraph in here, summarizing your experience as you presently see it, in terms of its strengths and your interests. Or you may wish to put here a precis of your Functional Summary. At each six months review point, you will want to add the old skills you have strengthened, the new skills you have developed, particularly those which you now know will help you to reach your later Objectives more easily and faster. Your Personal Efficiency Report will be of great help here, needless to say.

2. You will want to add that additional material can be found in Appendix III_a, in your filing system; specifically your autobiography, Efficiency Report, etc. By this time, you will realize the importance of writing your own autobiography as you go through the rest of your life, adding pages month-by-month.

B. My Skills & Qualities

1. A brief summary of your skills and qualities, perhaps listing your top ten clusters. This section should be updated each six months, when all this Summary is reviewed.

2. In Appendix III_b, of course, properly referenced here, you will want to put the Skill and Quality Lists you have recently developed for yourself, and as you add to your work autobiography, you will of course periodically analyze these new sections to discover what Skills and Qualities are there—adding them to your list in the Summary Paper, and revising your Objectives and Life Goal in their light, as you think best.

C. My Contacts

1. You might wish to list in this section of your Summary Paper which groups you would do well to constantly expand your future contacts—in view of your Objective and Life Goals. You should set yourself a goal there, as well: perhaps three new contacts in the appropriate activity, field, or geographical area, per week. Devote every minute you can spare, incidentally, to following up on this. Get off your chair, and get out to see them; you will enjoy it. Keep adding their names to your Contact list. Keep in touch with your old friends, also.

2. In Appendix III_c, and indicated here, will go your present Contacts List.

D. My Interests

1. In this section of your Summary Paper, list your intellectual interests and other avocations/hobbies. We encourage you, to the limit that you enjoy it, to make a conscious effort henceforth to go out and meet those fascinating people who share your interests, in whatever societies, associations, clubs or other places that they congregate. If you know what your interests really are, at their best—which is to say, your enthusiasms—this will not be difficult, and should turn out to be hugely enjoyable.

2. Reference here your Appendix III_d, and place in it any material from this course, or elsewhere, that you feel is pertinent. Keep adding to this file as time goes on, and your interests expand.

IV.
Financial

1. In this section of your Summary Paper, we suggest you list:
   A. Current Salary and Other Income
   B. Projected Salary, Other Income, Income Peak
   C. Present and Projected Budgets
   D. Estate Planning (investments, insurance, your will, etc.)

2. Place any additional material related to your financial plans, in a file folder labeled Appendix IV, and put a reference to that file folder here.

V.
Further Development of My Own Skills and Knowledge

1. In this section, list additional courses or training you would like to take, merely because they interest you. List additional non-academic skills you would enjoy developing, just for the fun of it. Then look hard at your Ultimate Goal and your various Objectives, and reflect upon what fields you have considered even briefly; go after whatever information you might want to gather, for exploring those fields. (We are not talking about the common error of signing up for courses merely for 'credentialing' purposes. You are, thank God, out of that trap for life.)

2. In Appendix V, footnoted here, file any description of courses or other material that is relevant to this section.

VI.
Current and Future State of My Areas of Interest

1. List the fields of activity that interest you, List what plans you have to grow in your mastery of them. Timelines too, if you want.

2. In your properly referenced files, labeled Appendix VI, and footnoted here, put all the more important information you collect on these matters. Keep adding to them, until you are at least as knowledgeable about them as is anyone else in each such field.

VII.
Geographical Interests

1. List here your current three top geographical preferences. These may change as time goes on, so keep up-dating this list.
2. In your file folder keyed to this section, Appendix VII, put articles etc. on other geographical areas that interest you. These may further suggest how you want to use your vacation—employing the surveying skills you have learned in this course.

VIII, IX, and X.

---

1. In these sections of your Summary Paper, put a summary of any other subjects (three, more or less) which *you* consider important to your lifework, for the future—drawn from the subjects covered in this course, or stemming from other sources. This is your Planning Process, so incorporate your own ideas.
2. Key your file folders to these sections, as you need to, placing supplementary or exploratory material in it—in them—that you want to consider later.

XI.
Broad Planning Outline

1. In this section of your Summary Paper, trace out in broad outline form your general plan—after giving due consideration and weight to every factor covered in previous sections here—for achieving your Ultimate Life Goal, using as a framework your Specific Objectives, in turn, that you outlined earlier. Now flesh these out, not attempting to cover every last detail but drawing up your own Master Plan Outline, with appropriate controls, measurements, milestones, etc.—as you did in your Personal Operations Plan, earlier in this course. Keep it flexible enough to accommodate changes in your own aims and in outside circumstances, unpredictable events, etc. Which is to say, revise it as time goes on.

2. In the file folder keyed to this section, place any relevant supplementary or implementary material.

DISCRIMINATION PROHIBITED. Title VI of the Civil Rights Act of 1964 states: "No person in the United States shall, on the ground of race, color, or national origin, be excluded from participation in, be denied the benefits of, or be subjected to discrimination under any program or activity receiving Federal financial assistance." Therefore, any program or activity supported by the Federal Manpower Development and Training Act, like every program or activity receiving financial assistance from the Department of Health, Education, and Welfare, must be operated in compliance with this law.

About the Authors

JOHN C. CRYSTAL,
President, Crystal Management Services, Inc. of McLean, Virginia. Founder and head of a firm which has provided highly professional and successful career transition counseling and guidance for many years, he is in wide demand as a speaker, leader, and trainer on the truth about the world of work. His techniques are taught in both the public and the private sector, in high schools, colleges, government, associations, women's groups, retirement seminars and elsewhere throughout the country. His wide experience in the world of work has included service as Manager for Europe, North Africa and the Middle East with Sears, Roebuck and Co., Vice President of an international firm in New York, executive in the Foreign Division of a major manufacturer in New Jersey, and with the government. He holds a B.A., with major in Economics, from Columbia University.

RICHARD N. BOLLES
National director of the Career Development project of United Ministries in Higher Education, which represents ten major Protestant communions working together nationwide. The project has four main thrusts: research, writing up the research, training professionals in new methods of helping the job-hunter, and developing a network among professionals in the world of education, the world of work, and the world of retirement, by means of a regular newsletter, occasional conferences, and other means. He is the author of the popular *What Color Is Your Parachute? A Practical Manual for Job-Hunters and Career-Changers* (1972, Ten Speed Press, Berkeley, California) and has contributed numerous articles to various periodicals or journals on the subjects of career education, career planning, and the job-hunt. He holds a B.A. (cum laude), with major in Physics, from Harvard University.

About the Authors

JOHN C. CRYSTAL

[illegible]

RICHARD N. BOLLES

[illegible]

WE ASK EVERY STUDENT TO FILL THIS OUT, UPON COMPLETING THE COURSE.

Evaluation Form

1. I have completed the course, *Where Do I Go from Here with My Life?* I took this course in order to:
   - ☐ change careers
   - ☐ find a new job
   - ☐ improve my performance right where I presently am
   - ☐ get a better fix on my personal goals and skills

2. I took this course:
   - ☐ by myself
   - ☐ under the tutelage of a counselor or instructor whose name and address is

   ____

   ____

   I found this counselor/instructor very helpful with

   ____

   ____

   and not as helpful as I might have wished with

   ____

   ____

3. As a result of this course, I was able to [tell us whatever good benefits you received in the way of increased self-esteem, better self-performance, getting a job, or a successful change of careers] :

   ____

   ____

   ____

Use other side if more space is needed.

PLEASE FILL OUT AND RETURN TO JOHN C. CRYSTAL, CMS, 6825 REDMOND DRIVE, McLEAN, VIRGINIA 22101.

pizza with gorgonzola, potatoes, and rosemary

Don't be put off by the thought of making your own pizza. This recipe is easy to make and very satisfying. Pack leftovers for a picnic and enjoy at room temperature.

1 package (2½ teaspoons) active dry yeast

¾ cup (6 fl oz/180 ml) lukewarm water (105°–115°F/40°–46°C)

2½ cups (12½ oz/390 g) all-purpose (plain) flour

½ teaspoon salt

3 tablespoons olive oil

3 red potatoes, about 1 lb (500 g) total weight

cornmeal for dusting

2 oz (60 g) gorgonzola cheese or 4 oz (125 g) blue cheese

leaves from 1 fresh rosemary sprig, chopped, or 2 teaspoons dried oregano

In a measuring cup, sprinkle the yeast over the warm water. Add a pinch of flour, stir briefly, and let stand until foamy, about 10 minutes.

In a bowl, stir together the flour and salt. Pour in the yeast mixture and 1 tablespoon of the olive oil and mix with a fork until the dough forms. Turn out onto a floured work surface and knead until smooth and elastic, about 5 minutes. Form into a ball and place in an oiled bowl; cover with plastic wrap and let rise in a warm place until doubled in bulk, about 1 hour.

Meanwhile, place the potatoes in a small saucepan, add cold water to cover, salt lightly, and bring to a boil over high heat. Boil until tender when pierced, about 20 minutes. Drain and, when cool enough to handle, peel. Set aside.

Position a rack in the lower third of an oven and preheat to 450°F (230°C).

Punch down the dough and turn out onto the floured work surface. Knead once or twice to expel the air. Using a rolling pin, roll the dough out to an 8-inch (20-cm) round. With your fingers, push and extend the dough out into a round about 10 inches (25 cm) in diameter, pinching up the edge to form a rim around the perimeter. Dust a baking sheet with cornmeal and transfer the dough to it. Brush the top of the dough with 1 tablespoon of the olive oil.

Slice the cooked potatoes as thinly as possible and arrange, slightly overlapping, in concentric circles on top of the pizza. Crumble the cheese evenly over the potatoes. Sprinkle the rosemary or oregano over the cheese. Drizzle with the remaining 1 tablespoon olive oil.

Bake until the crust is golden brown and the cheese is bubbly, about 25 minutes. Remove from the oven, slide onto a cutting board, cut into wedges, and serve.

serves four | per serving: calories 574 (kilojoules 2,411), protein 15 g, carbohydrates 92 g, total fat 16 g, saturated fat 5 g, cholesterol 12 mg, sodium 480 mg, dietary fiber 5 g

monkfish stew with fennel and olives

For a true taste of the Mediterranean, dissolve a few saffron threads in a little warm water and add to the stew during the last 5 minutes of cooking. Serve with crusty garlic bread.

3 tablespoons olive oil

1½ lb (750 g) skinless monkfish fillet, cut into 2-inch (5-cm) pieces

salt and ground pepper to taste

½ cup (2½ oz/75 g) all-purpose (plain) flour

3 Yukon gold or similar firm-fleshed boiling potatoes, about 1½ lb (750 g) total weight, peeled and diced

2 large fennel bulbs, trimmed and thinly sliced

1 yellow onion, thinly sliced

2 cups (16 fl oz/500 ml) fish stock

½ cup (4 fl oz/125 ml) dry white wine

2 tomatoes, peeled, seeded, and chopped

1 tablespoon finely chopped fresh thyme

½ cup (2½ oz/75 g) pitted black olives, coarsely chopped

1 tablespoon finely chopped fresh flat-leaf (Italian) parsley

In a large, deep frying pan over medium-high heat, warm 2 tablespoons of the oil. Pat the fish dry with paper towels, season well with salt and pepper, and then coat with the flour, tapping off any excess. Place in the pan and cook, turning often, until lightly browned on all sides, 5–7 minutes. Transfer to paper towels to drain.

Add the remaining 1 tablespoon oil to the pan along with the potatoes, fennel, and onion. Season with salt and pepper. Cover partially and cook, stirring often, until the fennel has wilted and the potatoes are slightly softened, about 10 minutes. Add the stock, wine, tomatoes, and thyme, raise the heat slightly, and cook uncovered, stirring often, until slightly thickened and the potatoes are tender, about 15 minutes. Add the olives, browned fish, and parsley, and cook until the fish is opaque throughout, 5–7 minutes longer. Season with salt and pepper.

Transfer to a warmed serving dish and serve very hot.

serves four to six | per serving: calories 407 (kilojoules 1,709), protein 26 g, carbohydrates 43 g, total fat 12 g, saturated fat 1 g, cholesterol 34 mg, sodium 413 mg, dietary fiber 6 g

risotto with red swiss chard and spinach

Feel free to alter this basic recipe to include the freshest produce available, such as wild and domestic mushrooms, English peas, and zucchini (courgettes). Serve the risotto as a main course in its own right or as a side dish to Ossobuco (page 220).

3 tablespoons olive oil

1 large leek, white part only, finely chopped

1 small bunch red Swiss chard, about ½ lb (250 g), leaves finely shredded and stalks thinly sliced

1 small bunch spinach, about ½ lb (250 g), tough stems removed and leaves finely shredded

salt and ground pepper to taste

5 cups (40 fl oz/1.25 l) chicken broth

½ cup (4 fl oz/125 ml) dry white wine

1½ cups (10½ oz/330 g) Arborio rice

2 tablespoons finely chopped fresh parsley

¾ cup (3 oz/90 g) grated Parmesan cheese

In a deep, heavy pot over medium heat, warm 1 tablespoon of the olive oil. Add the leek and sauté until softened, about 5 minutes. Add the chard and spinach, stir well, cover, and cook, stirring once or twice, until wilted, about 3 minutes. Uncover, raise the heat, and cook off the excess liquid, about 1 minute longer. Season with salt and pepper and remove from the heat.

In a saucepan over medium-high heat, combine the broth and wine and bring to a simmer. Adjust the heat so the liquid barely simmers.

In a heavy 4-qt (4-l) saucepan over medium heat, warm the remaining 2 tablespoons oil. Add the rice and stir well to coat with the oil. Pour in ½ cup (4 fl oz/125 ml) of the hot liquid and, using a wooden spoon, stir until all of the liquid is absorbed, 3–5 minutes. Continue adding the liquid ½ cup (4 fl oz/125 ml) at a time, stirring constantly and always making sure the previous liquid is absorbed before adding more, until the rice is just tender but still firm in the center and the mixture is creamy, about 20 minutes total.

Add the reserved vegetables with the final addition of hot liquid, mix well, and cook over low heat for 2 minutes. Remove from the heat and stir in the parsley and ½ cup (2 oz/60 g) of the Parmesan cheese. Season to taste with salt and pepper.

Serve immediately. Pass the remaining ¼ cup (1 oz/30 g) cheese at the table.

serves six | per serving: calories 350 (kilojoules 1,470), protein 12 g, carbohydrates 44 g, total fat 13 g, saturated fat 4 g, cholesterol 10 mg, sodium 1,170 mg, dietary fiber 5 g

extra-crusty baked rigatoni with beef ragù

Few meals are as comforting as a pan of baked pasta. Using rigatoni—large ridged tubes—gives you the pleasure of lasagna with less work.

1 lb (500 g) rigatoni

2 tablespoons olive oil, plus oil as needed

1 yellow onion, chopped

2 cloves garlic, chopped

1½ lb (750 g) ground (minced) beef

½ cup (¾ oz/20 g) chopped fresh parsley

1 tablespoon dried oregano

1 large can (28 oz/875 g) peeled and chopped tomatoes

1 cup (8 fl oz/250 ml) heavy (double) cream

salt and ground pepper

8 oz (250 g) whole-milk mozzarella cheese, shredded

1 cup (4 oz/125 g) grated Parmesan or aged Asiago cheese

Preheat an oven to 350°F (180°C).

Bring a large pot two-thirds full of salted water to a boil. Add the rigatoni, stir well, and cook until al dente (tender but firm to the bite), about 15 minutes or according to the package directions. Drain the rigatoni, place in a large bowl, and toss with a little olive oil to prevent sticking. Set aside.

In the same pot, heat the 2 tablespoons olive oil over medium-high heat. Add the onion and garlic and cook, stirring, until soft, about 5 minutes. Add the beef and cook, stirring to break up the meat, until no pink remains, about 10 minutes. Drain off any fat. Add the parsley, oregano, and tomatoes and stir well. Bring to a boil, then reduce the heat to low and simmer, uncovered, until the tomatoes break down and the flavors have melded, about 20 minutes.

Stir in the cream, raise the heat, and return to a boil. Remove from the heat and season to taste with salt and pepper. Return the rigatoni to the pot with the sauce and toss to coat well.

Oil the bottom of a shallow 3-qt (3-l) baking dish. Spread half of the pasta mixture in the bottom of the dish. Sprinkle with half of the mozzarella. Top with the remaining pasta, the remaining mozzarella, and the Parmesan or Asiago.

Bake until the sauce is bubbly and the top is crusty and golden brown, about 35 minutes. Remove from the oven, let stand for about 5 minutes, then serve.

serves six | per serving: calories 922 (kilojoules 3,872), protein 45 g, carbohydrates 68 g, total fat 52 g, saturated fat 25 g, cholesterol 165 mg, sodium 1,005 mg, dietary fiber 3 g

roast beef and spicy slaw sandwiches

These sandwiches are quick and easy to prepare when you use a good-quality roast beef from a local delicatessen. Take along a platter of raw vegetables and serve Oatmeal Chocolate-Chunk Cookies (page 242) for dessert.

½ cup (4 fl oz/125 ml) plus 6 teaspoons mayonnaise

2 tablespoons lemon juice

1 tablespoon plus 1 teaspoon prepared horseradish

1 garlic clove, minced

1 teaspoon caraway seeds

salt and ground pepper

3 cups (9 oz/280 g) finely shredded green cabbage

6 onion rolls, cut in half

1½ lb (750 g) thinly sliced rare roast beef

In a bowl, combine the ½ cup (4 fl oz/125 ml) mayonnaise, the lemon juice, horseradish, garlic, caraway seeds, and salt and pepper to taste. Mix to combine. Add the cabbage and toss to coat.

Spread the bottom half of each roll with 1 teaspoon of the remaining mayonnaise. Top with slices of the roast beef and then with the slaw. Place the top on each sandwich and secure with toothpicks. Cut in half, if desired. Wrap in aluminum foil and keep chilled until ready to serve.

serves six | per serving: calories 487 (kilojoules 2,045), protein 28 g, carbohydrates 35 g, total fat 27 g, saturated fat 5 g, cholesterol 64 mg, sodium 1,594 mg, dietary fiber 2 g

chicken pot pie

This is an excellent way to use up leftover chicken. If you don't have any on hand, poach boneless, skinless chicken breasts in chicken stock. Use the poaching liquid in place of the regular chicken broth to make the pot pie filling.

for the crust:

1 cup (5 oz/155 g) all-purpose (plain) flour

2 tablespoons grated Parmesan cheese

pinch of salt

7 tablespoons unsalted butter, chilled, cut into small pieces

3–4 tablespoons milk

for the filling:

2 tablespoons unsalted butter

1 leek, sliced

1 large carrot, chopped

1 sweet potato or baking potato, peeled and diced

1 tablespoon all-purpose (plain) flour

2 cups (16 fl oz/500 ml) chicken broth

2 cups (about ½ lb/250 g) cubed cooked chicken

1 cup (5 oz/155 g) peas (fresh or thawed frozen)

1 cup (8 fl oz/250 ml) half-and-half (half cream)

¼ cup (⅓ oz/10 g) chopped fresh parsley

½ teaspoon dried tarragon

salt and ground pepper

Preheat an oven to 400°F (200°C). To make the crust, in a bowl, stir together the flour, Parmesan, and salt. Using 2 knives or a pastry blender, cut in the butter until the mixture resembles coarse meal. Pour in 3 tablespoons of the milk and mix quickly with a fork until moistened; if the dough seems dry, add the remaining 1 tablespoon milk. Turn out onto a lightly floured work surface and gather together. Knead briefly until the dough just holds together. Enclose in plastic wrap and chill.

To make the filling, in a saucepan, melt the butter over medium-high heat. Add the leek, carrot, and potato and cook, stirring, until the leek is softened, about 5 minutes. Add the flour and stir for 1 minute. Stir in the broth. Bring to a boil, then reduce the heat to low and simmer until slightly thickened, about 3 minutes. Stir in the chicken, peas, half-and-half, parsley, and tarragon. Simmer until slightly thickened, about 5 minutes longer. Season to taste with salt and pepper. Spoon the filling into a deep 2-qt (2-l) baking dish.

On a lightly floured surface, roll out the dough to fit the inside dimensions of the dish. Trim off any rough edges. Place the dough on top of the filling. Bake until the crust is golden brown, 35–40 minutes. Serve at once directly from the dish.

serves four | per serving: calories 693 (kilojoules 2,911), protein 28 g, carbohydrates 55 g, total fat 40 g, saturated fat 22 g, cholesterol 146 mg, sodium 686 mg, dietary fiber 5 g

bake-ahead barbecued chicken

Marinating and roasting chicken before grilling it makes the meat flavorful and juicy. You can roast the chicken in the morning, refrigerate it, and then grill the pieces just before serving. Use your favorite purchased barbecue sauce for finishing the chicken on the grill.

½ cup (4 fl oz/125 ml) orange juice

1 shallot, finely chopped

2 teaspoons honey Dijon mustard

salt and ground pepper

2 frying chickens, about 3½ lb (1.75 kg) each, cut into pieces

¾ cup (6 fl oz/180 ml) barbecue sauce

In a small bowl, combine the orange juice, shallot, mustard, and salt and pepper to taste. Arrange the chicken pieces in a large, shallow, nonaluminum dish and pour the marinade evenly over the chicken to coat it well. Cover and marinate in the refrigerator for 2–4 hours.

Preheat the oven to 375°F (190°C).

Remove the chicken from the marinade and place in a roasting pan large enough to hold the pieces comfortably in a single layer. Pour the marinade over the chicken. Cover the pan tightly with aluminum foil. Roast until the juices run clear when the chicken is pierced, about 35 minutes. The chicken should be just barely done. Remove from the oven and transfer to a platter. Pour the juices into a bowl, add the barbecue sauce, and stir to combine. Keep chilled until ready to grill.

Prepare a fire in a grill. When the coals are medium-hot, place the chicken pieces on the rack and grill, turning once and basting occasionally with the sauce, until the skin is very crisp and brown, 10–15 minutes total. Remove from the grill and serve at once with the remaining sauce alongside.

serves six to eight | per serving: calories 510 (kilojoules 2,142), protein 55 g, carbohydrates 6 g, total fat 28 g, saturated fat 8 g, cholesterol 176 mg, sodium 383 mg, dietary fiber 0 g

bean and sausage chili

Modify this recipe according to your taste: use hot sausages for spicy chili or sweet sausages for a milder flavor. If you like, garnish with sour cream, chopped green (spring) onions, and shredded jack or cheddar cheese.

2 tablespoons vegetable oil

1 yellow onion, chopped

2 bell peppers (capsicums), 1 red and 1 green, chopped

2 cloves garlic, minced

1 lb (500 g) ground (minced) beef

¾ lb (375 g) hot or sweet Italian sausage, casings removed

2 tablespoons ground cumin

2 tablespoons paprika

1 tablespoon dried oregano

½ teaspoon cayenne pepper

¾ cup (6 oz/180 ml) dark beer, preferably Mexican

1 large can (28 oz/875 g) peeled and chopped tomatoes

2 cans (15 oz/470 g each) red kidney beans, drained

In a large, heavy pot, warm the oil over medium-high heat. Add the onion, bell peppers, and garlic and cook, stirring often, until the bell peppers are soft, about 7 minutes. Add the beef and sausage, stirring to break up the meat. Cook until the meat is no longer pink, about 10 minutes. Drain off any fat from the pot.

Stir in the cumin, paprika, oregano, and cayenne and cook for 1 minute. Add the beer and let simmer for 3–4 minutes, then add the tomatoes and beans. Bring the chili to a boil, then reduce the heat to low, cover, and simmer until thickened and the flavors have melded, about 30 minutes. Ladle into warmed bowls and serve at once.

serves four to six | per serving: calories 598 (kilojoules 2,512), protein 37 g, carbohydrates 36 g, total fat 35 g, saturated fat 11 g, cholesterol 94 mg, sodium 990 mg, dietary fiber 9 g

Wilson

lavash wrap with hummus and honey-roasted turkey

To make these Middle Eastern–influenced pinwheel sandwiches, seek out lavash, hummus, and honey-roasted turkey breast meat from a well-stocked food store or delicatessen. Allow three pinwheel slices per person, depending on how many other dishes you are serving.

1 lavash piece, about 14 by 22 inches (35 by 55 cm)

¾ cup (6 oz/185 g) hummus

¼ lb (125 g) thinly sliced, honey-roasted turkey breast

4–6 large spinach leaves, stems removed

Place the lavash on a work surface. Cover with a thin layer of hummus, spreading it all the way to the edges. Cover the hummus evenly with the turkey slices. Place the spinach leaves lengthwise down the center.

Starting with a long side, tightly roll the lavash and filling so they are compact. Trim the ends. Enclose in plastic wrap and refrigerate until set, about 30 minutes.

Cut the lavash roll into slices 1½ inches (4 cm) thick. Arrange in a large transportable container, cover, and keep chilled until ready to serve.

serves four | per serving: calories 224 (kilojoules 941), protein 14 g, carbohydrates 32 g, total fat 5 g, saturated fat 0 g, cholesterol 12 mg, sodium 578 mg, dietary fiber 3 g

grilled bratwurst with onion marmalade

Serve this dish at a tailgate picnic in the autumn months when there is a chill in the air and you want something substantial and satisfying. If you prefer, use your favorite sausages. Accompany with a selection of mustards and some crusty bread. Serve Roasted Beets with Orange Vinaigrette (page 89) on the side.

¼ cup (2 fl oz/60 ml) olive oil

2 leeks, white parts only, finely chopped

1 large red onion, finely chopped

1 large yellow or Maui onion, finely chopped

¾ cup (6 fl oz/180 ml) dry red wine

¼ cup (2 fl oz/60 ml) balsamic vinegar

1 tablespoon sugar

1 teaspoon finely chopped fresh thyme

salt and ground white pepper

12 bratwurst, 2½–3 lb (1.25–1.5 kg) total weight, halved lengthwise

In a Dutch oven or other large nonaluminum pot, warm the oil over medium-high heat. Add the leeks and onions and sauté, stirring frequently, until well softened, 10–15 minutes. Add the wine, vinegar, and sugar, reduce the heat to low, and simmer, stirring occasionally, until almost all of the liquid has evaporated, about 10 minutes. The onions should be very tender and slightly caramelized. Stir in the thyme and salt and pepper to taste. Remove from the heat and let cool. Transfer to a transportable container. Keep chilled until ready to serve.

Prepare a fire in a grill. When the coals are medium-hot, place the bratwurst halves on the grill rack. Grill, turning as needed, until browned all over, 5–7 minutes total. Remove from the grill and divide among individual plates. Spoon some of the onion marmalade alongside and serve at once.

serves six | per serving: calories 797 (kilojoules 3,347), protein 31 g, carbohydrates 21 g, total fat 63 g, saturated fat 21 g, cholesterol 125 mg, sodium 1,176 mg, dietary fiber 2 g

baked risotto with butternut squash

It's important to use Arborio or other similar short-grain rice. The high starch content lends risotto its characteristic creaminess.

3½ cups (28 fl oz/875 ml) chicken or vegetable broth

3 tablespoons olive oil

1 yellow onion, chopped

1½ cups (10½ oz/330 g) Arborio or other short-grain white rice

1 small butternut squash, peeled and cut into ½-inch (12-mm) cubes

½ cup (4 fl oz/125 ml) dry white wine or vermouth

1 cup (4 oz/120 g) grated Parmesan or aged Asiago cheese

ground pepper

Place the broth in a saucepan and bring to a simmer over medium heat. Adjust the heat to maintain a simmer. Preheat the oven to 350°F (180°C).

In a large ovenproof frying pan with a lid, warm the oil over medium-high heat. Add the onion and cook, stirring, until softened, about 5 minutes. Add the rice and squash and stir to coat with the oil. Pour in the wine or vermouth and stir until the liquid is absorbed. Add ½ cup (4 fl oz/125 ml) of the simmering broth and stir until it is absorbed. Continue cooking, adding ½ cup (4 fl oz/125 ml) broth at a time and stirring constantly, until you have used an additional 1½ cups (12 fl oz/375 ml) broth. Total cooking time from when you added the wine will be about 12 minutes.

Add the remaining 1½ cups (12 fl oz/375 ml) broth and bring to a boil, stirring. Remove from the heat and stir in ½ cup (2 oz/60 g) of the cheese. Cover and bake the risotto in the oven until tender, about 20 minutes. Stir in the remaining ½ cup (2 oz/60 g) cheese; let stand, partially covered, for 5 minutes. Season to taste with pepper and serve immediately.

serves four | per serving: calories 593 (kilojoules 2,491), protein 20 g, carbohydrates 81 g, total fat 21 g, saturated fat 7 g, cholesterol 22 mg, sodium 1,412 mg, dietary fiber 4 g

roasted turkey breast with root vegetables

Depending upon how many people you're serving, you may be able to get two meals from this generous recipe. Use leftover turkey for sandwiches or in a pot pie (page 190). If any of the vegetables are unavailable, substitute equal amounts of the others in any combination.

1 large bone-in turkey breast half, about 3½ lb (1.75 kg)

1 lb (500 g) sweet potatoes

½ lb (250 g) parsnips

1 large yellow or red onion

1 lb (500 g) white or red potatoes

½ lb (250 g) baby carrots or regular carrots

4 tablespoons (2 fl oz/60 ml) olive oil

1½ teaspoons dried thyme

salt and ground pepper

Place a rack in the lower third of the oven and preheat to 375°F (190°C). Rinse the turkey with cold water and pat dry with paper towels. Set aside.

Peel the sweet potatoes, parsnips, and onion. Cut the sweet potatoes, parsnips, onion, and red or white potatoes into 1-inch (2.5-cm) chunks. If using baby carrots, leave whole; if using regular carrots, cut into 1-inch (2.5-cm) lengths.

Spread the vegetables in a large roasting pan. Drizzle with 3 tablespoons of the olive oil and sprinkle with 1 teaspoon of the thyme. Toss the vegetables to coat well with the oil and season to taste with salt and pepper. Push the vegetables toward the sides of the pan, creating a space in the center for the turkey breast.

Place the turkey breast in the pan, skin side up, and brush with the remaining 1 tablespoon olive oil. Sprinkle with the remaining ½ teaspoon thyme and salt and pepper to taste.

Roast, stirring the vegetables once or twice, until the meat is no longer pink near the bone when cut in the thickest part and the vegetables are tender, about 1½ hours. Transfer the turkey breast to a serving platter and cover with aluminum foil.

Increase the oven temperature to 400°F (200°C), return the pan to the oven, and roast the vegetables until crisp, about 10 minutes longer. Carve the meat from the bone and serve with the roasted vegetables.

serves four to six | per serving: calories 670 (kilojoules 2,814), protein 55 g, carbohydrates 50 g, total fat 27 g, saturated fat 6 g, cholesterol 148 mg, sodium 175 mg, dietary fiber 8 g

potato-leek frittata

Potatoes and leeks are a natural pair.

12 eggs

2 tablespoons finely chopped fresh flat-leaf (Italian) parsley

salt and ground pepper

1½ cups (6 oz/185 g) shredded sharp cheddar cheese

2 tablespoons olive oil

1 lb (500 g) red or white waxy potatoes, peeled and finely diced

1 leek, including about ½ inch (12 mm) of green, finely chopped

1½ teaspoons chopped fresh thyme

6 oil-packed sun-dried tomatoes, drained and halved

Preheat the oven to 350°F (180°C). In a bowl, combine the eggs, parsley, and salt and pepper to taste and whisk until well blended. Stir in 1¼ cups (5 oz/155 g) of the shredded cheese.

Heat the oil in a 10-inch (25-cm) nonstick frying pan with an ovenproof handle over medium heat. Add the potatoes and leek and sauté, stirring frequently, until the potatoes are tender and the leek is golden brown, about 20 minutes. Stir in the thyme and season to taste with salt and pepper. Using a spatula, flatten the potato-leek mixture and pour in the egg mixture. Reduce the heat to medium-low and cook, stirring occasionally, until the bottom is slightly set, about 7 minutes. Arrange the sun-dried tomatoes around the perimeter of the pan. Sprinkle with the remaining ¼ cup (1 oz/30 g) cheese.

Bake the frittata until puffed and brown, 10–15 minutes. Let cool. Slide onto a transportable serving platter and bring to room temperature. Cut into slices, then wrap the entire frittata in aluminum foil. Keep cool until ready to serve. Serve chilled or at room temperature, cut into wedges.

serves six | per serving: calories 388 (kilojoules 1,630), protein 22 g, carbohydrates 19 g, total fat 25 g, saturated fat 10 g, cholesterol 455 mg, sodium 341 mg, dietary fiber 2 g

grilled marinated flank steak

This steak is ideal for a picnic. The slices can be layered with tomatoes and watercress on French rolls spread with a chile-flavored mayonnaise. Serve with Green Bean and Sweet Pepper Salad (page 105).

2 tablespoons olive oil

2 tablespoons chile sauce

1 tablespoon soy sauce

1 teaspoon grated orange zest

1 teaspoon grated lemon zest

2 tablespoons orange juice

1 tablespoon lemon juice

2 cloves garlic, minced

1 teaspoon peeled and minced fresh ginger

¼ teaspoon ground pepper

2 lb (1 kg) flank steak

In a small bowl, combine the oil, chile sauce, soy sauce, orange and lemon zest and juice, garlic, ginger, and pepper. Whisk until well blended. Taste and adjust the seasonings. Place the flank steak flat in a large, shallow, nonaluminum dish. Pour the marinade over the steak. Cover and marinate in the refrigerator for 2–4 hours.

Prepare a fire in a grill. When the coals are medium-hot, remove the steak from the marinade, letting the excess drip off. Discard the marinade. Grill the steak until grill marks appear, 5–7 minutes on each side for medium-rare. Transfer to a carving board and thinly slice across the grain. Let cool, place in a storage container, and pour the juices from the carving board over the meat. Chill for at least 4 hours or as long as overnight.

serves four to six | per serving: calories 331 (kilojoules 1,390), protein 35 g, carbohydrates 2 g, total fat 19 g, saturated fat 7 g, cholesterol 90 mg, sodium 256 mg, dietary fiber 0 g

ham, cheddar, and potato gratin

This luscious casserole is the perfect antidote to a cold day. Serve with a spinach salad or a big plate of steamed broccoli.

1½ cups (12 fl oz/375 ml) chicken broth

½ cup (4 fl oz/125 ml) heavy (double) cream

3 cloves garlic

5 or 6 fresh sage leaves, chopped, or 1 teaspoon dried sage

1 center-cut ham steak, about 1¼ lb (625 g), or 1¼ lb (625 g) good-quality baked ham, cut into slices about ½ inch (12 mm) thick

4 large baking potatoes, about 3 lb (1.5 kg) total weight, peeled and thinly sliced

½ lb (250 g) sharp cheddar cheese, finely shredded

ground pepper

Preheat the oven to 375°F (190°C). Butter a shallow 3-qt (3-l) baking dish.

In a small saucepan, combine the broth, cream, garlic, and sage. Bring to a boil, then reduce the heat to low and simmer, uncovered, for 15 minutes.

Meanwhile, trim any fat from the ham steak, if using, and remove and discard the center bone. Cut the ham steak or baked ham into ½-inch (12-mm) dice. Arrange one-third of the potatoes in a layer on the bottom of the prepared dish. Top with half of the diced ham and one-third of the shredded cheese. Repeat the layers of potatoes, diced ham, and shredded cheese. Top with the remaining potatoes and the remaining cheese.

Remove the broth-cream mixture from the heat. Remove and discard the garlic cloves. Season the broth-cream mixture to taste with pepper and pour over the layered vegetables, distributing it as evenly as possible. Bake, uncovered, until the potatoes are tender when pierced and the top is brown, about 1 hour. Remove from the oven and let stand for about 5 minutes before serving.

serves six | per serving: calories 554 (kilojoules 2,327), protein 32 g, carbohydrates 32 g, total fat 33 g, saturated fat 17 g, cholesterol 117 mg, sodium 1,757 mg, dietary fiber 3 g

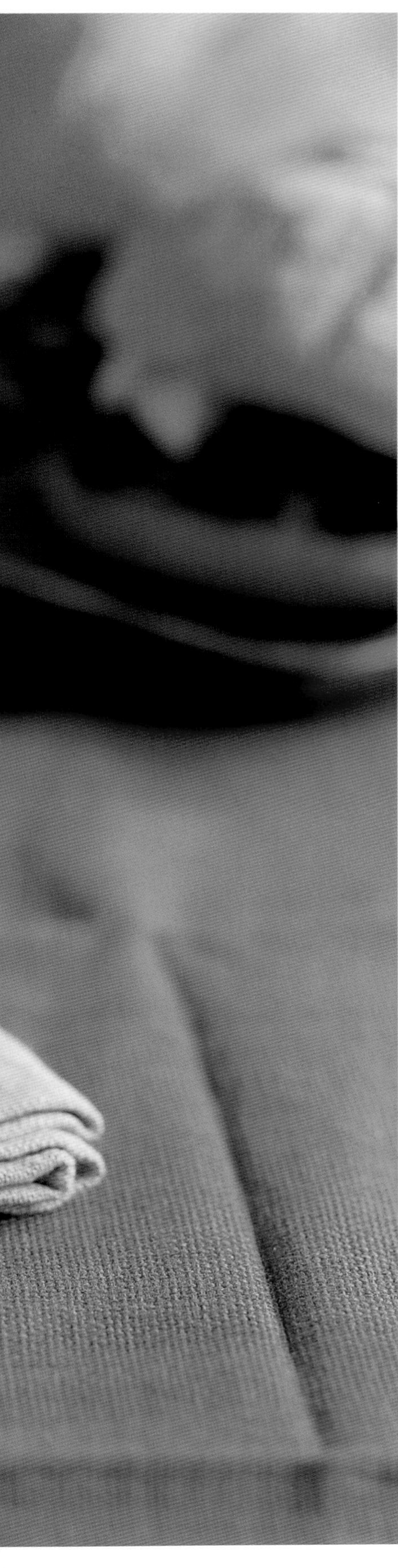

portobello mushroom and goat cheese sandwiches

The meaty texture of portobello mushrooms combined with creamy goat cheese, sun-dried tomatoes, and fresh basil makes a substantial sandwich. Marinating the mushrooms before grilling prevents them from drying out. The sandwiches can be served warm or chilled.

1 cup (8 fl oz/250 ml) plus 2 tablespoons olive oil

6 tablespoons (3 fl oz/90 ml) balsamic vinegar

3 cloves garlic, minced

2 shallots, minced

salt and ground pepper

6 portobello mushrooms, about 1½ lb (750 g), brushed clean and stems removed

6 round sourdough rolls, cut in half

1½ cups (7½ oz/235 g) crumbled goat cheese

12 oil-packed sun-dried tomatoes, drained and sliced in half

24 fresh basil leaves

In a small bowl, whisk together the oil, vinegar, garlic, shallots, and salt and pepper to taste. Arrange the mushroom caps in a single layer in a shallow, nonaluminum dish. Pour half of the marinade over the mushrooms and reserve the remainder. Cover and marinate at room temperature for 1 hour, turning after 30 minutes.

Prepare a fire in a grill. Lightly oil the grill rack. When the coals are hot, remove the mushrooms from the marinade, place on the grill rack, and weight with a large frying pan. Grill the mushrooms until tender and seared on each side, about 4 minutes total.

Drizzle about 1 tablespoon of the reserved marinade on each roll half. Place a mushroom on the bottom half of each roll. Sprinkle the top half with goat cheese, then cover with sun-dried tomatoes and basil leaves. Place the halves together. Secure each sandwich with toothpicks, cut in half, and wrap in aluminum foil. Keep chilled until ready to serve.

serves six | per serving: calories 606 (kilojoules 2,545), protein 17 g, carbohydrates 44 g, total fat 42 g, saturated fat 11 g, cholesterol 28 mg, sodium 653 mg, dietary fiber 5 g

winter

leg of lamb with mustard-herb glaze

Select your favorite herb combination to personalize this classic family pleaser. If fresh herbs are available, use them for the glaze and as a garnish. Potato Gratin with Caramelized Onions (page 226) and green beans make excellent accompaniments. Serve with a full-bodied Zinfandel or Merlot.

for the glaze:

½ cup (4 oz/125 g) Dijon mustard

1 tablespoon soy sauce

1 tablespoon olive oil

3 cloves garlic, minced

1½ teaspoons dried basil

¾ teaspoon dried thyme

salt and ground pepper to taste

1 leg of lamb, 5–6 lb (2.5–3 kg), trimmed of excess fat

2½ cups (20 fl oz/625 ml) water

salt and pepper to taste

Preheat the oven to 350°F (180°C). To make the glaze, in a small bowl, stir together the mustard, soy sauce, olive oil, garlic, basil, thyme, salt, and pepper.

Dry the lamb with paper towels and place on a rack in a roasting pan. Spoon the glaze evenly over the lamb. Pour 1½ cups (12 fl oz/375 ml) of the water into the bottom of the pan.

Roast the lamb until an instant-read thermometer inserted into the thickest part of the leg away from the bone registers 135°F (57°C) for medium-rare, 1½–1¾ hours, or 140°–150°F (60°–65°C) for medium-well, about 2 hours. Check periodically to make sure there is some liquid in the bottom of the pan and add more water if necessary. Transfer the lamb to a carving board and let rest for 10 minutes.

Meanwhile, place the pan on the stove top over medium-high heat and add the remaining 1 cup (8 fl oz/250 ml) water. Bring to a boil, stirring to dislodge any browned bits on the pan bottom. Season with salt and pepper. Skim the fat from the pan juices, then pour the juices into a small pitcher or bowl.

Carve the lamb into thin slices and arrange on a warmed platter. Pass the pan juices at the table.

serves six | per serving: calories 408 (kilojoules 1,714), protein 57 g, carbohydrates 1 g, total fat 17 g, saturated fat 6 g, cholesterol 178 mg, sodium 477 mg, dietary fiber 0 g

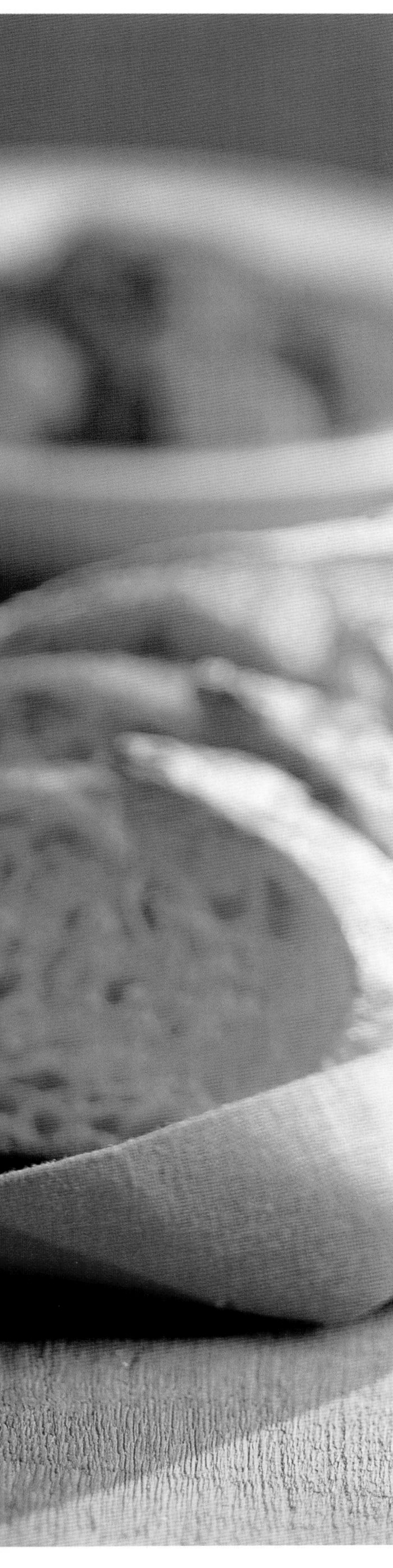

hearty winter beef stew

This cold-weather stew will revive you after a day in the snow. Serve with a warmed loaf of crusty bread, a tossed green salad, and a glass of your favorite red wine.

½ cup (2½ oz/75 g) all-purpose (plain) flour

salt and ground pepper to taste

5 tablespoons (3½ oz/105 ml) olive oil

3 lb (1.5 kg) boneless beef chuck, cut into 1½-inch (4-cm) cubes

2 large yellow onions, sliced

¼ cup (2 fl oz/60 ml) red wine vinegar

2 carrots, peeled and thinly sliced

4 cloves garlic, minced

1½ cups (12 fl oz/375 ml) beef broth

1 cup (8 fl oz/250 ml) dry red wine

¼ cup (2 oz/60 g) tomato paste

¼ teaspoon dried thyme

10 sun-dried tomatoes, soaked in water to cover for 20 minutes, drained, and quartered

3 parsnips, peeled and cut into ¾-inch (2-cm) chunks

1 lb (500 g) small boiling potatoes, cut into ¾-inch (2-cm) chunks

10 oz (315 g) frozen pearl onions, thawed and drained

2 tablespoons chopped fresh parsley

Combine the flour, salt, and pepper in a large bowl. In a large, deep nonstick frying pan over medium-high heat, warm 3 tablespoons of the olive oil. Dust the beef with the flour, shaking off any excess. Add the beef to the pan in batches and brown evenly on all sides, 5–7 minutes. Using a slotted spoon, transfer to paper towels to drain.

Add the remaining 2 tablespoons oil to the pan over medium-high heat. Add the onions and sauté until softened, about 5 minutes. Add the vinegar and continue sautéing until caramelized, about 15 minutes. Add the carrots and sauté until nearly tender, about 3 minutes. Add the garlic and sauté for 1 minute more. Add the broth, wine, tomato paste, thyme, and sun-dried tomatoes. Raise the heat and bring to a boil. Return the beef to the pan, reduce the heat to low, cover, and simmer, stirring occasionally, until the meat is almost tender, about 1½ hours.

Add the parsnips and potatoes, cover, and continue to simmer until both the vegetables and the meat are tender, about 15 minutes. Add the pearl onions and cook until tender, about 5 minutes longer. Adjust the seasonings. If the sauce is thin, raise the heat and reduce for a few minutes.

Spoon the stew into a large serving bowl or platter. Garnish with the parsley and serve.

serves six | per serving: calories 953 (kilojoules 4,003), protein 46 g, carbohydrates 52 g, total fat 62 g, saturated fat 21 g, cholesterol 164 mg, sodium 464 mg, dietary fiber 8 g

chicken and jack cheese quesadillas

Serve these quesadillas on their own for a light lunch or with Tomato-Rice Soup (page 135) for a heartier meal.

3 cups (24 fl oz/750 ml) chicken broth or water

½ teaspoon salt, if using water

3 skinless, boneless chicken breast halves

4 large flour tortillas, each 10–12 inches (25–30 cm) in diameter

2 cups (8 oz/250 g) shredded Monterey jack cheese

4 tablespoons (2 fl oz/60 ml) store-bought fresh tomato salsa, plus ½ cup (4 fl oz/125 ml) for serving

fresh cilantro sprigs for garnish

½ cup (4 fl oz/125 ml) sour cream

In a deep frying pan or a saucepan over medium-high heat, bring the broth or water to a simmer. If you're using water only, add the salt. Then add the chicken breast halves and simmer until just opaque throughout, 10–12 minutes. Remove from the heat and let the chicken cool in the liquid. Lift out the chicken breasts and shred into bite-sized pieces. You should have about 2 cups (12 oz/375 g). If you used broth, reserve for another use.

Spray a large nonstick frying pan with nonstick cooking spray and place over medium-high heat. When hot, place a tortilla in the pan and sprinkle with one-fourth of the shredded cheese. Top with one-fourth of the shredded chicken and 1 tablespoon of the salsa. Fold the tortilla in half, pressing down on top with a spatula. Cook until lightly browned on the underside, about 2 minutes. Turn and cook the second side until lightly browned, about 1 minute longer. Transfer to a warmed individual plate. Repeat to make 4 quesadillas in all. Garnish with cilantro sprigs and serve with the extra salsa and the sour cream.

serves four | per serving: calories 655 (kilojoules 2,751), protein 49 g, carbohydrates 42 g, total fat 32 g, saturated fat 15 g, cholesterol 145 mg, sodium 1,034 mg, dietary fiber 2 g

farfalle with chickpeas and winter vegetables

Two favorite Italian pasta sauces—bacony amatriciana *and bean-and-tomato* pasta e fagioli*—are combined for this robust dish.* Farfalle *means "butterflies" (also called bow ties). You can use other bite-sized pasta shapes if you prefer.*

1 tablespoon olive oil

2 slices thick-cut bacon, chopped

1 yellow onion, chopped

2 carrots, chopped

3 celery stalks, sliced

1 large can (28 oz/875 g) peeled and chopped tomatoes

1 can (15 oz/470 g) chickpeas (garbanzo beans), drained and rinsed

ground pepper

1 lb (500 g) farfalle *(see note)*

about ½ cup (2 oz/60 g) grated Parmesan or aged Asiago cheese

In a large frying pan, warm the oil over medium-high heat. Add the bacon and cook, stirring often, until browned, about 5 minutes. Add the onion, carrots, and celery. Cook, stirring often, until the vegetables are softened, about 5 minutes. Add the tomatoes and chickpeas, stir well, and bring to a boil. Reduce the heat to low and simmer, uncovered, until the sauce is thickened and the flavors have melded, about 15 minutes. Season to taste with pepper.

Meanwhile, bring a large pot two-thirds full of salted water to a boil over high heat. Add the pasta, stir well, and cook until al dente (tender but firm to the bite), about 12 minutes or according to the package directions. Drain the pasta and return to the pot or to a warmed large bowl. Add the tomato-chickpea sauce and toss well. Serve at once with the grated cheese.

serves four | per serving: calories 761 (kilojoules 3,196), protein 28 g, carbohydrates 113 g, total fat 22 g, saturated fat 7 g, cholesterol 22 mg, sodium 846 mg, dietary fiber 9 g

flank steak sandwiches

These versatile sandwiches can be made with warm or chilled steak. Some other good bread choices include sourdough, ciabatta, focaccia, or rustic country bread.

for the marinade:

2 tablespoons olive oil

1 tablespoon lemon juice

1 tablespoon Dijon mustard

1 teaspoon balsamic vinegar

1 teaspoon soy sauce

salt and ground pepper to taste

1 flank steak, 2 lb (1 kg)

½ cup (4 fl oz/125 ml) mayonnaise

3 tablespoons lemon juice

2 tablespoons bottled horseradish

1 clove garlic, minced

salt and ground pepper to taste

6 onion or poppy seed rolls, split horizontally

12 small lettuce leaves

To make the marinade, in a small bowl, whisk together the olive oil, 1 tablespoon lemon juice, mustard, vinegar, soy sauce, salt, and pepper. Place the flank steak in a large shallow dish and smear the marinade on both sides. Cover and refrigerate for at least 1 hour or for up to 4 hours.

Meanwhile, in a bowl, stir together the mayonnaise, 3 tablespoons lemon juice, horseradish, garlic, salt, and pepper. Cover and refrigerate until serving.

Preheat the broiler (grill) or place a large ridged stove-top grill pan over medium-high heat.

Remove the steak from the marinade, place on a broiler pan, and broil (grill), 3 inches (7.5 cm) from the heat source, turning once, 5–7 minutes on each side for medium-rare, or until an instant-read thermometer stuck into the thickest part registers 135°–140°F (57°–60°C). If using a stove-top grill pan, grill, turning once, using the same timing. Transfer the steak to a cutting board and let rest for about 10 minutes. Thinly slice against the grain.

Spread the cut sides of each roll half with some of the horseradish mayonnaise. Layer the sliced steak on the bottom halves, dividing it evenly among the rolls, and top each with 2 lettuce leaves. Drizzle a little bit more horseradish mayonnaise over the lettuce and then close the sandwiches. Cut in half, if desired, and serve.

serves six | per serving: calories 569 (kilojoules 2,390), protein 35 g, carbohydrates 30 g, total fat 34 g, saturated fat 8 g, cholesterol 89 mg, sodium 480 mg, dietary fiber 0 g

honey citrus salmon

These steaming packets carry a subtle sweet-and-sour Asian flavor. Make sure to wrap the foil packages tightly so the salmon cooks evenly. Serve with simple rice pilaf and steamed green beans.

¼ cup (2 fl oz/60 ml) lemon juice

1 tablespoon honey

1 tablespoon soy sauce

1 tablespoon peeled and finely chopped fresh ginger

1 small shallot, finely chopped

pinch of cayenne pepper

salt to taste

4 pieces salmon fillet, ½ lb (250 g) each

Preheat the oven to 400°F (200°C). In a small bowl, stir together the lemon juice, honey, soy sauce, ginger, shallot, cayenne pepper, and salt.

Place each piece of salmon in the center of a piece of aluminum foil large enough to enclose it fully. Evenly spoon the lemon juice mixture over the salmon pieces. Pull up the foil, fold over the edges, and seal securely. Place the packets on a baking sheet.

Bake until just opaque throughout, 15–18 minutes. The timing will depend on the thickness of the fillets; plan on 10 minutes for each inch (2.5 cm). You can open a packet to check for doneness.

Using pot holders to protect your hands, place the salmon packets on individual plates and open them to display the salmon. Serve immediately.

serves four | per serving: calories 439 (kilojoules 1,844), protein 46 g, carbohydrates 6 g, total fat 25 g, saturated fat 5 g, cholesterol 134 mg, sodium 395 mg, dietary fiber 0 g

alpine fondue

The traditional après-ski dish served in European chalets is best served in a fondue pot. What better place to keep one than at your cabin. If Gruyère cheese is unavailable, use good-quality Swiss cheese.

1 loaf coarse country bread

6 celery stalks, cut into 2-inch (5-cm) lengths

6 red potatoes, about 2 lb (1 kg) total weight, quartered and steamed

2 red bell peppers (capsicums), seeded and cut into wide strips

1 clove garlic, cut in half

1 cup (8 fl oz/250 ml) dry white wine such as sauvignon blanc or Sancerre

1 lb (500 g) Gruyère cheese, cut into cubes *(see note)*

pinch of cayenne pepper

3 tablespoons kirsch or vodka

1 tablespoon cornstarch (cornflour)

salt and ground white or black pepper

Cut or tear the bread, including the crusts, into 1½-inch (4-cm) chunks. Arrange the bread and cut-up vegetables on a platter and set aside.

Rub the interior of a 1–2-qt (1–2-l) heavy saucepan with the cut sides of the garlic clove. Place the pan over medium-high heat, add the wine, and bring to a boil. Reduce the heat to low and add the cheese and cayenne. Cook, stirring often with a wooden spoon, until the cheese melts, about 10 minutes; it is essential to keep the heat steady so that the mixture does not curdle. In a small bowl, blend the kirsch or vodka and cornstarch, then stir into the fondue. Stir until the mixture is smooth, 3–5 minutes. Season to taste with salt and pepper.

Warm a fondue pot by filling it with boiling water, then dry. Pour the fondue into the pot and set over a flame. (Alternatively, serve the fondue in a warmed ceramic serving dish and place on an electric warmer at the table.) Use fondue forks or long skewers to dip the bread and vegetables into the fondue.

serves four | per serving: calories 1,059 (kilojoules 4,448), protein 49 g, carbohydrates 108 g, total fat 41 g, saturated fat 22 g, cholesterol 125 mg, sodium 1,118 mg, dietary fiber 9 g

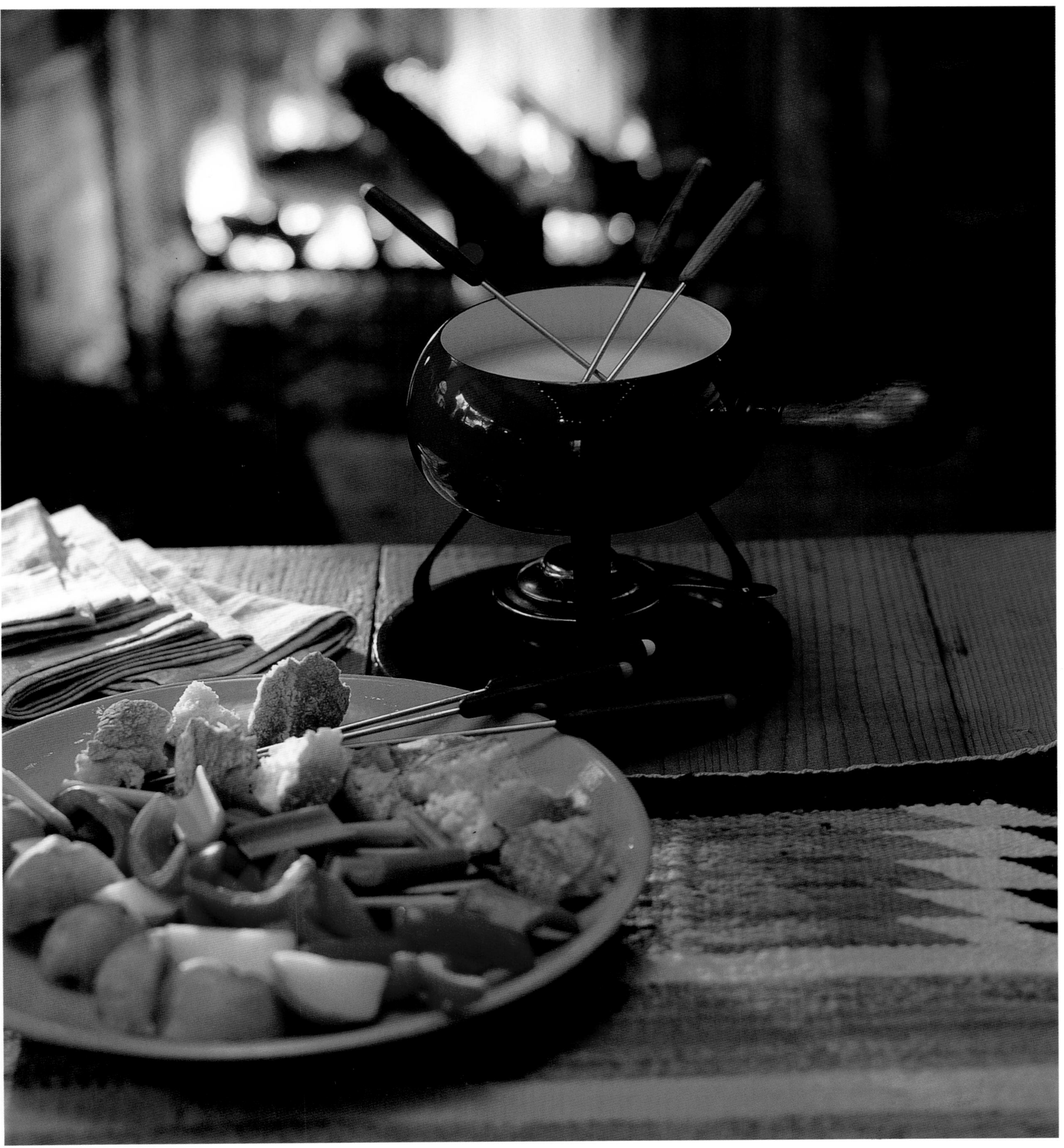

braised short ribs

Serve with your favorite mashed potatoes and bottled horseradish cream. Offer a simple green salad to begin the meal.

5 lb (2.5 kg) lean beef short ribs, cut into 3–4-inch (7.5–10-cm) pieces

salt and ground pepper to taste

3 tablespoons vegetable oil

3 large yellow onions, thickly sliced into rings

4 carrots, peeled and sliced ½ inch (12 mm) thick

4 cloves garlic, finely chopped

1½ cups (12 fl oz/375 ml) beer

1 cup (6 oz/185 g) canned crushed tomatoes

1 teaspoon Dijon mustard

Preheat an oven to 325°F (165°C). Season the ribs with salt and pepper. In a large nonstick frying pan over medium-high heat, warm 2 tablespoons of the vegetable oil. Add the ribs in batches and brown evenly on all sides, 7–10 minutes. Using tongs, transfer the ribs to paper towels to drain, then place in a large ovenproof pot.

Add the remaining 1 tablespoon oil to the same frying pan and place over medium-high heat. Add the onions and cook, stirring frequently, until browned, 7–10 minutes. Add the carrots and sauté until slightly softened, 2–3 minutes. Stir in the garlic and cook until softened, about 1 minute longer. Add the beer, tomatoes, and mustard; raise the heat to high and simmer for 1 minute. Pour the tomato mixture over the short ribs, stir to combine, cover, and bake, turning the ribs every 45 minutes, until the meat is very tender, 2½–3 hours. Season with salt and pepper and serve immediately.

serves six | per serving: calories 411 (kilojoules 1,726), protein 32 g, carbohydrates 19 g, total fat 23 g, saturated fat 8 g, cholesterol 92 mg, sodium 191 mg, dietary fiber 4 g

citrus-rosemary chicken

The secret of this delicious chicken is that it is first steamed and then roasted until the skin is brown and crisp.

1 roasting chicken, 5 lb (2.5 kg), wing tips removed

salt and ground pepper to taste

1 lemon

1 orange

1 tablespoon whole fresh rosemary leaves, plus 1 teaspoon finely chopped

2 tablespoons olive oil

6 cloves garlic

1½ lb (750 g) small potatoes, cut into 1-inch (2.5-cm) pieces

1 leek, white and light green parts only, finely chopped

1 cup (8 fl oz/250 ml) chicken broth

Preheat an oven to 450°F (230°C).

Season the chicken cavity with salt and pepper. Cut the lemon and the orange in half crosswise. Cut 1 lemon half in half again, and quarter half of the orange. Loosely stuff the cavity with the cut-up lemon and orange halves, the whole rosemary leaves, 1 tablespoon of the olive oil, and 3 of the garlic cloves.

Squeeze the juice from the remaining orange and lemon halves into a small bowl. Mince the remaining 3 garlic cloves. Add the garlic, the remaining 1 tablespoon oil, the chopped rosemary, salt, and pepper to the juice. Stir to combine. Smear the citrus mixture over the chicken, both under and all over the skin. Place the chicken, breast side up, in a large roasting pan with a lid.

Add the potatoes and leek to the roasting pan, spreading them evenly on the bottom. Season with salt and pepper and then pour the broth over them.

Cover the pan, place in the oven, and cook for 1½ hours. Uncover, stir the potatoes, and continue to cook until the chicken is golden brown and the juices run clear when the thigh is pierced at the thickest part, or until an instant-read thermometer inserted into the thickest part of the thigh away from the bone registers 165°–170°F (74°–77°C), about 15 minutes longer.

Transfer the chicken to a carving platter and let rest for 10 minutes. Transfer the potatoes to a platter and keep warm. Skim the fat off the pan juices and discard; pour the juices into a small pitcher.

Carve the chicken, place on the platter with the potatoes, and serve. Pass the pan juices at the table.

serves six | per serving: calories 668 (kilojoules 2,806), protein 50 g, carbohydrates 25 g, total fat 40 g, saturated fat 11 g, cholesterol 156 mg, sodium 320 mg, dietary fiber 2 g

ossobuco

Because you can prepare this popular Italian main course completely in advance and then reheat it just before serving, it is ideal for entertaining.

6 large veal shanks, each cut crosswise into pieces 2 inches (5 cm) thick

salt and ground pepper to taste

4 tablespoons (2 fl oz/60 ml) olive oil

2 large yellow onions, finely chopped

3 carrots, peeled and finely chopped

3 large celery stalks, finely chopped

4 cloves garlic, minced

1 cup (8 fl oz/250 ml) dry white wine

2 cans (14½ oz/455 g each) diced tomatoes with juice

1½ cups (12 fl oz/375 ml) beef or chicken broth

1 orange zest strip

1 lemon zest strip, plus 2 teaspoons finely chopped

½ teaspoon chopped fresh thyme or ¼ teaspoon dried thyme

1 bay leaf

4 tablespoons (⅓ oz/10 g) finely chopped fresh parsley

Season the veal with salt and pepper. In a large frying pan over medium-high heat, warm 2 tablespoons of the olive oil. Add the veal in batches and brown, turning once, about 4 minutes on each side. Transfer the veal to a bowl and set aside. Preheat an oven to 325°F (165°C).

In a large, deep ovenproof nonstick frying pan that will accommodate the veal in a single layer, warm the remaining 2 tablespoons oil over medium heat. Add the onions, carrots, and celery and sauté, stirring often, until all the vegetables are softened, 5–8 minutes. Add the garlic and cook until softened, about 1 minute longer.

Raise the heat to high, add the wine, and cook until most of the liquid evaporates, about 2 minutes. Add the tomatoes, broth, orange and lemon zest strips, thyme, and bay leaf and then place the browned veal in a single layer in the pan. Bring to a boil, cover, and bake in the oven until all the shanks are very tender, about 1½ hours. Discard the bay leaf and citrus zest strips and stir in 2 tablespoons of the parsley. To serve, garnish with the remaining 2 tablespoons parsley and the chopped lemon zest.

serves six | per serving: calories 435 (kilojoules 1,827), protein 38 g, carbohydrates 38 g, total fat 15 g, saturated fat 3 g, cholesterol 125 mg, sodium 579 mg, dietary fiber 7 g

pork stuffed with apples and apricots

Boneless center-cut pork loin is an excellent cut for this stove-top preparation because it retains moisture during slow cooking. Ask the butcher to make a pocket in and tie each loin for ease in stuffing. Serve with roasted potatoes and braised chard.

1 pippin or other firm, tart apple, peeled, cored, and coarsely chopped

1 cup (6 oz/180 g) whole dried apricots

½ cup (4 fl oz/125 ml) dry white wine

¾ cup (6 fl oz/185 ml) apple brandy

2 boneless center-cut pork loins, about 2 lb (1 kg) each *(see note)*

6 tablespoons (3 oz/90 g) unsalted butter

2 tablespoons olive oil

¼ cup (2 fl oz/60 ml) heavy (double) cream

salt and ground pepper to taste

2 tablespoons finely chopped fresh parsley

In a bowl, combine the apple and dried apricots. In a saucepan over medium heat, combine the wine and ½ cup (4 fl oz/125 ml) of the brandy and bring to a boil. Pour over the apple-apricot mixture and let stand until the apricots are softened, 1–2 hours.

Remove about half of the fruit from the marinade and, dividing evenly, stuff it into the hole in the center of each piece of pork by pushing it through with the handle of a wooden spoon. Reserve the remaining fruit and marinade.

In a pot large enough to hold both pork loins side by side, melt the butter with the olive oil over medium-high heat. Add the pork and brown evenly, 7–10 minutes. Pour in the remaining ¼ cup (2 fl oz/60 ml) brandy, ignite it with a match, and let the flames die out.

Cover, reduce the heat to low, and cook until an instant-read thermometer inserted into the pork (avoid the stuffing) registers 160°F (71°C), about 45 minutes.

Transfer the pork to a carving board and cover loosely with aluminum foil. Add the reserved fruit and marinade mixture to the pan juices, bring to a boil, and boil for 2 minutes. Add the cream, reduce the heat to medium, and simmer until slightly thickened, about 3 minutes. Season with salt and pepper.

To serve, cut the pork into slices ½ inch (12 mm) thick and arrange on a warmed platter. Spoon on the sauce and garnish with the parsley.

serves eight | per serving: calories 688 (kilojoules 2,890), protein 47 g, carbohydrates 16 g, total fat 44 g, saturated fat 18 g, cholesterol 186 mg, sodium 143 mg, dietary fiber 2 g

sausage and chicken ragù

Of northern Italian origin, a ragu is a meat-based sauce served with pasta. This version is particularly rich and flavorful.

4 sweet or hot Italian sausages, or a mixture, about 1 lb (500 g)

2 tablespoons olive oil

1 lb (500 g) boneless, skinless chicken breasts, cut into 1-inch (2.5-cm) pieces

1 yellow onion, sliced

4 cloves garlic, minced

1 cup (8 fl oz/250 ml) dry red wine

1 large can (28 oz/875 g) crushed tomatoes

1 small can (14½ oz/455 g) diced tomatoes with juice

3 tablespoons chopped fresh parsley

1 teaspoon dried basil

1 teaspoon dried oregano

salt and ground pepper to taste

1½ lb (750 g) penne, fusilli, or small pasta shells

½ cup (2 oz/60 g) grated Parmesan cheese

In a frying pan over medium heat, fry the sausages until evenly browned, 5–7 minutes. Using tongs, transfer to paper towels to drain. Let cool, then cut on the diagonal into slices 1 inch (2.5 cm) thick. Place in a bowl.

Pour off the drippings from the pan and add 1 tablespoon of the olive oil. Add the chicken pieces in batches and sauté until evenly browned, 3–4 minutes. Transfer with a slotted spoon to the bowl holding the sausages. Add the remaining 1 tablespoon oil to the pan over medium heat. Add the onion and sauté until softened and lightly browned, about 5 minutes. Add the garlic and sauté until softened, about 1 minute.

Pour in the wine and bring to a boil. Deglaze the pan, stirring with a wooden spoon to dislodge any browned bits on the pan bottom. Add the crushed and diced tomatoes, parsley, basil, oregano, salt, and pepper. Bring to a simmer, reduce the heat to medium-low, and simmer gently, uncovered, until the sauce is slightly thickened and no wine taste remains, 15–20 minutes. Add the reserved chicken and sausages and heat through, about 5 minutes. Taste and adjust the seasonings. Keep warm.

Bring a large pot three-fourths full of water to a boil. Add the penne or other pasta, stir well, and cook until al dente (tender yet firm to the bite), about 10 minutes or according to package directions. Drain and place in a warmed serving bowl. Pour on the sauce, toss well, and serve. Pass the Parmesan cheese at the table.

serves six | per serving: calories 819 (kilojoules 3,440), protein 49 g, carbohydrates 99 g, total fat 24 g, saturated fat 8 g, cholesterol 93 mg, sodium 1,049 mg, dietary fiber 5 g

winter pot roast

Just a handful of ingredients adds up to a tender, savory dinner. Serve each helping over mashed potatoes or wide egg noodles tossed with butter and chopped parsley.

1 boneless chuck roast, 3½–4 lb (1.75–2 kg), at room temperature

¼ cup (2 fl oz/60 ml) olive oil

2 lb (1 kg) yellow onions, thinly sliced

1 bottle (750 ml) full-bodied red wine

2 tablespoons tomato paste

salt and ground pepper

Preheat the oven to 350°F (180°C).

Pat the meat dry with paper towels. In a Dutch oven or other large, heavy pot with a lid, warm the olive oil over medium-high heat. When the oil is hot but not smoking, place the meat in the pot and brown on all sides, turning with a large fork and spoon as needed, about 15 minutes. The meat is properly browned when it releases from the pan without sticking.

Transfer the meat to a plate and set aside. Add the onions to the pot and cook, stirring often, until softened, about 10 minutes. Add the wine, tomato paste, and salt and pepper to taste; stir well and bring to a boil. Return the meat and any accumulated juices to the pot and bring to a boil. Spoon some of the liquid and onions over the top of the meat. Cover the pot and transfer it to the oven. Bake until the meat pulls apart easily with a fork, about 2½ hours.

Transfer the meat to a carving board. Cut across the grain into thick slices and arrange on a serving platter or individual plates. Spoon the sauce over the slices and serve at once.

serves six | per serving: calories 872 (kilojoules 3,362), protein 51 g, carbohydrates 16 g, total fat 66 g, saturated fat 24 g, cholesterol 204 mg, sodium 244 mg, dietary fiber 3 g

white bean stew

A crisp topping of Parmesan cheese, bread crumbs, and parsley crowns this thick, satisfying bean stew.

2 cups (14 oz/440 g) dried white beans such as Great Northern

2 tablespoons olive oil

1 yellow onion, finely chopped

2 cloves garlic, minced

4 cups (32 fl oz/1 l) chicken broth

1 cup (8 fl oz/250 ml) dry white wine

1 cup (6 oz/185 g) canned diced tomatoes, drained

¼ cup (2 fl oz/60 ml) plus 1 tablespoon balsamic vinegar

1 large bunch spinach, about 1 lb (500 g), tough stems removed and leaves torn into bite-sized pieces

salt and ground pepper to taste

¼ cup (1 oz/30 g) grated Parmesan cheese

¼ cup (1 oz/30 g) fine dried bread crumbs, toasted

1 tablespoon finely chopped fresh parsley

Pick over the beans, discarding any stones or misshapen beans. Rinse and drain. Place in a bowl, add plenty of water to cover, and let soak for at least 4 hours or for up to overnight. Drain and set aside.

In a heavy saucepan over medium heat, warm the olive oil. Add the onion and sauté until softened, 5–7 minutes. Add the garlic and sauté until softened, about 1 minute longer. Then add the broth, wine, tomatoes, the ¼ cup (2 fl oz/60 ml) vinegar, and the beans. Bring to a simmer, cover, reduce the heat to low, and cook until the beans are tender and beginning to fall apart, about 2¼ hours. Mash some of the beans with the back of a spoon to create a creamy consistency. Uncover the saucepan, increase the heat to medium, and reduce until thickened slightly, 5–10 minutes.

Add the spinach, re-cover, and cook over medium heat, stirring once, until the spinach is slightly wilted, about 3 minutes. Add the salt, pepper, and the remaining 1 tablespoon vinegar and stir to combine. Taste and adjust the seasonings.

To serve, preheat the broiler (grill). Spoon the beans into a flameproof gratin dish. In a small bowl, stir together the Parmesan cheese, bread crumbs, and parsley. Sprinkle evenly over the beans. Slip under the broiler 3–4 inches (7.5–10 cm) from the heat source and broil (grill) until the top is nicely browned, 3–4 minutes. Serve immediately, directly from the dish.

serves six | per serving: calories 357 (kilojoules 1,499), protein 20 g, carbohydrates 53 g, total fat 8 g, saturated fat 2 g, cholesterol 3 mg, sodium 904 mg, dietary fiber 29 g

potato gratin with caramelized onions

Serve this creamy potato dish with a large green salad or with Tomato-Rice Soup (page 135) for a satisfying vegetarian supper. It is also excellent offered as an accompaniment to Leg of Lamb with Mustard-Herb Glaze (page 206).

2 tablespoons olive oil

2 large yellow onions, thinly sliced

½ teaspoon sugar

1 teaspoon balsamic vinegar

salt and ground pepper to taste

2 cups (8 oz/250 g) grated Gruyère cheese

3 tablespoons finely chopped fresh parsley

4 cloves garlic, minced

4 lb (2 kg) baking or Yukon gold potatoes, unpeeled, cut into slices ¼ inch (6 mm) thick

2 cups (16 fl oz/500 ml) chicken broth

2 tablespoons unsalted butter, at room temperature, cut into small pieces

In a large frying pan over medium heat, warm the olive oil. Add the onions and sugar and sauté until the onions are browned and caramelized, about 15 minutes. Add the balsamic vinegar and cook until the liquid evaporates and the onions are very brown, about 2 minutes longer. Season with salt and pepper and set aside.

Preheat the oven to 375°F (190°C). Oil a 9-by-13-inch (23-by-33-cm) baking dish. In a small bowl, combine the cheese, parsley, garlic, and pepper.

Layer half of the potatoes on the bottom of the prepared baking dish. Spread the onion mixture evenly over the potatoes. Season with salt and pepper. Layer the remaining potatoes over the onion mixture and again season with salt and pepper. Pour the broth evenly over the potatoes and sprinkle the garlic-cheese mixture evenly over the top. Dot the surface with the butter. Cover the dish with buttered aluminum foil, buttered side down.

Bake for 30 minutes. Uncover and continue baking until the top is browned and crusty and the potatoes are fork-tender, about 30 minutes longer. Serve immediately, directly from the dish.

serves six to eight | per serving: calories 431 (kilojoules 1,810), protein 17 g, carbohydrates 50 g, total fat 19 g, saturated fat 9 g, cholesterol 45 mg, sodium 416 mg, dietary fiber 6 g

polenta bolognese

The polenta is also delicious cooled, cut into squares, and fried. Serve with the sauce, or on its own for a versatile, anytime side dish.

for the sauce:

3 tablespoons olive oil

1 lb (500 g) ground (minced) sirloin

1 yellow onion, finely chopped

1 carrot, finely chopped

1 celery stalk, finely chopped

2 large cloves garlic, minced

2 oz (60 g) prosciutto, chopped

2 cans (14½ oz/455 g each) diced tomatoes with juice

1 can (28 oz/875 g) crushed tomatoes

3 tablespoons minced fresh parsley

½ bay leaf

1 teaspoon dried oregano

2 teaspoons dried basil

¼ teaspoon dried thyme

1 cup (8 fl oz/250 ml) dry red wine

salt and ground pepper to taste

for the polenta:

1 tablespoon olive oil

1 small yellow onion, minced

1 clove garlic, minced

7 cups (56 fl oz/1.75 l) chicken broth

½ teaspoon salt

1 cup (6 oz/185 g) corn kernels

2 cups (10 oz/315 g) instant polenta

⅓ cup (1½ oz/45 g) grated Asiago or Parmesan cheese, plus ½ cup (2 oz/60 g) for passing

½ cup (2½ oz/75 g) finely diced fontina cheese

To make the sauce, in a large, heavy pot over medium heat, warm 1 tablespoon of the olive oil. Add the beef and sauté until browned, 4–5 minutes. Using a slotted spoon, transfer to a bowl.

Add the remaining 2 tablespoons oil to the same pan over medium heat. Add the onion, carrot, and celery and sauté until softened, 6–8 minutes. Add the garlic and prosciutto and sauté until just softened, about 1 minute. Add the tomatoes, herbs, red wine, and browned beef, cover partially, reduce the heat to medium-low, and simmer until the sauce has a well-rounded flavor, about 45 minutes. Remove the bay leaf. Season with salt and pepper. Keep warm.

To make the polenta, in a deep saucepan over medium heat, warm the olive oil. Add the onion and sauté until softened, about 5 minutes. Add the garlic and sauté for 1 minute. Add the broth and salt and bring to a boil. Add the corn, then slowly add the polenta in a stream while stirring. Reduce the heat to medium-low and cook, stirring constantly, until smooth and stiff, 3–5 minutes. Stir in the grated and diced cheeses.

To serve, divide the polenta among shallow bowls and spoon the sauce on top. Pass the extra grated cheese at the table.

serves six to eight | per serving: calories 588 (kilojoules 2,470), protein 30 g, carbohydrates 51 g, total fat 29 g, saturated fat 11 g, cholesterol 72 mg, sodium 1,985 mg, dietary fiber 8 g

turkey-vegetable cobbler

A cobbler dough replaces the traditional flaky pastry for this pot pie cousin. Frozen onions cut out extra steps without sacrificing quality. Serve with a simple salad of romaine (cos) and cucumbers tossed with a mustard vinaigrette.

10 oz (315 g) frozen pearl onions, thawed and drained

3 carrots or 10 oz (315 g) baby carrots, peeled and cubed

1 cup (5 oz/155 g) fresh or thawed frozen petite English peas

8 tablespoons (4 oz/125 g) unsalted butter

1 leek, white and light green parts only, finely chopped

1 lb (500 g) fresh mushrooms, brushed clean and coarsely diced

1 cup (6 oz/185 g) frozen corn kernels, thawed and drained

4 cups (1½ lb/750 g) diced cooked turkey breast (½-inch/12-mm dice)

7 tablespoons (2½ oz/75 g) all-purpose (plain) flour

2 cups (16 fl oz/500 ml) chicken broth

1 cup (8 fl oz/250 ml) half-and-half (half cream)

salt and ground white pepper to taste

2 tablespoons finely chopped fresh parsley

2 tablespoons finely chopped fresh dill

for the cobbler dough:

1¾ cups (9 oz/280 g) all-purpose (plain) flour

1 tablespoon baking powder

¼ teaspoon salt

4 tablespoons (1 oz/30 g) grated Parmesan cheese

6 tablespoons (3 oz/90 g) chilled unsalted butter, cut into small pieces

½ cup (4 fl oz/125 ml) heavy (double) cream

1 egg, beaten

Put the thawed onions in a large bowl. Bring a saucepan three-fourths full of water to a boil, add the carrots, and simmer until just tender, about 7 minutes. Using a slotted spoon, scoop out the carrots and add to the onions. If using fresh peas, return the water to a boil, add the peas, and cook until just tender, about 3 minutes. Drain well. Add the cooked fresh or thawed frozen peas to the bowl.

In a frying pan over medium heat, melt 2 tablespoons of the butter. Add the leek and sauté until softened, about 3 minutes. Add the mushrooms and sauté until softened, about 3 minutes longer. Add the contents of the pan to the bowl holding the vegetables. Then add the corn and turkey to the bowl and set aside.

In a large saucepan over medium heat, melt the remaining 6 tablespoons (3 oz/90 g) butter. Sprinkle in the flour and cook, stirring constantly, for about 3 minutes, making sure the flour does not darken. Slowly add the broth and half-and-half, whisking constantly, until thickened and smooth, about 4 minutes. Season with salt and pepper. Pour the sauce over the turkey-vegetable mixture, add the parsley and dill, and mix well. Taste and adjust the seasonings.

Preheat the oven to 400°F (200°C). Grease a deep 9-by-13-inch (23-by-33-cm) baking dish with butter. Pour the mixture into the prepared dish.

To make the cobbler dough, in a bowl, stir together the flour, baking powder, salt, and 3 tablespoons of the Parmesan. Using a pastry blender or 2 knives, cut in the butter until the mixture resembles coarse meal. Add the cream a little at a time, stirring and tossing with a fork just until the dough holds together.

On a lightly floured work surface, roll out the dough into a rectangle large enough to cover the top of the baking dish. Drape it around the rolling pin and carefully lay it over the dish, folding the edges under. Alternatively, drop the dough by spoonfuls on top of the turkey-vegetable mixture, distributing them evenly. Brush the dough with the beaten egg and sprinkle the remaining Parmesan evenly over the top. Place the dish on a baking sheet.

Bake until the crust is browned, about 30 minutes. Check regularly near the end of the cooking time to prevent burning. Serve immediately, directly from the dish.

serves six to eight | per serving: calories 746 (kilojoules 3,133), protein 43 g, carbohydrates 60 g, total fat 38 g, saturated fat 22 g, cholesterol 213 mg, sodium 756 mg, dietary fiber 5 g

easy coq au vin

The classic dish of chicken in red wine is simpler and faster made with thawed frozen pearl onions. It tastes even better the next day.

6 slices bacon, about 5 oz (155 g), cut into 1-inch (2.5-cm) pieces

¼ cup (1½ oz/45 g) all-purpose (plain) flour

salt and ground pepper to taste

3 each chicken breast halves, drumsticks, and thighs

5 tablespoons olive oil

¼ cup (2 fl oz/60 ml) brandy

2 cups (16 fl oz/500 ml) dry red wine

1 tablespoon tomato paste

3 cloves garlic, minced

½ lb (250 g) fresh white mushrooms, brushed clean and quartered

10 oz (315 g) frozen pearl onions, thawed and drained

1 tablespoon unsalted butter

4 carrots, peeled and cut into ¾-inch (2-cm) chunks

4 turnips, peeled, quartered, and cut into ¾-inch (2-cm) chunks

¾ cup (6 fl oz/180 ml) chicken broth

¼ cup (⅓ oz/10 g) chopped fresh parsley

In a large, heavy pot, fry the bacon until crisp, 4–5 minutes. Using a slotted spoon, transfer to paper towels to drain. Pour off all but 1 tablespoon of the bacon drippings from the pan.

In a bowl, stir together the flour, salt, and pepper. Lightly dredge the chicken.

Add 2 tablespoons of the oil to the same pan and place over medium-high heat. Brown the chicken in batches, 5–7 minutes. Pour off the drippings from the pan. Return all the chicken to the pan, add the brandy, ignite with a match, and let the flames die. Add the wine, tomato paste, and garlic. Cover, reduce the heat to medium-low, and cook until very tender and the sauce is slightly thickened, about 50 minutes.

Meanwhile, in a frying pan over medium heat, warm 1 tablespoon of the oil. Add the mushrooms and sauté until softened, 3–5 minutes. Raise the heat to high, add the onions, and stir until lightly glazed, 2–3 minutes longer. Season with salt and pepper and set aside.

About 20 minutes before the chicken is ready, in a large frying pan over medium heat, melt the butter with the remaining 2 tablespoons oil. Add the carrots and turnips and sauté until beginning to brown, 3–5 minutes. Add the broth, season with salt and pepper, reduce the heat to low, cover, and simmer until just tender, about 15 minutes. Uncover and boil down the liquid until it forms a glaze. Add the bacon and 2 tablespoons of the parsley.

When the chicken is ready, stir in the onion-mushroom mixture and the remaining 2 tablespoons parsley. Season with salt and pepper. Serve on a warmed platter with the turnips and carrots arranged around the chicken.

serves four to six | per serving: calories 705 (kilojoules 2,961), protein 52 g, carbohydrates 28 g, total fat 43 g, saturated fat 11 g, cholesterol 153 mg, sodium 547 mg, dietary fiber 5 g

four seasons pizza

Thanks to the benefits of canning, all four seasons are represented here without the use of out-of-season ingredients. For a vegetarian version, substitute oil-packed, sun-dried tomatoes for the prosciutto.

for the dough:

5 teaspoons (2 packages) active dry yeast

1 teaspoon sugar

1 cup (8 fl oz/250 ml) lukewarm water (115°F/46°C)

3 cups (15 oz/470 g) all-purpose (plain) flour

2 tablespoons yellow cornmeal

1½ teaspoons salt

2 tablespoons olive oil

1½ cups (15 oz/470 g) favorite store-bought tomato-basil sauce

1 cup (4 oz/125 g) shredded mozzarella cheese

¼ cup (1 oz/30 g) grated Parmesan cheese

6 canned artichoke hearts, well drained and quartered lengthwise

12 Kalamata olives, pitted and halved

6 fresh small white mushrooms, brushed clean, stems removed, and thinly sliced

2 thin slices prosciutto, shredded

To make the dough, in a bowl, sprinkle the yeast and sugar over ¼ cup (2 fl oz/60 ml) of the lukewarm water and let stand until foamy, 5–10 minutes. Stir to dissolve the yeast. In a bowl, stir together the flour, cornmeal, and salt. Add the remaining ¾ cup (6 fl oz/185 ml) water and the oil to the yeast mixture. Gradually pour the yeast mixture into the flour mixture, stirring until the dough comes together. If it is too dry, add 1 more tablespoon water. Turn out onto a lightly floured work surface and knead briefly until smooth. Place in an oiled bowl, turning to coat. Cover the bowl and let the dough rise in a warm place until doubled in volume, about 1 hour.

Oil a large rimless baking sheet. Punch down the dough and turn it out onto a floured work surface. Knead briefly until smooth, then divide in half. Press out each half into a 9-inch (23-cm) round, forming a slight rim. Transfer to the prepared baking sheet, cover, and let rise until tripled in height, about 30 minutes. Meanwhile, preheat the oven to 475°F (245°C).

Using a fork, pierce the rounds at even intervals. Spread the tomato sauce evenly over each. Sprinkle with the cheeses. Arrange the artichokes, olives, mushrooms, and prosciutto in 4 quadrants over the cheeses. Place in the oven, reduce the temperature to 425°F (220°C), and bake until the crust is golden brown and the cheeses are melted, 25–30 minutes. Let rest for 2 minutes, then cut into wedges and serve.

makes two pizzas; serves four | per serving: calories 791 (kilojoules 3,322), protein 27 g, carbohydrates 112 g, total fat 25 g, saturated fat 7 g, cholesterol 33 mg, sodium 1,931 mg, dietary fiber 6 g

turkey-ricotta burgers

Serve these moist, flavorful burgers with the classic condiments: ketchup, mustard, mayonnaise, and chile sauce.

2 tablespoons olive oil

2 shallots, minced

2 cloves garlic, minced

1½ lb (750 g) ground (minced) turkey

⅓ cup (2½ oz/75 g) ricotta cheese

1 tablespoon Dijon mustard

2 teaspoons Worcestershire sauce

salt and pepper to taste

6 Kaiser rolls, split horizontally and lightly toasted

6 slices fresh tomato, preferably beefsteak

6 lettuce leaves

In a frying pan over medium heat, warm the olive oil. Add the shallots and sauté until softened, about 2 minutes. Add the garlic and cook until softened, about 1 minute longer. Transfer to a bowl and add the turkey, ricotta cheese, mustard, Worcestershire sauce, salt, and pepper. Mix lightly and shape into 6 patties, each about 1 inch (2.5 cm) thick. Cover and refrigerate for at least 1 hour or for up to 4 hours.

Place a ridged stove-top grill pan or a sauté pan over medium-high heat. When hot, spray with nonstick cooking spray and add the patties. Cook on the first side until browned and crispy, 3–4 minutes. Flip and cook on the second side until browned and crispy, 4–6 minutes longer. Reduce the heat to medium, cover partially, and continue to cook until opaque throughout or until an instant-read thermometer stuck into the thickest part of a burger registers 160°F (71°C), 2–3 minutes longer.

Transfer the burgers to the roll bottoms and garnish each with a slice of tomato and a lettuce leaf. Top with the roll tops and serve at once.

serves six | per serving: calories 407 (kilojoules 1,709), protein 28 g, carbohydrates 34 g, total fat 17 g, saturated fat 4 g, cholesterol 89 mg, sodium 510 mg, dietary fiber 2 g

desserts

Buckle, Bundt, crumble, crisp. Just the names of these desserts cheer you up and make you feel like you're getting away from it all. Then there are the fillings: sour cherries, sunny apricots, crisp apples, plums, figs, berries, and more. Dessert puts you in touch with the outdoors, as you imagine picking fruits right off the tree or vine—even if you venture no farther than the local roadside farm stand.

Think of desserts as daylong treats, as something to snack on when you are hungriest. Pop a banana-oatmeal cookie into your mouth as you finish an early morning bike ride, or treat yourself to a mocha brownie or a lemon pudding square following an afternoon of sledding. Coffee-bourbon granita tastes great after a swim in the sea, or cap off a summertime outdoor supper with seasonal Peach-Raspberry Pie.

You will be surprised how easily this chapter's cookies, pies, and cakes pack up for transport to a picnic or tailgate party. Even ice cream can be toted along in a cooler with lots of ice. Regardless of where you are, or where you've been, anyone is happy to come home to a decadently rich hot-fudge sundae.

spring

sour cherry crisp

Tart, intensely flavorful sour cherries are at their peak for only a short time in the summer. Canned or bottled cherries (packed in water) can be used out of season. Serve with plenty of vanilla ice cream.

7 oz (220 g) frozen puff pastry, thawed

1 egg lightly beaten with 1 teaspoon warm water

4 cups (10 oz/315 g) pitted sour cherries

¾ cup (6 oz/185 g) sugar

¼ cup (1½ oz/45 g) all-purpose (plain) flour

1 tablespoon lemon juice

2 tablespoons unsalted butter, cut into pieces

On a floured work surface, roll out the pastry dough into an 8-by-12-inch (20-by-30-cm) rectangle about ⅛ inch (3 mm) thick. Place a 1½-qt (1.5-l) baking dish upside down on the dough. Using a sharp knife, carefully trace the outer edge of the dish; the dough must have exactly the same dimensions as the top of the dish. Set the dish aside.

Transfer the dough to a baking sheet and brush the pastry lightly with some of the egg-water mixture. Prick all over with a fork, cover with plastic wrap, and refrigerate for 30 minutes.

Preheat the oven to 375°F (190°C).

In a saucepan, combine the cherries, sugar, flour, and lemon juice. Stir well. Place over medium-high heat and cook until thickened, stirring occasionally, about 10 minutes. Remove from the heat, stir in the butter, and pour into the reserved baking dish. Set aside.

Remove the baking sheet from the refrigerator and brush the pastry with the remaining egg-water mixture. Bake until lightly golden and puffed, about 12 minutes. Using a wide spatula, carefully transfer the pastry to the baking dish, covering the cherry filling fully. Press down lightly.

Bake until the filling is bubbling and the pastry is crisp and golden brown, about 30 minutes. Transfer to a rack and let cool slightly before serving.

serves six to eight | per serving: calories 337 (kilojoules 1,415), protein 4 g, carbohydrates 48 g, total fat 15 g, saturated fat 4 g, cholesterol 39 mg, sodium 82 mg, dietary fiber 0 g

walnut-orange cake

Brimming with fresh orange zest and juice and ground walnuts, this cake has a crisp exterior and a moist and coarse-textured interior. Serve on its own or with a spoonful of Strawberries with Oranges and Balsamic Vinegar (right). It's also good with slices of fresh orange.

1½ cups (6 oz/185 g) chopped walnuts

1 cup (5 oz/155 g) all-purpose (plain) flour

1 tablespoon baking powder

4 eggs

1½ cups (12 oz/375 g) granulated sugar

grated zest and juice of 1 orange (about ½ cup/4 fl oz/125 ml juice)

½ cup (4 fl oz/125 ml) extra-virgin olive oil

confectioners' (icing) sugar for dusting

Preheat the oven to 350°F (180°C). Lightly coat a 9-inch (23-cm) springform pan with olive oil.

Place the walnuts in a food processor and process until finely ground, almost to the consistency of bread crumbs. In a bowl, combine the ground walnuts, flour, and baking powder.

Place the eggs in a large bowl and beat with an electric mixer until frothy. Slowly add the granulated sugar and beat until the mixture is light, thick, and lemon colored. Slowly add the walnut-flour mixture, beating continuously. Then, with the mixer on low speed, add the orange zest and juice and the olive oil and mix until just combined.

Pour into the prepared pan and bake until a wooden skewer inserted into the center comes out clean, 50–60 minutes. Set the pan on a rack to cool.

Remove the pan sides and transfer the cake to a transportable serving platter. Dust the top with confectioners' sugar, creating a decorative pattern if desired. Serve at room temperature, cut into wedges.

serves eight | per serving: calories 541 (kilojoules 2,272), protein 8 g, carbohydrates 64 g, total fat 30 g, saturated fat 4 g, cholesterol 106 mg, sodium 217 mg, dietary fiber 2 g

strawberries with oranges and balsamic vinegar

A splash of thickened balsamic vinegar enhances this colorful fruit concoction. Serve with your favorite biscotti or with slices of Walnut-Orange Cake (left) for a satisfying dessert.

½ cup (4 fl oz/125 ml) balsamic vinegar

4 small blood oranges or other small oranges

3 pt (1½ lb/750 g) strawberries, hulled and halved

Pour the balsamic vinegar into a small saucepan. Place over medium-high heat and simmer until the vinegar turns syrupy, about 5 minutes. Set aside and let cool.

Using a small, sharp knife, cut a slice off the top and bottom of each orange to expose the fruit. Place each orange upright on a cutting board and slice off the peel in thick strips to expose the flesh. Holding the orange over a transportable bowl, cut along either side of each section, letting the sections drop into the bowl. Remove any seeds and discard.

Add the strawberry halves to the orange sections and stir to combine. Pour the syrup over the fruit and refrigerate for at least 1 hour or for up to 4 hours. Keep chilled until ready to serve.

serves six | per serving: calories 81 (kilojoules 340), protein 1 g, carbohydrates 19 g, total fat 0 g, saturated fat 0 g, cholesterol 0 mg, sodium 2 mg, dietary fiber 5 g

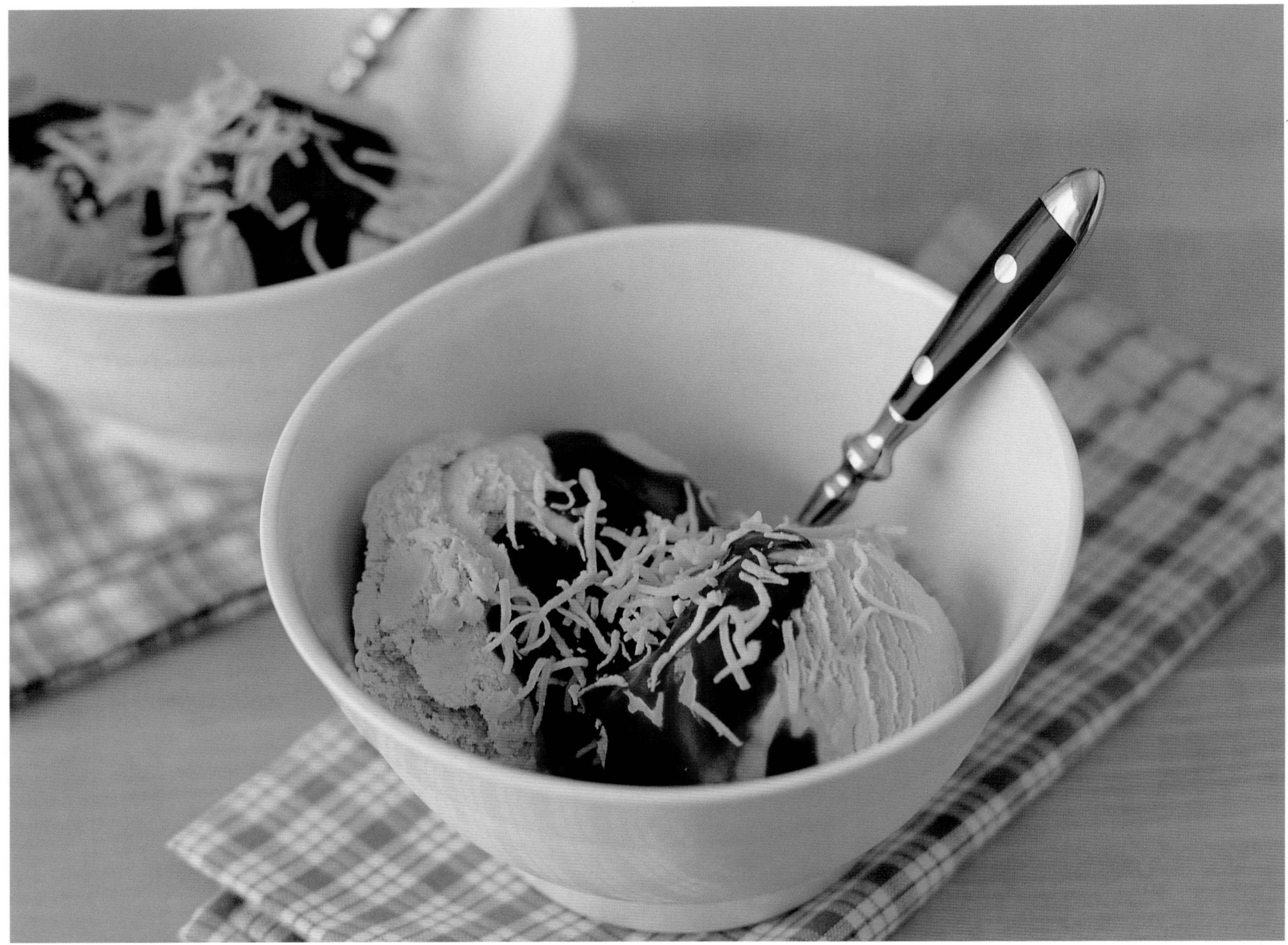

coffee-coconut sundaes

The sauce is so easy that you can make it in the time it takes to cool the coconut. If you prefer, splash the ice cream with warm Kahlúa instead of the sauce, then top with the toasted coconut.

¼ cup (¾ oz/20 g) flaked coconut

⅓ cup (3 fl oz/80 ml) heavy (double) cream

⅔ cup (4 oz/125 g) semisweet (plain) chocolate chips

2 tablespoons Kahlúa

1 pt (16 oz/500 g) coffee ice cream

Preheat the oven to 350°F (180°C).

Spread the coconut in a pie pan and toast, stirring once, until golden brown, 8–10 minutes. Remove from the oven and let cool.

While the coconut is cooling, in a small heavy saucepan, combine the cream and chocolate chips. Place over medium-low heat and cook, stirring, until the chocolate melts, 3–5 minutes. Add the Kahlúa and stir until the sauce is smooth.

Scoop the ice cream into bowls, top with the warm sauce, and sprinkle with toasted coconut. Serve immediately, as the sauce hardens if left to cool completely.

serves six | per serving: calories 253 (kilojoules 1,063), protein 3 g, carbohydrates 26 g, total fat 16 g, saturated fat 10 g, cholesterol 37 mg, sodium 50 mg, dietary fiber 0 g

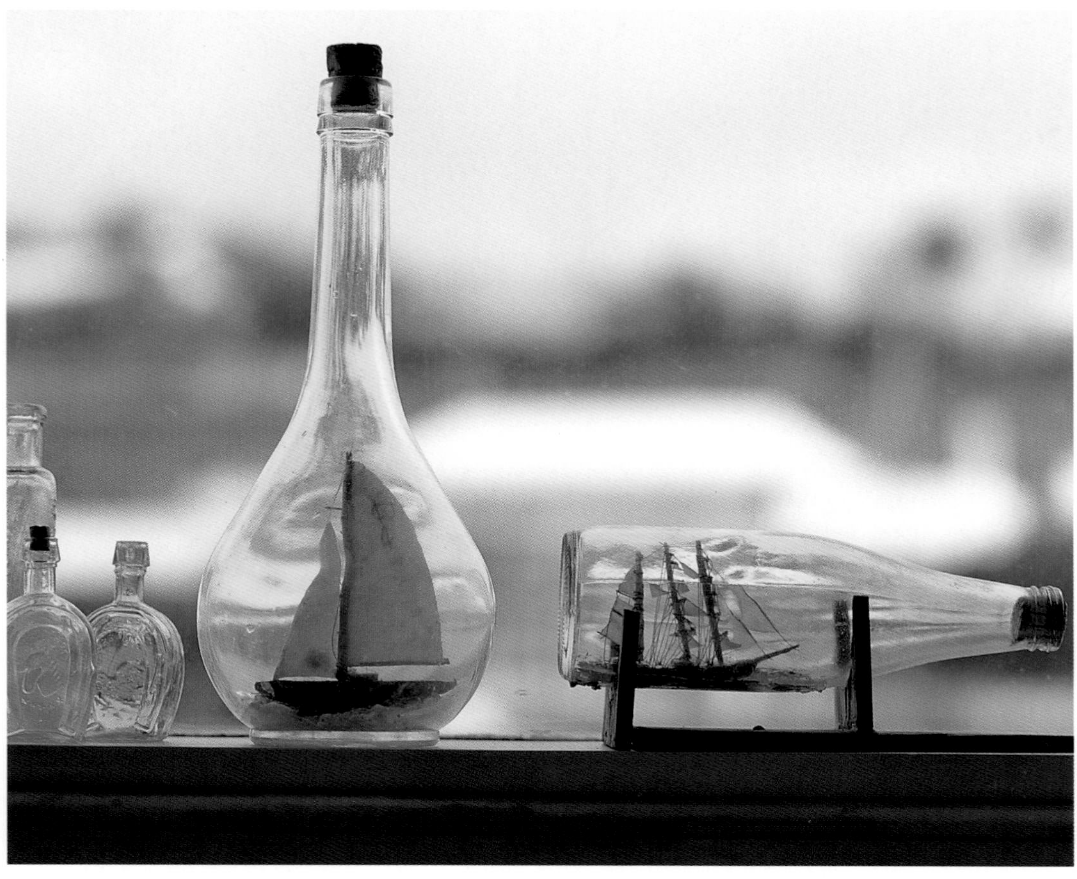

orange granita

The great thing about a granita, a flavorful Italian ice, is that you don't need an ice-cream machine to make it. Just freeze it in a metal container and scrape the crystals up with a fork. Serve with Lemon Pudding Squares (right), if you like.

¾ cup (6 oz/185 g) sugar

1¾ cups (14 fl oz/430 ml) water

1¼ cups (10 fl oz/310 ml) orange juice

3 tablespoons lemon juice, or to taste

In a saucepan over low heat, stir the sugar and water together until the sugar dissolves. Raise the heat to high and bring to a boil; boil for 5 minutes. Remove from the heat and stir in the citrus juices.

Pour into a metal bowl, metal baking pan, or other wide, freezer-safe container. Let stand at room temperature until tepid to the touch. Cover with plastic wrap or a lid and place in the freezer. When the mixture begins to get icy, after about 1½ hours, stir it well with a fork. Return to the freezer. Repeat one or two times until the mixture starts to freeze solid, about 4 hours total.

To serve, scrape the surface of the granita with the tines of a fork to create ice crystals. Scoop up the crystals and serve in a glass, cup, or mug. Store the remaining granita in the freezer for up to 1 week, scraping up the amount needed each time.

makes about one quart (one liter); serves four to six | per serving: calories 160 (kilojoules 672), protein 0 g, carbohydrates 41 g, total fat 0 g, saturated fat 0 g, cholesterol 0 mg, sodium 3 mg, dietary fiber 0 g

lemon pudding squares

Even people who rarely bake will be proud of the results when they make this simple recipe: lemon custard on the bottom with a meringuelike top layer. It's the perfect ending to casual meals year-round.

¾ cup (6 oz/185 g) sugar

¼ cup (1½ oz/45 g) all-purpose (plain) flour

2 pinches of salt

3 eggs, separated

1 cup (8 fl oz/250 ml) milk

grated zest of 1 Meyer or other small lemon

⅓ cup (3 fl oz/80 ml) Meyer lemon or other lemon juice

Preheat the oven to 350°F (180°C). Butter an 8-inch (20-cm) square baking pan. Bring a kettle of water to a boil.

In a bowl, stir together the sugar, flour, and 1 pinch of salt. In another bowl, whisk together the egg yolks, milk, lemon zest, and lemon juice. Pour over the flour mixture and stir until smooth. In a third bowl, beat the egg whites with the remaining pinch of salt until they hold stiff peaks. Using a rubber spatula, gently fold the whites into the egg yolk mixture until just a few streaks of white remain.

Pour the batter into the prepared pan and set in a larger baking pan. Place in the oven and pour boiling water into the large pan until it comes about halfway up the sides of the smaller pan.

Bake the pudding until golden brown on top, about 40 minutes. Let cool slightly, then cut into squares and serve warm or at room temperature.

makes nine squares; serves four to six | per square: calories 138 (kilojoules 580), protein 3 g, carbohydrates 25 g, total fat 3 g, saturated fat 1 g, cholesterol 76 mg, sodium 68 mg, dietary fiber 0 g

summer

sour-cream shortcakes with fresh berries

These shortcakes are made extra-tender with sour cream. Split and top with berries at their peak of sweetness and a dollop of whipped cream.

for the shortcakes:

2 cups (10 oz/315 g) all-purpose (plain) flour

½ cup (4 oz/125 g) sugar

1 teaspoon baking powder

½ teaspoon baking soda (bicarbonate of soda)

½ teaspoon salt

6 tablespoons (3 oz/90 g) chilled butter, cut into small pieces

1 cup (8 oz/250 g) sour cream

1 egg, at room temperature

for the berries:

1 qt (1 lb/500 g) mixed berries such as blackberries, blueberries, strawberries, and/or raspberries

1–2 tablespoons sugar, or to taste

½ cup (4 fl oz/125 ml) heavy (double) cream

½ teaspoon vanilla extract (essence)

Preheat the oven to 425°F (220°C). Lightly grease a baking sheet. Set aside.

To make the shortcakes, in a bowl, stir together the flour, sugar, baking powder, baking soda, and salt. Using 2 knives or a pastry blender, cut in the butter until the mixture resembles coarse meal. Stir in the sour cream and egg until moistened. Turn the dough out onto a lightly floured work surface and pat into a rough circle (the dough will be sticky). Working with about one-sixth of the dough at a time, shape into rough balls and place about 1 inch (2.5 cm) apart on the prepared baking sheet. Bake until golden brown, about 18 minutes.

Meanwhile, prepare the berries: If using strawberries, slice them. In a bowl, combine the fruit with sugar to taste. Stir, then let stand until ready to use.

Remove the shortcakes from the oven and let cool on the baking sheet. Whip the cream with the vanilla until it holds soft peaks. To serve, split each shortcake in half horizontally and place a bottom half on each of 6 individual plates. Top generously with the sugared berries and whipped cream. Replace the top half and serve.

serves six | per serving: calories 564 (kilojoules 2,369), protein 8 g, carbohydrates 69 g, total fat 29 g, saturated fat 17 g, cholesterol 110 mg, sodium 526 mg, dietary fiber 4 g

melon with lemon sorbet and raspberry sauce

For best results, have all ingredients chilled before assembling. Honeydew melon with lime sorbet makes a nice variation.

2 cups (8 oz/250 g) fresh or thawed frozen raspberries

½ cup (2 oz/60 g) confectioners' (icing) sugar

1 tablespoon lemon juice

1 cantaloupe, 2–2½ lb (1–1.25 kg), halved and seeded

1 pt (16 fl oz/500 ml) premium-quality lemon sorbet

fresh mint leaves

In a blender, combine the raspberries, sugar, and lemon juice. Blend for about 30 seconds, scrape down the sides, and blend again until smooth. Transfer to a fine-mesh sieve set over a small bowl. Using the back of a spoon, press the puréed raspberries through the sieve. Cover and chill thoroughly before serving. You should have about 1¼ cups (10 fl oz/310 ml).

Cut each melon half into 4 equal wedges. Using a sharp paring knife, carefully remove and discard the peel. Divide the melon pieces among chilled decorative plates. Top each serving with a scoop of lemon sorbet, and spoon a small amount of the raspberry sauce over the sorbet. Garnish with mint leaves and serve at once. Pass the remaining sauce at the table.

serves four | per serving: calories 239 (kilojoules 1,004), protein 2 g, carbohydrates 60 g, total fat 1 g, saturated fat 0 g, cholesterol 0 mg, sodium 24 mg, dietary fiber 4 g

blueberry fool

A fool is an old English dessert made of crushed fruit and whipped cream. The traditional favorite is made lighter here with the addition of yogurt. If blueberries are unavailable, use blackberries or raspberries instead; adjust the amount of sugar as needed.

2 cups (8 oz/250 g) firm but ripe blueberries

½ cup (4 oz/125 g) sugar

¼ teaspoon ground cinnamon

1 teaspoon finely grated lemon zest

¼ cup (1¼ oz/37 g) slivered blanched almonds

½ cup (4 fl oz/125 ml) heavy (double) cream

½ cup (4 oz/125 g) plain yogurt

In a large saucepan, stir together the blueberries, sugar, and cinnamon. Place over high heat, bring to a boil, reduce the heat to medium, and simmer until the berries are soft, 5–7 minutes. Using a fork, crush the berries to a thick, pulpy purée. Remove from the heat and stir in the lemon zest. Transfer to a bowl, cover, and refrigerate until well chilled.

Meanwhile, preheat the oven to 350°F (180°C). Spread the almonds on a baking sheet and toast in the oven until lightly browned and fragrant, about 5 minutes. Remove from the oven and let cool.

In a large bowl, stir together the cream and yogurt. Using an electric mixer set on high speed, beat until thick peaks form. Gently fold in the berry mixture; do not overmix. Spoon into 6 footed glasses such as parfait glasses. Refrigerate for 1–2 hours.

Sprinkle with the toasted almonds just before serving.

serves six | per serving: calories 210 (kilojoules 882), protein 3 g, carbohydrates 27 g, total fat 11 g, saturated fat 5 g, cholesterol 28 mg, sodium 24 mg, dietary fiber 2 g

orange icebox cookies

Double the recipe and keep wrapped cylinders of dough in the freezer for last-minute treats. Serve with sorbet or ice cream.

½ cup (4 oz/125 g) unsalted butter, at room temperature

½ cup (4 oz/125 g) sugar

1 egg yolk

1½ cups (7½ oz/235 g) all-purpose (plain) flour

1 teaspoon baking powder

⅛ teaspoon salt

¼ cup (2 fl oz/60 ml) orange juice

1 teaspoon finely grated orange zest

8 oz (250 g) good-quality bittersweet chocolate

In a large bowl, using an electric mixer set on high speed, beat together the butter and sugar until light and fluffy. Add the egg yolk and beat until smooth.

In another bowl, sift together the flour, baking powder, and salt and divide into 3 batches. Beat into the butter mixture alternately with the orange juice, beginning and ending with the flour mixture. The dough will be stiff. If it becomes too stiff to beat with a handheld electric mixer, revert to a wooden spoon. Mix in the orange zest.

Place a large sheet of plastic wrap on a work surface. Transfer the dough to the sheet and shape into a long cylinder about 1 inch (2.5 cm) in diameter. Wrap, then twist the ends to seal. Refrigerate for 1 hour.

Preheat the oven to 375°F (190°C). Lightly grease 1 or 2 baking sheets.

Cut the cookies into slices ¼ inch (6 mm) thick and arrange on the baking sheets, spacing them ½ inch (12 mm) apart.

Bake until lightly browned around the edges, about 10 minutes. Transfer to wire racks and let cool completely. Place the chocolate in a heatproof bowl placed over (not touching) simmering water in the lower pan. Melt until smooth, stirring occasionally. Let cool slightly.

Line a baking sheet with waxed paper. Dip one-half of each cookie in the chocolate and place on the lined baking sheet. Refrigerate until the chocolate is firm, about 10 minutes, then gently lift off. Refrigerate between layers of waxed paper in an airtight container for up to 1 week.

makes forty to forty-five small cookies | per cookie: calories 76 (kilojoules 319), protein 1 g, carbohydrates 10 g, total fat 4 g, saturated fat 2 g, cholesterol 11 mg, sodium 19 mg, dietary fiber 0 g

blackberry-nectarine buckle

A buckle is an old-fashioned dessert that makes a fine finish to any picnic. Try it with Cold Poached Salmon with Cucumber-Avocado Relish (page 147) and Cherry Tomato and Corn Salad (page 102).

½ cup (2 oz/60 g) coarsely chopped pecans

2½ cups (12½ oz/390 g) all-purpose (plain) flour

½ cup (3½ oz/105 g) firmly packed dark brown sugar

1 cup (8 oz/250 g) granulated sugar

½ teaspoon ground cinnamon

pinch of ground nutmeg

pinch of ground ginger

1 cup (8 oz/250 g) unsalted butter

1 egg

2 teaspoons baking powder

½ teaspoon ground ginger

½ cup (4 fl oz/125 ml) milk

1 pt (8 oz/250 g) blackberries

3 nectarines, peeled, pitted, and cut into ¼-inch (6-mm) pieces

Preheat the oven to 350°F (180°C). Butter and flour a 9-by-13-inch (23-by-33-cm) baking dish. Spread the pecans on a baking sheet and toast in the oven until lightly browned, 5–7 minutes. Let cool.

In a bowl, combine the pecans, ½ cup (2½ oz/75 g) of the flour, the brown sugar, ¼ cup (2 oz/60 g) of the granulated sugar, the cinnamon, the nutmeg, and the ginger. Cut ½ cup (4 oz/125 g) of the butter into small pieces, add to the pecan-sugar mixture, and, using your fingertips, blend in until the mixture is crumbly. Set aside.

In a large bowl, using an electric mixer, cream together the remaining ½ cup (4 oz/125 g) butter and the remaining ¾ cup (6 oz/190 g) granulated sugar until light and fluffy. Beat in the egg. In another bowl, combine the remaining 2 cups (10 oz/315 g) flour, the baking powder, and the ½ teaspoon ginger. Add to the butter-sugar mixture alternately with the milk.

Spoon the batter into the pan. Sprinkle the berries and nectarine evenly over the batter. Sprinkle the pecan-sugar mixture over the fruit. Bake until the top is golden brown and bubbling and a wooden skewer inserted into the center comes out clean, 45–55 minutes. Let cool in the pan. Cut into squares and place in a transportable container. Serve at room temperature.

serves six to eight | per serving: calories 727 (kilojoules 3,053), protein 8 g, carbohydrates 100 g, total fat 34 g, saturated fat 18 g, cholesterol 105 mg, sodium 168 mg, dietary fiber 4 g

plum crumble with hazelnuts

This versatile, nutty topping made with oatmeal and hazelnuts can also be sprinkled over peaches, apricots, and nectarines. When using these fruits, season with cinnamon instead of allspice.

⅔ cup (3½ oz/105 g) hazelnuts (filberts) or walnuts

3 lb (1.5 kg) firm, ripe plums, pitted and sliced

¼ cup (2 oz/60 g) sugar

2 tablespoons cornstarch (cornflour)

½ teaspoon ground allspice

1 tablespoon lemon juice

¾ cup (2½ oz/75 g) rolled oats

½ cup (3½ oz/105 g) firmly packed light brown sugar

5 tablespoons (2½ oz/75 g) chilled unsalted butter, cut into small pieces

vanilla ice cream (optional)

Preheat the oven to 375°F (190°C). Spread the hazelnuts or walnuts in a pie pan and toast until fragrant, about 7 minutes. Remove from the oven and, if using hazelnuts, place in a fine-mesh sieve. Working over a sink, rub the hazelnuts vigorously with a clean kitchen towel, letting the skin slough off against the sieve; do not worry if small bits remain. Lift the nuts from the sieve, discarding the skins. Finely chop the hazelnuts or walnuts.

Place the sliced plums in a large bowl. Sift the sugar, cornstarch, and allspice over the fruit. Add the lemon juice and stir until the fruit is evenly coated with the sugar mixture. Spread the fruit in a shallow 3-qt (3-l) baking dish.

In a bowl, stir together the oats, chopped hazelnuts, and brown sugar. Scatter the butter over the oat mixture and, using 2 knives or a pastry blender, cut in until the butter is in tiny pieces and the mixture looks lumpy. Scatter the topping over the fruit, covering it as evenly as possible.

Bake until the fruit is bubbly and the topping is browned, about 40 minutes. Remove from the oven and let cool for 5 minutes. Serve warm or at room temperature, topped with vanilla ice cream, if desired.

serves six | per serving: calories 462 (kilojoules 1,940), protein 6 g, carbohydrates 66 g, total fat 22 g, saturated fat 7 g, cholesterol 26 mg, sodium 10 mg, dietary fiber 7 g

plum-almond tart

Serve this French-style tart with crème fraîche or whipped cream.

for the pastry:

1¼ cups (6½ oz/200 g) all-purpose (plain) flour

1 tablespoon confectioners' (icing) sugar

pinch of salt

½ cup (4 oz/125 g) frozen unsalted butter, cut into small pieces

1 egg yolk

2 tablespoons ice water

for the filling:

1½ cups (6 oz/185 g) sliced (flaked), blanched almonds

¾ cup (6 oz/185 g) plus 2 tablespoons granulated sugar

¼ cup (2 oz/60 g) plus 2 tablespoons unsalted butter, cut into small pieces

2 tablespoons all-purpose (plain) flour

¼ cup (2 fl oz/60 ml) almond liqueur

2 eggs

1¼ lb (625 g) purple plums, pitted and thinly sliced

To make the pastry, place the flour, sugar, and salt in a food processor and pulse to blend. Add the butter and process until the mixture resembles coarse meal, 5–10 seconds. With the motor running, add the egg yolk and then the ice water, processing until the dough just begins to form a ball. On a lightly floured work surface, press into a disk. Roll out to fit a 10-inch (25-cm) tart pan with a removable bottom. Transfer the dough to the pan. Trim even with the pan rim and press with your fingers so it adheres to the sides of the pan. Place on a baking sheet and chill while preparing the filling.

Preheat the oven to 400°F (200°C).

To make the filling, process the almonds in the food processor until finely ground. Add the ¾ cup (6 oz/185 g) sugar, ¼ cup (2 oz/60 g) butter, the flour, and liqueur. Pulse until a paste forms. Add the eggs and process to incorporate.

Spread the filling in the dough-lined pan. Top with the plum slices, overlapping them in concentric circles and fitting them tightly together. Fill in the center with 2 rows of plum slices. Dot the plums with the remaining 2 tablespoons butter and sprinkle with the remaining 2 tablespoons sugar.

Bake until the top is brown, about 60 minutes. Set on a rack to cool. Remove the pan sides and wrap the tart in aluminum foil to transport. Serve at room temperature, cut into wedges.

serves eight to ten | per serving: calories 495 (kilojoules 2,079), protein 9 g, carbohydrates 51 g, total fat 30 g, saturated fat 13 g, cholesterol 119 mg, sodium 34 mg, dietary fiber 4 g

panna cotta with strawberries and plums

Panna cotta ("cooked cream" in Italian) is like a baked custard without the eggs. Here, plums and strawberries dress up the dessert. You can substitute currants for the strawberries and green plums for the red ones.

2 cups (16 fl oz/500 ml) heavy (double) cream

1 cup (8 fl oz/250 ml) milk

½ cup (2 oz/60 g) confectioners' (icing) sugar

5 lemon zest strips, each 3 inches (7.5 cm) long

1 vanilla bean, split in half lengthwise, or ¾ teaspoon vanilla extract (essence)

3¾ teaspoons unflavored gelatin

8 plums, about 1½ lb (750 g) total weight, pitted and thinly sliced

1 pt (8 oz/250 g) strawberries, halved

In a saucepan over medium-high heat, combine the cream, ⅔ cup (5 fl oz/160 ml) of the milk, the confectioners' sugar, the lemon zest, and the vanilla bean, if using. Bring to a simmer, stirring often. Remove from the heat, cover, and set aside for 10 minutes. Meanwhile, in a small bowl, combine the remaining ⅓ cup (3 fl oz/90 ml) milk and the gelatin. Set aside to soften for about 10 minutes.

Bring the cream mixture back to a simmer. Remove from the heat and whisk in the gelatin mixture until smooth. Strain through a fine-mesh sieve set over a large measuring pitcher. Stir in the vanilla extract, if using.

Pour into six ¾-cup (6–fl oz/180-ml) custard cups or ramekins. Cover and chill until set, about 3 hours.

To serve, run a small knife around the edge of each cup and unmold onto individual serving plates. Arrange the plum slices and strawberry halves around the molds. Serve at once.

serves six | per serving: calories 422 (kilojoules 1,772), protein 6 g, carbohydrates 33 g, total fat 31 g, saturated fat 19 g, cholesterol 114 g, sodium 53 mg, dietary fiber 2 g

blackberry cobbler

Strawberries, raspberries, cherries, or blueberries, alone or in combination, can be used in place of the blackberries. Serve the cobbler at room temperature with vanilla ice cream.

for the topping:

1 cup (5 oz/155 g) all-purpose (plain) flour

¼ cup (2 oz/60 g) sugar

1 teaspoon baking powder

½ teaspoon salt

¼ cup (2 oz/60 g) chilled unsalted butter, cut into small pieces

⅓ cup (3 fl oz/80 ml) milk

for the filling:

6 cups (1½ lb/750 g) blackberries

½ cup (4 oz/125 g) plus 2 tablespoons sugar

2 tablespoons all-purpose (plain) flour

1 tablespoon lemon juice

¼ teaspoon ground cinnamon

2 tablespoons unsalted butter, melted

To make the topping, in a large bowl, combine the flour, sugar, baking powder, and salt. Toss with a fork to blend. Using 2 knives or a pastry blender, cut in the butter until the mixture resembles coarse crumbs. Add the milk and, using the fork, stir until a stiff dough forms.

Turn the dough out onto a floured work surface and knead quickly into a ball. It will be sticky. Wrap in plastic wrap and refrigerate for 1 hour.

Flour the work surface and, using a rolling pin or your fingers, spread out the dough into a round ½ inch (12 mm) thick. Using a cookie cutter or wineglass 2½ inches (6 cm) in diameter, cut out 8 rounds.

Preheat the oven to 425°F (220°C). Lightly butter a shallow 2-qt (2-l) baking dish.

To make the filling, in a saucepan over medium-high heat, combine the blackberries, the ½ cup (4 oz/125 g) sugar, flour, lemon juice, and cinnamon. Bring to a boil, remove from the heat, and let cool slightly. Pour into the prepared baking dish, spreading evenly, and arrange the biscuit rounds evenly on top. Brush the rounds with the melted butter and sprinkle the remaining 2 tablespoons sugar over the top.

Bake until the filling is bubbling and the biscuits are golden brown, about 25 minutes. Let cool to room temperature before serving directly from the baking dish.

serves four to six | per serving: calories 472 (kilojoules 1,982), protein 5 g, carbohydrates 80 g, total fat 16 g, saturated fat 9 g, cholesterol 42 mg, sodium 341 mg, dietary fiber 7 g

mixed berry bundt cake

This moist Bundt cake is an easy dessert to prepare for a tailgate party. It's also terrific served at an early morning picnic with a big thermos of piping hot coffee. Be sure to select berries that are not overripe or they won't hold up well when baked.

5 eggs

1⅔ cups (13 oz/410 g) sugar

1¼ cups (10 oz/315 g) unsalted butter, at room temperature, cut into small pieces

2 tablespoons kirsch or other fruit liqueur

2½ cups (12½ oz/390 g) all-purpose (plain) flour

1 teaspoon baking powder

pinch of salt

1½ cups (6 oz/185 g) raspberries

1½ cups (6 oz/185 g) blueberries or blackberries

confectioners' (icing) sugar for dusting

Preheat the oven to 325°F (165°C). Butter and flour a 9-inch (23-cm) Bundt pan.

In a large bowl, blend the eggs and sugar using an electric mixer. Add the butter and liqueur and beat until fluffy. Add all but 2 tablespoons of the flour and the baking powder and salt and beat until well incorporated and no lumps remain.

In another bowl, combine the berries and the reserved 2 tablespoons flour. Toss to coat the berries evenly with the flour. Gently fold the berries into the batter.

Pour the batter into the prepared pan. Bake until a wooden skewer inserted in the center comes out clean, about 60 minutes. Remove from the oven and let cool in the pan for 20–25 minutes. Unmold the cake onto a rack to cool completely.

Lightly dust the top of the cake with confectioners' sugar. Transfer whole to a transportable cake dish or cut into pieces and arrange in a transportable container. Serve at room temperature.

serves ten to twelve | per serving: calories 494 (kilojoules 2,075), protein 7 g, carbohydrates 64 g, total fat 24 g, saturated fat 14 g, cholesterol 154 mg, sodium 90 mg, dietary fiber 2 g

coffee and bourbon granita

The beauty of a granita for beach house or cabin cooking is that you do not need any special equipment—just a metal baking pan or some old ice-cube trays with removable dividers.

3 cups (24 fl oz/750 ml) double-strength brewed coffee, preferably made from French roast beans

¾ cup (6 oz/185 g) sugar

1½ tablespoons bourbon

whipped cream (optional)

In a large bowl, combine the coffee, sugar, and bourbon and stir to dissolve the sugar.

Pour into a metal baking pan large enough to contain the liquid at a depth of 1 inch (2.5 cm) and place in the freezer. When the mixture begins to get icy, after about 1 hour, remove from the freezer and stir well with a fork to break up the ice crystals. Return to the freezer for another 45 minutes. Remove from the freezer and break up the crystals once again. Repeat this process 2 more times until the mixture starts to freeze solid.

To serve, scrape the surface of the granita with the tines of a fork to create ice crystals. Scoop up the crystals and spoon into chilled, small stemmed glasses. Top with a dollop of whipped cream, if desired, and serve at once.

serves six | per serving: calories 123 (kilojoules 517), protein 0 g, carbohydrates 29 g, total fat 0 g, saturated fat 0 g, cholesterol 0 mg, sodium 5 mg, dietary fiber 0 g

summer pudding

Dark berry juices soak through thin slices of bread to make this a particularly handsome dessert. If fresh red currants are unavailable, increase the raspberries by 1 cup (4 oz/125 g) and reduce the sugar to ⅔ cup (5 oz/155 g).

8–10 slices fine-textured white sandwich bread, crusts removed and cut in half on the diagonal

3 cups (12 oz/375 g) raspberries

1 pt (8 oz/250 g) blackberries

1 cup (4 oz/125 g) fresh red currants

¾ cup (6 oz/185 g) sugar

2½ teaspoons kirsch or brandy

1 cup (8 fl oz/250 ml) heavy (double) cream, whipped

Line a 1-qt (1-l) pudding mold, soufflé dish, or charlotte mold with the triangles of bread, arranging them across the bottom so that the pieces fit closely together. Line the sides with more triangles, then cut out scraps of bread and fit them into any open spaces. The bowl should be completely lined with bread.

In a large saucepan over medium heat, combine the berries, currants, and sugar. Bring to a simmer and cook, stirring often, until the berries give off some of their juice, about 5 minutes. Remove from the heat and stir in the kirsch or brandy.

Using a slotted spoon, transfer the berries to the lined mold. Pour on half of the berry juices and reserve the rest. Cover the berries completely with the remaining bread triangles. Cover any open spaces with scraps of bread. Trim the bread slices evenly along the top edge.

Place a plate slightly smaller than the diameter of the mold on the bread. Put the mold in a pan to catch any drips. Set a heavy can or other weight on the plate and refrigerate for 2 hours. Check the pudding and spoon over a little of the reserved berry juice if any of the bread slices on top are dry or white, then refrigerate overnight.

To serve, remove the weight and plate. Run the tip of a small knife around the sides of the mold and invert the pudding onto a serving plate. Serve with whipped cream and any reserved berry juices.

serves six | per serving: calories 412 (kilojoules 1,730), protein 5 g, carbohydrates 63 g, total fat 17 g, saturated fat 9 g, cholesterol 55 mg, sodium 221 mg, dietary fiber 5 g

peaches poached in sauternes

To help underripe peaches mature, store in a paper bag at room temperature for a few days before using.

4 firm but ripe peaches

ice water to cover

1 teaspoon lemon juice

½ cup (4 oz/120 g) sugar

1½ cups (12 fl oz/375 ml) Sauternes or similar sweet wine

1 lemon zest strip, about 2 inches (5 cm) long

½ vanilla bean, split lengthwise

fresh mint leaves

Bring a saucepan three-fourths full of water to a boil. Plunge the peaches into the boiling water for about 30 seconds, then transfer to a bowl of ice water, let cool, and slip off the skins. Halve the peaches, discard the pits, and place the halves in a bowl. Sprinkle with the lemon juice and ¼ cup (2 oz/60 g) of the sugar. Stir to coat. Set aside for 30 minutes.

In a large saucepan over high heat, combine the remaining ¼ cup (2 oz/60 g) sugar, the wine, lemon zest, and vanilla bean. Bring to a boil, stirring just until the sugar dissolves.

Reduce the heat to medium. Add the peach halves and cook, uncovered, until tender, 5–10 minutes. Using a slotted spoon, transfer the peaches to a glass dish; reserve the liquid in the pan. Let the peaches cool completely. Bring the poaching liquid to a boil and cook rapidly until reduced to ¾ cup (6 fl oz/180 ml). Strain through a fine-mesh sieve into a separate bowl and let cool. Cover the peaches and liquid and chill well, at least 2 hours or up to 1 day.

Divide the peaches among chilled dessert glasses and garnish with mint leaves. Spoon an equal amount of the poaching syrup over each serving.

serves four | per serving: calories 170 (kilojoules 714), protein 1 g, carbohydrates 44 g, total fat 0 g, saturated fat 0 g, cholesterol 0 mg, sodium 5 mg, dietary fiber 2 g

peach-raspberry pie

Make this luscious pie at the height of summer, when both peaches and raspberries are at their peak.

2 cups (10 oz/315 g) plus 3 tablespoons all-purpose (plain) flour

½ teaspoon salt

⅓ cup (3 oz/90 g) chilled vegetable shortening, cut into small pieces

⅓ cup (3 oz/90 g) chilled unsalted butter, cut into small pieces

7 tablespoons cold water

about 2½ lb (1.25 kg) ripe peaches

1½ pt (12 oz/375 g) raspberries

½ cup (4 oz/125 g) sugar

¾ teaspoon almond extract (essence)

1 egg, lightly beaten

In a bowl, stir together the 2 cups (10 oz/315 g) flour and the salt. Using 2 knives or a pastry blender, cut in the shortening and butter until the mixture resembles coarse meal. Sprinkle with the cold water and stir with a fork until moistened. Turn the dough out onto a lightly floured work surface and gather together. Knead briefly just until the dough holds together. Enclose in plastic wrap and refrigerate for about 20 minutes.

Meanwhile, bring a saucepan three-fourths full of water to a boil. Immerse the peaches in the boiling water for 30 seconds. Remove the peaches with a slotted spoon, and when cool enough to handle, peel off the skin. Pit and slice the peaches. In a bowl, combine the sliced peaches, raspberries, sugar, and the 3 tablespoons flour. Stir until the sugar and flour are dissolved. Let stand at room temperature for about 15 minutes.

Preheat the oven to 375°F (190°C). Cut the dough in half; rewrap one half and return to the refrigerator. On a lightly floured work surface, press the other half into a flat disk. Using a floured rolling pin, roll out to a 12-inch (30-cm) round. Transfer to an 8-inch (20-cm) pie dish. Stir the almond extract into the peach-raspberry mixture, then pour into the dough-lined pie dish. Trim off the excess dough, leaving a 1-inch (2.5-cm) overhang.

Roll out the remaining dough to a 12-inch (30-cm) round. Using a fluted pastry wheel or a knife, cut it into strips 1 inch (2.5 cm) wide. Arrange the strips atop the pie in a lattice pattern. Trim any overhanging dough and press gently on the strips all the way around to seal them to the bottom crust. Crimp as desired. Brush the top with the beaten egg. Bake until the crust is golden and the filling is bubbly, about 45 minutes. Transfer to a rack to cool completely. Serve at room temperature.

serves six to eight | per serving: calories 484 (kilojoules 2,033), protein 6 g, carbohydrates 64 g, total fat 23 g, saturated fat 9 g, cholesterol 57 mg, sodium 168 mg, dietary fiber 5 g

autumn

baked stuffed apples

Here's proof of the staying power of old-fashioned recipes. Don't be shy about serving baked apples any time of day; they're especially good for breakfast.

¼ cup (1 oz/30 g) chopped walnuts

4 good-quality red apples such as Fuji, Braeburn, McIntosh, or Rome Beauty

¼ cup (2 oz/60 g) packed brown sugar

2 tablespoons unsalted butter, at room temperature

½ teaspoon ground cinnamon

¼ cup (3 oz/90 g) honey

½ cup (4 fl oz/125 ml) apple juice

Preheat the oven to 350°F (180°C). Spread the walnuts on a baking sheet and toast in the oven until lightly browned and fragrant, about 7 minutes. Remove from the oven and let cool.

Working from the stem end, use a melon baller to remove the core from each apple, scooping out the stem and seeds and making a deep hole for filling; work to within about ½ inch (12 mm) of the bottom of the apple. (Alternatively, remove the core with an apple corer and widen the hole with a small spoon.) Peel the skin from the top half of each apple.

In a small bowl, blend together the brown sugar, butter, and cinnamon. Mix in the walnuts. Spoon equal amounts of the filling into the centers of the apples. Set the filled apples in an 8-inch (20-cm) square baking pan or other baking pan just large enough to hold them snugly.

In a small pan over medium heat, warm the honey with the apple juice, stirring until the honey dissolves. Pour around the apples. Spoon some of the liquid over the sides of the apples to moisten them, but do not spoon over the tops.

Bake, basting the sides once or twice with the pan juices, until the apples are tender when pierced, about 40 minutes. Remove from the oven, let cool, and serve in bowls with the pan juices spooned over the tops.

serves four | per serving: calories 332 (kilojoules 1,394), protein 1 g, carbohydrates 63 g, total fat 11 g, saturated fat 4 g, cholesterol 16 mg, sodium 9 mg, dietary fiber 4 g

gingerbread cake

This cake holds up well, and making it a day ahead improves the flavor. If you like, garnish each serving with whipped cream.

2 cups (10 oz/315 g) all-purpose (plain) flour
1 tablespoon ground ginger
2 teaspoons unsweetened cocoa powder
2 teaspoons ground cinnamon
½ teaspoon baking soda (bicarbonate of soda)
½ teaspoon salt
½ cup (4 oz/125 g) unsalted butter
½ cup (3½ oz/105 g) firmly packed dark brown sugar
½ cup (5½ oz/170 g) dark molasses
2 eggs
3 tablespoons finely chopped crystallized ginger
1 cup (8 fl oz/250 ml) buttermilk
¼ cup (2 oz/60 g) sour cream

Preheat the oven to 350°F (180°C). Butter a 9-inch (23-cm) square baking pan.

In a bowl, combine the flour, ground ginger, cocoa powder, cinnamon, baking soda, and salt. Stir to distribute the spices.

In another bowl, cream the butter using an electric mixer. Add the sugar and beat until creamy, about 3 minutes. Beat in the molasses, eggs, and crystallized ginger. Mix until well combined. Beat in half of the flour mixture alternately with the buttermilk and sour cream, then beat in the remaining flour mixture.

Pour into the prepared pan and bake until a wooden skewer inserted into the center comes out clean, 40–45 minutes. Transfer to a rack and let cool. Cut the cake into squares. Place in a transportable container. Serve at room temperature.

serves six to eight | per serving: calories 455 (kilojoules 1,911), protein 8 g, carbohydrates 68 g, total fat 18 g, saturated fat 10 g, cholesterol 103 mg, sodium 330 mg, dietary fiber 1 g

JUL
CALIFORNIA
52

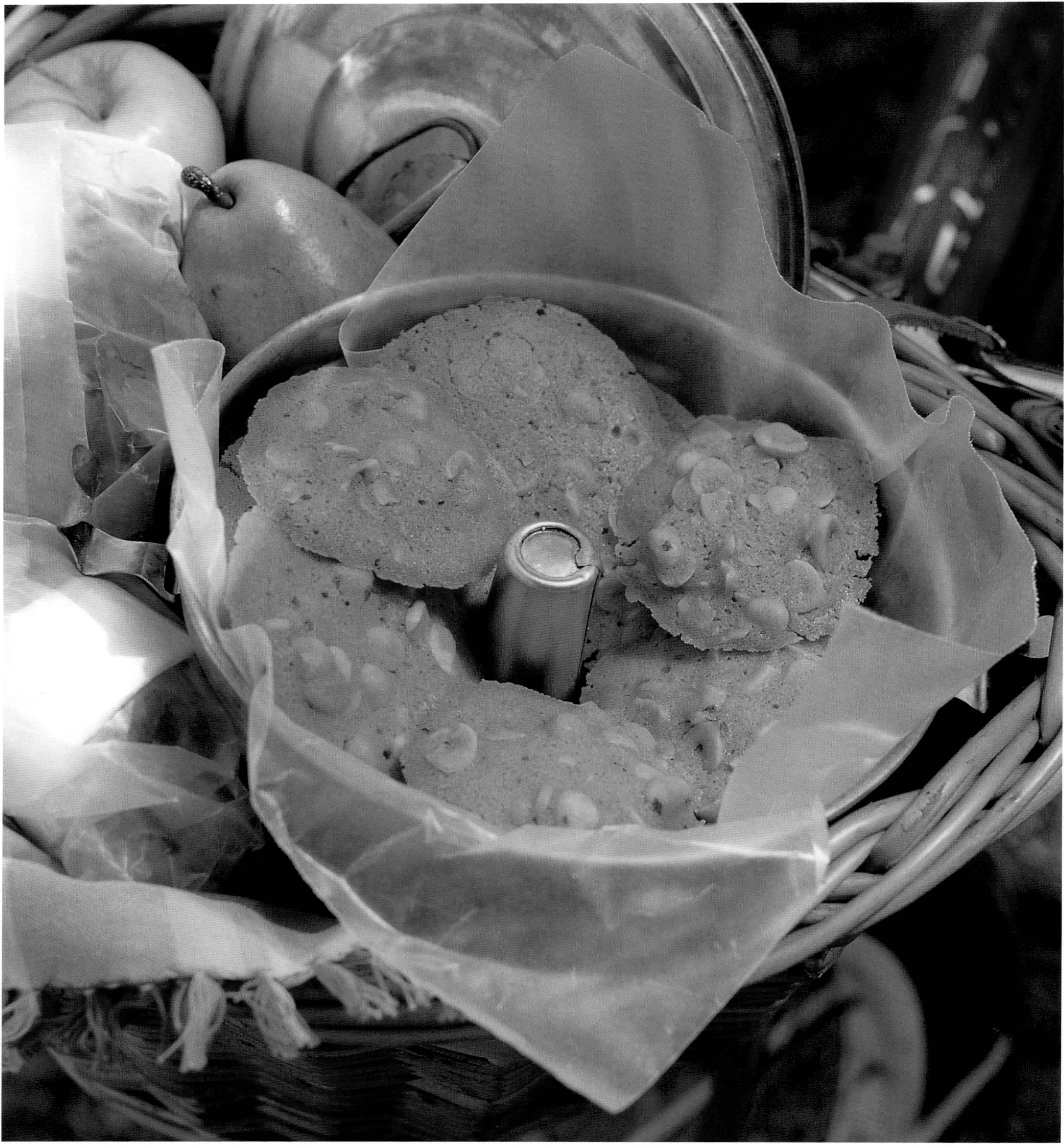

hazelnut cookies

Packaged hazelnuts are available already peeled and sliced. Toasting develops their full flavor. Serve these buttery nut cookies with Fruit Salad with Toasted Coconut (page 106) or Strawberries with Oranges and Balsamic Vinegar (page 245).

¾ cup (4½ oz/140 g) sliced hazelnuts (filberts)

½ cup (4 oz/125 g) unsalted butter, at room temperature

½ cup (3½ oz/105 g) dark brown sugar

1 teaspoon vanilla extract (essence)

1 egg

¾ cup (4 oz/125 g) all-purpose (plain) flour

confectioners' (icing) sugar for dusting (optional)

Preheat the oven to 350°F (180°C). Spread the hazelnuts on a baking sheet and toast until light brown, 3–5 minutes. Remove from the oven and let cool. Raise the oven temperature to 375°F (190°C).

In a bowl, combine the butter and brown sugar and beat with an electric mixer until well blended. Add the vanilla and egg and continue to beat until combined. Slowly add the flour, beating until incorporated. Carefully stir in the toasted hazelnuts.

Using a teaspoon, drop the batter onto 2 ungreased baking sheets, spacing the cookies about 1 inch (2.5 cm) apart. Bake until light brown, about 8 minutes. Transfer the cookies to a rack to cool.

Dust the cookies with confectioners' sugar, if desired. Place in a transportable container or store in an airtight container for up to 1 week.

makes about twenty-five cookies | per cookie: calories 100 (kilojoules 420), protein 1 g, carbohydrates 8 g, total fat 7 g, saturated fat 3 g, cholesterol 18 mg, sodium 5 mg, dietary fiber 1 g

spiced pear cake

Dense, moist, and nutty, this cake is superb on a cold day as an afternoon snack or dessert. It's also good for breakfast the next day, rewarmed in a low oven. Use baking pears such as Anjou or Comice.

3 firm, ripe pears, peeled, cored, and diced (*see note*)

1½ cups (12 oz/375 g) sugar

2 cups (10 oz/315 g) all-purpose (plain) flour

1½ teaspoons baking soda (bicarbonate of soda)

1 teaspoon ground cinnamon

½ teaspoon salt

2 eggs, at room temperature

¾ cup (6 fl oz/180 ml) vegetable oil

2 teaspoons vanilla extract (essence)

1 cup (6 oz/185 g) raisins

½ cup (2 oz/60 g) chopped pecans or walnuts

Place the pears in a large bowl with the sugar; stir, then set aside for 15 minutes. Preheat the oven to 350°F (180°C) and grease a shallow 3-qt (3-l) baking dish.

In another bowl, sift together the flour, baking soda, cinnamon, and salt. Then sift the flour mixture into the bowl containing the pears. Add the eggs, oil, vanilla, raisins, and nuts and mix well. Spread the batter evenly into the prepared dish.

Bake until a toothpick inserted in the center of the cake comes out clean, 50–55 minutes. Remove from the oven and let cool in the pan on a rack. Cut into 12 rectangles to serve.

makes twelve rectangles; serves six to eight | per rectangle: calories 444 (kilojoules 1,865), protein 5 g, carbohydrates 68 g, total fat 19 g, saturated fat 2 g, cholesterol 35 mg, sodium 261 mg, dietary fiber 3 g

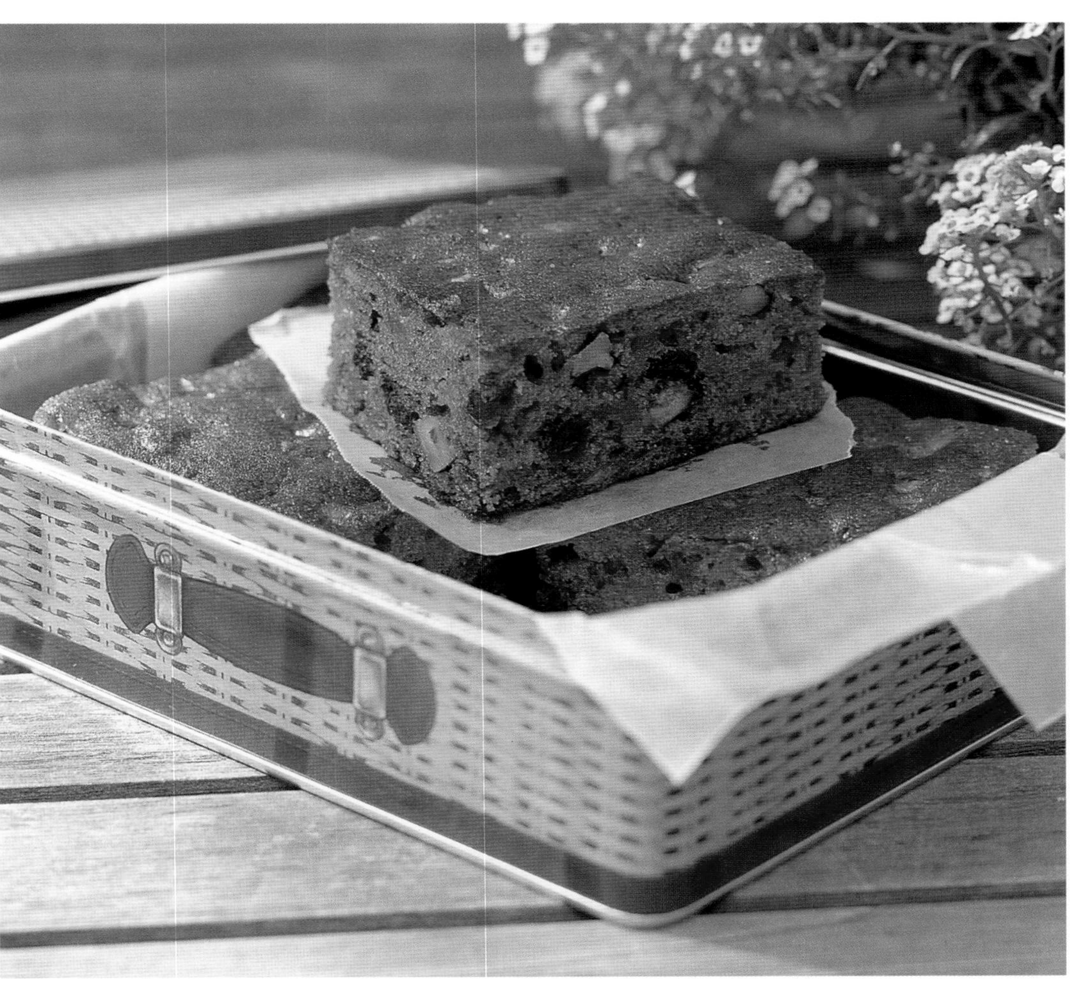

open-faced apple-pear tart

This no-fail tart is easy to make. You prepare the pastry, place the fruit on it, and then just pull up the edges of the crust for a rustic presentation.

for the pastry:

1¼ cups (6½ oz/220 g) all-purpose (plain) flour

1 teaspoon sugar

¼ teaspoon salt

½ cup (4 oz/125 g) frozen unsalted butter, cut into small pieces

2 tablespoons ice water, or as needed

for the filling:

5 tablespoons sugar

2 tablespoons all-purpose (plain) flour

3 medium or 2 large Granny Smith or Golden Delicious apples, peeled and cut into ½-inch (12-mm) pieces

3 medium or 2 large firm but ripe Bosc or Anjou pears, peeled and cut into ½-inch (12-mm) pieces

To make the dough, place the flour, sugar, and salt in a food processor. Process for about 5 seconds to blend. Add the butter and the ice water and process until the mixture has a crumblike texture and just begins to form a ball, 5–10 seconds, adding more ice water if the mixture is too dry.

On a lightly floured surface, press the dough into a disk. Place a 10-inch (25-cm) springform or tart pan on a heavy rimmed baking sheet. Roll out the dough into a 13-inch (33-cm) round. Drape over the rolling pin and transfer to the pan, allowing the 3-inch (7.5-cm) overhang to lay flat on the baking sheet. Refrigerate while making the filling.

Preheat the oven to 400°F (200°C). To make the filling, in a bowl, combine 1 tablespoon each of the sugar and flour, the apples, and the pears. Sprinkle 2 more tablespoons of the sugar and the remaining 1 tablespoon flour evenly over the tart pastry. Arrange the fruit mixture in the center and fold the dough edges up to create a free-form tart with the fruit visible in the center. Brush the dough with water and sprinkle the remaining 2 tablespoons sugar over the fruit.

Bake until the filling is bubbling and the crust is caramelized, 40–45 minutes. Let cool at least 20 minutes on a rack. Slide the tart pan onto a transportable basket. Serve at room temperature.

serves six | per serving: calories 390 (kilojoules 1,638), protein 4 g, carbohydrates 60 g, total fat 16 g, saturated fat 10 g, cholesterol 41 mg, sodium 93 mg, dietary fiber 4 g

figs with sweetened lemon sour cream

Simple yet elegant, this recipe makes an excellent light dessert. Use unblemished purple or green figs. Serve with slices of Orange and Almond Cake (page 283) and pour a dessert wine, such as Sauternes or Beaumes-de-Venise.

½ cup (4 fl oz/125 ml) sour cream

2 tablespoons sugar

1 teaspoon vanilla extract (essence)

1 teaspoon grated lemon zest, plus long, narrow lemon zest strips

6 large figs

In a small bowl, whisk together the sour cream, sugar, vanilla, and grated lemon zest until smooth. Cover and chill for at least 1 hour or up to 1 day.

Carefully remove the stems from the figs. Stand each fig upright and cut from the top almost to the bottom into quarters. Do not cut all the way through; leave the figs intact at the base. Spread the quarters open like a flower and place on individual plates.

Spoon an equal amount of the sour cream mixture into the center of each fig. Garnish with the lemon zest strips and serve at once.

serves six | per serving: calories 107 (kilojoules 449), protein 1 g, carbohydrates 17 g, total fat 4 g, saturated fat 3 g, cholesterol 8 mg, sodium 11 mg, dietary fiber 2 g

lemon-raspberry squares

These luscious squares have a colorful raspberry jam layer tucked between a crisp sugar-cookie crust and a creamy lemon topping. Make sure to provide forks, paper plates, and plenty of napkins for serving these old-fashioned favorites.

1¾ cups (9 oz/280 g) plus ⅓ cup (2 oz/60 g) all-purpose (plain) flour

½ cup (2 oz/60 g) confectioners' (icing) sugar, plus confectioners' sugar for dusting

½ teaspoon salt

1 cup (8 oz/250 g) chilled unsalted butter, cut into small pieces

1 teaspoon ice water, if needed

1 cup (10 oz/315 g) good-quality raspberry jam

2 cups (1 lb/500 g) granulated sugar

2 teaspoons grated lemon zest

4 eggs, beaten

¾ cup (6 fl oz/180 ml) lemon juice

Preheat the oven to 350°F (180°C). Butter a 9-by-13-inch (23-by-33-cm) baking pan.

Place the 1¾ cups (9 oz/280 g) flour, ½ cup (2 oz/60 g) confectioners' sugar, and salt in a food processor and pulse to blend. Add the butter and process until the dough begins to form a ball, adding the ice water if necessary.

Press the dough evenly over the bottom of the prepared baking pan. Bake until the crust is lightly golden, about 20 minutes. Let cool for at least 30 minutes, then evenly spread the jam over the crust.

In a bowl, whisk together the granulated sugar, remaining ⅓ cup (2 oz/60 g) flour, and the lemon zest. Place the eggs in a large bowl and slowly add the flour mixture, beating with an electric mixer until well blended, 1–2 minutes. Add the lemon juice and mix to combine.

Pour the lemon mixture carefully over the raspberry jam layer, making sure to keep layers separate. Bake until the lemon topping is just set, 25–30 minutes. Let cool in the pan. Dust with confectioners' sugar and cut into squares with a serrated knife. Place in a transportable container and keep cool until ready to serve.

makes two dozen squares | per square: calories 243 (kilojoules 1,021), protein 3 g, carbohydrates 40 g, total fat 9 g, saturated fat 5 g, cholesterol 57 mg, sodium 64 mg, dietary fiber 0 g

maple-pecan tart

This tart is perfect for an old-fashioned Thanksgiving celebration at a mountain retreat, but it's too good to save for a special occasion. Pack it whole in the tart pan for easy transportation to an autumn picnic.

for the pastry:

1½ cups (7½ oz/235 g) all-purpose (plain) flour

1 tablespoon confectioners' (icing) sugar

9 tablespoons (4½ oz/140 g) unsalted butter, cut into small pieces

¼ cup (2 fl oz/60 ml) water

for the filling:

½ cup (3½ oz/105 g) firmly packed dark brown sugar

2 tablespoons all-purpose (plain) flour

pinch of salt

½ cup (5½ oz/170 g) maple syrup

½ cup (5 oz/155 g) dark corn syrup

3 eggs

1 tablespoon unsalted butter, melted

3 cups (12 oz/375 g) pecan halves, lightly toasted

1 tablespoon confectioners' (icing) sugar

1 cup (8 fl oz/250 ml) chilled heavy (double) cream

¼ cup (3 oz/90 g) maple syrup, chilled

To make the pastry, in a bowl, stir together the flour and confectioners' sugar. Using a pastry blender or 2 knives, cut in the butter until the mixture resembles coarse meal. Sprinkle with the water and toss with a fork until evenly moistened. Turn out onto a lightly floured surface, knead briefly, and shape into a disk. Enclose in plastic wrap and refrigerate for 30 minutes.

Preheat the oven to 400°F (200°C).

To make the filling, in a bowl, whisk together the brown sugar, flour, salt, maple syrup, dark corn syrup, eggs, and melted butter until well combined.

On a floured work surface, roll out the dough into a 13-inch (33-cm) round. Transfer to an 11-inch (28-cm) tart pan, easing it into the bottom and sides. Trim the overhang even with the pan rim. Place the pan on a baking sheet.

Spread the pecans in the shell. Pour in the filling and bake for about 15 minutes. Reduce the oven temperature to 350°F (180°C) and bake until the pastry is golden brown and the filling is set, 15–20 minutes longer. Transfer to a rack to cool, place on a serving platter, and remove the pan sides. Dust with the confectioners' sugar.

In a bowl, whip together the cream and maple syrup until soft peaks form. Place in a serving bowl and pass at the table.

serves six to eight | per serving: calories 954 (kilojoules 4,007), protein 11 g, carbohydrates 91 g, total fat 64 g, saturated fat 21 g, cholesterol 182 mg, sodium 103 mg, dietary fiber 4 g

mocha-glazed chocolate bundt cake

This attractive, triple-chocolate cake is surprisingly light and moist. Serve with sweetened whipped cream or vanilla ice cream, if you like.

3 cups (15 oz/470 g) all-purpose (plain) flour

2 cups (1 lb/500 g) sugar

2 teaspoons baking soda (bicarbonate of soda)

½ teaspoon salt

½ cup (1½ oz/45 g) unsweetened cocoa powder

1 cup (8 fl oz/250 ml) hot water

1 cup (8 fl oz/250 ml) cold water

1 cup (8 fl oz/250 ml) plus ½ teaspoon vegetable oil

1 teaspoon vanilla extract (essence)

½ cup (3 oz/90 g) semisweet (plain) chocolate chips

2 tablespoons strong brewed coffee

3 oz (90 g) semisweet (plain) chocolate, broken into pieces

4 tablespoons (2 oz/60 g) unsalted butter

2 teaspoons light corn syrup

Preheat the oven to 350°F (180°C). Butter and flour a lightweight 10-inch (25-cm) Bundt pan.

In a bowl, sift together the flour, sugar, baking soda, and salt.

Place the cocoa in a large bowl. Slowly add the hot water while stirring constantly. When the mixture is smooth, stir in the cold water. Then mix in 1 cup (8 fl oz/250 ml) of the vegetable oil and the vanilla. Whisk in the flour mixture until incorporated. Pour into the prepared pan. Sprinkle the chocolate chips evenly over the surface, then press them into the batter.

Bake until the cake begins to come away from the sides of the pan, the top is springy to the touch, and a toothpick inserted into the center comes out almost clean, about 55 minutes. Transfer to a rack to cool for 30 minutes, then invert onto the rack and lift off the pan. Let cool completely.

Meanwhile, in a heatproof bowl or in the top pan of a double boiler, combine the coffee, chocolate, and butter to make a glaze. Place over (not touching) simmering water in a pan and stir until melted. Add the corn syrup and the ½ teaspoon vegetable oil and stir to combine.

Place the cake on the rack on a baking sheet lined with waxed paper. Drizzle the glaze evenly over the top. Transfer the cake to a platter and serve.

serves eight to ten | per serving: calories 711 (kilojoules 2,990), protein 6 g, carbohydrates 96 g, total fat 37 g, saturated fat 11 g, cholesterol 16 mg, sodium 422 mg, dietary fiber 4 g

winter

roasted pears with cranberry-wine glaze

Bosc pears have a creamy texture that holds up well during cooking, making them a good choice for this rustic bistro-style dessert. Serve with Spiced Molasses Cookies (page 288) or biscotti.

1 cup (8 fl oz/250 ml) dry red wine

1 cup (8 fl oz/250 ml) cranberry juice cocktail

⅔ cup (5 oz/155 g) sugar

1 cinnamon stick

finely chopped zest of 1 lemon

8 ripe Bosc pears with stems attached

fresh mint leaves

Preheat the oven to 350°F (180°C).

In a saucepan over medium-high heat, combine the red wine, cranberry juice, sugar, cinnamon stick, and lemon zest. Bring to a simmer, stirring to dissolve the sugar, and cook for about 3 minutes. Remove from the heat and remove the cinnamon stick.

Starting at the blossom end, core each pear (a melon baller works well for this), leaving the stem end intact. Then cut a slice off the bottoms so the pears will stand upright. Carefully wrap each pear stem in a small piece of aluminum foil to prevent burning during roasting.

Stand the pears in a 9-by-13-inch (23-by-33-cm) baking dish, stem ends up. Pour the wine mixture evenly over the pears.

Roast, basting every 15 minutes with the cranberry-wine sauce, until tender when pierced with a knife, about 1 hour and 20 minutes. Remove the pears from the oven and arrange on a serving platter. Carefully remove the foil from each stem.

Pour the wine mixture remaining in the baking dish into a saucepan and place over medium-high heat. Bring to a simmer and cook until reduced to a syrupy glaze, 10–15 minutes. Spoon the glaze over the pears.

Garnish with the mint leaves and serve warm or at room temperature.

serves eight | per serving: calories 187 (kilojoules 785), protein 1 g, carbohydrates 48 g, total fat 1 g, saturated fat 0 g, cholesterol 0 mg, sodium 2 mg, dietary fiber 4 g

orange and almond cake

The addition of almond paste in this recipe makes for a rich, moist, intensely flavored cake.

¾ cup (3 oz/90 g) sliced (flaked) almonds

2 cups (8 oz/250 g) cake (soft-wheat) flour

1 teaspoon baking powder

¾ cup (6 oz/185 g) unsalted butter, at room temperature

⅓ cup plus 1½ tablespoons (4 oz/125 g) almond paste

1¼ cups (10 oz/310 g) granulated sugar

4 teaspoons finely grated orange zest

1 teaspoon vanilla extract (essence)

6 eggs, at room temperature, separated

1 cup (8 fl oz/250 ml) heavy (double) cream

about ¼ cup (1 oz/30 g) confectioners' (icing) sugar

Preheat the oven to 350°F (180°C). Butter a 9-inch (23-cm) springform pan.

In a food processor, process the almonds until finely chopped. Alternatively, finely chop by hand. Place in a fine-mesh sieve and tap the side to remove the powder. Transfer the almonds to the prepared pan, rotate it to coat the bottom and sides, and tap out any excess.

In a bowl, whisk together the cake flour and baking powder. In a large bowl, using an electric mixer, combine the butter, almond paste, 1 cup (8 oz/ 250 g) of the granulated sugar, the orange zest, and vanilla. Beat on high speed until light and fluffy, about 10 minutes. Beat in the egg yolks. Divide the flour mixture and the cream into 3 batches each. Add them alternately to the butter mixture, beginning with the flour mixture and folding in each addition until just combined. Do not overmix.

In another large bowl, using clean beaters and with the mixer set on medium speed, beat the egg whites until they mound slightly. Increase the speed to high and gradually beat in the remaining ¼ cup (2 oz/60 g) granulated sugar until soft peaks form. Stir half of the egg whites into the batter to lighten it, then gently fold in the remaining egg whites just until no white streaks remain. Pour into the prepared pan and smooth the top.

Bake until the top of the cake is browned and a toothpick inserted into the center comes out clean, about 1 hour. Transfer to a rack and let cool in the pan for 15 minutes. Remove the pan sides and slide the cake onto a rack to cool completely. Transfer to a serving plate and dust the top with confectioners' sugar.

serves six to eight | per serving: calories 797 (kilojoules 3,347), protein 13 g, carbohydrates 81 g, total fat 48 g, saturated fat 23 g, cholesterol 283 mg, sodium 143 mg, dietary fiber 1 g

orange sponge pudding cake

Serve this ethereal soufflé-like dessert in front of the fire with a glass of Sauternes or vin santo, if you like.

⅔ cup (5 oz/155 g) sugar

2 tablespoons unsalted butter, at room temperature

2 teaspoons finely chopped orange zest

3 eggs, separated

3 tablespoons all-purpose (plain) flour

¼ cup (2 fl oz/60 ml) strained fresh orange juice

1 cup (8 fl oz/250 ml) half-and-half (half cream)

⅛ teaspoon salt

⅛ teaspoon cream of tartar

boiling water, as needed

Preheat the oven to 350°F (180°C).

In a bowl, using an electric mixer set on medium speed, beat together the sugar, butter, and orange zest until creamy and well blended. Beat in the egg yolks. Stir in the flour, orange juice, and half-and-half until well blended.

Fit the mixer with clean beaters. In a bowl, combine the egg whites, salt, and cream of tartar and beat on medium-high speed until stiff peaks form.

Fold the egg whites into the egg yolk mixture just until incorporated. Pour into a 1-qt (1-l) soufflé dish. Set the dish in a large baking pan and pour boiling water into the baking pan to reach halfway up the sides of the dish.

Bake until the pudding cake is set and the top is nicely browned, about 45 minutes. Remove from the oven. Serve immediately, spooning the pudding cake onto warmed individual plates.

serves four | per serving: calories 351 (kilojoules 1,474), protein 7 g, carbohydrates 45 g, total fat 17 g, saturated fat 9 g, cholesterol 197 mg, sodium 147 mg, dietary fiber 0 g

ginger applesauce cake

Well spiced and not too sweet, this homey cake makes a tasty snack at any time of day.

½ cup (4 oz/125 g) unsalted butter, at room temperature

1 cup (7 oz/220 g) firmly packed dark brown sugar

1 egg

2 cups (10 oz/315 g) all-purpose (plain) flour

1 teaspoon baking soda (bicarbonate of soda)

1 teaspoon ground cinnamon

1 teaspoon ground ginger

½ teaspoon ground nutmeg

½ teaspoon salt

3 tablespoons finely chopped crystallized ginger

1 cup (9 oz/280 g) unsweetened applesauce

¾ cup (3 oz/90 g) chopped walnuts

½ cup (3 oz/90 g) raisins

1 tablespoon confectioners' (icing) sugar

Preheat the oven to 350°F (180°C). Oil an 8½-inch (21.5-cm) springform pan. In a bowl, using an electric mixer set on medium speed, beat together the butter and brown sugar until fluffy. Add the egg and beat well. In another bowl, stir together the flour, baking soda, cinnamon, ground ginger, nutmeg, salt, and crystallized ginger. Add to the butter-sugar mixture in three batches, alternating with the applesauce. The batter will be thick. Add the nuts and raisins and mix just until combined. Pour into the prepared pan.

Bake until a knife inserted into the center comes out clean, about 55 minutes. Place on a rack and let cool completely. To serve, remove the pan sides and slide the cake onto a round platter. Dust the top with the confectioners' sugar.

serves eight | per serving: calories 478 (kilojoules 2,008), protein 6 g, carbohydrates 72 g, total fat 20 g, saturated fat 8 g, cholesterol 58 mg, sodium 330 mg, dietary fiber 3 g

chocolate brownie sundaes

Indulge chocolate lovers with this rich, kid-pleasing dessert. For best results, be sure to use good-quality chocolate and ice cream.

¾ cup (6 oz/185 g) unsalted butter

4 oz (125 g) unsweetened chocolate, broken into pieces

4 eggs

2 cups (1 lb/500 g) sugar

1 teaspoon vanilla extract (essence)

1 cup (5 oz/155 g) all-purpose (plain) flour

½ teaspoon baking powder

½ teaspoon salt

1 cup (4 oz/125 g) chopped walnuts

for the hot fudge sauce:

8 oz (250 g) bittersweet or semisweet (plain) chocolate

½ cup (4 oz/125 g) unsalted butter

¼ cup (2 fl oz/60 ml) heavy (double) cream

1 teaspoon vanilla extract (essence)

1 teaspoon corn syrup

1 qt (1 l) good-quality vanilla ice cream

Preheat the oven to 350°F (180°C). Butter a 9-by-13-inch (23-by-33-cm) baking pan.

In a heatproof bowl or the top pan of a double boiler, combine the butter and chocolate. Place the bowl or pan over (not touching) simmering water in a pan and melt together, stirring until smooth. Remove from over the water and let cool.

In a bowl, using an electric mixer set on medium speed, beat the eggs until blended. Add the sugar and beat until the mixture is thick and pale yellow and will hold a trail when the beaters are lifted, about 5 minutes. Add the vanilla and the butter-chocolate mixture and stir just until no streaks remain; do not overmix. Fold in the flour, baking powder, and salt just until incorporated. Stir in the nuts.

Pour the batter into the prepared pan. Bake until a toothpick inserted into the center comes out with slightly fudgy crumbs adhering to it, 25–30 minutes. Transfer to a rack and let cool.

Cut into 3-by-3¼-inch (7.5-by-8-cm) brownies. You should have 12 in all.

To make the hot fudge sauce, in a heatproof bowl or the top pan of a double boiler, combine the chocolate and butter. Place over (not touching) simmering water in a pan and melt together, stirring until smooth. Add the cream and whisk gently to incorporate. Add the vanilla and corn syrup and whisk to combine. Keep the sauce warm over hot water.

To assemble, place a brownie on each plate. Place a large scoop of ice cream on each brownie and then drizzle the hot fudge sauce over the top.

serves twelve | per serving: calories 699 (kilojoules 2,936), protein 9 g, carbohydrates 73 g, total fat 46 g, saturated fat 24 g, cholesterol 150 mg, sodium 181 mg, dietary fiber 3 g

rice pudding with dried apricots and golden raisins

Select a medium-grain rice to ensure this pudding's delicate character.

5 cups (40 fl oz/1.25 l) half-and-half (half cream)

1 cup (7 oz/220 g) medium-grain white rice

¾ cup (6 oz/185 g) granulated sugar

2 egg yolks

1 teaspoon vanilla extract (essence)

1 teaspoon finely chopped orange zest

½ cup (3 oz/90 g) dried apricots, finely chopped

½ cup (3 oz/90 g) golden raisins (sultanas)

2 tablespoons unsalted butter, at room temperature

cinnamon sugar (optional)

In a large saucepan over medium-high heat, combine the half-and-half and the rice and bring to a boil. Reduce the heat to medium and simmer, stirring occasionally at the beginning and constantly the last few minutes to avoid scorching, about 18 minutes. The rice should be soft, but the mixture should be very creamy, and not all the liquid should be absorbed. Remove from the heat and add the sugar, stirring to blend completely.

In a small bowl, whisk together the egg yolks, vanilla, and orange zest until blended. Stir ½ cup (3½ oz/105 g) of the hot rice mixture into the egg mixture, then return the egg yolk–rice mixture to the rice mixture, mixing well. Stir in the apricots, raisins, and butter until well combined and evenly distributed. Pour into a serving bowl and let cool to room temperature. Sprinkle with cinnamon sugar, if desired, and serve.

serves six | per serving: calories 621 (kilojoules 2,608), protein 10 g, carbohydrates 83 g, total fat 29 g, saturated fat 17 g, cholesterol 155 mg, sodium 89 mg, dietary fiber 2 g

banana-oatmeal power cookies

These cookies have it all—nuts, grains, fruit. Their portable size makes them perfect for taking on hikes, bike rides, and all sorts of expeditions.

1 cup (5 oz/155 g) all-purpose (plain) flour
½ cup (1½ oz/45 g) flaked coconut
½ cup (1½ oz/45 g) rolled oats
1 teaspoon baking soda (bicarbonate of soda)
½ teaspoon salt
¼ teaspoon ground cinnamon
¾ cup (6 oz/185 g) firmly packed light brown sugar
6 tablespoons (3 oz/90 g) unsalted butter, at room temperature
1 very ripe banana, mashed
1 egg, at room temperature
½ cup (3 oz/90 g) chopped dried apricots or golden raisins (sultanas)
½ cup (2 oz/60 g) chopped walnuts

Preheat the oven to 325°F (165°C). Lightly grease 2 baking sheets.

In a bowl, stir together the flour, coconut, oats, baking soda, salt, and cinnamon. In a large bowl, cream the brown sugar and butter with a wooden spoon until fluffy. Add the banana and egg and beat with a fork until blended. Stir in the flour mixture, about ½ cup (2½ oz/75 g) at a time, then stir in the apricots or raisins and the walnuts.

Spoon the dough by heaping tablespoonfuls onto the prepared baking sheet, spacing the cookies about 2 inches (5 cm) apart. Bake until golden brown, 12–15 minutes, switching pan positions halfway through baking. Remove from the oven and cool on the baking sheet(s) on a rack for about 5 minutes. Transfer the cookies to the rack to cool completely. The cookies can be stored in an airtight container for up to 3 days.

makes about eighteen cookies; serves six | per cookie: calories 104 (kilojoules 437), protein 2 g, carbohydrates 23 g, total fat 8 g, saturated fat 3 g, cholesterol 22 mg, sodium 146 mg, dietary fiber 1 g

spiced molasses cookies

Moist and chewy, these full-flavored cookies are perfumed with sweet spices. Serve with Mixed Dried Fruit Compote (page 292), fresh fruit desserts, or ice cream.

2¼ cups (11½ oz/360 g) all-purpose (plain) flour
2 teaspoons baking soda (bicarbonate of soda)
1 teaspoon ground cinnamon
1 teaspoon ground ginger
½ teaspoon ground nutmeg
½ teaspoon ground allspice
½ teaspoon ground cloves
¼ teaspoon salt
¾ cup (6 oz/180 g) unsalted butter, at room temperature
1 cup (7 oz/220 g) firmly packed dark brown sugar
1 egg
¼ cup (3 oz/90 g) molasses
about 3 tablespoons granulated sugar

In a bowl, stir together the flour, baking soda, cinnamon, ginger, nutmeg, allspice, cloves, and salt.

In a large bowl, using an electric mixer set on medium speed, beat together the butter and brown sugar until fluffy. Beat in the egg and molasses. Reduce the speed to low and add the flour mixture, mixing until blended. Cover the bowl and refrigerate for at least 1 hour or for up to 8 hours.

Preheat the oven to 350°F (180°C). Grease 2 baking sheets.

Place a large sheet of waxed paper on a work surface and sprinkle it with the granulated sugar. Using your palms, shape the dough into balls 1¼ inches (3 cm) in diameter. Then roll the balls in the granulated sugar, coating them evenly. Arrange the balls on the prepared baking sheets, spacing them about 2 inches (5 cm) apart. Using the tines of a fork, press the fork into each cookie, pushing down to create a decorative top.

Bake until just set and lightly browned, 10–12 minutes. Remove from the oven and let cool on the sheets for 10 minutes. Gently transfer to racks and let cool completely. Store the cookies in an airtight container for up to 1 week.

makes about forty cookies | per cookie: calories 92 (kilojoules 386), protein 1 g, carbohydrates 14 g, total fat 4 g, saturated fat 2 g, cholesterol 15 mg, sodium 82 mg, dietary fiber 0 g

tarte tatin

A nonstick frying pan makes this traditional caramelized apple tart easy to turn out. Accompany each slice with a scoop of vanilla ice cream.

for the pastry:

1 cup (5 oz/155 g) all-purpose (plain) flour

1 tablespoon sugar

pinch of salt

½ cup (4 oz/125 g) chilled unsalted butter, cut into 1-inch (2.5-cm) pieces

¼ cup (2 fl oz/60 ml) ice water

for the filling:

6 tablespoons (3 oz/90 g) unsalted butter

¾ cup (6 oz/185 g) sugar

5 or 6 pippin or Granny Smith apples, peeled, quartered, and cored

To make the pastry, in a bowl, stir together the flour, sugar, and salt. Using a pastry blender or 2 knives, cut in the butter until the mixture resembles coarse meal. Sprinkle with the ice water and stir and toss with a fork until the dough is evenly moistened. Turn the dough out onto a lightly floured work surface, gather it together, and shape into a disk. Roll out into an 11-inch (28-cm) round. Drape over the rolling pin and transfer to a piece of waxed paper. Cover with a second piece of waxed paper and refrigerate.

Preheat the oven to 400°F (200°C).

In an ovenproof 10-inch (25-cm) nonstick frying pan over medium heat, melt the butter. Stir in the sugar until almost dissolved, about 2 minutes. It may look slightly lumpy. Add the apple quarters, rounded sides down, using just enough to fit snugly. Reduce the heat to low and cook until the caramel is dark brown and the apples are barely tender, about 15 minutes.

Place the pan in the oven for about 5 minutes to cook the apples. Remove from the oven and raise the heat to 450°F (230°C). Carefully place the pastry round over the top, tucking the excess pastry inside the rim of the pan. Return to the oven and bake until the pastry is browned, about 20 minutes.

Remove from the oven. Run a knife around the inside edge of the pan to make sure the tart will unmold easily. Invert a serving platter over the pan, then flip the pan and the platter together. Lift off the pan. Serve warm or at room temperature.

serves six to eight | per serving: calories 439 (kilojoules 4,394), protein 3 g, carbohydrates 57 g, total fat 23 g, saturated fat 14 g, cholesterol 62 mg, sodium 24 mg, dietary fiber 2 g

warm winter fruit compote

Dried fruits keep well in the pantry and, when cooked, have the intense flavors of their fresh counterparts. Try this compote over ice cream or topped with sour cream or yogurt.

1 lb (500 g) dried Turkish or other apricots

8 oz (250 g) dried cranberries

½ cup (3 oz/90 g) golden raisins (sultanas)

2 firm, ripe pears, preferably Comice or Anjou, peeled, cored, and diced

½ cup (4 oz/125 g) sugar

2 cups (16 fl oz/500 ml) water

1½ cups (12 fl oz/375 ml) white dessert wine such as Moscato, late-harvest Riesling, or Sauternes

1 oz (30 g) crystallized ginger, finely chopped

In a heavy saucepan, combine the apricots, cranberries, raisins, pears, sugar, water, wine, and ginger and bring to a boil over medium-high heat, stirring often, until the sugar dissolves. Reduce the heat to low and simmer, uncovered, stirring occasionally, until the fruit is softened and the liquid is thickened, about 40 minutes.

Serve warm or let cool to room temperature, cover, and refrigerate for up to 1 week. Rewarm gently over low heat before serving.

serves six | per serving: calories 486 (kilojoules 2,041), protein 4 g, carbohydrates 124 g, total fat 1 g, saturated fat 0 g, cholesterol 0 mg, sodium 18 mg, dietary fiber 10 g

banana chocolate bread pudding

Be sure to use a high-quality egg bread, such as a good challah or brioche. You can dry the bread cubes by putting them out on the counter overnight or in a 250°F (120°C) oven for 30 minutes.

8 cups (16 oz/500 g) day-old cubed challah (1-inch/2.5-cm cubes)

4 oz (125 g) bittersweet chocolate, coarsely chopped

2 bananas, peeled and sliced

6 whole eggs, plus 2 egg yolks

1¼ cups (10 oz/315 g) granulated sugar

3 cups (24 fl oz/750 ml) milk

1 tablespoon vanilla extract (essence)

boiling water, as needed

1 tablespoon confectioners' (icing) sugar

whipped cream (optional)

Grease a 9-by-13-inch (23-by-33-cm) glass baking dish with butter.

Arrange the bread, chocolate, and bananas in the prepared dish, mixing them around and making sure they are evenly distributed.

In a bowl, using an electric mixer set on medium speed, beat together the whole eggs and egg yolks until frothy. Add the granulated sugar and beat until the mixture is thick and lemon colored, about 3 minutes. Reduce the speed to low, add the milk, and beat until combined. Mix in the vanilla.

Ladle the egg mixture over the bread and let stand for 30–60 minutes to allow the bread to absorb the liquid. Occasionally push down on the bread with a wooden spoon. (You can test to see if the bread cubes are absorbing the liquid by cutting into one.) Meanwhile, preheat the oven to 375°F (190°C).

Place the baking dish in a large baking pan and pour boiling water into the baking pan to reach halfway up the sides of the dish. Bake until a skewer inserted into the center of the bread pudding comes out clean, 40–45 minutes. Remove from the oven, dust the top with the confectioners' sugar, and let rest for about 10 minutes.

To serve, cut into squares and serve plain or with whipped cream. The bread pudding is also excellent served cold the next day.

serves six to eight | per serving: calories 613 (kilojoules 2,575), protein 17 g, carbohydrates 95 g, total fat 20 g, saturated fat 9 g, cholesterol 293 mg, sodium 435 mg, dietary fiber 2 g

mixed dried fruit compote

Cooking dried fruits in sweet wine such as Riesling brings out their sweet and slightly tart character. A small bowl of this compote, topped with lightly sweetened whipped cream, is a satisfying ending to lunch or dinner, or is even wonderful served warm in the morning. The compote will keep for up to 5 days in the refrigerator.

for the fruit compote:

¾ lb (375 g) dried whole apricots

¾ lb (375 g) dried pitted whole prunes

½ lb (250 g) dried pitted cherries

1 Granny Smith or pippin apple, peeled, cored, and finely chopped

1 Bosc or Comice pear, peeled, cored, and finely chopped

½ cup (4 oz/125 g) sugar

2 cups (16 fl oz/500 ml) Riesling or Gewürztraminer

1½ cups (12 fl oz/375 ml) water

for the whipped cream:

1 cup (8 fl oz/250 ml) chilled heavy (double) cream

2 tablespoons confectioners' (icing) sugar

In a large, heavy saucepan, combine the apricots, prunes, cherries, apple, pear, sugar, wine, and water. Bring to a boil over medium-high heat. Reduce the heat to low and simmer uncovered, stirring occasionally, until the fruits are soft and the liquid has thickened, about 25 minutes.

Meanwhile, to make the whipped cream, in a bowl, whip together the cream and confectioners' sugar until soft peaks form. Transfer to a small serving dish, cover, and refrigerate until serving.

When the fruits are cooked, transfer to a serving bowl and let cool until warm, or let cool completely, cover, and chill, if desired.

To serve, spoon the fruit compote into individual glass bowls. Top each with a dollop of the whipped cream.

serves eight | per serving: calories 504 (kilojoules 2,117), protein 5 g, carbohydrates 97 g, total fat 15 g, saturated fat 10 g, cholesterol 31 mg, sodium 26 mg, dietary fiber 7 g

glossary

Anchovies
Tiny saltwater fish most commonly sold as canned fillets that have been salted and preserved in oil.

Apples
Various apple varieties grace fall and winter tables. Among the most widely available are green, tart **Granny Smiths,** primarily used for cooking; **pippins,** a family of apples with a tartness suited to salads or cooking; red, tart-sweet **Romes,** ideal for baking or eating raw; and red, crisp **McIntoshes,** good for eating raw or cooking.

Apricots
If not eating immediately, select these favorite summer fruits when they are fairly firm, bright gold, and with no green areas. Complete ripening at room temperature until soft.

Artichokes
The flower buds of a type of thistle, available large, medium, and small (so-called baby artichokes). The tightly packed cluster of tough, pointed, prickly leaves conceals tender, gray-green flesh at the vegetable's center—the heart.

Arugula
Also known as rocket, this leafy Mediterranean green has deeply notched, slender leaves with a peppery, slightly bitter flavor. Often used raw in salads.

Avocados
The finest-flavored variety of this popular vegetable-fruit is the pear-shaped Hass, which has thick, bumpy, dark green skin. Ripe avocados yield slightly to fingertip pressure.

Beans
Canned and dried beans have a long shelf life, making them ideal pantry items for your cabin or beach house. Some of the more common bean varieties are used in this book. **Black beans** are relatively small in size and have deep black skins. **Cannellini beans** are an Italian variety of small, ivory, thin-skinned oval beans. Great Northern or navy beans may be substituted. **Kidney beans,** so called due to their kidneylike shape, have brownish red skins, a slightly mealy texture, and a robust flavor. White kidney beans are also available. **Navy beans,** also known as soldier or Boston beans, are small, white, thin-skinned oval beans. Great Northern beans may be substituted.

Belgian Endive
Leaf vegetable with mildly bitter spear-shaped leaves that are white to pale yellow-green—or sometimes red—and tightly packed in cylindrical heads 4–6 inches (10–15 cm) long. Also known as chicory or witloof.

Bell Peppers
Sweet-fleshed bell-shaped peppers (capsicums) are most commonly seen in their unripe green stage; red bells are a mature, or ripened, stage of green ones. Yellow bells are a different variety. Long, slender Italian sweet peppers are slightly sweeter than bells.

Berries
Various cultivated berries add bright color, flavor, and texture to outdoor menus. Usually sold in small baskets or other containers, they should be selected with care. Look for plump, firm specimens free of blemishes or mold. Frozen berries can be substituted for fresh in some desserts and sauces. Among fresh berry varieties most widely available are **blackberries,** lustrous purple-black berries at their best in high summer. **Blueberries** are small, round berries with smooth, dark blue skins. They are available late spring through summer. **Cranberries,** round, deep red, tart berries grown primarily in wet, sandy coastal lands—or bogs—in the northeastern United States, are available autumn through early winter. **Raspberries** are sweet, small, red berries with a delicate flavor and tender texture. They are in season June until October. Golden or black raspberries are also available. Probably the most popular berry variety is the **strawberry.** This plump and juicy, intensely sweet, red, heart-shaped fruit is best from spring into midsummer.

Cheeses

Feta White, salty, sharp-tasting cheese made from sheep's or goat's milk, with a crumbly, creamy-to-dry consistency.

Fontina Firm, creamy, delicate Italian cheese with a slightly nutty taste; made from cow's milk. Look for fontina from the Aosta Valley of northwestern Italy.

Goat Cheese Most cheeses made from goat's milk are fresh and creamy, with a distinctive sharp tang. They are sometimes coated with pepper, ash, or herbs, which mildly flavors them. Also known by the French chèvre.

Gorgonzola Creamy, blue-veined Italian cheese. Other creamy blue cheeses may be substituted.

Gruyère Type of Swiss cheese with a firm, smooth texture, small holes, and a relatively strong flavor.

Monterey Jack Semisoft white melting cheese with a mild flavor and buttery texture.

Mozzarella Rindless white, mild-tasting Italian cheese traditionally made from water buffalo's milk and sold fresh. Commercially produced and packaged cow's milk mozzarella is more common but less flavorful. Look for fresh mozzarella packed in water.

Parmesan Hard, thick-crusted aged Italian cow's milk cheese with a sharp, salty, full flavor. The finest Italian variety is designated Parmigiano-Reggiano. Buy in block form, to grate fresh as needed.

Ricotta Fresh Italian cheese made by heating the whey left over from making other cheeses. Traditionally based on sheep's milk, although today cow's milk ricotta is more common in most food stores.

Blood Oranges
Citrus fruits with red pulp and orange skins tinged with red. The flavor of blood oranges is more pronounced than that of regular oranges, which may be substituted.

Buttermilk
Form of cultured low-fat or nonfat milk that contributes a tangy flavor and thick, creamy texture to quick batters and doughs. Its acidity reacts with alkaline baking soda to create gas bubbles, causing baked goods to rise.

Capers
Small, pickled or, less often, salted buds of a bush native to the Mediterranean. Used as a savory flavoring or garnish. If using capers packed in salt, rinse before proceeding with the recipe.

Chickpeas
Round, tan member of the pea family, with a slightly crunchy texture and nutlike flavor. Also known as garbanzo beans or ceci beans.

Chile Oil
Popular seasoning made by steeping hot chiles in peanut, sesame, or other oil. Available in Asian markets and in the specialty-food section of most food stores.

Chile Sauce
Asian bottled blend of chiles, vinegar, and salt, plus other seasonings—ginger, garlic, soybeans, sesame oil—that vary depending on the origin of the sauce. Sometimes called chile paste. Used as an ingredient or a condiment.

Chocolate
Purchase the best-quality chocolate you can find. Many experienced cooks prefer the quality of European chocolate made in Switzerland, Belgium, France, or Italy. **Unsweetened chocolate,** also known as bitter chocolate, is pure chocolate liquor (half cocoa butter and half chocolate solids) ground and solidified in block-shaped molds. It provides intense chocolate flavor when combined with sugar and butter, milk, or cream in recipes. **Bittersweet chocolate,** a common term for European dark chocolate, is lightly sweetened eating or baking chocolate that generally contains about 40 percent cocoa butter. **Semisweet chocolate** is an American term for bittersweet chocolate. **Milk chocolate** is primarily a sweet eating chocolate that has been enriched with milk powder. Richly flavored **unsweetened cocoa** is ground from the solids left after most of the cocoa butter has been extracted from chocolate liquor.

Cornstarch
Powdery flour ground from the endosperm of corn—the white heart of the kernel. Used primarily as a thickening agent in sauces, stir-fries, and stews. Also known as cornflour.

Corn Syrup
Neutral-tasting syrup made from cornstarch and used as sweetener for desserts. Available in light and dark versions, with the dark more flavorful.

Cornmeal
Granular flour ground from the dried kernels of yellow or white corn, with a sweet, robust flavor that complements baked goods. In Italy, this same product is known as polenta. Most commercial cornmeal lacks the kernel's husk and germ and is available in fine, medium, and coarse grinds. Stone-ground cornmeal, made from whole corn kernels, produces a richer flour.

Chiles

Fresh Chiles

Habanero Incendiary small green or ripened red chile, about 1½ inches (4 cm) long, with a subtle citrus flavor.

Jalapeño Small, thick-fleshed, fiery chile, usually sold green, although red ripened specimens are sometimes found. Also available pickled in brine or smoke-dried. The latter, called chipotle chiles, are sold dried, canned in vinegar, or in a thick vinegar-based adobo sauce.

Serrano Small, slim, hot green chile also sold in its ripened red form, as well as pickled in brine.

Dried Chiles

Ripe red chiles are commonly preserved by drying. Dried chiles are often soaked in water to soften for easier blending with other ingredients.

Ancho chiles, the dried form of the large, fairly mild fresh poblano, are used in this book.

Eggplant
Vegetable-fruits, also known as aubergines, eggplants have tender, mildly earthy, sweet flesh. Their shiny skins vary in color from purple to red to yellow to white, and their shapes range from small and oval to long and slender to large and pear shaped. The most common variety is large, purple, and globular, but slender Asian eggplants, more tender and with fewer, smaller seeds, are available with increasing frequency.

Espresso Powder, Instant
Instant espresso powder (or granules) provides an easily blended source of intense coffee flavor to baked goods. Available in well-stocked food stores, in Italian delicatessens, and in specialty-coffee stores.

Extracts
Flavorings derived by dissolving essential oils of richly flavored foods—almond, anise, peppermint, vanilla—in an alcohol base. Use only products labeled "pure" or "natural" extract (essence) unless using coconut extract, which is only produced in imitation form.

Fennel
Crisp bulb vegetable with a sweet, faintly anise-like flavor, sometimes called by its Italian name, finocchio. Another related variety of the bulb is valued for its fine, feathery leaves, which are used as a fresh or dried herb, and for its small, crescent-shaped seeds, dried and used as a spice.

Fish Sauce
Southeast Asian seasoning prepared from salted, fermented fish, usually anchovies. Available in Asian markets and specialty-food sections of well-stocked food stores.

Ginger
The rhizome of the tropical ginger plant, which yields a sweet, strong-flavored spice. Whole brown, knobby ginger rhizomes, mistakenly called roots, are sold fresh in food stores.

Crystallized ginger pieces are available in the baking or Asian sections of well-stocked food stores.

Horseradish

Pungent, hot-tasting root sold fresh and whole, or already grated and bottled as a prepared sauce. The best prepared horseradish, freshly grated and combined with light vinegar, is found in the refrigerated section of food stores.

Hot-Pepper Sauce

Bottled commercial cooking and table sauce made from fresh or dried red chiles. Many brands are available, but Tabasco is the best known.

Jicama

Large Mexican tuber with light brown skin concealing crisp, juicy, slightly sweet ivory flesh. Usually eaten raw.

Kiwifruits

Also known as Chinese gooseberries, after their country of origin, these fruits are noteworthy for their fuzzy brown skins concealing sweet, juicy, bright green flesh. The fruit yields gently to the touch when ripe. Underripe fruits will ripen in the refrigerator within a few days.

Leeks

Long, cylindrical, moderately flavored member of the onion family, with a pale white root end and dark green leaves. Select small, firm leeks. Grown in sandy soil, the leafy-topped, multi-layered vegetables require thorough cleaning.

Maple Syrup

Syrup made from boiling the sap of the maple tree. The aromatic, deep amber, caramel-flavored syrup has an intense sweetness.

Meyer Lemons

Slightly larger and with thinner skins than common lemons, Meyers have a more pronounced, slightly sweeter aroma and taste. A mixture of 2 parts fresh lemon juice to 1 part fresh orange juice may be substituted for Meyer lemon juice in some recipes.

Molasses

Thick, robust-tasting, syrupy sugarcane by-product of sugar refining, a procedure that may or may not include the use of sulfur. Light molasses results from the first boiling of the syrup; dark molasses from the second boiling.

Herbs

Basil Sweet herb popular in Italian and French cooking, particularly as a seasoning for tomatoes and tomato sauces.

Chives Long, thin, hollow green shoots with a mild flavor reminiscent of the onion, to which it is related.

Cilantro Green, leafy herb resembling flat-leaf (Italian) parsley, with a sharp, aromatic, somewhat astringent flavor. Also called fresh coriander and Chinese parsley.

Dill Fine, feathery leaves with a sweet, aromatic flavor. Sold fresh and dried.

Mint Refreshing herb available in many varieties, with spearmint the most common. Used fresh to flavor savory and sweet dishes.

Parsley Popular fresh herb available in two varieties, curly leaf and flat leaf. The latter, also known as Italian parsley, has a more pronounced flavor and is preferred.

Rosemary Used fresh or dried, Mediterranean herb with a strong, aromatic flavor well suited to meats, poultry, seafood, and vegetables. Use sparingly except in grilling.

Thyme Fragrant, clean-tasting, small-leaved herb used fresh or dried as a seasoning for poultry, light meats, seafood, or vegetables.

Crushing Dried Herbs If using dried herbs, crush them first in the palm of the hand to release their flavor. Or warm them in a frying pan and crush with a mortar and pestle.

Mushrooms

Cultivated **white** and **brown** mushrooms are widely available in food markets and greengrocers; in their smallest form, with their caps still closed, they are often descriptively called **button** mushrooms. **Shiitakes,** meaty-flavored Asian mushrooms, have flat, dark brown caps usually 2–3 inches (5–7.5 cm) in diameter. Available fresh and dried, the latter must be softened in warm water to cover for about 20 minutes before use. **Portobello** mushrooms have wide, flat, deep brown caps, a rich, mildly meaty taste, and a silken texture. **Chanterelles** are subtly flavored, usually pale yellow, trumpet-shaped wild mushrooms 2–3 inches (5–7.5 cm) in length.

Nuts

Rich and mellow in flavor, crisp and crunchy in texture, many different kinds of nuts complement sweets and savories. Some popular options include **almonds,** mellow, sweet-flavored, oval nuts available whole roasted or blanched (skinned), as well as sliced (flaked) and slivered. **Almond paste,** made by finely grinding the nuts, and the sweetened form of almond paste known as marzipan, are commonly available in the baking section of food stores. **Hazelnuts,** also known as filberts, are small, usually spherical nuts with a slightly sweet flavor. Once toasted, hazelnuts may be stripped of their thin, papery skins by rubbing them while still warm in a kitchen towel. Despite the name, **peanuts** are actually legumes produced on a low-branching plant. When roasted, they have a rich, full flavor and satisfying crispness that make them the world's most popular nut. **Pecans** are brown-skinned, crinkly-textured nuts with a distinctive sweet, rich flavor and crisp, slightly crumbly texture. Small, ivory seeds with a rich, slightly resinous flavor, **pine nuts** are extracted from the cones of a species of pine tree. **Walnuts** are rich, crisp-textured nuts. English walnuts, grown worldwide, are the most familiar variety. American black walnuts, sold primarily as shelled pieces, have a stronger flavor.

Oats

Grain prized for its nutlike taste and texture when cooked as a breakfast porridge, stirred into batters for waffles or griddle cakes, or used in baking. For baking, use old-fashioned rolled oats—not quick-cooking or instant—unless otherwise specified.

Oils

Oils are used for cooking—sautéing, panfrying, deep-frying—and for flavoring foods. Store all oils in airtight containers away from heat and light. Some of the types that appear in this book include various grades of **olive oil.** Extracted from olives on the first pressing without use of heat or chemicals, **extra-virgin olive oil** is prized for its fruity flavor and golden to pale green color. Use it in dressings or as a seasoning. Products labeled "pure" or simply "olive oil" are less aromatic and flavorful and may be used for all-purpose cooking. Two types of **sesame oil** are available. Sesame oil from China and Japan is made with toasted sesame seeds, resulting in a dark, strong-flavored oil used primarily as a flavoring. Pale gold, nearly flavorless cold-pressed sesame oil, sold in health-food stores, is used for sautéing. **Vegetable oil** is the term used for general-purpose oils that may be composed of canola, corn, safflower, and other oils, blended and filtered to produce a pale-colored, neutral-flavored product.

Olives

Throughout Mediterranean Europe, black and green olives are cured in salt, oil, or brine and then usually seasoned to produce pungently flavored results. Good-quality olives, such as the tiny French Niçoise or the larger Greek Kalamata, are available in delicatessens and well-stocked food stores.

Onions

These multilayered bulbs, which are related to garlic and leeks, are staples in nearly every kitchen. The varieties used in this book include **green onions,** also known as spring onions or scallions, which are the mild-flavored immature shoots of the bulb onion. The green and white parts are eaten both raw and cooked. **Maui onions** are brown-skinned sweet onions cultivated in and around Maui, Hawaii. They are in season from spring to midsummer. Small, mild **pearl onions** are about 3/4 inch (2 cm) in diameter. They are also known as pickling onions. **Red onions** are mild and sweet with purplish red skin and red-tinged white flesh. Common white-fleshed, strong-flavored **yellow onions** are distinguished by their yellowish brown skin.

Papaya

Tropical fruit shaped somewhat like a large pear, with sweet orange flesh and smooth yellow skin. A ripe papaya yields gently to finger pressure; ripen green papayas in a bowl at room temperature. Halve lengthwise and scoop out the black seeds before peeling.

Parsnips

Root vegetable similar in shape and texture to the carrot, but with ivory flesh and an appealingly sweet flavor.

Pears

Anjou pears, available from autumn through midspring and among the largest and plumpest of the pear family, have short necks, yellow-green skins, a rich flavor, and a smooth texture. Long, slender, tapered **Bosc** pears, with their yellow and russet skins and slightly grainy, solid-textured flesh, are good for cooking. Short-necked **Comice** pears, available from autumn through early winter, are large, round, sweet and juicy, and have greenish yellow skins tinged with red.

Peas

Also known as English or garden peas, freshly shelled peas are one of early summer's great delicacies. At other times of the year, frozen peas, particularly those labeled "petite peas," are an acceptable and convenient substitute.

Pineapples

These popular tropical fruits should always be purchased fully ripe. To test, smell the fruit, which should have a distinctively sweet aroma. Then pull a center leaf from the top, which should release easily.

Plums

Thanks to crossbreeding, hundreds of varieties of this smooth, shiny-skinned, sweet-tart fruit exist. They range in color from green and red to the deep blue-black of Italian plums, the variety dried to make prunes. Purchase firm, plump fruits free of blemishes.

Potatoes

While the kinds of potatoes and the names they go by vary from region to region, some common varieties include **baking potatoes,** also known as russet or Idaho potatoes, which are large potatoes with thick brown skins and a dry, mealy texture when cooked. **White boiling potatoes** are medium-sized with thin tan skins and a waxy flesh. When cooked, the texture is finer than that of baking potatoes. Usually of the round red or round white variety, **new immature potatoes** are harvested in spring and early summer and have sweet, tender flesh.

Prosciutto

Italian raw ham, a specialty of Parma, cured by dry-salting for 1 month, followed by air-drying in cool curing sheds for up to 2 years. Quality prosciutto is best eaten raw in tissue-thin slices or briefly cooked, such as in egg dishes or pasta sauces.

Puff Pastry

Type of pastry in which the dough of flour, salt, water, and butter is repeatedly layered to form thin leaves that puff up to flaky lightness when baked. Commercial frozen puff pastry dough is available in most food stores.

Rice

Thousands of distinct varieties of rice are grown, milled, and cooked around the world. A favorite Italian variety is short-grain **Arborio,** which creates a creamy, saucelike consistency during cooking due to its high starch content. The term "long-grain white" is applied to any variety with grains three to five times longer than they are wide. These slender grains cook to a light, fluffy consistency.

Sausages

Many recipes, from scrambled eggs to jambalaya, benefit from the addition of a full-flavored sausage. Cajun **andouille,** a smoked pork sausage, is highly seasoned with red pepper and garlic. Mexican- or Spanish-style **chorizo** is a coarse-textured pork sausage spiced with chiles and other seasonings. Seek out both sausages in good-quality meat markets and better food markets.

Shallots

Small member of the onion family with bronze or reddish skin, white flesh usually streaked with red, and a flavor that resembles a cross between sweet onion and garlic.

Soy Sauce

Asian seasoning and condiment made from soybeans, wheat, salt, and water. Look for imported brands labeled "naturally brewed."

Squash, butternut

A pale yellowish-tan winter squash with yellow to orange flesh. Commonly 8–12 inches (20–30 cm) long, with a broad bulblike base and a slender neck.

Stock

Flavorful liquid derived from slowly simmering chicken, meat, or fish and aromatic vegetables and herbs in water. Many good-quality canned stocks or broths, in regular or concentrated form, are readily available; they tend to be saltier than homemade stock, however, so taste and adjust recipe seasoning as necessary. Excellent stocks may also be found in the freezer section of quality food stores.

Sweet Potatoes

Tubers similar in shape and consistency to potatoes, but unrelated. They have yellow-brown skin and yellow flesh, or dark reddish or purplish skin and dark orange flesh. The latter are commonly known in the United States as yams, although a different species than the true yam.

Swiss Chard

Also known as chard, a leafy, dark green vegetable with thick, crisp white or red stems and ribs. The green part, often trimmed from the stems and ribs, may be cooked like spinach and has a somewhat milder flavor.

Tomatillos

Although the small green tomatillo resembles a tomato, the two are unrelated. Fresh tomatillos, available in the produce section of Latin American markets and well-stocked food stores, have brown papery husks that slip off easily before the tomatillos are cut. Canned tomatillos are found in most markets. Tomatillo salsa is also available, either fresh in the refrigerated case or bottled on the shelf.

Tomatoes, Sun-Dried

When sliced or halved, then dried in the sun, tomatoes develop an intense, sweet-tart flavor and a pleasantly chewy texture that enhance savory recipes. Available either dry or packed in oil, with or without seasonings. Sold in specialty-food shops and well-stocked food stores.

Tomato Paste

A commercial concentrate of puréed tomatoes, used to add flavor and body to sauces. Although typically sold in small cans, imported double-strength tomato concentrate, packed in tubes and sold in Italian delicatessens and well-stocked food markets, has a superior flavor.

Spices

Allspice Sweet spice of Caribbean origin with a flavor suggesting a blend of cinnamon, cloves, and nutmeg, hence its name. Sold as whole dried berries or ground.

Cayenne Pepper Very hot ground red pepper made from dried cayenne and other chiles.

Chile Powder Commercial spice blend of ground dried chiles and other seasonings such as cumin, oregano, cloves, coriander, pepper, and salt. Purchase in small quantities, as flavor diminishes rapidly after opening.

Cinnamon Aromatic bark of a type of evergreen tree. Sold as whole dried strips—cinnamon sticks—or ground.

Cloves Cloves are a rich and aromatic East African spice used to flavor both savory and sweet dishes. Used as whole buds or ground.

Cumin Middle Eastern spice with a strong, dusky, aromatic flavor. Sold ground or as whole crescent-shaped seeds.

Curry Powder Generic term for spice blends commonly used to flavor South Asian dishes. Among the most common ingredients are cardamom, coriander, cumin, chile, fenugreek, curry leaves, fennel seeds, mace, and turmeric. Purchase in small quantities, as flavor diminishes rapidly after opening.

Paprika Powdered spice derived from the dried paprika pepper; available in sweet, mild, and hot forms. Hungary and Spain produce the finest paprika. Buy in small quantities to ensure a fresh, flavorful supply.

Turmeric Pungent, earthy-flavored, yellow-orange ground spice that adds vibrant color to any dish.

Vanilla Beans

The dried aromatic pods of a variety of orchid. One of the most popular flavorings in dessert making, vanilla is most commonly used in the form of an alcohol-based extract (essence); only purchase products labeled "pure vanilla extract."

Vinegars

Vinegar results when certain strains of yeast cause wine—or some other alcoholic liquid such as apple cider or Japanese rice wine—to ferment for a second time, turning it acidic. **Balsamic vinegar,** a specialty of Modena, Italy, is made from reduced grape juice; the best is aged for many years. **Cider vinegar** has the sweet tang and golden color of the apple cider from which it is made. The best-quality **wine vinegars** begin with good-quality wine. **Red wine vinegar,** like the wine from which it is made, has a more robust flavor than vinegar produced from white wine. **Rice wine vinegar,** a specialty of Japan, possesses a delicacy well suited to Asian dishes. **Sherry vinegar** has its own rich flavor and color reminiscent of the fortified, cask-aged aperitif wine.

Watercress

Refreshing, slightly peppery, dark green leaf vegetable commercially cultivated and also found wild in freshwater streams. Used primarily in salads and as a popular garnish.

Worcestershire Sauce

This intensely flavorful and aromatic traditional English seasoning or condiment is a blend of many ingredients, including molasses, soy sauce, garlic, onion, and anchovies. Popular as a marinade ingredient or table sauce for grilled foods, especially red meats.

Yeast, Active Dry

Baker's yeast is commonly sold in individual packages containing a scant 1 tablespoon (1/4 oz/7 g) in the baking section of most food stores. For faster action, seek out one of the new strains of quick-rise yeast.

Zest

Thin, brightly colored outermost layer of a citrus fruit's peel, containing most of its aromatic essential oils, and thus a lively source of flavor.

Zucchini

Slender, tube-shaped summer squash with edible green, yellow, or green-and-cream-striped skin and pale, tender flesh. Also known as courgette. Seek out smaller-sized squashes for a finer texture and flavor and fewer seeds.

index

acknowledgements

The publisher wishes to thank: Annette Sandoval, Donita Boles, Vicky Carter, Ken DellaPenta, Jennifer Hanson, Wendely Harvey, Patty Hill, Sharilyn Hovind, Ruth Jacobson, Lisa Lee, Melinda Levine, Kathryn Meehan, Jan Newberry, Annette Sandoval, Cecily Upton.

The photographers wish to thank: Richard and Pauline Abbe, Elba Borgen, Joyce Anna Bowen, Doug Gibbs, Sandra Griswold, Sarah Hammond, Finn and Pascale Jorgensen, Stephan Juilusburger, Sue Fisher King, Kim Konecny, Beverly McGuire, Anthony Mello, Judy Montgomery-Moore, Lorraine and Jud Puckett, Micheal Procopio, Hellie Robertson, Beverly and Andy Stern, Mr. and Mrs. deForest Trimingham, John, Tom, and Nancy Wadson, Hubert and Penny Watlington, Judith Watson and J. Goldsmith Antiques, The Coral Beach & Tennis Club, Pottery Barn, Seadrift Co, Williams-Sonoma